W9-DFG-384

Investments
Fourth Edition

Student Resource Manual

Investments
Fourth Edition

Student Resource Manual

Robert W. Kolb
Adam E. Carlin

KOLB *Kolb Publishing Company*
6395 Gunpark Drive, Suite N, Boulder, CO 80301
(303) 530-7778   FAX (303) 530-7773

Copyright © Kolb Publishing Company, Inc., 1995.
All rights reserved.

Printed in the United States of America.

Library of Congress Catalog Card Number 94–78775

Student Resource Manual Only:
   ISBN 1–878975–55–2
Text + Student Resource Manual:
   ISBN 1–878975–46–3

K Kolb Publishing Company
6395 Gunpark Drive, Suite N, Boulder, CO 80301
KOLB (303) 530–7778   FAX (303) 530–7773

Preface

Investments Fourth Edition includes three different computer programs and data sources that this *Manual* describes. These resources are: STUDY!, Investmaster, and REALDATA. Together, these three programs can dramatically improve your learning experience. Before you can use these programs, you must follow the installation instructions in the next section. The remainder of this preface briefly describes each chapter of this manual. Consult the relevant chapter for detailed instructions on using the software.

Software Installation

The software that accompanies *Investments Fourth Edition* is delivered in a highly compressed form. **You must install the software before it can be used**. The next section provides the installation instructions. Installation to a hard disk should take less than five minutes.

STUDY!

STUDY! is a self–testing and review program. The program allows you to select any combination of chapters from *Investments*. The program utilizes a data bank of multiple–choice questions from these chapters and presents them to you one by one for your solution. After you indicate your solution, the program determines if your answer is correct and updates your score. If you make a mistake, the program reveals the correct answer and updates your score. You can use this program to review for a test or merely to check your understanding of each chapter as you work through the text.

Investmaster

Investmaster is a number crunching program that can solve many of the problems that you will encounter in studying investments. Investmaster contains ten modules that cover virtually all areas of investments. It is extremely easy to use to solve time value of money problems, bond pricing problems, and so on.

REALDATA

REALDATA is a collection of more than 35 spreadsheets containing real–world financial and economic data. Data include stock price, mutual fund indexes, interest rate series, money supply figures, exchange rates, and so on. **To use the data in REALDATA, you must access the data using a spreadsheet program, such as Lotus 123, Quattro Pro, or Excel.** The REALDATA chapter describes each data series in detail to make the information easy to access. In addition, the REALDATA chapter contains more than 100 exercises that your instructor may assign to you or that you can work on your own. At the end of appropriate chapters of *Investments*, selected exercises relevant to that chapter are recommended.

Contents

CHAPTER THREE
The Stock Market: An Overview   52

CHAPTER FOUR
The Primary Market and Investment Banking   78

CHAPTER FIVE
Sources of Investment Information

CHAPTER SIX
The Security Market: Regulation and Taxation

CHAPTER SEVEN
Bond Pricing Principles

114

CHAPTER EIGHT
Bond Portfolio Management

134

CHAPTER NINE
Preferred and Common Stock Valuation

155

CHAPTER TEN
Economic Analysis and the Stock Market

172

CHAPTER ELEVEN
Industry Analysis

185

CHAPTER TWELVE
Company Analysis   **198**

CHAPTER THIRTEEN
Diversification and Portfolio Formation   **211**

CHAPTER FOURTEEN
The Market Price of Risk

230

CHAPTER FIFTEEN
Efficient Markets and the Capital Asset Pricing Model

249

CHAPTER SIXTEEN
Investment Companies and Performance Evaluation

267

CHAPTER SEVENTEEN
The Futures Market

280

CHAPTER EIGHTEEN
The Options Market

CHAPTER NINETEEN
The Swap Market

CHAPTER TWENTY
Financial Engineering   **333**

Software Installation   **347**

STUDY!   **351**

Investmaster   **358**

REALDATA   367

REALDATA Exercises   418

CHAPTER ONE

Introduction

Chapter Objectives

Upon completion of this chapter, you should be able to:
1. Explain the trade–off between risk and expected return.
2. Compute WR, return, and annualized WR.
3. Measure the mean return on a single investment or on a group of investments.
4. Calculate and define variance and standard deviation.
5. Compare investments with different mean returns and standard deviations given risk aversion.
6. Discuss the different asset classes and their relationship to risk.
7. Define and calculate exchange rates.
8. Calculate the WR for domestic currencies.
9. Explain the goals of investing in financial assets, and the three keys to successful investing.
10. Understand the characteristics of investing in debt and equity.
11. Define and give examples of financial derivatives.

Chapter Outline

I. Overview

A. This book deals with investment in financial claims such as stocks and bonds.
B. Investment in financial claims requires reducing consumption in the present in the hope of increasing consumption opportunities in the future.
   1. Investing in financial claims involves the choice of some level of risk.
   2. Risk can be thought of as the chance that the investment will have an unexpected result.

3. Investment opportunities with high expected return are almost invariably accompanied by high risk.

C. There is a trade–off between the good (high returns) and the bad (high risk), and the investor must know how to measure both returns and risk.

II. Securities Investment

A. This book introduces the world of investing in securities. A **security** is a financial claim, usually evidenced by a piece of paper, on some other good. Some securities, such as a share of stock, represent a fractional ownership in all of the real assets and productive resources of a corporation. Other securities, like U.S. Treasury bonds, give someone the right to expect periodic cash payments from the government. This security does not represent any ownership interest in the government.

B. The principles that govern securities investment are very close in spirit to those that govern capital budgeting decisions, but there is an important difference in the goods that are acquired by the two investment processes.

III. The Goals of Investing

A. The goal of investing is to make money. In order to do so, investors must choose a certain level of risk. The book makes several simplifying assumptions about typical investors:
1. They are interested in monetary benefits only.
2. They prefer more wealth to less.
3. They are risk–averse, which means that they will demand compensation, in the form of a greater anticipated investment profit, for the bearing of risk.

B. The goals of investing can be summarized.
1. For a given level of risk, to secure the highest expected return possible.
2. For a given required rate of return, to secure the return with the lowest risk possible.

IV. The Measurement of Return

A. The Wealth Relative (WR)

$$WR = \frac{\text{Current Value of Investment}}{\text{Original Value of Investment}}$$

1. We define the **holding period** as the length of time an investment is held.
2. If there is a profit on an investment during a given holding period, the WR will be greater than 1.0; a loss means that the WR would be less than 1.0, and a WR equal to 1.0 means no profit or loss.

B. Returns and Yields
  1. The WR must be converted into a **return** or **yield** to be stated in percentage terms. The formula is:

$$\text{Return} = \text{WR} - 1$$

  2. To be meaningful tools in the comparison of different investments' performances, the returns and yields must be annualized.
C. Annualized WRs and Returns
  1. The simple wealth relative can be converted to an annual basis by applying the following formula:

$$\text{Annualized WR} = \text{WR}^{\left(\frac{1}{n}\right)}$$

  where n = number of years the investment is held.
  2. The annualized return bears the same relationship to the annualized WR as the simple return does to the simple WR:

$$\text{Annualized Return} = \text{Annualized WR} - 1$$

  3. This method assumes that the earnings on the investment can be compounded at an interval equal to the period over which the WR was originally measured. You must be sure to use comparable assumptions when trying to compare returns on two or more investments.

V. The Measurement of Mean Return

A. Measuring Mean Return for a Single Investment
  1. For investment over successive time periods, the mean return can be calculated by multiplying the WRs from the successive periods and taking the nth root of the product, where n equals the number of time periods. This is known as the **geometric mean**.
B. Measuring the Mean Return for a Group of Investments
  1. When managing a group of investments, it is often important to know what the mean return was across the whole set of investments. In such a situation, there are still two different cases to consider:
     a. There could be an equal investment in all of the different assets.
     b. Alternatively, there might be different amounts invested in the various assets.
  2. The calculation of the mean return for both cases can use the same basic formula:

$$\text{Mean WR} = \sum_{t=1}^{N} w_i \, \text{WR}_i$$

VI. The Measurement of Risk

A. The variance (σ^2) and the standard deviation (σ) measure the risk of the WR of investments.

B. The standard deviation (σ) is simply the square root of the variance (σ^2).

C. The decision to measure risk by the variance or standard deviation implies that the investor is interested in the dispersion of WRs or returns from their means.

D. The greater the chance of getting a result far away from the mean, the greater the risk of a particular investment.

E. The variance of the WR is defined by the following equation:

$$\sigma^2_{WR} = \sum_{t=1}^{T} \frac{(WR_1 - \text{Mean } WR)^2}{T}$$

where T is the number of individual WRs being used to make the calculation.

F. The variance and standard deviation can be compared with those of other assets to provide a comparison of the risk levels; of the two, standard deviation is probably the more useful because its units have the same magnitude as the variable being measured.

VII. Historical Returns and Risk

A. Historical data shows that investment among different asset classes involves substantially different risks.

B. For the 65 years from 1926–1990, the standard deviation of returns has been greatest for stocks, second for T–bonds, and lowest for T–bills.

VIII. Measuring Returns on Foreign Investments

A. Investing in foreign securities generally involves investing in an asset with cash flows denominated in a foreign currency.

B. Measuring return in a foreign investment requires that we consider not only the return on the foreign security, but that we also evaluate the effect of the exchange rate between the domestic and the foreign currency.

   1. The **exchange rate** is the price of one currency in terms of another.

C. There are two ways to take the effect of changing exchange rates into account as we measure WRs.

   1. First, we can express all cash flows in the domestic currency, which would be dollars for a U.S. investor.

   2. Second, we can find the WR measured in the domestic currency as:

$$WR_d = WR_f \frac{FX_t}{FX_i}$$

IX. Risk and Expected Return: The Keys to Investment

    A. It is absolutely critical that the investor understand the concepts of risk and return, and the relationship between them.

    B. There is a risk/return trade–off. The investor who demands high returns must be willing to bear high risk.

    C. In investing, there is no "free lunch." You cannot have something desirable without paying for it one way or another. In other words, if you want a high return, you must be willing to bear the accompanying high risk.

    D. Investors must correctly understand performance measurement. We cannot measure performance simply by the profits reaped in a given trading period. Rather, we must always consider how well the investor did in relationship to the risk that was being borne.

X. Organization of the Text

    A. Market Fundamentals and Organization

        1. Part One of the book provides special vocabulary and ideas of investments.

        2. Two terms that you should add to your vocabulary are primary and secondary securities markets.

            a. The **secondary market** is a market for already existing securities.

            b. The **primary market** is the market for the original issuance of securities. Because all stocks and bonds are created in this market, it is of crucial importance.

        3. Many of the most prestigious and highly paid jobs are to be found in **investment banking**—the segment of the securities industry that deals with the original distribution of securities in the primary market.

        4. The Government, through regulation, and more importantly, taxation, plays an important role in the working of the securities markets.

    B. Investing in Debt Instruments

        1. Part Two of the book introduces bonds, which can be defined as securities that promise a fixed periodic payment.

        2. Although there are some bonds that do not promise a fixed payment, the similarities between types of bonds lead to general principles about bond pricing and behavior.

    C. Investing in Equities

        1. Part Three focuses on stocks, which are securities that represent title to the productive assets of corporations. As such, they represent an ownership position in the firm.

        2. Stockholders cannot expect fixed or promised payments.

            a. Stockholders hold a residual position. They own what is left after others are paid.

            b. Because of the residual claim, stocks tend to be riskier than bonds.

3. The process of security analysis is traditionally divided into three phases: analysis of the economy, analysis of the industry, and analysis of the firm.

D. Portfolio Management

1. Two key concepts discussed in this section of the book are portfolios and diversification.

   a. A **portfolio** is the collection of securities held by an investor and may include a variety of stocks, bonds, and other instruments. The way in which funds are allocated to different investments determines the riskiness and expected return of the investment.

   b. The term **diversification** stands for the allocation of funds to a variety of securities with different characteristics. It is one of the most successful ways of controlling risk in securities investment.

   c. Certain financial organizations, called **mutual funds**, provide investors with "ready made" diversification at low cost. These organizations accept funds from a large number of investors in order to pool those funds and use them to invest in a portfolio of securities.

2. To be able to compare the performance of various portfolios, financial experts have developed a performance standard which considers both risk and return.

3. An **efficient market** is one in which the prices reflect a given body of information. Researchers in this area have developed evidence that shows that much of the information used by investors in their decision–making process is already reflected in security prices.

E. Financial Derivatives and Portfolio Risk Management

1. A **derivative instrument** is a financial obligation that has value depending on the value or performance of some more basic underlying financial security.

2. The three basic types of derivative instruments are futures, options, and swaps.

   a. Futures contracts, which exist on physical as well as financial instruments, provide an opportunity for much exciting speculation. While it is easy to make and lose large sums of money with futures, they do play an important role in portfolio management.

   b. Options are a kind of security representing a **contingent claim**, or one that has payoff only in certain conditions that are specified at the outset of the investment.

   c. Swaps are the newest type of derivative instruments, and they involve the exchange of one sequence of cash flows for another.

3. Techniques of portfolio risk management have become so important that they have given rise to the specialized risk management branch of finance known as **financial engineering**—the construction of specialized financial arrangements from the simpler building blocks of futures, options, and swaps.

Key Terms and Concepts

arithmetic mean	the sum of the products of the WRs of individual investments at a point in time multiplied by the percentage of funds invested in each asset
bonds	legal claims on a firm's assets which usually promise fixed periodic payments and have a defined maturity date
compound interest	a method of accruing interest which assumes that intermediate interest payments can be reinvested to earn additional interest
contingent claim	one that has a payoff only in certain conditions that are specified at the outset of the investment
derivative instrument	a financial obligation that has value depending on the value or performance of some more basic financial security
diversification	the allocation of funds to a variety of securities with different risk/return characteristics to minimize the risk of the total holding
efficient market	a market where prices reflect a given body of information
exchange rate	the price of one currency in terms of another
financial investment	investing in financial claims, such as stocks or bonds
futures contract	a contract for the sale of a good at some point in the future at a price specified today
geometric mean	the nth root of the product created by multiplying together a time series of n WRs
holding period	the length of time an investment is held
investment banking	the segment of the securities industry that aids issuers in distributing securities in the primary market

mutual funds	financial organizations that pool the funds of small investors to purchase large, diversified portfolios of securities
options contract	a contingent claim that pays off only in certain situations
portfolio	a collection of securities held by an investor which may include a variety of instruments
primary market	the market for the original issuance of securities
risk	the chance that an actual result will differ from the expected result
risk–averse investor	one who is willing to bear more risk only in return for the promise of greater expected reward
risk/return trade–off	the rule stating that the benefit of high expected return occurs only if one is willing to bear the detriment of higher risk
secondary market	the market for existing securities
security	a financial claim on a good, usually evidenced by a piece of paper
standard deviation	the square root of the variance
stock	represents an ownership position in a firm—a claim on the assets of a firm that remain after all prior claimants have been satisfied
U.S. treasury debt	claims on the U.S. government which promise periodic cash payments
variance	the sum of the squared deviations from the arithmetic mean divided by the number of observations

Multiple–Choice Questions

1. The nth root of the product of n numbers is known as the ____.
   A. arithmetic mean
   B. variance
   C. standard deviation
   D. compound mean
   E. geometric mean

2. Squaring the WR of a six–month investment creates a(n) ____ WR.
   A. annualized
   B. geometric
   C. mean
   D. variance
   E. finalized

3. A WR that is less than one implies that the return is ____.
   A. greater than one
   B. greater than zero
   C. compounded
   D. negative
   E. geometric

4. The sum of the squared deviations from the arithmetic mean divided by the number of observations is known as the ____.
   A. annualized WR
   B. variance
   C. standard deviation
   D. compounded mean
   E. volatile mean

5. If one assumes that interim interest is reinvested, the annualized WR reflects ____.
   A. compounding
   B. volatility
   C. risk aversion
   D. risk preference
   E. the risk/expected return trade–off

6. Subtracting 1 from the WR calculates the ____.
   A. geometric mean return
   B. annualized mean return
   C. holding period yield
   D. holding period variance
   E. holding period deviation

7. An arithmetic mean return is calculated by ____.
    A. summing the number of observations and dividing the sum by the number of observations
    B. summing the squared deviations from the mean
    C. taking the square root of the variance
    D. taking the nth root of the product of n observations
    E. subtracting 1 from the holding period yield

8. If you invest an equal amount of money in each of a series of investments, your mean holding period return is equal to the ____ return.
    A. geometric mean
    B. simple average
    C. compounded mean
    D. standard deviate
    E. portfolio variance

9. If one investment has a higher variance than another, there is a greater chance that its ____.
    A. geometric mean exceeds its arithmetic mean
    B. price is lower
    C. actual return will differ from its expected return
    D. actual return is higher
    E. downside risk is lower

10. Dividing the current value of an investment by its initial value computes the ____ return.
    A. standard deviation
    B. arithmetic mean
    C. geometric mean
    D. variance
    E. holding period

11. A three–month investment that cost $20 is now worth $21.50. The investor's annualized WR is ____%.
    A. 7.50
    B. 15.00
    C. 15.56
    D. 30.00
    E. 33.55

12. If a portfolio's returns are normally distributed, the probability that an investor's return will lie between the mean return and one standard deviation above the mean return is ____%.
    A. 2.50
    B. 5.00
    C. 33.50
    D. 67.00
    E. 97.50

13. Every investor in the securities market faces a trade–off between ____.
    A. real asset investment and financial asset investment
    B. the standard deviation of return and the variance of return
    C. risk and expected return
    D. investing in futures contracts versus investing in options contracts
    E. investing in primary securities versus investing in mutual funds

14. An investment that has a WR of zero implies that ____.
    A. the investment is worthless at the end of the holding period
    B. the investor received title to the corporation's real assets at the end of the holding period
    C. the investor received the original investment at the end of the holding period
    D. the holding period yield is equal to one
    E. the investor placed his or her funds in an efficient market

15. A financial claim on a good, usually evidenced by a piece of paper, is a ____.
    A. yield
    B. security
    C. stake
    D. writ
    E. option

16. From 1926–1990, the standard deviation of returns has been greatest for ____ second for ____ and lowest for ____.
    A. stocks, T–bills, Eurodollars
    B. T–bills, T–bonds, stocks
    C. stocks, T–bonds, T–bills
    D. Eurodollars, stocks, T–bills
    E. stocks, Eurodollars, T–bonds

17. Which of the following is a financial asset?
    A. a Ford truck
    B. a U.S. army truck
    C. a U.S. government bond
    D. an automated teller machine
    E. a U.S. government warehouse

18. The fundamental trade–off present in all investment decisions has evolved because investments with high expected returns tend to have ____.
    A. low marketability
    B. low actual returns
    C. low cost
    D. high risk
    E. high transactions costs

19. Which of the following is *not* a form of financial investment?
    A. purchasing corporate stock
    B. purchasing savings bonds
    C. liquidating a savings account to pay college tuition
    D. selling a stock option
    E. trading a futures contract

20. Allocating funds to securities with different risk/return characteristics is known as ____.
    A. mutual funding
    B. diversifying
    C. speculating
    D. efficient marketing
    E. optioning

21. A market where prices fully reflect all available information is ____.
    A. diversified
    B. personalized
    C. efficient
    D. speculative
    E. primary

22. An important difference between investing in stocks and investing in bonds arises because stocks ____.
    A. are less risky than bonds
    B. do not carry fixed payments
    C. must be purchased through a mutual fund
    D. are traded only in primary markets
    E. are issued only by the U.S. government

23. A portfolio is a ____.
    A. contract for the sale of a good in the future at a price specified today
    B. contingent claim that pays off only in certain situations
    C. market for the original issuance of securities
    D. market for trading existing securities
    E. collection of securities with different risk/expected return characteristics

24. Which of the following is an example of a secondary market trade?
    A. opening a savings account
    B. purchasing a savings bond
    C. selling shares in a new corporation
    D. borrowing money to purchase a home from a bank
    E. selling a share of IBM stock

25. An organization that pools the assets of small investors to purchase a variety of securities is known as a(n) _____.
    A. mutual fund
    B. corporation
    C. investment banker
    D. options fund
    E. futures fund

26. A derivative instrument is a _____.
    A. long–term instrument
    B. short–term instrument
    C. high risk instrument
    D. financial obligation that has a value depending on the value or performance of some more basic financial security
    E. financial obligation that is valued based on a derived basis

27. Futures contracts exist on _____.
    A. physical goods
    B long–term contracts only
    C. financial instruments
    D. A and C
    E. none of the above

Review Problems

1. A share of stock you purchased one month ago for $20.00 is now worth $20.50. Compute your WR, return, annualized WR, and annualized return.
2. A share of stock you bought five years ago for $100 is now worth $150. Compute your WR, return, annualized WR, and annualized return.
3. A stock you purchased three years ago has had annual WRs of 1.06, 1.01, and 1.20. Compute the arithmetic and geometric mean WRs and the corresponding mean return.
4. A share of stock you purchased three months ago for $18 is now worth $20. Compute your three–month return and your annual return with and without compounding. Which annual return is most realistic? Why?

5. A portfolio you invested $18,000 in two years ago was worth $25,000 one year ago and is worth $24,000 now. Compute the annual WR for each year and the arithmetic mean and geometric mean return over the two–year period. Which mean return is most realistic? Why?

6. A share of stock you purchased four years ago has had annual returns of 12%, –2%, 8%, and 4%. Compute the annual WRs and the geometric WR and return for the investment.

7. Six months ago, you created the following portfolio with $10,000:

Stock	Amount Invested	Original Share Value	Current Share Value
A	$5,000	$100	$106
B	$2,500	$75	$85
C	$1,500	$50	$30
D	$1,000	$125	$110

Calculate the annual WRs for each of the stocks and the portfolio. Would your actual return have been larger or smaller if you had invested an equal amount in each stock? Why?

8. You have invested your money in the following stocks:

Stock	Percentage Invested	Original Value	Current Value
A	20%	$20	$22
B	30%	$15	$13
C	5%	$80	$92
D	10%	$40	$36
E	35%	$5	$8

Calculate the arithmetic mean WR on the portfolio and the return that it implies.

9. You hold an equally weighted portfolio of the following stocks:

Stock	Original Value	Current Value
A	$10	$12
B	$8	$6
C	$30	$35
D	$20	$16

Calculate your arithmetic mean WR, the return that it implies, the portfolio variance, and the portfolio standard deviation.

10. You hold two equally weighted portfolios of stocks:

Stock	Portfolio 1	
	Original Value	Current Value
A	$5	$6
B	$15	$12
C	$30	$32

Stock	Portfolio 2	
	Original Value	Current Value
W	$100	$104
X	$160	$150
Y	$95	$100
Z	$120	$116

Calculate the arithmetic mean WR, the variance, and the standard deviation for each portfolio. Which portfolio is riskier? Why? Are these actual returns consistent with the theoretical trade–off between risk and expected return? Why or why not?

11. A U.S. investor buys a German stock for DM 100 and sells it one year later for DM 130. At the time of the stock purchase the exchange rate between the U.S. dollar and the German mark was $.60 and at the end of the year the exchange rate was $.62. What is the return on this stock to a German investor and to the American investor?

Answers

Multiple–Choice Questions

1. E	10. E	19. C
2. A	11. E	20. B
3. D	12. C	21. C
4. B	13. C	22. B
5. A	14. A	23. E
6. C	15. B	24. E
7. A	16. C	25. A
8. B	17. C	26. D
9. C	18. D	27. D

Review Problems

1. The WR is equal to the current value divided by the original value:

   $20.50/$20 = 1.025.

   The return is equal to the WR minus one:

   $1.025 - 1 = 2.5\%$.

   One month is $1/12 = 8.33\%$ of a year, so the annualized WR is equal to:

   $(1.025)^{(1/.0833)} = (1.025)^{12} = 1.3449$, and

   annualized return $= 1.3449 - 1 = 34.49\%$.

2. WR = $150/$100 = 1.5

   return $= 1.5 - 1 = 50\%$.

   Since this is a five–year investment:

   annualized WR $= (1.5)^{(1/5)} = 1.08447$, and

   annualized return $= 1.08447 - 1 = 8.447\%$.

3. The arithmetic mean WR is the simple average:

   $(1.06 + 1.01 + 1.20)/3 = 3.27/3 = 1.09$, and

   return $= 1.09 - 1 = 9\%$.

   The geometric mean WR is the cube root of the product of the three WRs:

   $[(1.06)(1.01)(1.20)]^{1/3} = (1.28472)^{1/3} = 1.0871$, for a

   return $= 1.0871 - 1 = 8.71\%$.

4. The three–month WR is equal to the current value divided by the original value:

   $20/$18 = 1.11, for a

   three–month return $= 1.11 - 1 = .11 = 11\%$.

There are four three–month compounding periods in one year, so the annual compounded WR is equal to:

$(1.11)^4 = 1.52$, for an

annual return $= 1.52 - 1 = .52$ or 52%.

Without compounding, a three–month return of 11% leads to an annual return of $4(11\%) = 44\%$. For an investment whose value changes over time, the compound return best measures the true return to the investor. If you liquidate the investment today, you will have $20 to invest in other projects, or in consumption. Any opportunity whose value grows by 11% each quarter for four consecutive quarters will attain a value 52% larger than its original value at the end of one year.

5.   The annual WRs depend on the portfolio's beginning and ending values each year:

Year	Beginning Value	Ending Value	WR
1	$18,000	$25,000	25/18 = 1.39
2	$25,000	$24,000	24/25 = .96

The arithmetic mean WR is the simple average of the two annual returns:

$(1.39 + .96)/2 = 1.175$.

The geometric mean WR is the square root of the product of the two annual returns since this is a two–year investment:

$[(1.39)(.96)]^{.5} = (1.3344)^{.5} = 1.155$.

The geometric mean return is more realistic because it measures the change in the value of your holdings over time with compounding, or reinvesting. For example, an annual compound return of 17.5% per year, (the arithmetic average) on an $18,000 investment suggests that the portfolio will be worth:

$(\$18,000)(1.175)^2 = (\$18,000)1.381 = \$24,851.25$.

This value is higher than the true market worth of the holdings.

The geometric mean return of 15.5% per year does reflect the current market value of the holdings, (except for a small rounding error) since:

$(\$18,000)(1.155)^2 = (\$18,000)(1.334) = \$24,012.45$.

6. The WR is simply the return plus 1, to reflect the original amount invested:

Year	Return		WR = return + 1	
1	12% =	.12	1 + .12	= 1.12
2	−2% =	−.02	1 − .02	= 0.98
3	8% =	.08	1 + .08	= 1.08
4	4% =	.04	1 + .04	= 1.04

The geometric mean is the fourth root of the product of the four annual WRs:

$$[(1.12)(.98)(1.08)(1.04)]^{.25} = (1.2328)^{.25}$$

$$= 1.0537, \text{ for a mean return of } 1.0537 - 1 = .0537$$

$$= 5.37\%.$$

7. The annual WR of a six–month investment is the square of the six–month WR since there are two six–month periods in one year:

Stock	Six–Month WR		Annual WR	
A	$106/$100	= 1.06	$(1.06)^2$	= 1.12
B	$85/$75	= 1.13	$(1.13)^2$	= 1.28
C	$30/$50	= 0.60	$(.60)^2$	= 0.36
D	$110/$125	= 0.88	$(.88)^2$	= 0.77

The six–month portfolio WR is the weighted average of the individual stock WRs, with the weights determined by the percentage investment in each stock:

Stock	Investment	Percentage	
A	$5,000	$5,000/$10,000	= 50%
B	$2,500	$2,500/$10,000	= 25%
C	$1,500	$1,500/$10,000	= 15%
D	$1,000	$1,000/$10,000	= 10%

$$= .50(1.06) + .25 (1.13) + .15(.60) + .10(.88)$$

$$= .53 + .2825 + .09 + .088 = .9905,$$

for an annual WR of $(.9905)^2 = .981$.

Your annual return would have been lower with equal amounts invested in each stock. With hindsight, you were lucky to have placed most of your money (75%) into the two stocks that had positive returns. Only 25% of your money was invested in shares with negative returns. In this case, the more money invested in Stocks C and D, the lower your return would have been since those two stocks lost money over your holding period.

8. First, find the WRs:

Stock	WR
A	$22/$20 = 1.10
B	$13/$15 = 0.87
C	$92/$80 = 1.15
D	$36/40 = 0.90
E	$8/$5 = 1.60

Now find the mean WR by incorporating the percentage weights:

$$.2(1.1) + .3(.87) + .05(1.15) + .1(.9) + .35(1.6)$$

$$= .22 + .261 + .0575 + .09 + .56 = 1.1885, \text{ or}$$

return $= 1.1885 - 1 = 18.85\%$.

9. First, find the WRs:

Stock	WR
A	$12/$10 = 1.20
B	$6/$8 = 0.75
C	$35/30 = 1.17
D	$16/20 = 0.80

Now, find the arithmetic mean:

$$(1.20 + .75 + 1.17 + .8)/4 = 3.92/4 = .98, \text{ for a}$$

return $= .98 - 1 = -2\%$.

Now, divide the sum of the squared deviations by the number of observations:

$$[(1.20 - .98)^2 + (.75 - .98)^2 + (1.17 - .98)^2 + (.8 - .98)^2]/4$$

$$= [(.22)^2 + (-.23)^2 + (.19)^2 + (-.18)^2]/4$$

= (.0484 + .0529 + .0361 + .0324)/4 = .1698/4

= .04245 = Variance.

To find the standard deviation, take the square root of the variance:

$(.04245)^{.5}$ = .206 = 20.6%.

10. For each portfolio:

	Portfolio 1		Portfolio 2
Stock	**WR**	**Stock**	**WR**
A	$6/$5 = 1.20	W	$104/$100 = 1.04
B	$12/$15 = 0.80	X	$150/$160 = 0.94
C	$32/$30 = 1.07	Y	$100/$95 = 1.05
		Z	$116/$120 = 0.97

For each portfolio, the arithmetic mean is the average of the WRs.

Portfolio 1:

(1.20 + .80 + 1.07)/3 = 3.07/3 = 1.023.

Portfolio 2:

(1.04 + .94 + 1.05 + .97)/4 = 4.000/4 = 1.000.

For each portfolio, the variance is the sum of the squared deviations from the mean and the standard deviation is the square root of the variance.

Portfolio 1:

$[(1.20 - 1.023)^2 + (.80 - 1.023)^2 + (1.07 - 1.023)^2]/3$

$= [(.177)^2 + (-.223)^2 + (.047)^2]/3$

= [.0313 + .0497 + .0022]/3 = .027755 = Variance.

$(.027755)^{.5}$ = .1666 = 16.66% = Standard Deviation.

Portfolio 2:

$$[(1.04 - 1)^2 + (.94 - 1)^2 + (1.05 - 1)^2 + (.97 - 1)^2]/4$$

$$= [(.04)^2 + (-.06)^2 + (.05)^2 + (-.03)^2]/4$$

$$= [.0016 + .0036 + .0025 + .0009]/4 = .00215 = \text{Variance.}$$

$$(.00215)^{.5} = .046368 = 4.64\% = \text{Standard Deviation.}$$

Portfolio 1 is the riskier portfolio since it has a higher variance and standard deviation of returns. This shows that there is a greater chance that actual returns on Portfolio 1 will be different than the expected returns on Portfolio 1 in the future if the past is a guide to the future. These historical results are consistent with the risk/expected return trade–off because Portfolio 1 had a higher realized return than Portfolio 2. The higher actual return compensated the investor for the increased uncertainty.

11. The return to the German investor is simply:

$$\text{Return}_{\text{Foreign}} = \frac{130}{100} - 1 = .3, \text{ or 30 percent}$$

The return to the U.S. investor is:

$$\text{Return}_{\text{U.S.}} = 1.3 \frac{\$.62}{\$.60} - 1 = .34, \text{ or 34 percent}$$

Due to the appreciation of the German mark, the U.S. investor had a higher return than the German investor.

CHAPTER TWO

The Debt Market

Chapter Objectives

Upon completion of this chapter, you should be able to:

1. Distinguish between pure discount and coupon instruments.
2. Understand the differences between a par, premium, and discount bond.
3. Compare and contrast money market and bond market instruments.
4. Calculate prices and yields for pure discount instruments.
5. Find the price of a coupon bond if you are given its yield.
6. Use the two yield approximation formulas for coupon bonds.
7. Compare and contrast the three categories of issuers in the bond market.
8. Compare and contrast the different types of money market instruments.
9. Calculate current yield, discount yield, equivalent tax–exempt yield, and bond equivalent yield.
10. Explain the different types of security typically found in corporate bond indentures.
11. Explain the other features typically found in a bond indenture.
12. Explain the investment characteristics and calculations for convertible bonds.
13. Describe and apply the trading, payment, and price quotation conventions for coupon bonds.
14. Explain the features of the municipal bond market.
15. Be able to discuss and describe the different types of mortgages available.
16. Discuss the debt instruments available in the international bond market.

Chapter Outline

I. Overview

    A.   The bond pricing formula expresses the relationship among yields, prices, and promised payments on bonds—relationships that hold for all debt instruments.

    B.   Although the bond pricing formula applies to all debt instruments, it is traditional to divide the debt market into two segments—the money market and the bond market.

         1.   The money market is comprised of those debt instruments that are issued with a maturity of one year or less.

         2.   All debt instruments originally issued with maturities greater than one year are considered to be bonds.

    C.   The prices of debt instruments depend on the relationship expressed in the **bond pricing formula**.

    D.   For money market instruments, the general bond pricing principles all hold, but there are some special methods used to calculate various yields, such as the **discount yield** and the **bond equivalent yield**.

    E.   The U.S. Bond market is typically divided into three distinct segments.

         1.   The U.S. government debt market.

         2.   The corporate bond market.

         3.   The Municipal bond market.

II. The Bond Pricing Formula

    A.   Pure Discount Instruments

         1.   A **pure discount bond** promises to pay a certain amount, once, at a specified time in the future. This instrument trades for less than the promised future payment.

         2.   Normally, the promised future payment is the **par value** or **face value** of the bond—the final promised payment on a bond.

         3.   The difference between the par value and the selling price is the **bond discount**.

         4.   The value of a pure discount bond is expressed as:

$$P = \frac{C_m}{(1 + r)^t}$$

where:

        P = the price today

        C_m = the promised future payment at time m

        r = the annual yield to maturity on the instrument

        t = the time, in years, until the payment is received

5. The yield to maturity is the yield that will be realized if the promised payment is made. The riskier the promised payment, the higher the promised yield or expected return must be in order to induce investors to hold such bonds.

B. Coupon Bonds

1. Coupon bonds make regularly scheduled payments, called **coupons**, between the original date of issue and the maturity date. They also have a par value that is paid to the owner of the bond at a specified time in the future. In most cases, the coupon payments are made semiannually.

2. The value of a coupon bond is expressed as:

$$P = \sum_{t=1}^{m} \frac{C_t}{(1 + r)^t}$$

where: C_t = the cash flow received by the bondholder at time t

3. Both coupon payments and stated yield must be altered to reflect a bond's cash flows if the flows do not occur annually; this usually means dividing these by 2, as most bonds have semiannual cash flows and must therefore be valued with a semiannual rate of interest.

C. Par, Premium, and Discount Bonds

1. When the market price exceeds the face value, the bond is a **premium bond**.

2. If the market price equals the face value, the bond is a **par bond**.

3. When the price is less than the face value, the bond is a **discount bond**.

D. Yield Approximations

1. The yield approximation formula is a very useful alternative to making yield calculations by hand:

$$YTM = \frac{C + (FV - P)/n}{(FV + P)/2}$$

where C = the annual coupon payment, FV = the bond's face value, P = the bond's market price, and n = the number of years until the bond matures.

2. A recent contribution in the continuing effort to improve the approximation of yield to maturity formula is the following formula:

$$YTM = \frac{C + (FV - P)/n}{(FV + 2P)/3}$$

E. Accrued Interest

For most bonds, the bond price does not reflect the actual price that must be paid. Instead, one must pay the stated price plus the **accrued interest**— the portion of the next coupon payment that has been earned by the bondholder, but which the bondholder has not yet received.

$$\text{Accrued Interest} = \text{Coupon Payment} \times \frac{\text{days since last coupon payment}}{\text{days between coupon payments}}$$

III. The Bond Market in the United States

A. The U.S. bond market can be divided into three categories by issuer—the U.S. government, corporations, and municipalities.

B. The Market for U.S. Government Bonds
1. The U.S. government is the world's single largest debtor.
2. Treasury Debt
   a. The three principal kinds of U.S. Treasury obligations are Treasury bills, notes, and bonds.
      (1) T–bills are pure discount instruments with an initial maturity of one year or less.
      (2) Treasury notes and bonds are similar in the structure of their payment streams. Each bears coupons, but notes have an initial maturity of one to ten years while bonds have an initial maturity of greater than 10 years (often 30 years).
   b. During the past 65 years, returns on investments in Treasury securities have been similar, but very different in their risk levels.
   c. Average Maturity of Treasury Debt
      (1) In the last fifteen years, the average maturity of Treasury debt has increased to about 6.5 years.
      (2) The schedule showing the relationship between the maturity of bonds in the same risk class and the yields on those bonds is known as the **yield curve**.
   d. Zero Coupons and STRIPS
      (1) **Coupon stripping** is the act of removing the individual interest coupons from the bond and treating each payment as a separate security.
      (2) The resulting instruments are zero coupon bonds, because each represents a single payment due on a particular date.
   e. Treasury Auctions
      The U.S. Treasury holds weekly T–bill auctions in the money market, where purchasers bid for the new securities by offering either competitive or non–competitive bids through one of the 12 Federal Reserve Banks.
   f. Death and Taxes: Flower Bonds
      A **flower bond** is a specially designated U.S. Treasury bond that is redeemable at its owner's death for its face value plus accrued interest in payment of federal estate taxes.
3. Federal Agency Debt

      a. A **federal agency** is a direct arm of the U.S. government that does not issue debt on its own, but meets its financing needs through issues of the Federal Financing Bank.

      b. A **federally sponsored agency** is a privately owned entity that raises funds in the market.

      c. With one exception, there is no federal guarantee of agency securities; however, a perception that the federal government will not allow these securities to default has resulted in yields that are slightly higher than those of comparable Treasury issues.

    4. Ownership of U.S. Government Securities and the Burden of Federal Debt

      a. One developing public issue that promises to be of great importance is the continuing growth of the federal deficit and the burden that it creates.

      b. The major owners of federal securities are private nonbank financial and nonfinancial holders.

      c. Financing of the federal debt places a large burden on the taxpayer and consumes a significant portion of the annual budget of the federal government each year.

IV. The Corporate Bond Market

A. Corporate bonds constitute a smaller amount of long–term borrowing than either mortgages or the issues of state and local governments.

B. Corporate Bond Quotations

    1. The **current yield** of a bond is reported in the bond quotation columns and can be calculated as follows:

$$CY = \frac{\text{Annual Coupon Payment}}{\text{Bond's Current Market Price}}$$

    2. In some cases, the current yield column carries the designation "cv," which indicates that the bond is a **convertible bond**, a bond that may be converted into another security, usually common stock, at the option of the bond's owner.

    3. In rare cases, the current yield column may show an "f," which indicates that the bond is traded **flat**, and the purchasers need not pay the accrued interest in addition to the bond price.

    4. Although *The Wall Street Journal* is the most readily available source of daily quotations, it is limited in many respects.

C. The Corporate Bond Over–the–Counter Market

    1. The **over–the–counter market (OTC)** is a loose organization of traders without a centralized physical location; instead, participants communicate with each other electronically from their own offices.

    2. When a corporation issues a bond, it promises to make a series of payments of a certain amount on pre–specified dates.

3. A bond purchaser hopes at best for the issuer to keep his promise.

4. To aid bond investors in making their assessment about the future payment prospects of a particular bond, there are services (S&P, Moodys) that rate the quality of various bonds by measuring **default risk**—the chance that one or more payments on the bond will be deferred or missed altogether.

D. History of Corporate Bond Returns

1. From the period 1926 to 1990, a portfolio of high–quality, long–term corporate bonds returned an annual rate of 5.2 percent, which translated into a real return of only 2.01 percent.

2. However, there are many other types of bonds with different yields as well, with the differences in yields due largely to differences in risk.

E. High–Yield Corporate Bonds

1. The high–yield corporate bond market developed into special prominence in the 1980s; these bonds are lower rated or speculative grade bonds and are commonly referred to as **junk bonds**.

2. Standard & Poor's regards BB and lower grade bonds as "predominantly speculative with respect to capacity to pay interest and principal in accordance with the terms of the obligation."

3. If junk bonds have a sufficiently high expected return, it might compensate for the greater chance that junk bonds would default.

4. A variety of studies have sought to measure the default experience of corporate bonds, with the rough consensus being that bond portfolios might lose 1–2 percent of their value each year through default; however, if yields are high enough to compensate for this loss through default, junk bonds could still be an attractive investment.

V. The Municipal Bond Market

A. A **municipal bond** is a debt security issued by a government or a quasi–governmental agency, other than those associated with the federal government. Most municipal bond interest is exempt from federal income taxation.

B. A given rate of return on a tax–free bond is more valuable than the same rate on a taxable bond. The relationship can be expressed as follows:
Equivalent Tax-Exempt Yield = (1 – Marginal Tax Rate) (Taxable Yield)

C. In general, the higher the tax rate, the greater the preference for tax–exempt securities.

D. In addition to exemption from federal taxation, some municipal bonds are also **triple tax–exempt**—exempt from income taxation by the state and municipality in which they were issued.

E. The municipal bond market is huge, but it is not a very liquid market. A market is **liquid** if assets can be sold easily, at close to their true value.

F. Issues in the municipal bond market can be divided into general obligation bonds and revenue bonds.

        1.   A **general obligation bond** is one backed by the full taxing power of the issuer.

        2.   A **revenue bond** is backed only by the revenue from some specific project.

VI. The Mortgage Market

A. One of the largest components of debt is the mortgage, or the debt owed on real estate.

B. It is important to distinguish between real estate mortgages and mortgages as a type of collateral for a debt obligation.

C. Most mortgages are for residential properties.

D. In **balloon mortgages**, the final payment is much larger than the ordinary monthly payments.

E. Historically most residential mortgages carried a fixed interest rate over the loan's life. In recent years, however, **variable rate loans**, whose interest rate moves up and down with a market index over time, have become popular.

F. Most residential mortgages are typically **amortized loans**. In an amortized loan, the amount of the payment remains constant over the life of the loan, but the proportion going to principal and interest changes over time.

G. Mortgage Pass–Through Securities

    1.   It has become very common to create a **mortgage pool**—a collection of individual mortgages that can be treated as a unit; once the pool is created, securities are created based on the mortgages in the pool.

    2.   Investors can buy a participation in the entire pool of mortgages, instead of investing in a single mortgage.

    3.   These securities are a **mortgage pass–through security** because the original lender continues to collect payments from the borrower and passes them through to the investors in the mortgage pool.

    4.   Agency–guaranteed mortgage pass–throughs (GNMA, FNMA & FHLMC) provide an attractive means for individual investors or managers of bond portfolios to invest in safe residential mortgages with yields higher than Treasury issues.

VII. The Bond Contract

A. The **bond contract**, or **bond indenture**, is a legal document stating in precise terms the promises made by the issuer of a bond and the rights of the bondholders.

B. For all corporate bonds issued by firms engaging in interstate commerce with an issue size exceeding $5 million, the Trust Indentures Act requires that an independent trustee be established to insure that the terms of the indenture are fulfilled.

C. The bond indenture also contains numerous covenants. Some define the security that the issuer is offering for the bond and some specify how the bond is to be retired.
D. Corporate bonds may or may not have specific security pledged.
  1. Mortgage bonds have specific assets pledged as security. **First mortgage bonds** have the first claim on the assets specified in the mortgage, while second mortgage bonds have the next claim, and so forth.
  2. In addition to mortgage bonds, some firms offer security under slightly different arrangements. For example, **collateral trust bonds** are secured by financial assets and **equipment trust certificates** are secured by equipment, such as railroad cars.
  3. Most bonds issued by corporations have no security. This type of bond is known as a **debenture**.
  4. **Subordinated debentures** are unsecured bonds that have an inferior claim to other outstanding debentures and are paid only after straight debentures, which were issued earlier.
  5. Debentures may seem to be a risky investment, but bond contracts for debentures, as well as for mortgage bonds, often have covenants that protect the bondholders by restricting the behavior of the issuer.
E. The bond contract will also specify how the bond is to be retired.
  1. With **callable bonds** the issuer has the right to call the bonds in before maturity and pay them off at a certain price stipulated in the bond contract. Callable bonds are not usually called unless they can be refunded at a lower interest rate. Also, the price the issuer must pay to call the bond, the **call price**, usually gives a premium over the par value to the bondholder.
  2. Many bonds also have a **sinking fund** which is used to retire a portion of the bond issue over time.
  3. Sometimes bonds are scheduled for retirement with a certain principal amount becoming due at predetermined dates. These bonds are called **serial bonds**.
  4. Another method of retiring bonds is through conversion. A **convertible bond** is a bond that gives the bondholder the option of surrendering the bond and receiving in return a specified number of shares of common stock, thereby converting the bond into stock.
    a. The **conversion ratio** determines the number of shares received for each bond.
    b. The **conversion price** is the market price of the convertible bond divided by the conversion ratio. It determines the implied price paid for the stock by converting.
    c. The **conversion premium** is the additional amount per share of stock that one pays to obtain the share by converting the bond rather than by buying the stock in the marketplace.

d. Without a positive conversion premium, purchasers of a convertible bond could create an arbitrage opportunity to earn a riskless profit with no investment.

e. **Arbitrage** is the opportunity to earn a return without risk or investment.

VIII. The Money Market

A. The **money market** is the market for debt instruments with a maturity of one year or less at the time of issuance.

B. Money Market Yield Concepts

1. In the money market, **interest–bearing instruments** are issued with a given par value and a stated coupon rate.

2. **Discount paper** is a money market instrument that is issued with a stated par value and no coupon rate.

3. The Discount Yield

   a. Many money market securities are quoted in terms of the **discount yield**, d. The formula for d is:

$$d = \left(\frac{360}{t}\right)\left(\frac{DISC}{FV}\right)$$

   b. The actual dollar price, P, depends on the face value, FV, and the amount of the dollar discount, DISC: P = FV − DISC

4. The Bond Equivalent Yield

   To make discount instruments comparable to bonds, there is a **bond equivalent yield** (EBY):

$$EBY = \frac{(365)\ (d)}{360 - (d)(t)}$$

C. Major Money Market Instruments

1. Treasury Bills

   a. Treasury bills are pure discount obligations of the U.S. Treasury with an initial maturity of 365 days or less.

   b. The quotation of this instrument is based on the discount yield.

2. Commercial Paper

   a. **Commercial paper** is short–term pure discount obligations of the largest and most creditworthy industrial and financial firms.

   b. This instrument is quoted using the discount yield method.

   c. To escape registration requirements of the SEC, the maturity cannot exceed 270 days.

   d. The issuer offers no collateral, except the firm's good faith and credit.

3. Bankers' Acceptances

   a. **Bankers' acceptances** are used almost exclusively to finance international trade.

      b. These instruments are pure discount drafts against a bank where the bank has promised to pay a specified amount at a future date.

      c. When the bank accepts the obligation and stamps the draft **accepted**, it creates a bankers' acceptance.

      d. Bankers' acceptances are normally **two–name paper** where the bank and the original firm for whom the acceptance was created are both obligated to make the payment.

4. Certificates of Deposit

      a. Certificates of deposit are interest–bearing liabilities of banks. With CDs, interest is added to a given principal amount.

      b. CDs may be either negotiable or non–negotiable. Small CDs are often held by individual investors and are typically non–negotiable. Large CDs, $100,000 or more, are negotiable and form an important part of the money market, exceeding even T–bills in market size.

5. Eurodollars

      a. A **Eurodollar** is a dollar–denominated bank deposit held in a bank outside the United States.

      b. A **Eurodollar CD** is a dollar–denominated CD issued by a bank outside the United States; the most important part of the Eurodollar market is the CD sector.

      c. The greater risk inherent in Eurodollar CDs arises from the fact that the issuing banks are not as tightly regulated as U.S. banks.

6. Repurchase Agreements

      a. A **repurchase agreement**, or **repo**, arises when one party sells a security to another party with an agreement to buy it back at a specified time and at a specified price.

      b. Repos are used mainly for short–term financing, usually for just one day, and as such they are often called **overnight repos**.

      c. Repos held for longer periods are called **term repos**.

7. Federal Funds

Federal Funds or **Fed funds** make up another type of short–term market. They involve the trading of reserve balances between banks that are members of the Federal Reserve system. Most federal funds are loaned on an overnight basis.

8. Yield Relationships in the Money Market

      a. Even though the money market is defined as consisting of those securities issued with original maturities of one year or less, there is a considerable difference in yields within the market.

      b. For those instruments with longer maturities, the T–bill offers the lowest rate. This is due to its having the best backing of all instruments, the promise of the U.S. Treasury.

      c. Figure 2.21 in the text offers a breakdown of the yield relationships in the money market.

IX. The International Bond Market

A. An **international bond** is a bond available for sale outside the country of its issuer.

B. If a U.S. firm issues a bond denominated in a foreign currency for sale exclusively in the country of the foreign currency, the bond is a **foreign bond**.

C. An **external bond** is either an international bond or a foreign bond.

D. A **straight bond** is a bond with a fixed payment schedule with no special features, such as convertability into stock or a floating interest rate.

E. A **floating rate note (FRN)** is a bond that pays a different coupon rate over time as the general level of interest rates fluctuates.

F. Equity–Related Bonds
1. **Equity–related bonds** include both convertible bonds and bonds with equity warrants.
2. An **equity warrant** is a security that gives the holder the right to acquire a newly issued share of common stock from a company for the payment of a stated price.
3. Equity warrants are often attached to bonds as a way of enticing prospective bond investors.

G. A **Eurodollar bond** or **Eurobond** is a bond issued by a borrower in one country, denominated in the borrower's currency, and sold outside the borrower's country.

H. Composition of the International Bond Market
1. Of the new international bond issues in 1990, 70 percent were issued as straight bonds; equity–related bonds made up the next largest category, with FRNs being relatively scarce.
2. The **ECU** is a special composite currency of the European Economic Community (the common market). It consists of a basket of currencies of its member nations, such as Germany, France, and Britain.

X. The International Money Market

A. Syndicated Loans
1. One of the dominant forms of credit in the international market is a form of bank lending called a **syndicated loan**—a loan made by a consortium of banks to a single borrower.
2. Syndicated loans are priced as a spread above **LIBOR—London Interbank Offered Rate**. LIBOR is the rate that banks participating in the international debt market charge each other for short–term loans.
3. Therefore, most syndicated loans are floating rate loans.
4. In 1990, average spreads for syndicated loans were 52 basis points above LIBOR. A **basis point** is 1/100 of 1 percent.

5. For lenders, syndicated loans have important advantages because this form of lending allows them to participate in a loan without having to commit too large a portion of their capital.

B. **Euro–commercial paper (ECP)** is commercial paper traded in the international market, usually denominated in dollars.

C. A **note–issuance facility (NIF)** is a form of medium–term lending through a variety of instruments, usually floating rate notes.

D. Committed versus Back–Up Facilities
1. For the most part, NIFs represent a **committed facility**—the banks issuing the facility commit themselves to making the loans as promised to the borrower.
2. It is also possible for a syndicate of lenders to offer an **uncommitted back–up facility**—an expressed intention, but no commitment, to lend under specified circumstances.

Key Terms and Concepts

accrued interest	the portion of the next coupon payment that has been earned by the bondholder, but which the bondholder has not yet received
amortized loan	a loan where equal payments over the life pay off all principal and interest, common in residential mortgages
arbitrage	the opportunity to earn a riskless profit with no investment
ask price	the price demanded by the owner of an instrument
balloon mortgage	a loan that is structured so that the final payment is much larger than the ordinary monthly payments
bankers' acceptance	a money market instrument represented by a draft on a bank that the bank has promised to honor at some point in the future
basis point	equal to 1/100 of one percent
bid price	the price a buyer is willing to pay for a good
bond contract	or bond indenture, is a legal document stating in precise terms the promises made by the issuer of a bond and the rights of the bondholders

bond discount	the par value minus the selling price of a bond
bond equivalent yield	a money market yield measure that converts a discount yield to a return that is comparable to the returns on bonds
bond market	trading of legal claims against governments, corporations, or municipalities
bond rating	an analyst's assessment of default risk—the chance that one or more payments on the bond will be deferred or missed altogether.
call price	the price the issuer must pay to redeem a callable bond, usually above par, or par if the issue is close to maturity
callable bond	a bond that may be retired early at the option of the issuer, usually if interest rates have fallen
collateral trust bond	a bond secured by financial assets
commercial paper	short–term unsecured debt of large, creditworthy corporations which is traded in the money market
committed facility	when the banks issuing the facility commit themselves to making the loans as promised to the borrower
conversion premium	the additional amount per share of stock that one pays to obtain the share by converting the bond rather than by buying the stock in the marketplace
conversion price	the market price of a convertible bond divided by the conversion ratio
conversion ratio	the number of shares of stock a convertible bond may be surrendered for
convertible bond	a bond that may be turned in for the issuer's common stock if the owner so desires
corporate bond	a legal claim against the assets of a corporation, usually long term with interim coupon payments

coupon	regularly scheduled payments made by coupon bonds between the original date of issue and the maturity date
coupon bond	a bond that promises interim interest payments, (coupons), most often paid semiannually, in addition to paying par value at maturity
coupon stripping	the act of removing the individual interest coupons from the bond and treating each payment as a separate security
current yield	the annual dollar coupon divided by the current market price
debenture	bonds issued by corporations that have an inferior claim on the firm's assets
default risk	the chance that one or more promised payments will not be made as promised
discount bond	a coupon bond trading below face value
discount paper	a money market instrument that is issued with a stated par value and no coupon rate
discount yield	a yield calculation traditionally applied in the money market that uses a 360–day year and considers the dollar return as a percentage of face value
equipment trust certificate	debt secured by physical equipment such as railroad cars
equivalent tax exempt yield	the after–tax yield on taxable debt, or (1 – marginal tax rate)(taxable yield)
Eurobond	a bond issued by a borrower in one country, denominated in the borrower's currency, and sold outside the borrower's country
Euro–commercial paper	commercial paper traded in the international market, usually denominated in dollars
Eurodollar	dollar–denominated bank deposits held outside the United States, traded in the money market

Eurodollar CD	a dollar–denominated CD issued by a bank outside the U.S.
equity–related bonds	include both convertible bonds and bonds with equity warrants
equity warrant	a security that gives the holder the right to acquire a newly issued share of common stock from a company for the payment of a stated price
external bond	can be either an international bond or a foreign bond
federal agency	a direct arm of the U.S. government that does not issue debt on its own, but meets its needs through issues of the Federal Financing Bank
federal funds	or fed funds, is the borrowing and lending of reserve balances by member banks in the money market, usually on an overnight basis
federally sponsored agency	a privately owned entity that raises funds in the market
first mortgage bond	debt secured by the first claim on specific assets
flat bond	a bond that trades without accrued interest because the issue is in default or there is a great deal of uncertainty regarding the receipt of the next interest payment
floating rate note	a bond that pays a different coupon rate over time as the general level of interest rates fluctuates
flower bond	a specially designated U.S. T–bond that is redeemable at its owner's death for its face value plus accrued interest in payment of federal estate taxes
foreign bond	a bond a U.S. firm has issued that is denominated in a foreign currency for sale exclusively in the country of the foreign currency
general obligation bond	a bond backed by the issuer's taxing power, such as a state or local government

indenture	a legal document that contains the specific promises made by a bond issuer to the bondholders
interest–bearing instruments	in the money market these instruments are issued with a given par value and a stated coupon rate
international bond	a bond available for sale outside the country of its issuer
junk bonds	high–yield corporate bonds that are lower rated or speculative grade, which came into prominence in the 1980s
LIBOR or London Interbank Offered Rate	the rate that banks participating in the international debt market charge each other for short–term loans
money market	the market for debt instruments with a maturity of one year or less at the time of issuance
mortgage	debt owed on real estate
mortgage pass–throughs	a security where the original lender continues to collect payments from the borrower and passes them through to the investors in the mortgage pool
mortgage pool	a collection of individual mortgages that can be treated as a unit
municipal bond	a debt security issued by a government or a quasi–governmental agency, other than those associated with the federal government
mutual funds	portfolios of securities that are owned in common by a group of investors
negotiable CD	short–term liability of banks traded in the money market in units of $100,000 or more
note–issuance facility	a form of medium–term lending through a variety of instruments, usually floating rate notes
overnight repo	a repo used for short–term (one day) financing
par bond	a coupon bond trading at face value

par value	or face value is the amount a bond will pay at maturity
premium bond	a coupon bond trading above face value
pure discount bond	a bond that does not carry interim interest payments, but pays only face value at maturity
repurchase agreement	or repo is an agreement to sell an asset today with a promise to buy it back at a later date at a price specified today
revenue bond	a municipal bond secured by the revenues generated by the project it finances
serial bond	a bond issue where predetermined portions of the debt are retired at specified dates
sinking fund	a fund established by the issuer for the orderly retirement of a bond issue
straight bond	a bond with a fixed payment schedule with no special features
subordinated debenture	an unsecured bond that has an inferior claim to other outstanding debentures
syndicated loan	a loan made by a consortium of banks to a single borrower
term repo	a repo held for more than one day
Treasury bill	or T–bill is a pure discount debt of the U.S. Treasury with an initial maturity of less than one year
Treasury bond	or T–bond is a long–term, coupon bearing, debt of the U.S. government with an initial maturity in excess of 10 years
Treasury note	or T–note is a long–term, coupon bearing, debt of the U.S. government with an initial maturity between one and 10 years
triple tax–exempt	a debt issue whose interest is exempt from state, local, and federal income taxation

trustee	an individual or institution charged with insuring that a bond issuer complies with the terms of the indenture
two–name paper	a bankers' acceptance in which the bank and the original firm for whom the acceptance was created are both obligated to make the payment
uncommitted back–up facility	an expressed intention, but no commitment, to lend under specified circumstances
variable–rate mortgage	a loan secured by real property whose interest rate moves up and down with economic conditions
yield approximation formula	the approximate annual return on a coupon bearing instrument that is determined by applying a fixed formula instead of trial and error calculations
yield curve	the schedule showing the relationship between the maturity of bonds in the same risk class and the yields on those bonds
yield to maturity	the annualized return that would be earned over the life of the bond if all interim cash flows are reinvested at that same yield to maturity

Multiple–Choice Questions

1. The money market is comprised of those debt instruments that have ____ or less to maturity when issued.
    A. six months
    B. nine months
    C. one year
    D. two years
    E. five years

2. Bonds secured by financial assets are known as ____ bonds.
    A. serial
    B. sinking fund
    C. collateral trust
    D. equipment trust
    E. mortgage

3. The difference between par value and selling price for a pure discount bond is called the ____.
   A. bond premium
   B. bond coupon
   C. bond differential
   D. bond discount
   E. price bond differential

4. A bond that has a face value of $1,000, a yield of 12 percent, a semiannual coupon of $50, and a maturity of one year is priced at $____.
   A. 576.96
   B. 867.98
   C. 965.87
   D. 981.67
   E. 998.45

5. Bond equivalent yield differs from discount yield in that the bond equivalent yield is a return on ____.
   A. price paid
   B. a 360–day year
   C. the date of call
   D. the premium over par
   E. the serial maturity

6. If the market price of the bond equals the face value, the bond is a ____ bond.
   A. premium
   B. discount
   C. coupon
   D. pure discount
   E. par

7. All of the following money market instruments are pure discount instruments *except* ____.
   A. bankers' acceptances
   B. commercial paper
   C. Treasury bills
   D. fed funds
   E. negotiable CDs

8. The ability to earn riskless profits without investment is known as ____.
   A. convertability
   B. callability
   C. serialization
   D. fundability
   E. arbitrage

9. Commercial paper usually carries a higher return than Treasury bills do because ____.
   A. corporations are better credit risks than banks
   B. domestic banks are better credit risks than foreign banks
   C. the U.S. government is a better credit risk than a corporation
   D. commercial paper has a shorter maturity
   E. commercial paper interest is exempt from income taxes

10. The price an issuer pays to redeem a bond early is known as the ____ price.
    A. conversion
    B. call
    C. serial
    D. sinking fund
    E. face

11. The current yield is calculated as ____.
    A. annual coupon divided by market price
    B. market price divided by annual coupon
    C. annual coupon minus market price
    D. market price plus annual coupon
    E. annual coupon times market price

12. The designation "cv" means that the bond is ____.
    A. coupon value
    B. cash variance
    C. convertible
    D. convex
    E. current value

13. Municipal bonds usually have lower yields than corporate bonds because ____.
    A. the municipal market is more liquid
    B. municipals are secured by residential mortgages
    C. municipal interest is exempt from Federal income taxation
    D. corporations are poorer credit risks than governments
    E. corporate bonds are secured by specific assets

14. Bonds issued in one currency and sold in countries that do not use that currency are known as ____.
    A. discount bonds
    B. Eurobonds
    C. federal funds
    D. commercial papers
    E. bankers' acceptances

15. An overnight loan of reserve balances is known as a ____ trade.
    A. repo
    B. fed funds
    C. bankers' acceptance
    D. general obligation
    E. sinking fund

16. If you are in a 36 percent tax bracket, a bond with a before–tax yield of 12 percent has an equivalent tax exempt yield of ____ percent.
    A. 4.32
    B. 6.00
    C. 7.68
    D. 8.20
    E. 12.00

17. The document that details a bond issuer's promises to the bondholders is known as the ____.
    A. sinking fund
    B. serial
    C. discount
    D. acceptance
    E. indenture

18. The interim payments that bond issuers make to bondholders are known as ____.
    A. coupons
    B. discounts
    C. yields
    D. returns
    E. municipals

19. Yield spreads between bonds of different credit quality tend to widen in recessions because ____.
    A. weaker bonds have shorter maturities
    B. the probability of default rises faster for weaker bonds as the economy worsens
    C. higher quality bonds are less liquid
    D. higher quality bonds have higher coupons
    E. higher quality bonds require smaller tax payments

20. Bonds that carry no specific security and have a weaker claim than other outstanding debentures of the same firm are known as ____.
    A. subordinated debentures
    B. debentures
    C. first mortgage bonds
    D. second mortgage bonds
    E. serial bonds

The following information applies to the next three problems.

A convertible bond with a par value of $1,000 has a market price of $920. The common stock of the issuing company is currently selling for $35. The bond contract allows the bondholder to convert the bond into 25 shares of common stock.

21. The conversion ratio is ____.
    A. 15
    B. 20
    C. 25
    D. 35
    E. 920

22. The conversion price is $____.
    A. 34.70
    B. 35.00
    C. 35.86
    D. 36.80
    E. 37.65

23. The conversion premium is $____.
    A. 0.00
    B. 0.86
    C. 1.80
    D. 2.30
    E   2.65

24. A mortgage where a series of equal payments pay off all principal and interest over the life of the loan is known as a(n) ____ loan.
    A. amortized
    B. variable rate
    C. balloon
    D. serial
    E. indenture

25. A $1,000,000 T–bill with 180 days to maturity selling for $940,000 has a discount yield of _____ percent.
    A. 6.00
    B. 6.38
    C. 6.93
    D. 12.00
    E. 13.85

26. _____ is the act of removing the individual interest coupons from the bond and treating each payment as a separate security.
    A. Coupon stripping
    B. Coupon dividing
    C. Coupon separating
    D. Security dividing
    E. Security stripping

27. A(n) _____ is a specially designated U.S. Treasury bond that is redeemable at its owners death for its face value plus accrued interest in payment of federal estate taxes.
    A. death bond
    B. enhanced bond
    C. flower bond
    D. estate bond
    E. discount bond

28. Most mortgages are for _____.
    A. residential properties
    B. mobile homes parks
    C. farm land
    D. rental properties
    E. one to two years in maturity

29. Bankers' acceptances are also known as _____.
    A. no–name paper
    B. two–name paper
    C. domestic paper
    D. low yield paper
    E. junk bonds

30. A(n) _____ bond is either an international bond or a foreign bond.
    A. flower
    B. convertible
    C. straight
    D. external
    E. junk

Review Problems

1. A pure discount bond has a face value of $1,000 and matures in three years. If it has a yield to maturity of 10 percent per year, what is its price?

2. A pure discount bond having a yield to maturity of 10 percent per year and maturing in 10 years has a face value of $1,000. What is its price?

3. A pure discount bond that matures in two years with a face value of $5,000 has a price of $3,986. What is its annual yield?

4. A pure discount bond that has a face value of $9,000 is priced at $6,762 for an annual yield of 10 percent. What is its term to maturity?

5. A $100,000 face T–bond with an 8 1/2 percent annual coupon and three years to maturity is priced at $98.01 bid, $98.09 asked. Compute its current yield and its approximate yield to maturity using both yield approximation formulas.

6. A coupon bond that pays an annual rate of 8 percent and has a face value of $1,000 matures in four years. If the bond yields 11 percent, what is its price?

7. A bond with two years to maturity has a face value of $1,000 and a 10 percent coupon rate with semiannual payments. If it yields 12 percent, what is its price?

8. You are trying to decide between two bonds that have equal default risk. The corporate bond yields 12 percent and the municipal yields 7.5 percent. What tax bracket makes you indifferent between the two bonds? If your tax bracket is lower than the indifference bracket, which bond should you pick?

9. A corporate bond that makes semiannual interest payments carries a coupon rate of 12 percent and a face value of $1,000. It made the last interest payment on October 15. If you purchase the bond on December 1, how much accrued interest will you pay the seller? If you sell the bond for the same price on December 21, how much accrued interest will you receive? How could you calculate the accrued interest return directly?

10. A Treasury bond with semiannual payments has a coupon rate of 10 percent, four years to maturity, a $1,000 face value, and a yield to maturity of 8 percent. A similar Treasury bond has a coupon rate of 6 percent, six years to maturity, and a yield to maturity of 7.5 percent. Calculate the current yield for each bond. Why is the current yield always between the coupon rate and the yield to maturity?

11. A bond selling for $900 is convertible into 50 shares of stock. The stock is currently selling at $15 per share. Compute the conversion ratio, the conversion price, and the conversion premium. If the stock goes to $20 per share and the bond price remains at $900, what should you do? How will the market prices react?

12. A $1,000,000 face T–bill with 40 days to maturity is priced at $985,000. Compute the discount yield and the bond equivalent yield.

13. A $1,000,000 T–bill with 120 days to maturity has an annual discount yield of 11.7 percent. What is its price?

14. A $10,000 T–bill that matures in 73 days has an annual bond equivalent yield of 12 percent. What is its price?

15. There are two bonds with a face value of $1,000 and both mature in five years. One bond has a coupon rate of 10 percent and a yield to maturity of 10 percent. The other bond has a coupon rate of 11 percent and a yield to maturity of 11 percent. Which bond is worth more today?

Answers

Multiple–Choice Questions

1. C	11. A	21. C
2. C	12. C	22. D
3. D	13. C	23. C
4. D	14. B	24. A
5. A	15. B	25. D
6. E	16. C	26. A
7. E	17. E	27. C
8. E	18. A	28. A
9. C	19. B	29. B
10. B	20. A	30. D

Review Problems

1. The price of the pure discount bond is the present value of the single future payment occurring in three years discounted at 10 percent per year.

   $P = \$1,000/(1.1)^3 = \$1,000/1.331 = \$751.31.$

2. Discounting the payment promised in 10 years back to today at a rate of 10 percent per year is:

   $P = \$1,000/(1.10)^{10} = \$1,000/2.5937 = \$385.54$

3. Applying the bond pricing formula for a pure discount bond with two years to maturity:

   $\$3,986 = \$5,000/(1 + x)^2$, or

   $(1 + x)^2 = \$5,000/\$3,986 = 1.2544$, or

   $1.2544 =$ the square of (one plus the annual yield)

   $(1 + x) = (1.2544)^{.5} = 1.12$, so $x = .12$ or 12 percent.

4. Now using x to represent years to maturity:

    $6,762 = $9,000/(1.1)^x$, or

    $(1.1)^x = $9,000/$6762 = 1.331$.

    x must exceed 1, so by trial and error:

    $(1.1)^2 = 1.21$

    $(1.1)^3 = 1.331$, so the bond matures in three years.

5. If you buy a bond, you pay the seller's price, the ask of $98.09. Remember that the numbers to the right of the decimal place in government bond quotes represent 32nds, so the price of a $100,000 bond at 98 9/32 per $100 is $98,281.25.

    To use the yield to maturity approximation formula, accrue ($100,000 –$98,281.25)/3 = $572.92 of the discount per year for each of the three years. The annual coupon is $8,500 and the average investment is ($100,000 + $98,281.25)/2 = $99,140.63.

    Therefore, the approximate yield is:

    ($8,500 + $572.92)/$99,140.63 = 9.15 percent.

    The more sophisticated approximation formula changes the denominator to (FV + 2P)/3, or:

    [$100,000 + 2($98,281.25)]/3 =

    ($100,000 + $196,562.50)/3 = $98,854.17.

    Now the approximate yield to maturity is:

    $9,072.92/$98,854.17 = 9.18 percent.

    To give you an idea of the accuracy of the two approximations, the true yield to maturity of the bond is 9.17 percent.

    The current yield is the annual interest payment divided by the current price: $8,500/$98,281.25 = 8.65 percent.

6. The price of a coupon bond is the present value of each coupon plus the present value of the face value discounted at an annual rate of 11 percent.

$$P = \$80/(1.11)^1 + \$80/(1.11)^2 + \$80/(1.11)^3$$

$$+ \$80/(1.11)^4 + \$1000/(1.11)^4$$

$$= (\$80/1.11) + (\$80/1.2321) + (\$80/1.3676)$$

$$+ (\$80/1.5181) + (\$1000/1.5181)$$

$$= 72.07 + 64.93 + 58.50 + 52.70 + 658.72$$

$$= \$906.92.$$

7. An annual 10 percent coupon on a $1,000 bond is $100 per year or $50 every six months. A 12 percent annual rate is equivalent to 6 percent every six months. Find the present value of all the payments:

$$P = \$50/(1.06)^1 + \$50/(1.06)^2 + \$50/(1.06)^3$$

$$+ \$50/(1.06)^4 + \$1000/(1.06)^4$$

$$= 47.17 + 44.50 + 41.98 + 39.60 + 792.09$$

$$= \$965.34.$$

8. The equivalent tax–exempt yield is equal to the taxable yield times (1 – the marginal tax bracket), so the tax bracket that creates indifference is represented by x in the following equation:

7.5 percent = (1 – x)12 percent, or:

(1 – x) = 7.5 percent/12 percent = 62.5 percent, so x = 37.5 percent.

If your tax bracket is below 37.5 percent, you would choose the corporate bond since you would lose less than 37.5 percent of your return to taxes and would net more than 7.5 percent. For example, if you are in a 30 percent bracket, your after–tax yield would be:

(1 – .3)12 percent = .7(12 percent) = 8.4 percent.

9. The annual payment is .12($1,000) = $120, for a semiannual payment of $120/2 = $60.

    Calculating the days since the last payment, there are 16 days left in October plus 30 days in November for a total of 46 days. In addition, there are 182 days between interest payments, so the accrued interest is:

    (46/182)($60) = (.253)$60 = $15.16.

    On December 21, accrued interest for the original 46 days plus 20 days in December are traded, (a total of 66 days), so the accrued interest is:

    (66/182)($60) = (.363)$60 = $21.78.

    This is an increase of $21.78 – $15.16 = $6.62.

    The increase can be calculated directly by realizing that one day's interest is $60/182 = $.33. Therefore, 20 days' interest is $.33(20) = $6.60.

10. The current yield is equal to the annual interest payment divided by the price. For the 10 percent bond:

    $100/$1,067 = .0937 = 9.37 percent.

    For the 6 percent bond:

    $60/$929 = .0646 = 6.46 percent.

    The current yield is always between the coupon rate and the yield to maturity because of the assumptions built into the yield calculations. The 10 percent bond is a premium bond so the purchaser pays more than face value. Thus, the coupon rate, which assumes the payment of face value, overstates the return to the investor. The current yield reflects the price paid, reducing the over-statement, but assumes that the purchaser receives the price paid for the bond at maturity. Since the purchaser receives only face value, there is still some overstatement here. Only the yield to maturity, which reflects both the price paid and the face value returned, does not overstate the return to the investor.

    For the discount bond, the opposite relationships hold. The purchaser pays less than face value, a return reflected in the current yield but not the coupon rate, and receives face value at maturity, a return reflected in the yield to maturity but not the current yield. These relationships hold for all coupon bonds.

11. The conversion ratio is the number of shares the bond can be converted into: 50 shares.

    The conversion price is the market price of the bond divided by the number of shares it carries:

    $900/50 = $18.

    The conversion premium is the excess of the conversion price over the market price:

    $18 – $15 = $3.

    If the stock rises to $20 and the bond price does not change, you, and every one else, will buy the bond for $900, turn it in for 50 shares worth $20 each, sell those shares for $1,000 total, and pocket the $100 difference as a riskless profit. This cannot occur in an efficient market. People wishing to buy the bond bid its price up. People selling the stock force its price down. These adjustments continue until the conversion premium exceeds $0.

12. The bond discount is its face value minus its price:

    $1,000,000 – $985,000 = $15,000

    The discount yield is:

    (360/40)($15,000/$1,000,000) = 9(.015) = 13.5 percent.

    The bond equivalent yield is: (365)(.135)/[360–(.135)(40)] =

    [49.275/(360 – 5.4)] = 13.9 percent.

13. We must solve the discount yield equation to find the amount of the discount (DIS):

    .117 = (360/120)(DIS/$1,000,000), or

    (.117/3) = .039 = (DIS/$1,000,000), so

    DIS = .039($1,000,000) = $39,000, and

    Price = $1,000,000 – $39,000 = $961,000.

    Or, $1,000,000 [1 – .117(120/360)] = $961,000

14. First, find the discount yield (d) by solving from the bond equivalent yield formula:

    $.12 = 365d/(360 - 73d)$, or $.12(360 - 73d) = 365d$, or

    $43.2 - 8.76d = 365d$, or $43.2 = 365d + 8.76d$, or

    $43.2 = 373.76d$, so $d = 43.2/373.76 = 11.56$ percent.

    Now, find the price from the discount yield as in Problem 9:

    $.1156 = (360/73)(DIS/\$10,000)$, or

    $.1156 = 4.932(DIS/\$10,000)$, or

    $.1156/4.932 = .02344 = DIS/\$10,000$, so

    $DIS = .02344(\$10,000) = \$234.40$, and

    $Price = \$10,000 - \$234.40 = \$9,765.60$.

15. Because both bonds are par bonds, they both sell for $1,000, or the face value. Therefore, both bonds are worth the same today.

CHAPTER THREE

The Stock Market: An Overview

Chapter Objectives

Upon completion of this chapter, you should be able to:
1. Explain the rights and responsibilities of common stock ownership.
2. Calculate WRs and returns on common stock trades.
3. Compare and contrast cash dividends, stock dividends, and stock splits.
4. Compare and contrast organized exchanges and the over–the–counter market.
5. Compare and contrast the functions of specialists and market makers.
6. Be able to explain the functions of a floor broker.
7. Be able to describe and explain the order flow.
8. Distinguish between the different types of stock trade orders.
9. Calculate dividend yield and the P/E ratio.
10. Explain and calculate the returns from margin trading and short sales.
11. Describe the third and fourth markets.
12. Compare and contrast discount and full–line brokerage houses.
13. Compare and contrast the major stock market indexes.

Chapter Outline

I. Common Stock Rights and Responsibilities

    A. Common stock represents an ownership interest in a corporation.
       1. The management of the firm is charged with advancing the interests of the common stock owners, implying that management should maximize the price of a share of common stock.
       2. Therefore, managers of the firm act as agents for the stockholders.

3. The interests of the agent–managers are not always the same as those of the shareholders. For example, managers may purchase unnecessary luxury items.

4. Common stock constitutes a **residual claim** on the assets and proceeds of the firm, that is, a claim on the value of the firm after other claimants have been satisfied.

5. Common stock is the riskiest position of all claimants against the firm; the hope of large returns normally goes with the acceptance of greater risk.

6. Common stock ownership does contain the risk–limiting feature of limited liability. The most that can be lost is the amount invested.

7. Holders of common stock commit their funds and assume the last place claim on the value of the firm in hopes of securing substantial profits.

8. Payoffs to shareholders can come in two forms:
   a. The price of shares could increase, generating a capital gain.
   b. The firm could pay a cash dividend.

9. The WR formula for common stock is:

$$WR = \frac{\text{Current Stock Price + Cash Dividends Received}}{\text{Original Stock Price}}$$

10. While the stock is owned, the only cash flow from the shares is the cash dividends, if any.

11. Most firms that pay dividends do so on a quarterly basis, although that is not always the case.

12. Most common stock shares convey voting rights to their owners. Stockholders can empower some other party to vote for them at the annual meeting by giving them a **proxy**.

13. The struggle by two or more parties to acquire voting rights from shareholders, and thus control of the firm, is known as a **proxy fight**.

14. In some firms, common stock is classified, usually as either Class A or Class B. Normally, the primary difference is Class A will have voting rights while Class B will not having voting rights.

15. Occasionally, owners of common stock receive **stock dividends** or **stock splits**.
   a. Stock dividends and splits raise no new funds for the firm or the owners. Rather, they increase the number of shares held by the current owners.
   b. A stock dividend occurs when the firm increases the number of shares outstanding by 25 percent or less. An increase of more than 25 percent is a stock split.
   c. Stock splits or stock dividends may be beneficial to investors if the dividend is not reduced proportionately. In addition, some managers appear to believe that keeping share prices within some popular trading range helps the stock's liquidity.
   d. Although some believe that investors perceive additional stock as some kind of benefit, it may not be any benefit at all.

e. Stock transaction costs are cheapest for a **round lot**—a block of stock of 100 shares or some multiple of 100. If a stock dividend or split leaves an investor with an **odd lot**—a holding not evenly divisible by 100—then the transaction costs can be higher on a percentage basis.

II. General Organization of the Stock Market

A. The **secondary market**, (for existing securities), is made up of organized stock exchanges, such as the New York Stock Exchange (NYSE), the American Stock Exchange (AMEX), and a dealer market, called the over–the–counter market (OTC).
B. There is also a **primary market**, a market for the sale of new securities.
C. Organized Exchanges
 1. A **stock exchange** is a voluntary organization formed by a group of individuals to provide an institutional setting in which common stock, and other securities, can be bought and sold.
 2. Members of stock exchanges own memberships or **seats** on the exchange, and only members or their representatives are allowed to trade on the exchange.
 3. Each stock exchange allows trading only on the floor of the exchange and only during approved trading hours.
 4. The floor of an exchange is an actual physical location to which orders are transmitted for execution.
 5. The floor of the exchange houses regular and business news wire services to serve the participants' vast informational needs.
 6. People working on the floor of the exchange fall into several groups:
  a. **Exchange employees**, who oversee the trading activity and report the outcomes of trades to the public on a continuous basis.
  b. **Exchange members**, who trade for their own accounts.
  c. **Brokers**, who receive orders from the public outside the exchange and execute the orders
  d. **Specialists** for each security, who stand ready to trade at least 100 shares of the stock they are assigned to, and record all orders awaiting execution in the stock
D. The Specialist
 1. The **specialist**, who always holds a seat on the exchange, has the responsibility of making a market in an assigned security. The specialist has two main functions:
  a. The specialist acts as a broker on some transactions for other trading parties.
  b. The specialist may also act as a dealer, buying and selling for his or her own account.

2. As a dealer, the specialist stands ready to buy or sell securities on order from other members of the exchange or to the public. As compensation for the capital investment and the assumption of the risk the specialist necessarily takes, the specialist attempts to make a profit on each share of stock traded.

3. Acting as a dealer or **market maker**, the specialist maintains a **bid–asked spread**—the difference between the price at which she is willing to buy and sell a share.

4. A specialist must respond to new information and correctly manipulate his bid and asked prices, so that he does not receive orders for one side of the market only.

5. The spread between the bid and asked prices represents the gross profit margin for the specialist; therefore, the wider the bid–asked spread, the greater the specialist's profits, other things being equal.

6. At times, traders outside the exchange may know more about the future of the stock price for a given share than the specialist. These traders are known as **informed traders**.

7. In contrast, **liquidity traders** buy because they have funds to invest or sell because they need cash.

8. One of the richest sources of a specialist's information comes from the limit order book in which all limit orders awaiting execution are recorded. A **limit order** is an order to be executed only at a certain price, if that price becomes available.

9. Specialists do not trade for their own accounts in most stock transactions; in 1990, specialists were neither buyers nor sellers in 80.1 percent of the volume.

10. Exchange rules regulate the specialists' trading.
    a. The specialist is obligated to reveal the highest bid price and the lowest asked price.
    b. To participate as a buyer or seller, the specialist must bid more than any limit order to buy, or ask less than any limit order to sell.
    c. Public orders at the same price as a specialist's have precedence over the specialist's.

11. In summation, in return for the monopoly positions granted by the exchange, specialists are required to make a market in the stock, to keep the bid–asked spread reasonably small, and to trade to stabilize prices.

E. The Floor Broker
   1. Typically, floor brokers facilitate the execution of larger orders.
   2. The floor broker may be an employee of a large brokerage firm or may be a free–lance broker.
   3. Because floor brokers work larger orders, they generally have the discretion to **work an order**—to try to fill the order at the best price.
   4. Floor brokers are paid based on shares traded, so they have an incentive to trade as quickly as possible.

F. Order Flow
1. Orders can be initiated from virtually anywhere. Consider an individual in Miami, Florida, wishing to purchase a share of stock from the NYSE. Since the individual is not a member of the NYSE, he or she must trade through a member, in our case, a brokerage firm:
    a. The first step would be to open an account.
    b. Once the account is opened, the customer may contact the broker by telephone and place an order.
    c. Once the order reaches the NYSE, it may be completed in one of two fundamentally different ways.
        (1) It can go to a floor broker for execution.
        (2) If the order is small and requires no special treatment, the order may be handled electronically through SuperDOT (Designated Order Turnaround).
    d. Exchanges arrange their trading floors with particular physical locations, or **trading posts** for each security; all orders to buy or sell a security must ultimately come to the trading post for the particular stock.
    e. Once the trade is executed, the transaction must be reported to the customer, the customer's brokerage firm, and the public at large.
    f. The entire transaction described takes only a few minutes. Usually, the customer can place the order and receive confirmation of the order during the same two–minute phone call.
G. The New York Stock Exchange
1. The New York Stock Exchange dominates the stock exchanges in the United States and matches any exchange in the world.
2. Domestically, the NYSE accounts for about 50 percent of share volume and about 64 percent of dollar volume, due to the higher average price of NYSE shares.
3. Only firms meeting certain minimum requirements regarding financial strength, total value of outstanding stock, and number of shareholders are eligible for listing. These requirements often mean that only larger firms qualify for NYSE listing.
4. Transactions for all NYSE–listed securities are shown on one reporting system, called the **consolidated tape**, no matter where the transaction actually took place.
5. Exchange membership confers valuable rights to the owner of the seat, and, as such, these memberships are traded openly as capital assets.
6. Among the data on NYSE stocks you will find in *The Wall Street Journal* are the **dividend yield** and the **price–earnings ratio**:

$$\text{Dividend Yield} = \frac{\text{Current Annual Dividend}}{\text{Current Stock Price}}$$

$$\text{P-E Ratio} = \frac{\text{Current Stock Price}}{\text{Current Annual Earnings}}$$

7. Of the other organized exchanges, the American Stock Exchange is clearly the largest.

III. The Secondary Market: The Over–the–Counter Market

A. Trading on the over–the–counter market has been growing faster than trading on organized exchanges, even the NYSE. Further, recent and future advances in computer technology will probably benefit the OTC market more than the organized exchanges.

B. General Organizational Features
    1. In the OTC market, there is no central trading place, but electronic communications are used to link participants all over the world.
    2. The OTC market does not make use of specialists. Instead, there are a number of **market makers**—firms and individuals making a market in particular stocks.
    3. The privilege of trading in the OTC market is granted by the National Association of Securities Dealers (NASD), and is granted based on financial soundness and qualification examinations.

C. Flow of Orders
    1. Only a member of NASD is allowed to trade in the OTC market, and one must use a broker and a brokerage account to buy or sell shares.
    2. For all practical purposes, placing an order in this market is as easy as placing an order on the NYSE.
    3. Brokers and other traders in the OTC market use the National Association of Securities Dealers Automated Quotation (NASDAQ) System.

D. Stock Trading on the OTC Market
    1. Firms traded OTC tend to be quite a bit smaller than NYSE firms. Historically, smaller firms tend to have greater returns than larger firms, as well as more risk.
    2. The OTC market consists of about 15,000 securities, yet many of these have only a local market, such as the stock of local banks.
    3. Only the larger, more important firms are carried on NASDAQ.

E. The National Market System
    The most important stocks on the over–the–counter market are listed on the National Market System (NMS), and transactions for these securities are reported more rapidly and more fully than for the less important stocks.

F. Contrasts with Organized Exchanges
    1. The criticism of the dealer market used in the OTC market is now much weaker in light of NASDAQ and the NMS. In the major OTC stocks, the trader has information about current stock prices that is just as good as the information available to the trader on an organized exchange.
    2. With further developments in computer technology, the reporting requirements now in place for NMS securities can be expected to be extended to many others.

IV. *Trading Procedures and Practices*

A. Types of Orders
    1. A **market order** instructs the broker to buy or sell a security at whatever price prevails on the market floor at that time. A market order is an order for immediate execution.
    2. **Limit orders** are orders to transact only if certain conditions are met, rather than being an order for immediate execution.
    3. A **not held order** can be either a limit order or a market order, where marking the order as "not held" gives the floor broker the freedom to seek a better price.
    4. A **percentage order** instructs the broker to make a transaction only as a certain percentage of the order flow in a given stock.
    5. A **stop order** is an order that becomes active when a certain price condition is met. It can be either a stop market order or a stop limit order.
    6. In addition to specifying the conditions under which orders will be executed, the trader can also control the time dimension of stop or limit orders or the portion of an order that can be filled.
        a. A **day order** is in effect just for the current trading day.
        b. A **good until canceled order** is an order that is left in effect until it is canceled, so it can stay in effect virtually forever.
        c. An **at the opening** order instructs that the order be executed only at the opening of the trading session.
        d. A **fill or kill order** instructs the broker to fill the entire order at a particular price immediately or cancel the order.
        e. An **immediate or cancel** order instructs the broker to fill the entire order, or any part, at a particular price immediately or cancel the order.
        f. An **all or none** order instructs the broker to fill the entire order or not to transact.
        g. A **market–on–close** order is an order to transact at the market price as close to the close of trading as possible.
        h. A **limit** or **market–on–close** order is a limit order left in effect during the trading day. If the order is not executed during the day, it becomes a market order at the close of trading.

B. Margin Trading
  1. If one wishes to invest in stocks in an amount that exceeds the cash available to pay for them, one can buy the shares through **margin trading.**
  2. Here, one borrows some of the share price from the brokerage firm, which itself borrows money at the **broker's call rate**—the rate charged by banks for loans to brokerage houses on loans secured with securities.
  3. The proportion of the share value that the investor must invest out of personal funds is called the **initial margin**.
  4. Currently, the maximum percentage of the shares' value that one may borrow is 50 percent.
  5. In addition to the initial margin, stipulated by the Federal Reserve Board, the broker also imposes a **maintenance margin** requirement. If the stock price later falls far enough that the security value is less than the required level, the purchaser will face a **margin call** to provide additional cash.
  6. Since the Great Depression, the initial margin that one can borrow has been regulated by the Federal Reserve Board.
C. Short Sales
  1. If one sells shares that one does not currently own, this transaction is called a **short sale**. In the stock market, this is a legitimate form of trading, referred to as **selling short** or **short selling**.
  2. In a short sale, a trader begins by selling shares that he does not own, with the intention of buying them back later at a lower price.
  3. A short sale is normally accomplished by borrowing the shares to be sold from another trader. A broker helps accomplish this.
  4. Brokers have a ready supply of shares to borrow for most stocks, since they hold shares for many customers in **street name**. That is, customers simply leave their shares in the custody of their brokers, and the brokers are specifically authorized to loan these shares by the agreement which opens the brokerage account.
  5. Later, the short seller must purchase and return the borrowed shares to close the position. In addition, the short seller must pay the owner of the shares any dividends received during the short sale.
  6. The short sale is profitable if the stock falls in price, so short selling is a way to make profits from falling stock prices.

V. The Third and Fourth Markets

A. Transactions for stock in excess of 10,000 shares are called **block trades**. Block trading is an important activity for the organized exchanges, particularly the NYSE, but it is less important now than it has been.
B. The **third market** is a market for large blocks of shares that operates outside the confines of the organized exchanges and the OTC market.

    C. The major traders in this market are large institutions who have a frequent need to move large blocks of shares.

    D. In the third market, brokers assist the institutions by bringing buyers and sellers together.

    E. The **fourth market** is composed mainly of institutional traders who, like third market traders, are seeking to economize on transaction costs.

    F. The difference between them is that in the fourth market, institutions trade among themselves without the aid of brokers.

    G. Both markets developed in response to the fixed commission structure of the NYSE. This policy of fixed commission rates was later changed on **Mayday**, May 1, 1975. Brokers who are now able and willing to negotiate commissions on block trades have attracted much business back to the NYSE.

VI. The Brokerage Industry

    A. The brokerage industry is rapidly evolving.

    B. The key function of a brokerage firm is the execution of customers' orders for securities purchases and sales. Many firms provide research, which is one of the main competitive tools used.

    C. For the investor who does not consider research to be an important service, **discount brokers** are useful.

    D. Full–line brokerage firms continue to supply research reports and a much higher level of service, with brokers functioning largely as salesmen who drum up orders from a client list.

    E. On the other hand, discount brokers wait for calls from clients, and an investor may not even know the name of the broker executing the order.

    F. Differences in service and philosophy can lead to sizable differences in commission costs, which can be an important factor in the profitability of the investment.

VII. Transaction Costs and Portfolio Management

    A. In addition to commissions and the bid–asked spread, large traders face a third type of cost, a **price impact**—a change in the price of a share due to a transaction being made.

    B. Commissions
       1. The commission charged usually depends on both the number of shares and on the share price.
       2. Commission costs appear to be the largest component of the transaction costs facing traders.
       3. The transaction cost per share drops dramatically for larger orders.

    C. The Bid–Asked Spread
       1. Factors like activity, volatility, informational effects, and competition can all affect the size of the bid–asked spread.

2. Therefore, estimates of the bid–asked spread vary, depending on the stock and the market being examined.

3. The full bid–asked spread is a direct estimate of the round–trip (purchase and sale) transaction costs due to the bid–asked spread.

4. Components of the Bid–asked Spread

   a. Studies have sought to decompose the specialist's or market maker's bid–asked spread into its relevant components:

   (1) Order processing costs—costs that a specialist or market maker charges simply for filling an order.

   (2) Inventory holding costs.

   (3) **Adverse information** is information unknown to the specialist or market maker that may affect the price of the security.

D. Price Impacts

1. An excess demand for shares of a certain stock, in combination with the price prevailing when the order is initiated, can cause the price to rise. In this case, the very act of attempting to buy the shares can have a significant price impact.

2. Price impacts are likely to arise only for large traders. Individual traders are unlikely to generate price impacts.

3. Large institutions carefully manage their orders in order to minimize or avoid price impacts.

E. Transaction Costs and Trading

1. Very low transaction costs are available only to very large traders; individual traders face much higher transaction costs.

2. Buying and selling together constitute a round–trip transaction, which is also known as the **turnover** of a share.

3. For large portfolios, it is common to measure the **turnover ratio** of the entire portfolio.

VIII. Market Indexes

A. Market indexes provide a useful tool to summarize and to conceptualize the vast array of information generated by the continuous buying and selling of securities.

B. Many different indexes compete for attention; they differ in construction and can differ widely in interpretation.

C. There are indexes for almost all kinds of instruments.

D. The Dow Jones Industrial Average (DJIA) reflects price movements of 30 of the largest industrial firms (**blue chip stocks**) listed on the NYSE. It is the most widely reported market index, but it is extremely limited as a gauge of the stock market.

E. Because the prices are all added, the DJIA is a **price–weighted** index, in which each stock contributes to the index value in proportion to its price.

F. Because the index depends on the number of dollars from summing all the prices, the DJIA does not reflect the percentage change in the price of a share.

G. The Dow is computed as follows:

$$\text{DJIA} = \frac{\sum_{n=1}^{30} P_n}{\text{Divisor}}$$

where, P_n is the price of stock n and Divisor is the special DJIA divisor.

H. The S&P 500 Index consists of 500 of the largest stocks on the NYSE, although a few OTC–traded firms are also included. It is a broader market index than the Dow.

I. The S&P 500 is a **value–weighted index**—the importance of the price movement in a given share depends upon its market value relative to the total market value of all of the shares in the index.

J. The value of the S&P 500 index is reported relative to the average value during the period of 1941–1943, which was assigned an index value of 10.

K. The NYSE Composite Index is a value–weighted index of all stocks listed on the NYSE.

L. Comparison of the Indexes
   1. The more stocks in an index, the less volatile the percentage price change.
   2. Because big firms tend to be more stable than small firms, we would expect a value–weighted index to be less volatile than a price–weighted index.
   3. Historically, broader market indexes have tended to outperform narrower measures. This result occurs because the broad indexes include returns for small companies, which have tended to perform better than large firms.
   4. It is important to remember that most of these indexes consider only price changes, not dividends, so they typically do not provide a good indication of the total returns earned on the stocks in the index.
   5. In general, each index gives a measure of performance for some segment of the stock market. Following the major indexes can give a good guide to general stock market activity.

IX. The Worldwide Stock Market

A. Alternative Trading Procedures
   1. The U.S. stock market is a **continuous market**—a market in which a good is available for trading throughout the trading session.
   2. By contrast, some markets use an entirely different system. In a **call market**, each security is called for trading at a specific time and can be traded only at that time.

B. World Equity Market Capitalization
   1. In recent years, Japan has overtaken the U.S. in market capitalization, and its higher growth rate suggests that it may far outstrip U.S. markets before long.

2.   Virtually every European country has its own stock market. Markets are forming among eastern European countries, often with assistance from western nations.
3.   In emerging nations, market capitalization is universally thin and is reported in millions of dollars. All of these markets together amount to only about one–thousandth of the value of the shares listed on the NYSE.

C.   Dual Listing and American Depositary Receipts
1.   Some stocks are listed on several exchanges in different countries. Rules for listing differ markedly in different countries, with U.S. requirements being among the most restrictive.
2.   To avoid U.S. trading restrictions, the **American Depositary Receipt (ADR)** was created.
   a.   An ADR is a document showing that shares of stock have been deposited with a bank that acts as a depositary for the shares.
   b.   The purchaser of an ADR holds a claim on a certain number of shares deposited with the bank. The company whose stocks are held by the depositary pays dividends to the bank, which exchanges those foreign funds into dollars, and then pays the American investor a dollar dividend.

D.   Foreign Stock Market Indexes
1.   Virtually every stock market has some stock market index designed to summarize trading results.
2.   The Financial Times Stock Exchange (FTSE) from London and the Nikkei from Tokyo are reported daily in *The Wall Street Journal*.
3.   The MSCI and the FT–Actuaries indexes summarize stock activities from many countries, and are published widely.

Key Terms and Concepts

adverse information	information unknown to the specialist or market maker that may affect the price of the security
all or none order	instructs the broker to fill the entire order or not to transact
American Depository Receipt (ADR)	a document showing that shares of stock have been deposited with a bank that acts as a depository for the shares
at the opening order	instructs that the order be executed only at the opening of the trading session
bid–asked spread	the difference between the buying price and the selling price of a commodity

block trade	a trade of 10,000 shares or more
blue chip stocks	shares of high investment value; issued by established, financially sound firms
broker	one who arranges trades for others in return for compensation
broker's call rate	the rate charged by banks to brokerage houses for loans
call market	a market in which each security is called for trading at a specific time and can be traded only at that time
cash dividends	intermittent voluntary cash payments from a firm to its shareholders
common stock	the residual ownership claim on the net assets of a corporation
consolidated tape	a reporting system for trades on major exchanges which is dominated by NYSE trades
continuous market	a market in which a good is available for trading throughout the trading session
day order	an order in effect only for the current trading day
dealer	a specialist that buys and sells for his or her own account
discount broker	one who executes trades for a fee without providing research or advisory services
Dow Jones Industrial Average	a price–weighted index of the 30 largest industrial firms on the New York Stock Exchange
exchange floor	the physical location where trades on an exchange take place
fill or kill order	instructs the broker to fill the entire order at a particular price immediately or cancel the order

fourth market	is where direct trades between institutional investors takes place, without the need of any broker or agent involvement
full–line broker	one who executes trades for a fee and provides research and advisory services
good until canceled order (GTC)	is an order that is left in effect until it is canceled, so it can stay in effect virtually forever
informed trader	a trader outside the exchange who knows more about the future of the stock price for a given share than the specialist
immediate or cancel order	instructs the broker to fill the entire order, or any part, at a particular price immediately or cancel the order
initial margin	the proportion of the share value that the investor must invest out of personal funds
limit or market–on–close order	a limit order left in effect during the trading day; if the order is not executed during the day, it becomes a market order at the close of trading
limit order	an order to transact only if certain conditions are met
limit order book	a list held by an exchange specialist which shows the price, amount, and direction of outstanding limit orders
liquidity traders	traders who buy because they have funds to invest or sell because they need cash
maintenance margin	the minimum cash deposit required to hold stock on margin
margin call	the additional required cash deposit if the price of margined shares fall
margin trade	buying stock by depositing a portion of the purchase price and borrowing the rest from the broker
market index	a measure of price movements in the underlying shares over time

market–on–close order	an order to transact at the market price as close to the close of trading as possible
market maker	a firm or individual who holds an inventory of shares and stands ready to buy or sell the shares
market order	an order that instructs the broker to buy or sell a security at whatever price prevails on the market floor at that time
Mayday	May 1, 1975; the date on which the NYSE lifted its fixed commission policy
National Market System (NMS)	a compilation of price quotes and trades for important over–the–counter stocks
NASDAQ	the National Association of Securities Dealers Automated Quotation—the computer system that is used in over–the–counter trading between geographically disbursed dealers
NYSE	the New York Stock Exchange—one of the largest stock exchanges in the world and limits trading to only the biggest, most financially sound firms
NYSE Composite Index	a value–weighted index of all shares traded on the New York Stock Exchange
not held order	can either be a limit order or a market order, where marking the order "not held" gives the floor broker the freedom to seek a better price.
odd lot	a holding not evenly divisible by 100
organized exchange	an exchange organized for securities trading, located at a single location, and governed by specific rules
OTC	the over–the–counter market—a network of market makers in smaller stocks who trade by telephone or through electronic equipment
percentage order	instructs the broker to make a transaction only as a certain percentage of the order flow in a given stock

price–earnings (P–E) ratio	the current price of a share divided by the most recent annual earnings per share
price impact	a change in the price of a share due to a transaction being made
price–weighted index	an index in which each stock contributes to the index value in proportion to its price, such as the DJIA
primary market	the market for the sale of new securities
proxy	the legal conveyance of a shareholder's voting rights to another party
proxy fight	the struggle to gain voting rights from shareholders who will not be attending the annual meeting
residual claim	a claim on the assets of a firm after all other claims have been satisfied
round lot	a trade in multiples of 100 shares
seat	represents a membership on an exchange and conveys the right to trade
secondary market	the market for already existing securities
short sale	selling shares that one does not own, but has borrowed from another investor, with the hope of repurchasing the shares at a lower price in the future and returning them to the owner
S&P 500	a value–weighted index of shares from 500 companies in various industries compiled by the Standard & Poors Corporation
specialist	will always hold a seat on an organized exchange and makes a market in an assigned security; the two basic functions of a specialist are acting as a broker for other trading parties and acting as a dealer, buying and selling for his own account
stock dividend	creation of new shares for existing shareholders in an amount that is 25 percent or less than the existing shares

stock exchange	a voluntary organization formed by a group of individuals to provide an institutional setting in which common stock, and other securities, can be bought and sold
stock split	creation of new shares for existing shareholders in an amount that is more than 25 percent of the existing shares
stop order	an order that becomes active when a certain price condition is met
street name shares	securities held by brokers in trust for their customers
third market	a market for large blocks of shares that operates outside the confines of the organized exchanges and the OTC market
trading post	the physical location on the floor of an organized exchange used for the trading of a specific security
turnover	or a round–trip, is the buying and selling of a share
value–weighted index	an index in which each stock in the index is weighted according to the market value of its outstanding shares, such as the S&P 500
work an order	the discretion floor brokers have to try to fill an order at the best price

Multiple–Choice Questions

1. Trades between institutional investors that take place without the aid of brokers or agents are known as ____ trades.
   A. day
   B. odd–lot
   C. limit
   D. fourth market
   E. stop–loss

2. An increase in the price of shares that have been purchased creates a ____.
    A. price profit
    B. price gain
    C. capital gain
    D. capital profit
    E. capital revenue

3. A(n) ____ occurs when the percentage increase of shares that are created by the firm and distributed to the current shareholders is more than 25 percent.
    A. stock dividend
    B. cash dividend
    C. stock split
    D. extra dividend
    E. revenue dividend

4. If you buy a share for $50, hold it for a year in which it pays a $1.00 dividend, and sell it at the end of the year for $48, your WR is ____ percent.
    A. 2.00
    B. 2.08
    C. 4.00
    D. 6.00
    E. 98.00

5. The market for existing shares is known as the ____ market.
    A. primary
    B. secondary
    C. specialist
    D. maintenance
    E. round lot

6. One of the richest sources of the specialist's information comes from the fact that the specialist maintains the ____ book showing unfilled orders.
    A. limit order
    B. information
    C. confidential
    D. trading
    E. stock order

7. The reporting system for trades on major exchanges is known as the ____ tape.
    A. fourth market
    B. limit order
    C. market index
    D. consolidated
    E. exchange

8. A shareholder conveys its voting rights to another party through a(n) ____.
   A. proxy
   B. odd lot
   C. limit order
   D. street name agreement
   E. block

9. Transactions for stock in excess of 10,000 shares are called ____ trades.
   A. block
   B. round
   C. large
   D. even
   E. flat

10. Brokers borrow from banks to finance their inventory of securities at the broker's ____ rate.
    A. specialist
    B. limit
    C. call
    D. maintenance
    E. Dow Jones

11. The dividend yield is calculated by dividing ____.
    A. stock price by annual earnings
    B. current capital gains by dividends
    C. bid price by ask price
    D. current annual dividend by current price
    E. brokerage commission by price

12. An order that remains in effect until the end of the trading day is known as a ____ order.
    A. stop
    B. day
    C. limit
    D. market
    E. third

13. ____ orders become market orders if certain pre–specified conditions are met.
    A. Deferred
    B. Conditional
    C. Limit
    D. Stop
    E. Transaction

14. The advantage, and potential disadvantage, of margin trading is ____ for the investor.
    A. extra income
    B. greater leverage
    C. extra profit
    D. taxable revenue
    E. deductible loss

15. ____ brokers offer cheaper commissions than their full–service counterparts.
    A. Discount
    B. Odd lot
    C. Specialist
    D. Remission
    E. Sale

16. As compared to some foreign markets, the U.S. stock market is considered a _____ market.
    A. call
    B. continuous
    C. premium
    D. discount
    E. developing

17. If the price of shares you have borrowed money from your broker to purchase falls, you may be faced with a ____ call.
    A. broker's
    B. odd lot
    C. specialist
    D. margin
    E. maintenance

18. The quote system for important over–the–counter stocks is known as the ____.
    A. S&P 500
    B. National Market System
    C. Dow Jones Industrial Average
    D. NYSE Composite
    E. Wilshire 5000

19. A trade in a multiple of 100 shares is known as a(n) ____ lot.
    A. block
    B. round
    C. odd
    D. third market
    E. specialist

20. Shares in established companies with proven performance and high investment value are known as ____.
    A. round lots
    B. blue chips
    C. proxies
    D. indexes
    E. specialists

21. The computer system that connects the many geographically disbursed dealers in the over–the–counter market is known as the ____.
    A. NYSE
    B. S&P 500
    C. Wilshire 5000
    D. NASDAQ
    E. DJIA

22. Organized exchange trading occurs at a specific location for each stock, known as a trading ____.
    A. post
    B. seat
    C. floor
    D. index
    E. spread

23. If you think that the price of a share will fall, which trade should you undertake?
    A. margin purchase
    B. limit order
    C. day order
    D. short sale
    E. stock dividend

24. If you buy a share at $25, hold it for six months, receive a $.50 dividend, and sell the share for $26, your annual return is ____ percent.
    A. 4.00
    B. 6.00
    C. 7.84
    D. 8.16
    E. 12.36

25. The limited liability feature of common stock means that ____.
    A. a stock owner will not lose more than 10 percent over the original investment
    B. there is no limit to the amount of personal assets a stockholder might lose
    C. the maximum loss incurred by a stockholder will not exceed the amount invested
    D. stockholders are responsible for additional compensation only when the environment is involved
    E. only the major stockholders are liable

Review Problems

1. Two years ago, you purchased shares at $50. You have received dividends of $1.25 and $1.30. You could sell the shares today at $56 bid, $58 asked. Calculate your WR, return, annualized WR, and annualized return.
2. Three months ago, you purchased shares at $120. You have received a dividend of $2 and you can sell the shares today for $117. Calculate your WR, return, annual WR, and annual return.
3. A stock you purchased a year ago for $73 paid an annual dividend of $1. If your annual return is 4.1 percent, what is the current price?
4. A stock you purchased a year ago for $68 is now trading at $65. If your annual return is –2.2 percent, what was the annual dividend?
5. You purchased 100 shares of stock at $25 per share. It has been paying an annual dividend of $1.25. If the stock splits 6 for 5, how many shares will you have? If the dividend remains constant, how much will the stock dividend generate in increased cash?
6. Stock that is trading for $200 per share and pays a $16 annual dividend splits 4 for 1. Compute the new price and the new dividend on a proportional basis. Why might the firm's managers have declared the split?
7. A stock with a P/E ratio of 6 pays an annual dividend of $2.50, 80 percent of most recent earnings. Calculate the price and the dividend yield.
8. A firm pays 50 percent of its $5 earnings per share in dividends. It is trading at $20 per share. Compute the P/E ratio and the dividend yield.
9. You buy 1,000 shares of stock at $40, borrowing 50 percent on margin at an annual call rate of 12 percent. Six months later, the shares pay a dividend of $2 and you can sell them for $43. Calculate your WR, return, annualized WR, and annualized return. Recalculate the same return statistics for a non–margin purchase. Why has the margin arrangement increased your yield? What would margin buying do to your yield if the share price falls?
10. A stock is trading at $85, but you think its price will fall. What should you do to trade on your belief? One year later, the price has fallen to $80 but the shares have paid a $2 dividend. Calculate your dollar profit or loss. What is the danger in this type of trade?

Answers

Multiple–Choice Questions

1. D	10. C	19. B
2. C	11. D	20. B
3. C	12. B	21. D
4. E	13. D	22. A
5. B	14. B	23. D
6. A	15. A	24. E
7. D	16. B	25. C
8. A	17. D	
9. A	18. B	

Review Problems

1. Your two–year WR is determined by dividing the current price, plus dividends, by the original price:

    ($56 + $1.25 + $1.30)/$50 = $58.55/$50 = 1.171

    return = 1.171 – 1 = 17.1 percent.

    Annualizing the two–year WR by taking the square root:.

    $(1.171)^{1/2}$ = 1.0821, and return = 1.0821 – 1 = 8.21 percent.

2. On a three–month basis:

    WR = ($117 + $2)/$120 = .9917

    return = .9917 – 1 = –.0083 = –.83 percent.

    Since there are four three–month periods in a year, the three–month WR must be compounded to the fourth power to determine the annual WR:

    $(.9917)^4$ = .9672, and the annual return

    = .9672 – 1 = –.0328 = –3.28 percent.

3. The return is equal to the WR minus 1, so the WR is 1.041. Given the WR formula:

   $(x + 1)/73 = 1.041$, or $(x + 1) = 73(1.041) = \$76$.

   The current price must be $\$76 - \$1 = \$75$.

4. The annual WR is now $(1 - .022) = .978$.

   $(65 + x)/68 = .978$, or

   $(65 + x) = .978(\$68) = \$66.50$.

   The annual dividend must be $\$66.50 - \$65 = \$1.50$.

5. Before the stock dividend, you have 20 sets of 5 shares each. After the dividend, you have 20 sets of 6 shares, or 120 shares in total. You received cash dividends of $\$1.25(100) = \$125$ before the stock dividend. If the payments remain at $\$1.25$ per share, you will receive $\$1.25(120) = \$150$ after the stock dividend, an increase of $\$25$.

   Notice that the stock dividend itself does not increase your cash returns. They rise because the firm has held the dividend per share constant over a larger number of shares.

6. $\$200$ for one old share implies $\$200/4 = \$50$ for each new share, and $\$16$ in dividends annually for one old share implies dividends of $\$16/4 = 4$ for each new share. The firm's managers may feel that the $\$200$ stock price is so high that the average investor cannot afford to purchase a round lot for $\$200(100) = \$20,000$. A round lot of new shares will cost only $\$50(100) = \$5,000$. In addition, the managers may not believe the academic research that argues that stock dividends and stock splits do not create value, believing instead that the share price will not drop all the way to $\$50$ per share.

7. If $\$2.50$ is 80 percent of the firm's most recent earnings, earnings are $(\$2.50/.8) = \$3.125$.

   A P/E ratio of 6 means that a share is selling for six times earnings, or $\$18.75 = 6(\$3.125)$.

   Dividends of $\$2.50$ on a share trading at $\$18.75$ create a dividend yield of $(\$2.50/\$18.75) = 13.3$ percent.

8. The dividend is $.5(\$5.00) = \$2.50$, so the dividend yield is $\$2.50/\$20 = 12.50$ percent. A P/E ratio of $\$20/\$5 = 4$ results from dividing price by earnings per share.

9. The 1,000 shares cost you $40(1,000) = $40,000, of which you put up 50 percent, or $20,000, borrowing the rest.

    In six months, your investment is worth $43,000, but you owe the principal on your $20,000 loan, plus half of a year's interest at an annual rate of 12 percent, or:

    $20,000 + (.12/2)($20,000) = $21,200.

    In addition, you have received $2,000 in dividends, so your six–month WR is:

    ($43,000 – $21,200 + $2,000)/$20,000

    = $23,800/$20,000 = 1.19.

    Return = 1.19 – 1 = .19 or 19 percent.

    Squaring the six–month WR will provide an annual WR since there are two six–month periods in one year:

    $(1.19)^2 = 1.4161$, for an annual return of 41.61 percent.

    If you did not create a margin trade, you would invest $40,000 at the beginning, but you would claim the entire $43,000 market value, plus the dividends:

    WR = ($43,000 + $2,000)/$40,000 = 1.125

    Return = 1.125 – 1 = .125 or 12.5 percent.

    Annual WR = $(1.125)^2$ = 1.2656, return = 26.56 percent.

    Margin buying has increased your leverage, because the cost of the borrowing is fixed. Any price increases in excess of the borrowing cost belong to you. The danger is that the price of the stock will fall. Then you will suffer any losses out of a smaller equity value. It must be kept in mind that no matter what happens to the share price, the investor must repay the loan with interest. Any loss has a greater impact on the $20,000 investment (with the margin) than on the $40,000 investment (without it).

10. If you think that the price of a stock will fall, you should sell it short. This type of transaction involves borrowing the shares to sell with the hope of buying them back later at a cheaper price to return them to the owner.

If you borrow 100 shares and sell them at $85 each, you will receive $8,500. If the price falls to $80, you can repurchase the shares for $8,000, keeping the $500 difference as a profit. You owe the owner $200 in dividends, however, so your net profit is $300. Keep in mind that in this transaction, the short seller will not have the use of the full $8,500 because the broker will keep some as collateral. The danger in this type of trade is that the price of the shares will rise. Then you will have to buy them back for more than you sold them for. In addition, you still owe the dividends to the owner.

CHAPTER FOUR

The Primary Market and Investment Banking

Chapter Objectives

Upon completion of this chapter, you should be able to:
1. Define and explain the differences between the primary and secondary market.
2. Explain the advantages and disadvantages of public offerings and private placements.
3. Discuss the types of services provided by investment bankers.
4. Explain the roles of the various participants in an underwriting syndicate.
5. Explain the process of an initial public offering.
6. Explain the advantages of shelf registration.

Chapter Outline

I. Overview

A. Securities traded on the New York Stock Exchange are being traded on a **secondary market**—the market for already existing securities.
B. The initial offering of securities takes place in the **primary market**—the market for the issuance of new securities.
C. The primary market is much less visible than the secondary market, but it is crucial to the world of investments.
D. In the United States, investment banking has been kept almost totally distinct from the more familiar commercial banking by a law known as the Glass–Steagall Act.

II. The Primary Market: Size and Scope

A. **Preferred stock** is a hybrid security, with features of both bonds and common stock.
   1. Like bonds, preferred stock carries scheduled payments, but the issuer is not obligated to make these disbursements if enough funds are not available.
   2. Like common stock, preferred stock never matures.
B. Only corporations issue common stock and preferred stock.
C. Private Placements and Public Offerings
   1. In a **public offering**, the security is offered to the public, giving any investor the right to purchase part of the new issue. The issuing process is governed by the Securities and Exchange Commission regulations.
   2. In a **private placement**, the entire issue is sold to a single buyer, or a small consortium of buyers, without the issue ever being made available to the public.
   3. Issuers may prefer private placements because they do not have to disclose information about the firm, or its plans, in registration documents.
   4. In private placements, the buyers of the securities tend to be large cash–rich institutions, such as insurance companies.
   5. Private placements typically carry higher yields, since the owner cannot resell them. The issuer can afford the higher yield because it saves on flotation costs.
   6. The holder of a privately placed security cannot sell it, because it has never undergone the process of scrutiny required for a public offering.
   7. Essentially, the buyer of a privately placed issue sacrifices liquidity in order to obtain the higher rate of interest paid on private placements.
   8. **Liquidity** is a measure of how easily an asset may be converted into cash without loss of value.
D. Relative Size of Issuers
   1. The vast majority of stock issues are for common stock.
   2. In recent years, preferred stock has fallen out of favor as a financing vehicle, in part because corporations must pay preferred stock dividends from after–tax income. This is in contrast with bonds.
   3. Bonds dwarf stocks by a ratio of about five–to–one in the primary market, but secondary stock market volume is much greater than secondary bond market volume.
   4. The largest issuer of securities in the world is the U.S. government.
   5. State and local governments also issue vast quantities of securities, called **municipals**, or **municipal bonds**. Interest on municipals is often exempt from federal and state income taxation.

III. The Process of Issuing Securities

A. For corporations, the development of a good relationship with an investment banker is very important to the financial management of the firm.

B. The investment banker will normally fulfill three functions:
   1. Consulting
   2. Forming a distribution network
   3. Bearing the risk involved in the issuance of the new security

C. The Investment Banker as Consultant
   1. The consulting duties of an investment banker typically require three tasks:
      a. Preparing the necessary registration and informational materials
      b. Timing the issue
      c. Pricing the issue
   2. One of the important SEC requirements for the public offering of new securities is the formal disclosure of the firm's financial condition and future plans.
      a. This disclosure is accomplished in a **prospectus**, which is a legal document required by the SEC.
      b. The information in a prospectus will include:
         (1) A report on the firm's financial condition.
         (2) The names of the principal officers in the corporation, and an accounting of their holdings in the firm.
         (3) Information on the firm's line of business.
         (4) The firm's plans for future expansion.
   3. Investment bankers often give firms advice on the issue of timing.
      a. For stocks, the ideal would be to issue securities when the stock market peaks.
      b. For bonds, the ideal time to issue occurs when interest rates are very low.
   4. Since investment bankers are constantly engaged in the primary market, they should be in a good position to advise on the proper pricing of a new security.
      a. The goal of the pricing strategy is to set the highest price that will allow all of the issue to be sold in a fairly short period of time.
      b. An issue that sells out rapidly is said to go **out the window**.
      c. If the price is set too low, the issue will sell out virtually immediately, but will not bring the firm as much cash as if it had been properly priced.
      d. An issue that is priced too high will not be sold out promptly and is referred to as a **sticky issue**.

D. The Distribution Network
   1. Usually one investment bank is the **lead bank** for the issue. It has primary responsibility for the issuance of a particular security.
   2. The **syndicate members** are other investment banking firms that have committed themselves to assisting in the flotation of a given security.

3. The **flotation** is the initial sale of the security.

4. The **selling group** consists of those investment houses that are participating to a smaller degree in the distribution process.

5. Advertisements, known as **tombstones**, announce the firm making the issue, the price, the number of securities, and the members of the syndicate.

6. The **spread** is the difference between the price paid by the final investor and the amount the issuing firm receives from the sale of the security.

E. The Service and Cost of Risk–Bearing

   1. The investment banker has two basic ways of distributing securities for the issuer.

      a. The investment banker may act as an **underwriter**, where the bank actually buys the securities from the issuing firm and then tries to sell them to the public at a profit.

      b. The investment banker may distribute the issue on a **best efforts basis**, where the investment bank promises to sell the securities at the best price it can obtain.

   2. The costs of issuing securities—known as **flotation costs**—have a strong impact on the cost of acquiring funds and also on the investment desirability of new issues.

   3. Corporations pay their investment bankers in two ways.

      a. First, they typically pay out–of–pocket expenses for consulting services, legal fees, and document preparation.

      b. Second, the issuer offers securities at a price that allows the investment bankers, and other members of the distribution network, to make a profit.

   4. Spreads are typically lower for debt issues than for issues of common stock.

   5. Further, the spread, as a percentage of the proceeds, is smaller the larger the issue size.

F. The Green Shoe Option

   1. The **Green Shoe option** is the right of the investment banking firm to buy an additional number of securities from the issuer at the original price.

   2. The **aftermarket** is the market for a security shortly after its issuance.

   3. Generally, the Green Shoe option has considerable value.

G. Investment Bankers and Investing in New Issues

   1. Pricing of new issues is really an art, rather than a science.

   2. A price set too low means that the issuer does not receive full value, while a price set too high means that security purchasers are likely to have low returns.

   3. It seems that an equilibrium can be achieved only when the new issues offer a return comparable with investment opportunities available elsewhere.

IV. Initial Public Offerings

A. A firm engages in an **initial public offering (IPO)** when it offers securities to the public for the first time.

B. A period of intense IPO issuance is called a **hot issue market**.

C. Asymmetric Information and the Pricing of IPOs
   1. Kevin Rock points out that potential investors in an IPO security possess **asymmetric information**, a condition that arises when one party has information that is superior to another's.
   2. The investors with the good information are said to be **informed investors**.
   3. Underwriters, according to Rock, must price securities in a way that gets them sold, attracting both the informed and the uninformed investor.
   4. In short, IPO underpricing compensates uninformed investors for the risk of trading against superior information.

D. Are IPOs Underpriced?
   1. It has become widely accepted that IPOs are underpriced, as their very high returns appear to indicate.
   2. Evidence indicates that new issues of shares and bonds for existing firms are also underpriced, but only by a relatively small amount, compared to IPOs.
   3. For the largest potential underpricing, investors might seek issues underwritten by less prestigious firms.
   4. Underpricing appears to be quite short–lived, lasting only a few days or a few weeks.

E. Shelf Registration
   1. **Shelf registration** allows firms to register with the SEC once, and then to offer securities for sale through agents and through the secondary markets for a period of two years following the registration.
   2. The chief advantages of this procedure are:
      a. The corporation can reduce the expense of offering securities by avoiding numerous registrations.
      b. Corporations receive greater flexibility in timing an offering.
   3. There are potential disadvantages to shelf registration.
      a. The short period required to issue a new security may not provide enough time for the investment banker handling the shelf registration to assure that no misstatements or omissions appear in the registration statement.
         (1) The requirement for the investment banker to verify the claims made in the registration statement is known as a **due diligence obligation**.
      b. It may lead to higher concentration in the investment banking industry, with smaller regional investment banking firms not being able to participate in the syndicate.

4. In general, the evidence on shelf registration supports the view that shelf registration has led to lower issuing costs for firms that have used it.

F. The Condition of the Investment Banking Industry
1. Firm Size and Concentration in Investment Banking
Figures showing the percentage of the industry represented by the largest three, five, and ten firms are known as **industry concentration ratios**.
2. Compensation and Source of Profits
a. Compensation in the industry consists of a salary and bonus, with the bonus often being as large or larger than the salary.
b. **Proprietary trading** is trading of securities that a firm engages in for its own account, often using its own privately developed trading techniques.

V. The International Primary Market

A. Major Investment Banking Firms in the International Market
Major investment banking firms in the international market come mostly from five countries: Japan, the United States, Great Britain, Switzerland, and Germany.
B. Investment Banking in Great Britain and Japan
1. In 1986, Great Britain experienced the **Big Bang**—a major liberalization of regulation governing securities dealing.
2. In Japan, investment banking is dominated by the **Big Four** securities firms: Nomura, Daiwa, Nikko, and Yamaichi.

Key Terms and Concepts

aftermarket	the market for the security shortly after its issuance
asymmetric information	a condition that arises when one party has information that is superior to another's
best efforts basis	when an investment bank promises to sell a security at the best price it can obtain
Big Bang	the major liberalization of regulations governing securities dealing which Great Britain experienced in 1986
Big Four	the firms that dominate Japanese investment banking

bond	debt instrument representing a legal claim to future payments
commercial bank	an institution that specializes in making loans and taking deposits
due diligence obligation	the requirement for investment bankers to verify the claims made in the registration statement
flotation	the initial sale of securities
flotation costs	the spread and the out–of–pocket costs an issuer pays to issue new securities
Glass–Steagall Act	legislation that required the separation of commercial banking and investment banking
Green Shoe option	the right of an investment banker to purchase additional securities at the original price
hot issue market	a period of intense IPO issuance
industry concentration ratio	the percentage of an industry's volume controlled by its largest firms
informed investor	the investors with the good information concerning securities
initial public offering (IPO)	the first time a firm issues securities to the public
investment banks	institutions specializing in helping firms issue new securities
lead bank	the investment bank primarily responsible for an issue of new securities
liquidity	the ease with which an asset can be converted into cash without loss of value
municipal bonds	bonds issued by state and local governments
out the window	a new issue that sells out rapidly

preferred stock	an ownership claim that has no maturity, and scheduled dividends the issuer is not obligated to pay
primary market	the market for the issuance of new securities
private placement	the sale of a new issue to a single buyer, or small group of buyers, without SEC registration
proprietary trading	securities trading an investment banking firm engages in for its own account, often using its own privately developed trading techniques
prospectus	a legal document issued in advance of a flotation that contains relevant facts about the issue and the issuer
public offering	issuing new securities to the public at large
SEC	the Securities and Exchange Commission, a government agency that regulates public offerings and secondary markets
secondary market	a market for trading of existing securities
selling group	investment bankers that participate to a smaller degree in distributing a new issue
shelf registration	an SEC rule that allows an issuer to register once and distribute securities when it chooses any time during the next two years
spread	the total price difference between the price paid by the final buyer of a new security and the amount received by the issuer
sticky issue	a new issue that does not sell well
syndicate members	investment bankers that are committed to helping distribute a new issue
tombstone	an advertisement of a new public offering
underwriter	an investment banker that buys new securities from the issuer, hoping to resell them at a profit

Multiple-Choice Questions

1. If a new issue sells out quickly, it is referred to as _____.
    A. sticky
    B. privately placed
    C. shelved
    D. out the window
    E. concentrated

2. The Glass–Steagall Act requires the separation of _____.
    A. underwriters and the selling group
    B. public offerings and private placements
    C. municipal bonds and corporate bonds
    D. commercial banks and investment banks
    E. preferred stock and common stock

3. In a _____, an entire bond issue is sold to a single buyer or a small consortium of buyers.
    A. private placement
    B. private offering
    C. private contract
    D. regulated contract
    E. consortium contract

4. The vast majority of stock issues are for _____.
    A. preferred stock
    B. common stock
    C. high priced stock
    D. subordinated stock
    E. closely held stock

5. A firm issuing new securities to the public must disclose its financial condition and future plans in a(n) _____.
    A. prospect report
    B. SEC report
    C. prospectus
    D. initial report
    E. annual report

6. An issue that is not sold out quickly is said to be _____.
    A. out the door
    B. sticky
    C. stuck at home
    D. shelved
    E. tombstoned

7. The ____ bank has the primary responsibility for the issuance of a particular security.
   A. selling
   B. lead
   C. primary
   D. issuing
   E. SEC

8. Those investment houses that are participating to a smaller degree in the distribution process constitute the ____.
   A. buying group
   B. purchasing group
   C. distributing group
   D. selling group
   E. lending group

9. Securities are often announced in *The Wall Street Journal* with advertisements known as ____.
   A. milestones
   B. tombstones
   C. prospectuses
   D. underwritings
   E. shelves

10. The difference between the price paid by the final investor and the amount the issuing firm receives is known as the ____.
    A. spread
    B. risk differential
    C. risk spread margin
    D. risk margin
    E. price differential

11. An investment banker's right to purchase additional securities after the issue at the original price is known as the ____ option.
    A. blue chip
    B. red line
    C. trading post
    D. aftermarket
    E. Green Shoe

12. The percentage of an industry's volume controlled by its largest firms is known as a _____ ratio.
    A. liquidity
    B. concentration
    C. flotation
    D. syndication
    E. leading

13. Initial public offerings differ from other security offerings in that IPOs _____.
    A. are underwritten
    B. have smaller spreads
    C. are the first primary market transaction for the firm
    D. are secondary market trades
    E. require the formation of a selling group

14. An investment banker's compensation for risk–bearing services differs from its compensation for fixed flotation costs in that risk–bearing services are paid for by _____.
    A. a fixed fee for services rendered
    B. the Green Shoe option
    C. the underwriting and selling groups
    D. the proceeds of a shelf registration
    E. the difference between the price paid by the public and the price received by the issuer

15. The Big Four refers to _____.
    A. the U.S., Japan, UK, and Germany
    B. the biggest four firms in an industry
    C. the dominant investment banks in Japan
    D. the four most informed investors
    E. primary, secondary, third, and fourth markets

16. In percentage terms, flotation costs tend to be lower for _____.
    A. larger issues than for smaller issues
    B. public offerings than for private placements
    C. underwritten offerings than for shelf registrations
    D. initial public offerings than for subsequent offerings
    E. stock issues than for bond issues

17. New issues of securities that are sold to the public are governed by _____.
    A. the Securities and Exchange Commission
    B. the Glass–Steagall Commission
    C. the government of the municipality that issues them
    D. the underwriting syndicate
    E. the Tombstone Commission

18. Shelf registration gives an issuer flexibility in ____.
    A. timing the offering
    B. disclosing information about the firm
    C. selecting an investment banker
    D. timing dividend payments
    E. supporting the aftermarket

19. Which of the following functions is *not* typically performed by an investment banker?
    A. forming the distribution network
    B. timing the issuance
    C. choosing the underwriter
    D. helping to prepare the prospectus
    E. consulting

20. A prospectus must include all of the following *except* ____.
    A. a report of the firm's financial condition
    B. the names of the principal officers in the corporation
    C. an accounting of the principal officers' holdings in the firm
    D. information about the firm's line of business
    E. the spread earned by the issue's underwriters

21. In a ____, the security is offered to the public, giving any investor the right to purchase part of the new issue.
    A. private placement
    B. public placement
    C. public offering
    D. consortium contract
    E. regulated contract

22. Preferred stock is a cross between ____.
    A. common stock and investment stock
    B. real estate stock and financial stock
    C. private placements and financial stock
    D. private placements and common stock
    E. common stock and bonds

23. Which of the following is *not* correct concerning private placements?
    A. Buyers tend to be small, cash–rich institutions.
    B. They offer a chance to avoid disclosing business plans.
    C. They often offer higher yields than publicly issued securities.
    D. They are often less liquid than publicly issued securities.
    E. A privately placed bond cannot be resold.

24. If a firm is issuing common stock, a good time to do it would
    be ____.
    A. before the public has too much time to research the firm
    B. after the public has sufficient time to research the firm
    C. after the prospectus goes "out the window"
    D. when the stock market peaks
    E. after the product line has been through its life cycle

25. The ease with which a security can be converted into cash is referred to as ____.
    A. flotation
    B. spread
    C. placement
    D. liquidity
    E. concentration

26. State and local governments issue securities called _____.
    A. tombstones
    B. locals
    C. commons
    D. high yield strips
    E. municipals

27. When an investment bank distributes an issue on a best efforts basis, it
    promises to _____.
    A. sell only a small amount of the issue
    B. sell only the best securities available
    C. sell the securities at the best price it can obtain
    D. distribute only to buyers that make the best effort to buy the issue
    E. make its best effort to put together a good selling group

28. The _____ is the market for a security shortly after its issuance.
    A. post market
    B. out the window market
    C. testing market
    D. aftermarket
    E. short–term market

Answers to Questions

Multiple–Choice Questions

1. D	11. E	21. C
2. D	12. B	22. E
3. A	13. C	23. A
4. B	14. E	24. D
5. C	15. C	25. D
6. B	16. A	26. E
7. B	17. A	27. C
8. D	18. A	28. D
9. B	19. C	
10. A	20. E	

CHAPTER FIVE

Sources of Investment Information

Chapter Objectives

Upon completion of this chapter, you should be able to:

1. Compare and contrast the following sources of investment information: general business periodicals; federal government publications; industrial publications; information provided by investment banking houses, investment advisory services, and the companies themselves.
2. Be familiar with charting services.
3. Discuss academic journals.
4. Explain the role computerized data bases play in investment.
5. Discuss sources of data on the international economy and multinational and foreign companies.

Chapter Outline

I. General Business Periodicals

A. The premier business periodical in the United States is *The Wall Street Journal,* published every business day by Dow Jones Company, Inc. It contains more information on security prices than any daily publication in the country.

B. While *The Wall Street Journal* offers the most comprehensive single listing of securities transactions, it does not carry quotations of securities of more local interest, such as the current price of minor bank stocks.

C. The *Commercial and Financial Chronicle* is published weekly and carries exhaustive securities quotations. It is the only publication to carry complete NASDAQ quotations on a weekly basis.

D. The *Wall Street Transcript*, published daily, carries very detailed information about business, such as the full text of speeches made by major corporate executives.

E. *Barron's*, the weekly sister publication to *The Wall Street Journal*, carries quotations for securities as of the end of trading for the week, and many columns on topics relevant to investing.

F. *Business Week*, *Forbes*, and *Fortune* are three major business magazines. *Dun's Review* and *Financial World* are similar in many respects to the three magazines just mentioned, although they are not as popular. These two magazines often feature longer articles with more analysis.

G. *Financial World* often has reports on the stocks of particular industries and reports on different segments of the mutual fund industry.

H. *Institutional Investor* and *Pensions and Investment Age* contain articles geared toward professionals engaged in pension fund trading.

II. Indexes to Further Information

A. The *Business Periodicals Index* provides a monthly subject index that covers hundreds of periodicals with items about businesses.

B. *The Wall Street Journal Index* is organized in a similar way, but it focuses only on stories that originally appeared in *The Wall Street Journal*.

C. Two commercial on–line computer information services, *Bibliographical Retrieval Service* and *Dialog*, allow users to specify key words that might occur in titles or subject descriptions of interest.

III. Federal Government Publications

A. One of the most widely available sources of reliable information about the U.S. economy is the U.S. government.

B. The *Federal Reserve Bulletin*, published monthly, carries articles on major economic trends.

C. The *Treasury Bulletin* focuses mainly on the activities of the Treasury Department, including the debt of the United States. One of the most useful regular features of this publication is the yield curve.

D. The *Business Conditions Digest*, published monthly by the Commerce Department, features many graphs illustrating general movements in the economy.

   1. One of the most closely followed sections is the one on "Cyclical Indicators."

   2. Economic variables that tend to respond to the economic cycles more quickly than the economy as a whole are called **leading indicators**.

   3. Other types of indicators are **coincident indicators** and **lagging indicators**.

E. *The Survey of Current Business* was also published monthly by the Commerce Department until recently. Now much of the information formerly reported in the survey now appears in *Business Conditions Digest*. One example of the information provided is monthly data on the Consumer Price Index.

F.   Each of the 12 Federal Reserve Banks in the United States publishes an economic review on a quarterly or monthly basis.

G.   The two main publications of the Securities and Exchange Commission are the "SEC Monthly Statistical Review" and an "Annual Report."

H.   A useful source of visual information is the annual *Federal Reserve Historical Chart Book*.

I.   *Economic Indicators*, published monthly by the Council of Economic Advisers, is prepared for members of Congress and contains data on major macroeconomic variables.

J.   The *Quarterly Financial Report* of the Federal Trade Commission presents aggregated financial reports, such as balance sheets and income statements.

K.   The *Economic Report of the President* is published annually and contains the president's interpretation of recent economic events and an analysis of forthcoming economic concerns.

L.   The *Statistical Abstract of the United States* is published annually, and contains statistical information on all phases of the national life in its approximatley 1,000 pages.

IV. Information About Specific Industries

A.   Some of the publications already mentioned, such as *Forbes*, *Business Week*, *Fortune*, and *The Wall Street Journal*, include a great deal of information about particular industries.

B.   Federal government publications also often provide statistical information about different industries.

C.   Trade associations of particular industries can be a source of useful information about industry trends.

D.   Most of the major brokerage firms, particularly the full–service brokerage houses, make research reports available to their existing and potential customers.

E.   Dun and Bradstreet's *Key Business Ratios* is a publication that computes industry specific financial statement ratios for many different industries.

F.   Standard & Poor's *Industry Surveys* provides basic information on individual industries and their prospects.

G.   The *Media General Industriscope*, which appears weekly, focuses on the performance of different industries and individual companies.

H.   Standard & Poor's *Outlook*, published weekly, gives opinions about which industries and which firms have good prospects.

I.   Each week the *Value Line Investment Survey* focuses on about six to ten industries and the stocks within those industries. It discusses each industry, and particular firms within the industry, giving unequivocal recommendations and the reasons behind them.

V. Information Prepared by Individual Companies

A. Potential investors may generally rely on the prospectus as a conservatively stated view of a company's forthcoming prospects.

B. Every publicly owned firm must also make an annual report available to its shareholders.

C. Public firms must also file more complete financial data with the Securities and Exchange Commission. This report is called a 10–K and goes beyond the information in the annual report. One of the easiest ways to acquire a 10–K is through Disclosure, Inc.

D. Standard & Poor's and Moody's

   1. Standard & Poor's and Moody's are the two dominant firms in the investment information business.

   2. Standard & Poor's *Corporation Records* and Moody's *Manuals* provide basic information about particular firms.

   3. Two sources of timely information on particular companies are the S&P *Stock Market Encyclopedia* and Moody's *Handbook of Common Stocks*.

   4. For bond information, Standard & Poor's publishes its *Bond Guide* while Moody's has its *Bond Record* and *Bond Survey*, both published monthly.

   5. For stocks, Standard & Poor's also publishes its *Stock Guide*, which is roughly comparable to Moody's *Stock Survey*.

E. Brokerage Firm Reports

   1. Most full–line brokerage houses have active research departments. The reports they publish are available to the customers of the firm.

   2. Many of these reports are somewhat ambiguous. After reading a recommendation, the layperson is often confused about whether to buy or sell the security.

   3   The reports prepared by brokerage firms are very often positive in nature.

F. Value Line

   1. The *Value Line Investment Survey* is one of the best sources of information about particular firms that might help an investor make an actual and immediate decision about investing in a certain common stock.

   2. In the *Survey*, the appraisal of the firm's prospects is made concrete in its ranking system for "timeliness" and "safety."

   3. In this ranking system, a ranking of 1 is the highest, on a scale of 1 to 5.

G. Chart Services

   1. One popular way of predicting future stock price movements is to extrapolate from past movements.

   2. Commercially prepared charts assist those investors who believe that past stock price movements can provide a reliable guide to future movements.

VI. *Academic Journals*

A. These sources of information are for the investor willing to spend considerable time learning about pricing relationships in the security markets.

B. Some of the most respected journals in the field are *The Journal of Finance*, *The Journal of Financial Economics*, and *The Journal of Financial and Quantitative Analysis*.

C. *Financial Management*, the journal of the Financial Management Association, has a less mathematical, more practical orientation.

D. Two journals that are quite readable, yet still give a flavor of the kinds of research being undertaken by the academic community, are the *Financial Analysts Journal* and the *Journal of Portfolio Management*.

E. The American Association of Individual Investors (AAII) serves the interests of individual investors and publishes the *AAII Journal*, which contains many interesting and accessible articles about all aspects of investing. While not strictly an academic journal, many articles are written by academics.

VII. *Computerized Data Bases*

A. Standard & Poor's provides *Compustat*, which comes in different parts to focus on different industries.

B. The Center for Research in Security Prices (CRSP) sells its data base, generally called the **CRSP tapes**. Its most prominent feature is data on the common stock returns of more than a thousand companies on a daily basis.

C. *Compuserve* and *The Source* offer a wide range of data services to the home computer user.

D. Value Line also produces Value Screen II, a product that is ideal for home computers. It contains balance sheet and income statement data for about 1,700 companies.

VIII. *International Securities Information*

A. Information about investing in foreign securities is much scarcer than the information available for domestic firms.

B. Two daily newspapers contain general news: the *Financial Times*, which covers Great Britain and the European continent, and the *Asian Wall Street Journal*, which covers the Orient.

C. *Euromoney* focuses principally on the European markets, but it also contains articles on the Orient.

D. *The Economist*, a British weekly publication, is another excellent source for following world business.

E. The monthly *International Financial Statistics* covers exchange rates, interest rates, industrial production, imports and exports, and commodity prices with reports on specific countries.

F. Further sources of international statistical data can be obtained from the following:
    1. *Balance of Payment Statistics*
    2. *Direction of Trade Statistics*
    3. *Government Finance Statistics Yearbook*
    4. *Staff Papers*
    5. *Monthly Bulletin of Statistics*

G. The U.S. Department of Commerce publishes the *International Economic Indicators* quarterly, which focuses on the role of the United States in the world economy.

H. The *International Letter*, published every two weeks by the Federal Reserve Bank of Chicago, contains brief articles about important trends in international finance.

I. Many other publications of the U.S. government, such as the *Quarterly Review* of the Federal Reserve Bank of New York, carry some international information, even if they are not devoted to the international scene exclusively.

J. *The World Directory of Multinational Enterprises* features short reports on major multinational corporations.

K. The *Columbia Journal of World Business* and the *Journal of International Business Studies* carry articles related to finance, but not necessarily about international securities.

Key Terms and Concepts

coincident indicators

economic variables that tend to respond to the economic cycles at the same time as the economy as a whole

lagging indicators

economic variables that tend to respond to economic cycles after the economy as a whole

leading indicators

economic variables that tend to respond to the economic cycles more quickly than the economy as a whole

Multiple–Choice Questions

1. The _____ is the premier business periodical in the United States.
    A. *Dow Jones Daily*
    B. *Financial Times*
    C. *Wall Street Journal*
    D. *U.S. Treasury Bulletin*
    E. *Wall Street Transcript*

2. All of the following are current business periodicals, except _____.
    A. *Business Week*
    B. *Fortune*
    C. *Forbes*
    D. *Business World*
    E. *Dun's Review*

3. The world of pension investing is covered in _____.
    A. *Pensions and Investment Age*
    B. *Pension Investor*
    C. *Investor Weekly*
    D. *Pension Weekly*
    E. *Investment Review*

4. Which of the following is *not* an example of an index for further information?
    A. *Business Periodicals Index*
    B. Dialog
    C. Bibliographical Retrieval Service
    D. *Wall Street Journal Index*
    E. *Index of Financial Matters*

5. Which of the following is *not* an example of a federal government publication?
    A. *Economic Report of the President*
    B. *Treasury Bulletin*
    C. *Quarterly Business Review*
    D. *Business Conditions Digest*
    E. *Federal Reserve Bulletin*

6. _____ is prepared for members of Congress and contains data on major macroeconomic variables.
    A. *Quarterly Financial Report*
    B. *Economic Indicators*
    C. *Statistical Abstract of the United States*
    D. *Federal Reserve Bulletin*
    E. *Fortune*

7. One of the most useful features of the *Treasury Bulletin* is(are) the ____.
   A. bond curve
   B. callable issues plot
   C. yield curve
   D. market yields
   E. coupon equivalencies

8. One of the greatest problems in investment management is ____.
   A. lack of information
   B. information overload
   C. deciphering graphs
   D. cost of information
   E. over–reliance on the federal government

9. An economic variable that tends to respond to the economic cycles more quickly than the economy as a whole is called a _____ indicator.
   A. coincident
   B. lagging
   C. cyclical
   D. leading
   E. trend

10. For Great Britian, and good coverage of the European continent, the _____ is(are) very usefull.
   A. *Financial Times*
   B. *Economic Indicators*
   C. *Treasury Bulletin*
   D. *Federal Reserve Bulletin*
   E. *Wall Street Transcript*

11. While Standard & Poor's publishes its *Bond Guide*, Moody's has its _____ dedicated to bonds.
   A. *Bond Handbook*
   B. *Bond Record*
   C. *Bond Trader*
   D. *Bond Investor*
   E. *Bond Journal*

12. Which of the following is *not* an example of a Federal Reserve Bank location?
   A. Washington, DC
   B. Minneapolis
   C. Atlanta
   D. Richmond
   E. Kansas City

13. There are ____ Federal Reserve Banks in the United States.
    A. 10
    B. 11
    C. 12
    D. 13
    E. 14

14. Which of the following statements is *false*?
    A. Just by finding the prospering industries, investors can greatly increase the chance of rapid returns.
    B. There are some publications devoted entirely to a specific industry.
    C. Nearly every industry has one or more trade journals or industry magazines.
    D. Trade journals are generally a helpful source for potential investors.
    E. Most of the major brokerage houses make research reports available to their customers.

15. Standard & Poor's ____ indicates the firms in an industry that it believes to be good prospects.
    A. *Prospective*
    B. *Financial Management*
    C. *Survey of Current Business*
    D. *Outlook*
    E. *Investment Profile*

16. All publicly owned firms must file a detailed financial report, called a ____, with the SEC.
    A. corporate record
    B. C–R
    C. 10–K
    D. K–11
    E. S&P

17. One of the most useful sources of industry analysis and recommendations is provided by the ____.
    A. *Value Line Investment Survey*
    B. *Key Business Service*
    C. *General Investment Survey*
    D. *Specific Industry Report*
    E. *Transcript of Financial Transactions*

18. The two dominant firms in the investment information business are Standard & Poor's and ____.
    A. Hinckle's
    B. Whiteburn's
    C. Moody's
    D. Module's
    E. Black and Smithton's

19. Which of the following statements is *incorrect*?
    A. Each new issue of securities requires a prospectus.
    B. Every publicly owned firm must make an annual report available to its shareholders.
    C. Annual reports contain statistics prepared by the SEC about the company.
    D. An annual report contains the audited financial reports of a firm.
    E. Sometimes, annual reports raise false hopes about the prospects for the coming year.

20. ____ are sources of information for the investor willing to spend considerable time learning about pricing relationships in the security markets.
    A. Chart services
    B. Value lines
    C. Brokerage firm reports
    D. Annual reports
    E. Academic journals

21. Which of the following statements concerning brokerage houses is *false*?
    A. Most of the full–line brokerage houses have active research departments.
    B. Brokerage house reports are always presented in an industry–wide format.
    C. Of the reports prepared by brokerage firms, the overwhelming majority are positive.
    D. Many of the brokerage house reports are somewhat ambiguous.
    E. Discount brokers provide little or no research to their customers.

22. The *Value Line Investment Survey* appraises a firm's prospects with a ranking for ____ and ____.
    A. liquidity; risk
    B. liquidity; safety
    C. consistency; timeliness
    D. timeliness; safety
    E. consistency; risk

23. The *Value Line Investment Survey* uses a ranking scale of ____, with ____ being the highest.
    A. 1 to 10; 10
    B. 1 to 10; 1
    C. 1 to 5; 1
    D. 1 to 5; 5
    E. 0 to 5; 5

24. You are an investor who believes that past stock price movements provide a reliable guide to future movements. Therefore, you should ___.
    A. use a chart service
    B. subscribe to the *Value Line Investment Service*
    C. follow the "Selection and Opinion" reports
    D. keep accurate journals
    E. not need a full–service broker

25. Which of the following is *not* an example of an academic journal?
    A. *Journal of Finance*
    B. *Journal of Financial Economics*
    C. *Financial Management*
    D. *Financial Analysts Journal*
    E. *Journal of Investment Decisions*

Answers

Multiple–Choice Questions

1. C	10. A	19. C
2. D	11. B	20. E
3. A	12. A	21. B
4. E	13. C	22. D
5. C	14. D	23. C
6. B	15. D	24. A
7. C	16. C	25. E
8. B	17. A	
9. D	18. C	

CHAPTER SIX

The Security Market: Regulation and Taxation

Chapter Objectives

Upon completion of this chapter, you should be able to:
1. Review the major legislation affecting the security markets, and the rationale behind each act.
2. Understand the specific provision of the various acts.
3. Define corporate insiders.
4. Explain the current rules regarding taxation for individuals and corporations at the ordinary and investment income level.
5. Calculate individual and corporate income taxes.
6. Discuss the problem of the double taxation of dividends.

Chapter Outline

I. Overview

A. Most of the important regulations of securities markets now in force in the United States stem from the 1930s.
B. Taxation is one of the most complicated and rapidly changing subjects in business.
C. The Tax Reform Act of 1986 revolutionized the tax treatment of securities investing.

II. The Legislation of Regulation

A. Glass–Steagall Act (The Banking Act of 1933)
   1. The essential provision of the act is to prohibit commercial banking concerns from acting as security underwriters for initial security offerings.

2. The separation of the commercial banking and investment banking functions is unique to the United States.

3. The Glass–Steagall Act is now starting to erode rapidly. A 1988 ruling by the Supreme Court allowed commercial banks to underwrite commercial paper, municipal revenue bonds, mortgage–backed securities, and securities collateralized by consumer debt.

4. In 1989, the Federal Reserve extended this trend of deregulation by allowing J.P. Morgan and Co. to underwrite corporate debt through its securities trading firm.

B. Securities Act of 1933

1. The Securities Act of 1933 was the first major piece of legislation directed specifically toward the securities market. It is basically a "truth in securities" law.

2. The law states that issuers of new securities must provide truthful information about the securities to potential investors and it prohibits fraud in security sales.

3. An important provision of the law is the requirement that the prospective issuer file a registration statement with the Securities and Exchange Commission.

4. The law covers large, long–term issues and excludes short–term (270 days to maturity or less) issues and small (less than $500,000) issues.

C. Rule 144a

1. Rule 144a of the Securities Act of 1933 governs private placements and stipulates that a security originally issued as a privately placed security cannot be sold for two years from the date of issue.

2. In essence, Rule 144a permits the immediate resale of privately placed securities to a Qualified Institutional Buyer (QIB)—an institution, other than a bank or savings and loan association, that engages in transactions of more than $100 million of securities per year.

3. Because it contains no requirement to register with the SEC, Rule 144a may offer a way for sophisticated financial institutions in the U.S. and abroad to trade in this new market niche.

D. Securities Exchange Act of 1934

1. This act extended federal regulation to the organized exchanges operating in the secondary market.

2. The other main contribution was the establishment of the Securities and Exchange Commission (SEC), a federal agency charged with all facets of security market regulation.

3. The law specifically requires that securities exchanges register with the SEC, comply with the laws governing them, and organize their own procedures consistent with SEC guidelines.

4. The act defines a **corporate insider** as an employee or officer of a corporation who has access to non–public information about the firm.

5. The act prohibits insiders from making speculative profits on the shares of the company about which they have inside information.

6. Every shareholder with more than 10 percent of the outstanding shares of the firm, as well as the officers and directors of the firm, must report their transactions in the shares of the firm.

7. In addition, the act gives the Federal Reserve Board the power to set margin requirements for security purchases made with borrowed funds.

E. The Public Utility Holding Company Act of 1935

1. Public utilities hold one of the world's largest monopolies. Physical limitations make it difficult to sustain competition in the market for the products of public utility firms.

2. Believing that this monopoly power was not being used in the public interest, the Public Utility Holding Company Act of 1935 brought major parts of the financial dealings of these firms under the jurisdiction of the SEC.

3. The SEC was empowered to examine and control the corporate structure of public utilities, regulate their accounting practices, and determine the types of securities the companies could issue.

F. The Maloney Act (1939)

1. The Maloney Act amended the Securities Exchange Act of 1934, the original terms of which gave authority over organized exchanges to the SEC.

2. The essential purpose of the Maloney Act was to extend similar control to the over–the–counter (OTC) market.

G. The Trust Indenture Act of 1939

1. Prior to the passage of the Trust Indenture Act of 1939, there was no legal safeguard which insured that the trustee for a bond issue could act independently and strongly on behalf of the bondholders.

2. The Act requires that the trustee maintain its financial independence from the issuing firm, so that it is free to enforce the terms of the indenture.

H. The Investment Advisors Act of 1940

1. Investment advisors, those who give investment advice for compensation, were brought under the regulation of the SEC by the Investment Advisors Act of 1940.

2. The act prohibits fraud and deception and requires advisors to keep records, which can be inspected by the SEC. In addition, the act controls some advertising practices.

3. The law does not require proof of competence on the part of the advisor as a condition of registering with the SEC.

I. The Securities Investor Protection Act of 1970

1. In 1970, the Securities Investor Protection Act established the Securities Investor Protection Corporation (SIPC).

2. The SIPC is a government corporation that acts as an insurance company to protect investors against failed brokers and securities dealers.

J. The Employee Retirement Income Security Act of 1974
1. This act brought pension funds under federal regulation.
2. Pension fund managers are charged with the preservation of capital and must make prudent investments that contribute to the growth of capital.
3. The **prudent manager rule**, which requires that pension fund managers behave prudently when making investment decisions, results in the managers' consciously amassing evidence of their prudence.

K. The Securities Act Amendments of 1975
1. In 1975, Congress amended the Securities Act of 1933, ordering the SEC to move toward the establishment of a single nationwide securities market.
2. The act also outlawed fixed commission rates, but it allowed the NYSE to continue to require its members to trade all NYSE–listed securities only on the NYSE.
3. The act also directed the SEC to establish minimum capital requirements for brokers.

III. Insider Trading

A. The Securities Exchange Act of 1934 limits the trading of corporate insiders and requires the reporting of their transactions in stocks for which they hold inside information.
B. The act applies to principals of firms and to others who learn of material, non–public, information.
C. Insider Trading by Corporate Employees
A U.S. court upheld the SEC's position in the Texas Gulf Sulphur Company insider trading case.
D. Insider Trading by a Non–Employee
1. Occasionally, someone who is not a director, officer, or employee of a firm may gain access to information about a firm's prospects that is material to making an investment decision.
2. If that information has not been made public, it is illegal to use that information as a basis for trading.
E. Increases in Insider Trading and Increasing SEC Activity
1. As a response to an increase in alleged insider activity, or perhaps as the reason insider activity has received more attention, the SEC enforcement actions have escalated dramatically in recent years.
2. In spite of the recent dramatic increase in the number of SEC actions, the number is pathetically small in comparison to the range of insider trading that is probably taking place.

IV. Taxation

A. Taxable Income Derived from Securities Investing
   1. Investing in securities gives rise to taxable income from two major sources.
      a. Cash flows from owning the securities (dividends or interest payments).
      b. Changes in the value of the securities (capital gains or losses).
B. Taxation of Interest and Dividends
   1. Interest received by individuals or corporations, whether it be interest on long–term bonds, money market accounts, or bank accounts, is all taxable income.
   2. An important exception is the interest paid on tax–exempt municipal debt obligations, which is free of federal income taxation.
   3. For individuals, all dividend income is subject to taxation.
   4. For corporations that own securities and receive dividends, 80 percent of all dividends received are tax–exempt.
C. Capital Gains and Losses
   1. An increase in the price of a security during the time it is held is known as a **capital gain**, while a decrease in price is known as a **capital loss**.
   2. Capital gains and losses may be either realized or unrealized.
   3. In most cases, a capital gain or loss is realized when an investor sells a security and receives the cash flow associated with a gain or suffers a cash outflow associated with a loss.
   4. For the most part, only realized capital gains and losses give rise to tax consequences.

V. Personal Tax Rates

A. Taxable personal income consists of all income, including wages and investment income, adjusted for many factors.
B. The **marginal tax rate** is the tax paid on each additional dollar of income.

VI. Corporate Tax Rates

A. **Double taxation** occurs because corporations paying dividends must pay them out of after–tax earnings, and the dividends are taxed again when the individual receives them as regular income.

Key Terms and Concepts

capital gain (loss)   an increase (decrease) in the price of a security during the time it is held

corporate insider	an employee or officer of the corporation who has access to non–public information about the firm
double taxation	the taxation of dividends at the individual level and the corporate level (since they are paid out of a firm's after–tax income)
Employee Retirement Income Security Act of 1974	ERISA brought pension funds under federal regulation
Glass–Steagall Act	legislation passed in 1933 that separated the investment banking and commercial banking functions
insider trading	the speculative purchase or sale of securities by entities that possess non–public information about the firm
Investment Advisors Act	legislation of 1940 that placed entities which give investment advice for compensation under the jurisdiction of the SEC
Maloney Act	legislation of 1939 that extended the Securities Exchange Act of 1934 to over–the–counter markets
margin requirement	the proportion of the position value that the investor must invest out of personal funds
marginal tax rate	the tax paid on each additional dollar of income
prudent manager rule	requires that pension fund managers behave prudently when making investment decisions
Public Utility Holding Company Act	legislation of 1935 that gave the SEC regulatory authority over the financial dealings of public utility firms
Securities Act	legislation of 1933 that requires the issuers of new securities to provide truthful information about the securities to potential investors
Securities Act Amendments	legislation of 1975 that outlawed fixed brokerage commissions, ordered the SEC to try to establish a single nationwide securities market, and directed the SEC to establish minimum capital requirements for brokers

Securities Exchange Act	legislation of 1934 that brought organized exchanges under federal control, established the SEC, regulated insider trading, and gave the Federal Reserve Board the power to set margin requirements
Securities and Exchange Commission (SEC)	the federal agency charged with regulating all facets of the securities industries for the benefit of the investing public
Securities Investor Protection Act	legislation of 1970 that established the Securities Investor Protection Corporation (SIPC) to provide insurance against failing brokers and securities dealers
Trust Indenture Act	legislation of 1939 that required bond trustees to be financially and physically independent from bond issuers

Multiple–Choice Questions

1. A firm that pays all of its earnings in dividends is in a 48 percent tax bracket. If it has income before taxes of $100,000 and its shareholders are in a 38 percent tax bracket, the shareholders net $____ in after–tax income.
    A. 32,240
    B. 29,760
    C. 24,240
    D. 19,760
    E. 42,090

2. The federal agency charged with regulating most facets of the securities markets is the ____.
    A. Federal Reserve Board
    B. National Association of Securities Dealers
    C. Investment Advisory Board
    D. Securities and Exchange Commission
    E. Public Utility Advisory Board

3. The Securities Act of 1933 does *not* ____.
    A. cover short term securities
    B. require issuers of new securities to provide information about the securities to potential investors
    C. prohibit fraud in security sales
    D. require that a potential investor be given a prospectus before investing
    E. require a registration statement from the prospective issuer

4. According to the tax table in the text, the tax bill owed by a married couple filing jointly with $100,000 in taxable income is $____.
   A. 23,190
   B. 27,000
   C. 36,788
   D. 25,670
   E. 24,116

5. Cash payments from a corporation to its owners are ____.
   A. prudent income
   B. capital gains
   C. exempt income
   D. registered income
   E. dividends

6. The SEC was established by the ____.
   A. Securities Exchange Act of 1934
   B. Securities Investor Protection Act of 1970
   C. Securities Act of 1933
   D. Securities Act Amendments of 1975
   E. Glass–Steagall Act of 1933

7. Entities within a firm with access to non–public information about a firm are known as ____.
   A. corporate traders
   B. corporate insiders
   C. regulated brokers
   D. general agents
   E. corporate agents

8. The ____ was an amendment to the Securities Exchange Act of 1934.
   A. Public Utility Holding Act of 1935
   B. Maloney Act of 1939
   C. Banking Act of 1938
   D. Securities Exchange Act of 1937
   E. Investments Act of 1942

9. The Maloney Act extended SEC control to the ____.
   A. over–the–counter (OTC) market
   B. New York Stock Exchange
   C. American Stock Exchange
   D. United States Stock Exchange
   E. Inter–American Stock Exchange

10. The _____ outlawed fixed brokerage commissions.
    A. Glass–Steagall Act of 1933
    B. Maloney Act of 1939
    C. Employee Retirement Income Security Act of 1974
    D. Investment Advisors Act of 1940
    E. Securities Act Amendments of 1975

11. The Employee Retirement Income Security Act (ERISA) of 1974 brought _____ under federal regulation.
    A. corporate employees
    B. mutual funds
    C. all corporate insiders
    D. pension funds
    E. the stock market

12. The insurance fund that protects investors from brokerage house bankruptcy was established by the _____.
    A. Securities Investor Protection Act
    B. Employee Retirement Income Security Act
    C. Glass–Steagall Act
    D. Public Utility Holding Company Act
    E. Securities Act

13. According to the tax table in the text, under the Tax Reform Act of 1986, the tax bill owed by an individual with $100,000 in taxable income is $_____.
    A. 15,000.00
    B. 24,133.00
    C. 25,538.00
    D. 25,680.00
    E. 26,875.50

14. An increase in the price of a security while it is held is called a _____.
    A. price increase
    B. profit taking
    C. capital increase
    D. capital winning
    E. capital gain

15. If corporations receive dividends, _____ percent of the payment is exempt from taxation.
    A. 5
    B. 10
    C. 15
    D. 20
    E. 80

16. The Federal Reserve Board was given the power to set margin requirements by the ____.
    A. Securities Exchange Act of 1934
    B. Employee Retirement Income Security Act of 1974
    C. Securities Act Amendments of 1975
    D. Trust Indenture Act of 1939
    E. Investment Advisors Act of 1940

17. Bond trustees are required to be independent of bond issuers under the ____.
    A. Securities Act of 1934
    B. Employee Retirement Income Security Act of 1974
    C. Securities Act Amendments of 1975
    D. Trust Indenture Act of 1939
    E. Investment Advisors Act of 1940

18. Brokers are required to keep accurate records under the ____.
    A. Securities Act of 1934
    B. Employee Retirement Income Security Act of 1974
    C. Securities Act Amendments of 1975
    D. Trust Indenture Act of 1939
    E. Investment Advisors Act of 1940

19. The Securities and Exchange Commission was directed to establish a single nationwide securities market by the ____.
    A. Securities Act of 1934
    B. Employee Retirement Income Security Act of 1974
    C. Securities Act Amendments of 1975
    D. Trust Indenture Act of 1939
    E. Investment Advisors Act of 1940

20. Pension fund managers are required to conform to the prudent manager rule by the ____.
    A. Securities Act of 1934
    B. Employee Retirement Income Security Act of 1974
    C. Securities Act Amendments of 1975
    D. Trust Indenture Act of 1939
    E. Investment Advisors Act of 1940

21. Which of the following acts mandates the separation of commercial banking and investment banking?
    A. Employee Retirement Security Act of 1974
    B. Glass–Steagall of 1933
    C. Investment Advisors Act of 1940
    D. Maloney Act of 1939
    E. Public Utility Holding Company Act of 1935

22. Which of the following acts is designed to curb abuses of monopoly power?
    A. Employee Retirement Security Act of 1974
    B. Securities Exchange Act of 1934
    C. Investment Advisors Act of 1940
    D. Maloney Act of 1939
    E. Public Utility Holding Company Act of 1935

23. Which of the following acts required the financial and physical separation of bond issuers and issue trustees?
    A. Securities Act of 1933
    B. Securities Exchange Act of 1934
    C. Securities Act Amendments of 1975
    D. Securities Investor Protection Act of 1970
    E. Trust Indenture Act of 1939

24. The ____ mandated truth in advertising for the issuance of new securities.
    A. Securities Act of 1933
    B. Securities Exchange Act of 1934
    C. Securities Act Amendments of 1975
    D. Securities Investor Protection Act of 1970
    E. Trust Indentures Act of 1939

25. The possessor of non–public information about a firm or a security is known as a(n) ____.
    A. investor
    B. broker
    C. insider
    D. reformer
    E. advisor

Answers

Multiple–Choice Questions

1. A	10. E	19. C
2. D	11. D	20. B
3. A	12. A	21. B
4. E	13. E	22. E
5. E	14. E	23. E
6. A	15. E	24. A
7. B	16. A	25. C
8. B	17. D	
9. A	18. E	

CHAPTER SEVEN

Bond Pricing Principles

Chapter Objectives

Upon completion of this chapter, you should be able to:

1. Explain how the relationship between coupon rate and coupon yield causes bond prices to move over time if interest rates do not change.
2. Explain and give examples of the five principles of bond pricing.
3. Explain the advantages of and calculate Macaulay's duration.
4. Compute the simplified duration measure.
5. Explain and be able to calculate convexity.
6. Explain Fisher's relationship between the real rate of interest, expected inflation, and the nominal rate of interest.
7. Explain how the real rate of interest and the marginal productivity of capital interact to determine equilibrium capital investment.
8. Compute the Realized Compound Yield to Maturity, with and without reinvestment.
9. Explain how the relationship between expected yield to maturity and the reinvestment rate determine the relationship between RCYTM and the expected yield.

Chapter Outline

I. Overview

A. Well–established principles explain and predict the movement of bond prices as a result of changes in market rates of interest.
B. Only by understanding the price relationships between interest rates and bonds of different descriptions can one develop the skills necessary for good bond investing.
C. The key variables of bond pricing are: the maturity, the coupon rate, and the market rate of interest.

D. **Duration** is a measure of a bond's price sensitivity to changing interest rates.
E. **Convexity** is another measure of bond price sensitivity.
F. To measure performance in maximizing the value of the bond investment at some future date, the **realized compound yield to maturity** (RCYTM) is used.

II. The Effect of Time on Bond Price Movements

A. Bond prices change over time, due to the passage of time, even if interest rates do not change at all.
  1. An investor must realize that a premium bond's price will fall toward its face value even if interest rates do not change.
  2. If a bond is selling at a discount, its price must rise, reaching the par value by the maturity date.

III. The Effect of Interest Rates on Bond Price Movements

A. The effect of a given change in interest rates on the price of a bond depends upon three key variables.
  1. The maturity of the bond.
  2. The coupon rate.
  3. The level of interest rates at the time of the change in interest rates.
B. The basic valuation equation of finance, applied to bonds, states that the price of a bond (P), equals the present value of all promised cash flows from the bond (C_t), when those cash flows are discounted to the present at the bond's yield to maturity, (r):

$$P = \sum_{t=1}^{M} \frac{C_t}{(1 + r)^t}$$

C. The Bond Pricing Principles
  1. **Bond prices move inversely with interest rates.** A decrease in interest rates creates an increase in the price of any bond, and any increase in interest rates will cause the price of any bond to fall, but the amount of the price change depends on the particular features of the bond.
  2. **The longer the maturity of a bond, the more sensitive is its price to a change in interest rates, holding other factors constant.**
  3. **The price sensitivity of bonds increases with maturity, but at a decreasing rate.**
  4. **The lower the coupon rate on a bond, the more sensitive is its price to a change in interest rates, holding other factors constant.**
  5. **For a given bond, the capital gain caused by a yield decrease exceeds the capital loss caused by a yield increase of the same magnitude.**

D. The Need for a Summary Measure
1. Since each of the bond pricing principles assumes that all other factors are being held constant, except for the one under consideration, it is still difficult to compare the price sensitivity of different bonds.
2. Accordingly, it would be very useful to have some summary measure of a bond's price sensitivity that reflects all of the factors affecting the sensitivity—the maturity, the coupon rate, and the yield to maturity.

IV. Duration

A. **Duration** is a single number for each bond that summarizes the three key factors (maturity, coupon rate, and yield to maturity) that affect the sensitivity of a bond's price to changes in interest rates.
B. Macaulay's duration is given by the following equation:

$$D_m = \frac{\sum_{t=1}^{M} t \left(\frac{C_t}{(1+r)^t} \right)}{P}$$

C. How to Calculate Duration
The duration equation computes the present value of each of the cash flows and weights each by the time until it is received. The weighted cash flows are then summed, and the sum is divided by the current price of the bond.
D. Duration as an Elasticity Measure
1. There is another equation for Macaulay's duration that expresses duration as the negative of elasticity of the bond's price with respect to a change in the discount factor $(1 + r)$:

$$D_m \approx - \frac{\frac{\Delta P}{P}}{\frac{\Delta (1+r)}{(1+r)}}$$

2. Duration is essentially an elasticity measure, for it gives a single measure of the way in which a bond's price changes for a change in the discount factor $(1 + r)$.
E. The Duration Price Change Formula and Modified Duration
1. We can rearrange the previous equation to form:

$$\Delta P \approx -D \, \frac{\Delta(1+r)}{1+r} \, P$$

2. The concept of **modified duration (MD)** equals Macaulay's duration divided by $(1 + r)$:

$$MD = \frac{D_m}{1 + r}$$

3. The price change of a bond equals the negative of modified duration multiplied by the change in the yields, multiplied by the original price before the yield changed:

$$\Delta P \approx -(MD)(\Delta r)(P)$$

F. Duration Tracking Errors
    1. The duration price change formula takes into account the curvature of the price/yield line at a given point.
    2. It does not take into account how the shape of the curve changes, and how duration changes, away from the initial point at which duration is measured.
    3. Duration can change dramatically for the same bond with the same maturity and coupon due solely to a change in yields.
    4. The following principles summarize how duration changes as the yield, coupon rate, and maturity vary individually.
        a. For a given coupon rate and maturity, duration is inversely related to the yield on a bond.
        b. For a given yield and maturity, duration is inversely related to the coupon rate.
        c. For a given yield and coupon rate, duration is inversely related to the bond's maturity.

V. Convexity

A. **Convexity** reflects the way in which duration changes for different yields on the same bond and tries to account for the duration tracking error previously discussed.
B. We denote convexity as VEX, and letting R = 1 + r, we define convexity as:

$$VEX = \frac{1}{P R^2} \sum_{t=1}^{M} \frac{t (t + 1) C_t}{R^t}$$

C. Estimating Price Changes with Duration and Convexity
    To use convexity to better approximate the price change for a bond, we use the following equation:

$$\Delta P \approx -MD (\Delta R) (P) + .5 \, VEX(\Delta R)^2 \, P$$

D. Convexity and Bond Selection
    1. Other factors being equal, investors should prefer greater convexity.
        a. In a price/yield curve, we have seen that duration essentially measures the slope of a curve at a given point.
        b. Convexity, by contrast, reflects the severity of the curve.

2. Convexity is the tendency of the price/yield graph to curve away from the tangent line.
    a. The greater the degree of this curvature, the better, because it means the price will be higher for a given yield.
    b. Therefore, the more convexity a bond has, the better.

VI. Duration and Convexity: Some Qualifications

A. The conclusions we have reached about the benefits of duration and convexity are based on four assumptions.
    1. First, we assume that the bonds being analyzed are not callable by the issuer.
    2. Second, we have assumed that the yield curve is flat at the time the yield change occurs.
    3. Third, we assume that if yields change, they all change by the same amount.
    4. Finally, the analysis holds for a single change in yields.
B. Focus on Non–Callable Bonds
    1. If yields fall by a large amount, the price of a non–callable bond would rise along the type of price/yield curve that we have considered in this chapter.
    2. If the bond is callable, the bond holders know that the issuer may call the bonds and pay them only the call price.
    3. Therefore, the price of the bond will not rise as we have assumed if the bond holder is threatened by a call.
    4. As a practical matter, the analysis that we have conducted holds for small changes in yields if the bond is not in imminent danger of being called.
C. Restriction to Flat Yield Curves
    By considering only a common yield for all of a bond's payments, we have implicitly assumed that the yield curve is flat.
D. Restriction to Parallel Shifts in Yield Curves
    1. If we consider a change in the one common yield applied to all of the bond's cash flows, we are assuming that the yield curve shifts in parallel fashion.
    2. Researchers have found that concerns about the flat yield curve and parallel shift assumptions have only very small practical results.
E. Restriction to a Single Change in Yields
    1. In actual markets, yields change frequently. This can be important, because we have seen that duration and convexity change as yields change, even when time to maturity does not change.
    2. A changing yield environment requires periodic adjustments to a bond portfolio to reflect the changing duration and convexity.

VII. *The Level of Interest Rates*

A. The Nominal Rate of Interest
   1. The **nominal rate of interest** reflects only the promised dollar payments without reference to the expected purchasing power of the payments.
   2. Following the work of the great economist Irving Fisher, we express the nominal rate of interest on a default–free security as being composed of the real rate of interest and the expected rate of inflation.
   3. For a bond with no default risk, the relationship can be expressed as follows:
$$(1 + r) = (1 + r^*)[1 + E(I)]$$
   where:

   r = the nominal rate of interest

   r^* = the real rate of interest

   $E(I)$ = the expected rate of inflation over the period

B. The Real Rate of Interest and the Expected Inflation Rate
   1. The **real rate of interest** has many names, including the **pure price of time** and the **marginal productivity of capital**.
   2. The pure price of time label results because the **real rate of interest** is the expected change in purchasing power necessary to induce investors to postpone consumption.
   3. The **pure price of time** is the change in purchasing power investors demand for postponing their consumption.
   4. The **marginal productivity of capital** is the rate of return that can be earned by the next unit of capital to be invested.
   5. As long as the marginal productivity of capital exceeds the real rate of interest, more funds will be demanded for investment. Equilibrium is reached when the real rate of interest equals the marginal productivity of capital.
   6. For the years 1926–1990, the real rate of return on investment in U.S. Treasury securities, whether in bonds or bills, was about 0.5 percent.
   7. The best estimate of the real rate of return is somewhere in the range of 0 to 2 percent.
   8. The real rate is not very important in determining interest rates. Instead, the nominal interest rate is composed mainly of the expected inflation rate.
   9. Quoted interest rates pertain to investment over some future time period, and as such, they cannot depend on the actual inflation rate to be sustained during the investment period, since that is not known. Instead, **expected** inflation is the key component.

VIII. Realized Compound Yield to Maturity (RCYTM)

A. Expectations of future changes in levels of interest rates are very important to bond investors for two reasons:
   1. First, we have already seen that changing rates mean that bond prices change.
   2. Second, the rate earned on reinvested coupons also depends on how interest rates change.
B. The **realized compound yield to maturity (RCYTM)** takes into account the rates earned on reinvested coupons.
C. Because bond investment is often directed toward some specific date in the future, the rate earned on reinvested coupon payments or on proceeds from maturing bonds is very important in determining the amount of funds available on the target date.
D. The best measure of progress toward wealth maximization on a target date is the RCYTM because it is a geometric mean growth rate over a given period:

$$RCYTM = \sqrt[n]{\frac{\text{Terminal Wealth}}{\text{Initial Wealth}}} - 1$$

where:
   Initial Wealth = the value of the funds at the outset of the investment period
   Terminal Wealth = the value of the funds at the conclusion of the investment period
   n = the number of periods between the outset and the conclusion of the investment period

E. There are three general rules about reinvestment rates:
   1. If the reinvestment rate for the interim cash flows exceeds the yield to maturity, the RCYTM is greater than the yield to maturity.
   2. If the reinvestment rate for the interim cash flows equals the yield to maturity, the RCYTM equals the yield to maturity.
   3. If the reinvestment rate for the interim cash flows is less than the yield to maturity, the RCYTM is less than the yield to maturity.

Key Terms and Concepts

bond table   gives prices for bonds of different maturities, different coupon rates, and different yields

convexity	is an additional measure of the price sensitivity of a bond which reflects the way in which duration changes for different yields on the same bond and tries to account for the duration tracking error that one encounters
coupon rate	the percentage that determines the coupon payments on a coupon bond
duration	is a measure of the sensitivity of a bond's price to a change in yield that incorporates the bond's coupon rate, maturity, and its existing yield
expected rate of inflation	the rate of increase in the price level expected by the financial market
marginal productivity of capital	the rate of return on the next unit of capital employed
modified duration	a concept closely related to Macaulay's duration which says that the price change of a bond equals the negative of modified duration times the change in yield times the original price before the yield changed
nominal rate of interest	reflects only the promised dollar payments without reference to the purchasing power of the payments
price sensitivity	the change in the price of a given bond for a given change in yield
pure price of time	the change in purchasing power investors demand for postponing their consumption
real rate of interest	the inflation adjusted return on an investment
Realized Compound Yield to Maturity (RCYTM)	the geometric mean return on the investment over a given period, which also reflects the rate of return realized on all proceeds from the investment

Multiple–Choice Questions

1. The price sensitivity of a bond is an increasing function of its ____.
   A. coupon rate
   B. maturity
   C. purchasing power
   D. default risk
   E. investment grade

2. A bond's yield to maturity is a(n) ____ rate of interest.
   A. current
   B. inflated
   C. real
   D. nominal
   E. compounded

3. The lower the ____ rate on a bond, the more sensitive is its price to a change in interest rates, holding other factors constant.
   A. marginal
   B. discount
   C. premium
   D. coupon
   E. equality

4. If the real rate of interest is 4 percent and expected inflation is 8 percent, the nominal rate of interest is ____ percent.
   A. 10.385
   B. 11.232
   C. 12.000
   D. 12.320
   E. 12.694

5. The interest rate that determines the amount of a bond's annual interest payments is known as the ____ rate.
   A. discount
   B. coupon
   C. yield
   D. current
   E. compound

6. The real return that can be earned on the next unit of physical capital employed is known as the ____.
   A. nominal rate of interest
   B. expected rate of inflation
   C. pure price of time
   D. marginal productivity of capital
   E. yield to maturity

7. Duration is a measure of the way a bond price changes for a given change in its ____.
   A. yield
   B. default risk
   C. premium
   D. standard deviation
   E. expected inflation

8. The ____ is the expected change in purchasing power needed to induce investors to postpone consumption.
   A. real rate of interest
   B. nominal rate of interest
   C. expected rate of inflation
   D. marginal rate of interest
   E. marginal productivity of capital

9. The crucial difference between an expected yield and the RCYTM is that the RCYTM considers ____.
   A. default risk
   B. the pure price of time
   C. the marginal productivity of capital
   D. the reinvestment rate on interim cash flows
   E. the real rate of interest

10. Which of the following is *not* one of Malkiel's five bond pricing principles?
    A. Bond prices move inversely with interest rates.
    B. The nominal interest rate is determined by the interaction between the expected real rate of interest and expected inflation.
    C. The longer the maturity of a bond, the greater its price sensitivity to changes in yield.
    D. The lower the coupon rate on a bond, the greater its price sensitivity to changes in yield.
    E. Price sensitivity increases with maturity at a decreasing rate.

11. The Realized Compound Yield to Maturity is ____.
   A. positively related to duration
   B. positively related to maturity
   C. positively related to the reinvestment rate
   D. negatively related to the coupon rate
   E. negatively related to expected inflation

12. Equilibrium in the capital market occurs when the marginal productivity of capital equals the ____.
   A. nominal interest rate
   B. expected inflation rate
   C. duration of default–free government securities
   D. default risk of the obligation
   E. real rate of interest

13. The price sensitivity of a coupon bond is a decreasing function of its ____.
   A. coupon rate
   B. maturity
   C. duration
   D. par value
   E. face value

14. The change in the price of a given bond for a given change in yield is known as its ____.
   A. purchasing power
   B. pure price
   C. expected inflation
   D. marginal productivity
   E. price sensitivity

15. The change in purchasing power generated by an investment in a bond is a(n) ____ rate of interest.
   A. current
   B. inflated
   C. nominal
   D. compounded
   E. real

16. If the real rate of interest is 10 percent and the expected rate of inflation is 4 percent, the nominal rate of interest is ____ percent.
   A. 10.385
   B. 11.232
   C. 12.000
   D. 14.400
   E. 12.694

17. Other things being equal, a bond's duration ____.
    A. increases with its maturity
    B. increases with its coupon rate
    C. increases with its price
    D. decreases with face value
    E. is larger than its term to maturity

18. Duration is calculated by ____.
    A. multiplying the present value of each bond payment by the time period until received and dividing that sum by the bond price
    B. dividing the annual coupon payment by the price
    C. adding the present value of each coupon payment to the present value of the face value
    D. multiplying (one plus the real rate of interest) and (one plus the expected inflation rate)
    E. dividing (one plus the nominal yield) by (one plus the actual inflation rate)

19. Relative purchasing power is calculated by ____.
    A. multiplying the present value of each bond payment by the time period until received and dividing that sum by the bond price
    B. dividing the annual coupon payment by the price
    C. adding the present value of each coupon payment to the present value of the face value
    D. multiplying (one plus the real rate of interest) and (one plus the expected inflation rate)
    E. dividing (one plus the nominal yield) by (one plus the actual inflation rate)

20. A bond's price is determined by ____.
    A. multiplying the present value of each bond payment by the time period until received and dividing that sum by the bond price
    B. dividing the annual coupon payment by the price
    C. adding the present value of each coupon payment to the present value of the face value
    D. multiplying (one plus the real rate of interest) and (one plus the expected inflation rate)
    E. dividing (one plus the nominal yield) by (one plus the actual inflation rate)

21. The nominal rate of interest is calculated by _____.
    A. multiplying the present value of each bond payment by the time period until received and dividing that sum by the bond price
    B. dividing the annual coupon payment by the price
    C. adding the present value of each coupon payment to the present value of the face value
    D. multiplying (one plus the real rate of interest) and (one plus the expected inflation rate)
    E. dividing (one plus the nominal yield) by (one plus the actual inflation rate)

22. A bond's current yield is calculated by _____.
    A. multiplying the present value of each bond payment by the time period until received and dividing that sum by the bond price
    B. dividing the annual coupon payment by the price
    C. adding the present value of each coupon payment to the present value of the face value
    D. multiplying (one plus the real rate of interest) and (one plus the expected inflation rate)
    E. dividing (one plus the nominal yield) by (one plus the actual inflation rate)

23. A bond that is yielding 10 percent is priced at $950 and has a duration of 7.75 years. If its yield rises to 12 percent, the new approximate price is $_____.
    A. 133.86
    B. 775.00
    C. 816.14
    D. 1,027.50
    E. 1,083.86

24. A bond that is yielding 12 percent is priced at $1,020 and has a duration of 8.25 years. If its yield falls to 10 percent, the new approximate price is $_____.
    A. 150.27
    B. 869.73
    C. 918.00
    D. 1,102.00
    E. 1,170.27

25. The geometric mean return earned on a bond that considers the rate at which coupons are reinvested is known as the _____.
    A. RCYTM
    B. relative purchasing power
    C. discount bond table
    D. expected inflation duration
    E. capital gain coefficient

Review Problems

1. A $1,000 face, 8 percent annual payment coupon bond with three years to maturity has a yield of 12 percent.
    a. What is its price?
    b. What is its duration?
    c. If the yield on the bond changes to 10 percent, which way do you expect its price to move? Why? What financial market factors might cause this to happen?
    d. Calculate the bond's new price using the bond pricing formula.
    e. Calculate the bond's change in price using the duration price change relationship.
    f. Why do the two price changes differ?
    g. Is this bond's price change greater or less than what you would expect on an 8 percent 10–year bond with the same initial yield and yield change? Why?
    h. Is this bond's price change greater or less than what you would expect on a 6 percent three–year bond with the same initial yield and yield change? Why?

2. A $1,000 face value, 10 percent coupon bond with semiannual payments and two years to maturity has a yield to maturity of 8 percent.
    a. Compute its price.
    b. Compute its Macaulay duration.
    c. If the bond's yield rises to 9 percent, compute its new price using the duration measure relationship equation.
    d. If the bond has only one and one half years to maturity at an 8 percent yield, what is its price?
    e. Why is this price lower than your answer to (a)?

3. You are trying to decide between purchasing $1,000 face value bonds with 10 percent annual coupons and one year or two years to maturity. The expected real rate of interest is 3 percent and the expected inflation rate is 6 percent.
    a. Compute the nominal yield for the one–year bond.
    b. What is its price?
    c. Compute the nominal yield for the two–year bond.
    d. What is its price?
    e. If actual inflation is 5 percent the first year and 7 percent the next year, compute the relative purchasing power of the cash flows from the two–year bond.
    f. How does the relationship between actual and expected inflation affect the real return you earn each year if you purchase the two–year bond?

4. A $1,000 face value, 6 percent coupon bond with annual payments and three years to maturity is priced at $948.46 to yield 8 percent per year. Compute the RCYTM if:
    a. the interim cash flows are reinvested at 4 percent.
    b. the interim cash flows are reinvested at 10 percent.
    c. the interim cash flows are not reinvested (flows are used for consumption).
    d. Explain the relationship shown between expected yield, the actual reinvestment rate, and the realized compound yield to maturity.

Answers

Multiple–Choice Questions

1. B	10. B	19. E
2. D	11. C	20. C
3. D	12. E	21. D
4. D	13. A	22. B
5. B	14. E	23. C
6. D	15. E	24. E
7. A	16. D	25. A
8. A	17. A	
9. D	18. A	

Review Problems

1a. The price is the present value of the three years worth of coupon payments plus the present value of the face amount in three years discounted at 12 percent.

$$P = \frac{\$80}{(1.12)^1} + \frac{\$80}{(1.12)^2} + \frac{\$80}{(1.12)^3} + \frac{\$1,000}{(1.12)^3}$$

$$= \$71.43 + \$63.78 + \$56.94 + \$711.78 = \$903.93.$$

b. The first step in finding duration is to calculate the present value of the payments weighted by the time until received.

$$P = \frac{\$80(1)}{(1.12)^1} + \frac{\$80(2)}{(1.12)^2} + \frac{\$80(3)}{(1.12)^3} + \frac{\$1,000(3)}{(1.12)^3}$$

$$= \$71.43 + \$127.55 + \$170.83 + \$2,135.34$$

$$= \$2,505.15.$$

Now divide the sum by the price found in (a):
Duration = $2,505.15/$903.93 = 2.77 years.

c. The prices of coupon bonds with fixed payments are inversely related to their yields. As one discounts (divides) the fixed payments by a smaller yield, a larger price results. A coupon bond's nominal yield could fall because the real rate of interest has fallen or, more likely, because the market's opinion of expected inflation has fallen.

d. Repeating the calculations in (a) with a 10 percent yield:

$$P = \frac{\$80}{(1.1)^1} + \frac{\$80}{(1.1)^2} + \frac{\$80}{(1.1)^3} + \frac{\$1,000}{(1.1)^3}$$

$$= \$72.73 + \$66.12 + \$60.11 + \$751.31$$

$$= \$950.27.$$

Notice that the present value of each coupon payment has risen as the discount factor has fallen.

e. According to the duration relationship, for a change in yield of –2 percent, (from 12 percent down to 10 percent):

$$\text{Change in Price} = (-D)\left(\frac{\text{Change in r}}{1 + r}\right)(\text{Current Price})$$

$$= -2.77 \left(\frac{-2\%}{1.12}\right)\$903.93$$

$$= \left(\frac{.0554}{1.12}\right)\$903.93 = \$44.71.$$

f. The actual price change is ($950.27 – $903.93) = $46.34. The duration estimate is close, but not exact, since duration is derived from calculus and refers to infinitesimal changes in yield. While it may not seem so at first, two days worth of bond quotes in *The Wall Street Journal* will show you that 2 percent is a large change in yield from one point in time to the next. Nevertheless, duration provides a very accurate estimate of the price change.

g. The 8 percent, 10–year bond has a longer maturity so you would expect a bigger price change. More payments are affected by the change in yield.

h. The 6 percent, three–year bond has a lower coupon rate. More of its return comes from the last, face value payment so you would expect a bigger price change on the low coupon bond for a given change in yield.

2a. The price is the present value of the actual payments. With semiannual payments, the investor will receive an annual payment of .1($1,000) = $100 as two payments of $100/2 = $50 every six months. The annual yield of 8 percent must also be converted to a semiannual basis for a semiannual yield of (.08/2) = .04.

$$P = \frac{\$50}{(1.04)^1} + \frac{\$50}{(1.04)^2} + \frac{\$50}{(1.04)^3} + \frac{\$1,050}{(1.04)^4}$$

$$= \$48.08 + \$46.23 + \$44.45 + \$897.54$$

$$= \$1,036.30.$$

b. The time–weighted present value of the payments is:

$$P = \frac{\$50(1)}{(1.04)^1} + \frac{\$50(2)}{(1.04)^2} + \frac{\$50(3)}{(1.04)^3} + \frac{\$1,050(4)}{(1.04)^4}$$

$$= \$48.08 + \$92.46 + \$133.35 + \$3,590.18$$

$$= \$3,864.07.$$

Dividing by the price yields a duration of:
$3,864.07/$1,036.30 = 3.73 semiannual payments, or
3.73/2 = 1.865 years.

c. The duration measure relationship equation suggests a 1 percent increase in yield will cause a price change of:
−1.865(.01/1.08)$1,036.30 = −$17.90

for a new price of:
$1,036.30 − $17.90 = $1,018.40.

d. The new price with 1.5 years (three payments) to maturity and an 8 percent annual yield would be:

$$P = \frac{\$50}{(1.04)^1} + \frac{\$50}{(1.04)^2} + \frac{\$1,050}{(1.04)^3}$$

$$= \$48.08 + \$46.23 + \$933.45 = \$1,027.76.$$

e. This price is lower than the answer to (a) because this is a premium bond. Its yield (8 percent) is less than its coupon rate (10 percent) so its price exceeds face value. Price must equal face value at maturity so the price must decline over the bond's life, as maturity approaches, even if yields remain constant. The opposite price pattern must also hold true for discount bonds (those trading below face value).

3a. The nominal interest rate is determined by the expected real rate and the expected inflation rate:

$(1 + r) = (1.03)(1.06) = 1.0918$, so $r = 9.18$ percent.

b. The price of the one–year bond is just the present value of the terminal payments, $(.1)(\$1,000) = \$100$ in interest, plus the face value:

$P = \$1,100/1.0918 = \$1,007.51$.

c. The two–year nominal rate is determined by compounding the annual relationships:

$(1 + r)^2 = (1.03)^2(1.06)^2 = (1.0609)(1.1236) = 1.192$

$(1 + r) = (1.192)^{1/2} = 1.0918$, so $r = 9.18$ percent.

Notice that this is identical to the nominal one–year yield since the same interest rates are expected to hold over the two–year interval.

d. The price of the two–year bond is the present value of the two payments discounted at 9.18 percent:

$$P = \frac{\$100}{(1.0918)^1} + \frac{\$1,100}{(1.0918)^2}$$

$$= \$91.59 + \$922.80 = \$1,014.39.$$

e. If actual inflation is 5 percent during the first year, relative purchasing power for the first interest payment is:

$RPP = (1.0918)/(1.05) = 1.04$

implying a real return of $(1.04 - 1) = 4$ percent.

If actual inflation is 7 percent during the second year, relative purchasing power for the final interest payment and the face value is:

RPP = (1.0918)/(1.07) = 1.02

implying a real return of (1.02 − 1) = 2 percent.

f. The nominal yield of 9.18 percent assumed expected inflation of 6 percent. Actual inflation at a lower rate, like the 5 percent first year value, gives a real return greater than the 3 percent assumed in calculating the nominal yield. On the other hand, higher than expected inflation (7 percent in the second year) eats away at the real return, making it less than expected.

4a. Annual coupon payments are .06($1,000) = $60.

Reinvesting the first payment for two years and the second payment for one year adds:

($60)$(1.04)^2$ + ($60)$(1.04)^1$

= $64.90 + $62.40 = $127.30 to terminal wealth.

Combining this with the last coupon payment and the face value gives terminal wealth of:

$127.30 + $1,060 = $1,187.30.

The three–year geometric mean return (RCYTM) is:

($1,187.30/$948.46)$^{1/3}$ = $(1.252)^{1/3}$ = 1.078, or 1.078 − 1 = 7.8 percent.

b. Reinvestment at 10 percent adds:

($60)$(1.10)^2$ + ($60)$(1.10)^1$

= $72.60 + $66.00 = $138.60 to terminal wealth, for a total of:

terminal wealth = $1,060 + $138.60 = $1,198.60

and an RCYTM of:

($1,198.60/$948.46)$^{1/3}$ = 1.081, or 8.1 percent.

c. With no reinvestment, terminal wealth is simply the last payment of $1,060 total, so the RCYTM is:

($1,060/$948.46)$^{1/3}$ = 1.04, or 4 percent.

d. As long as the reinvestment rate is less than the 8 percent expected yield, the RCYTM is also less than the expected yield. If the reinvestment rate exceeds the expected yield, so does the RCYTM. This occurs because the expected yield calculation, which was used to determine the price of the bond, implicitly assumed reinvestment at the expected yield.

For example, reinvestment at 8 percent leads to reinvested coupons worth:

$60(1.08)^2 + $60(1.08)^1 = 134.78

and terminal wealth of:

$1,060 + $134.78 = $1,194.78$

for an RCYTM of:

$(\$1,194.78/\$948.46)^{1/3} = 1.08$, or 8 percent.

CHAPTER EIGHT

Bond Portfolio Management

Chapter Objectives

Upon completion of this chapter, you should be able to:
1. Define the term structure of interest rates.
2. Explain and calculate forward rates.
3. Compare and contrast the three theories of the term structure.
4. Explain the risk structure of interest rates and the determinants of how the risk premium changes over time.
5. Explain the advantages and disadvantages of the ladder and dumbbell strategies.
6. Apply the three term structure theories to the problems of interest rate forecasting and yield curve slope determination.
7. Describe, and give numerical examples of, the bank immunization and planning period immunization strategies.
8. Explain contingent immunization and calculate trigger points.
9. Discuss the real–world complications encountered in applying immunization strategies.
10. Explain the concept of dedicated portfolios.

Chapter Outline

I. Overview

A. Yields on bonds can be graphed as a **yield curve**, a graph that shows the relationship between the maturity of a bond and its yield to maturity.
B. **Default risk** is the risk that one or more of the payments on a bond will not be paid as promised.
C. The **risk structure of interest rates** is the relationship between the yields of different securities as a function of their level of default risk.

D. In practice, choosing the correct maturity composition of the portfolio and selecting the appropriate risk level are two of the prime functions of the bond portfolio manager.

E. An **immunization strategy** seeks to make the value of the bond portfolio immune, or insensitive, to changes in interest rates.

II. The Term Structure of Interest Rates

A. The difference in yields, due solely to differences in maturity, is described by the yield curve or the term structure of interest rates.

B. The **term structure of interest rates** is the relationship between the term to maturity and yield to maturity for bonds similar in all respects except maturity.

C. The shape of the yield curve is important because it contains information about the future course of interest rates, and this information is the most valuable asset a bond investor could have.

D. Forward Rates
   1. **Forward rates** of interest are rates covering future time periods implied by current spot rates.
   2. A **spot rate** is a yield prevailing on a bond for immediate purchase.

E. The Principle of Calculation of forward rates is derived as follows.
   1. Forward rates are calculated on the assumption that returns over a given period of time are all equal, no matter which maturities of bonds are held over that span of time.
   2. Given the relevant spot rates, it is possible to calculate any forward rate.

III. Theories of the Term Structure

A. Three theories of the term structure have received the greatest attention.
   1. The pure expectations theory.
   2. The liquidity premium theory.
   3. The market segmentation theory.

B. The Pure Expectations Theory
   1. The pure expectations theory states that forward rates are unbiased estimators of future interest rates, or forward rates are equal to expected future spot rates.
   2. According to this theory, many bond investors will switch their funds to any maturity with a higher yield, so, after the maturity switching has stopped, there must be an equal expected return for any investment period, no matter what maturities are held over that period.
   3. If expected returns from all maturity strategies are the same, forward rates must necessarily equal expected future spot rates.

4. The truth of this theory depends upon the presence of bond investors who are indifferent to the maturities of the bonds they hold and who seek the greatest expected returns.

C. The Liquidity Premium Theory

1. This theory states that forward rates are upwardly biased estimates of expected future spot rates, or forward rates are greater than expected future spot rates.

2. This theory also states that bondholders greatly prefer to hold short–term bonds rather than long–term bonds, because the short–term bonds have less interest rate risk.

3. Thus, investors are willing to pay more for short–term bonds, and the extra amount they are willing to pay is the **liquidity premium**.

4. Long–term bonds must pay a greater return than short–term bonds to induce investors to commit their funds to the long–term instruments, and the expected return on a succession of one–year bonds must be less than the expected rate of return on a long–term bond.

D. The Market Segmentation Theory

1. Unlike the pure expectations theory and the liquidity premium theory, the market segmentation theory is not expressly stated in terms of forward rates.

2. According to this theory, the yield curve reflects the actions and preferences of certain major participants in the bond market, mainly large financial institutions.

3. These participants have different maturity preferences due to the nature of their businesses and a desire to match the maturity of their assets and liabilities in order to control risk.

4. Therefore, they tend to trade bonds only in their respective maturity ranges; this desire leads directly to the segmented markets hypothesis.

    a. The yield curve is determined by the interplay of supply and demand factors in different segments of the maturity spectrum of the bond market. Financial institutions with strong maturity preferences occupy those different segments and effectively cause the bond market to splinter into different market segments based on maturity.

E. How the Three Theories Explain Different Observed Yield Curves

1. Each of the theories has a different interpretation of the causes of the shape of a given yield curve, and, therefore, a different interpretation of the expected future course of interest rates.

2. According to the pure expectations theory: if the yield curve slopes upward, short–term interest rates should rise; if the yield curve is flat, interest rates will remain constant; and if the yield curve slopes downward, then short–term interest rates should fall.

3. According to the liquidity premium theory's more complicated analysis of the yield curve: assuming that the market expects short–term rates to be constant forever, long–term bonds would pay a higher yield, and

the yield curve will slope slightly upward even when short–term rates are expected to remain constant.

4. For a downward–sloping yield curve, the liquidity premium theory argues that interest rates are expected to fall by an amount greater than the effect of the liquidity premium.

5. The market segmentation hypothesis explains all observed yield curve shapes as resulting from the supply and demand factors in each segment of the bond market, and it emphasizes interest and maturity preferences of institutional participants.

F. Evidence on the Three Theories

1. In spite of some evidence in support of the market segmentation theory, there does seem to be a consensus that it alone cannot explain the yield curve.

2. As a consequence, the real struggle is between the pure expectations theory and the liquidity premium theory.

3. Most theorists would agree on the fundamental proposition that the shape of the yield curve expresses the market's opinion about future interest rates.

4. In general, an upward–sloping yield curve implies that rates are expected to rise; a downward–sloping yield curve implies that rates are expected to fall.

5. Further, if a liquidity premium does exist, it is not very large, so forward rates are a good guide to market expectation of future interest rates.

IV. The Risk Structure of Interest Rates

A. The risk structure of interest rates analyzes the differences in risk among different classes of bonds.

B. For two classes of bonds differing only in their risk level, the yield difference that results from a difference in risk is called a **yield differential, yield spread**, or **risk differential**.

C. In comparing risk–free Treasury bonds and risky corporate bonds, the yield differential is also known as the **risk premium**.

D. Determinants of the Risk Premium

1. The risk premium varies inversely with the business cycle.

2. In general, when interest rates are high, risk premiums tend to be large.

3. Evidence on the relationship between the yield spread and maturity is somewhat mixed, but tends to suggest that longer maturities lead to higher yield spreads.

4. Lastly, there is evidence that the marketability of the particular bond issue has an effect on the risk premium.

5. The risk premium essentially measures the risk of default.

E. The Risk Premium as a Measure of Default Risk
    1. The greater the chance of default, the larger the risk premium necessary to attract investors.
    2. Bond rating services, such as Moody's and Standard & Poor's, attempt to summarize all factors that affect default risk and determine the risk premium in their bond ratings.
    3. While it is not possible to specify a general rule for how much default risk should be undertaken, it is clear that the promised return will increase with greater default risk.

V. Bond Portfolio Maturity Strategies

A. The maturity structure of the portfolio concerns the way in which funds are allocated to bonds of differing maturities.
B. Two popular approaches are the **laddered strategy** and the **dumbbell** or **barbell strategy**.
    1. In the laddered portfolio strategy, funds in the bond portfolio are distributed approximately evenly over the range of maturities.
        a. The main advantage of this strategy is ease of management. It is very easy to maintain the same kind of maturity distribution with very low transaction costs.
        b. The disadvantage of this strategy is the difficulty in changing the maturity composition of the portfolio.
    2. The dumbbell strategy places bonds only in very short and very long maturities.
        a. The active bond manager using this strategy can easily shift the maturity structure of the portfolio.
        b. This strategy has the disadvantage of requiring considerably greater management effort and higher transaction costs.

VI. Interest Rate Forecasting

A. A number of tests that compare more sophisticated forecasting techniques with the most naive of all forecasts, that of no change, indicate that, as a group, neither experts nor sophisticated econometric models are able to outperform the naive forecast.

VII. Portfolio Immunization Techniques

A. Given the lack of success of models and experts in predicting interest rates, some managers have taken a different approach to portfolio management.
B. If one holds the position that it is impossible to forecast interest rates, active bond portfolio management has little appeal.

C. Immunization strategies attempt to create portfolios in which investment returns are not affected by increases or decreases in interest rates. As such, immunized portfolios are managed passively once the immunization is in place.

D. The Bank Immunization Case
1. This form of immunization gets its name from the fact that it first came into prominence in commercial banking.
2. One of the problems in commercial banking is the short duration of the deposit portfolio, because most deposits can be withdrawn on very short notice. By contrast, the loan portfolio consists of obligations to provide funds for longer periods.
3. If interest rates fall, the value of a bank's assets and liabilities will rise, but the asset portfolio (loans) will be more sensitive because its duration is larger.
4. If interest rates rise, the same change in rates creates a much larger drop in the loan portfolio's value.
5. If a bank starts from a position of no owners' equity and interest rates rise, the bank can move to a position of negative equity, or technical insolvency.
6. By careful management of its liabilities and assets, a bank can achieve immunization by having the liability and asset portfolios have the same duration.
7. With identical durations, the value of both portfolios will rise and fall by the same amount.
8. It must be noted that perfect immunization is very difficult for many financial institutions to achieve.

E. The Planning Period Case
1. This type of immunization concerns managing a portfolio toward a horizon date.
2. The problem confronting the bond manager in this case concerns the effect of changing interest rates on the immediate value of the bond portfolio and on the **reinvestment rate**—the rate at which cash thrown off by the bond portfolio can be reinvested.
3. In planning period immunization, if the duration of the portfolio equals the number of years in the planning period, the portfolio will be immunized.
4. When duration equals planning period, a change in interest rates will have a reinvestment rate effect that almost exactly offsets the capital gain or loss, which is also caused by the change in interest rates.

VIII. Contingent Immunization

A. **Contingent immunization** occurs when the investor accepts a guaranteed minimum return that is less than the return that could be achieved with immunization. In return, the manager is permitted to manage the portfolio as long as its value is large enough to cover the minimum guaranteed return.

1. The manager promises to implement full immunization if the portfolio's value falls to the **trigger point**, the value necessary to guarantee the minimum return with immunization under current market conditions.

2. The investor risks earning a return less than that which could be achieved on a portfolio immunized throughout its life in return for the chance that the active strategy pursued initially will generate higher returns.

IX. Some Complications with Immunization

A. Duration for Yield Curves with Shape

1. For any particular duration measure, there is some possible yield curve change that will interfere with immunization.

2. D_2, an alternative duration measure, reflects the slope of the yield curve but still assumes that yield curves shift in a parallel fashion. This measure reflects shape in the yield curve by allowing each cash flow to be discounted at the rate uniquely appropriate to its timing.

B. Multiple Shifts in Interest Rates

1. A second complication with duration arises from the fact that the immunization result holds only for a single change in interest rates, even when rates change by the same amount for all maturities.

2. Duration depends on the interest rate. So, if a portfolio is immunized and interest rates change, the portfolio loses its immunization.

X. Dedicated Portfolios

A. Faced with these duration complications in immunizing a portfolio, many managers choose to create **dedicated portfolios** instead.

1. A dedicated portfolio is a bond portfolio created such that its cash inflows from coupons and maturing bonds cover cash outflows that result from a given liability stream.

2. This task is not as simple as it sounds given the infinite number of securities with different characteristics that the manager must choose from.

3. A manager may want to follow a **cash–flow matching strategy**—to create a bond portfolio that will generate cash flows that will allow it to pay each of the liability cash flows as they come due.

4. The bond portfolio manager's job is to find the portfolio of bonds that generates the matching set of cash flows.

5. In this instance, the manager will have to work within client constraints, which may include:

a. The quality of bonds in the portfolio.

b. Whether the included bonds are callable.
c. Requirements on the industry concentration of the portfolio.
d. Restricting the overall portfolio duration.
e. Avoiding concentration of investment in a single issue.
6. In order to select the best collection of bonds to constitute the dedicated portfolio, managers often use linear programming techniques to find the optimal set of bonds.

Key Terms and Concepts

alternative duration measure	D2, a duration calculation that allows for the slope of the existing term structure but assumes parallel yield curve shifts
bank immunization strategy	immunization strategy designed to equalize the duration of assets and liabilities, protecting owner's equity from the danger of unequal interest rate sensitivities in the two components
cash–flow matching strategy	creation of a bond portfolio that will generate cash flows that will allow it to pay each of the liability cash flows as they come due
contingent immunization	immunization strategy that guarantees a minimum RCYTM less than that which could be achieved with total immunization, in return for the chance of greater returns from active management
dedicated portfolio	a bond portfolio created such that its cash inflows from coupons and maturing bonds cover cash outflows that result from a given liability stream
default risk	the chance that bond payments will not be made at the time or in the amount scheduled
dumbbell strategy	also the barbell strategy; allocating funds only to very short and very long maturity bonds
expected future spot rates	rates for current investments expected to prevail in the future
forward rate	a rate which covers an investment beginning in the future and is implied by currently available spot rates

immunization	attempting to make the value of a portfolio insensitive to a change in interest rates
interest rate forecasting	attempting to estimate future spot rates
laddered strategy	allocating funds evenly across the available spectrum of bond maturities
liquidity premium	the extra amount investors are presumed to be willing to pay to hold short–term bonds instead of long–term bonds
Liquidity Premium Theory	a term structure theory that argues that because investors prefer short maturities, forward rates are upwardly biased estimates of future spot rates
Macaulay's duration	a measure of a bond's price sensitivity to changes in interest rates which assumes a flat term structure in calculating the time–weighted present value of the bond's payments
Market Segmentation Theory	also the Preferred Habitats Theory; a term structure theory which argues that supply and demand within individual maturity classes determines yields
planning period strategy	an immunization strategy which balances reinvestment risk with capital gains or losses on unmatured obligations by setting the portfolio duration equal to the investment horizon
Pure Expectations Theory	a term structure theory that argues that investors are indifferent to the maturity of their holdings, so forward rates are unbiased estimates of future spot rates
rebalancing	reallocating investments in an immunized portfolio as changes in interest rates change the portfolio's duration away from the desired value
reinvestment rate	the rate at which cash thrown off by the bond portfolio can be reinvested
risk premium	the difference between the yield on a risky bond and the yield on a similar risk–free bond; a measure of default risk

risk structure of interest rates	the relationship between the yields of different securities as a function of their level of default risk
spot rate	the rate available on an investment made today
term structure of interest rates	the relationship between yield to maturity and term to maturity for bonds alike in all respects except maturity
trigger point	the minimum portfolio value at each point in time that signals that immunization must be adopted to meet the guaranteed minimum return
unbiased estimate	a forecast whose expected value equals the true value of the parameter being estimated
yield curve	a graph that relates term to maturity and yield to maturity for bonds that are alike in all other respects

Multiple–Choice Questions

1. If you allocate your bond portfolio only to the longest and shortest maturities available, you are following a ____ strategy.
    A. preferred habitat
    B. barbell
    C. liquidity premium
    D. forward rate
    E. risk premium

2. A yield prevailing at the present time is called a ____ rate.
    A. spot
    B. current
    C. forward
    D. future
    E. momentary

3. One advantage of a laddered strategy is that it ____.
    A. is easy to maintain
    B. is easy to alter the maturity distribution of the portfolio
    C. relies on the ability to make accurate interest rate forecasts
    D. immunizes the portfolio against default risk
    E. avoids reliance on forward rates

4. Which term structure theory argues that one can read the market's opinion regarding future interest rate moves in the slope of the yield curve?
   A. Risk Premium Theory
   B. Preferred Habitat Theory
   C. Market Segmentation Theory
   D. Liquidity Expectations Theory
   E. Pure Expectations Theory

5. A graph of the relationship between term to maturity and yield to maturity for similar bonds is called a ____ curve.
   A. forward
   B. liquidity
   C. default
   D. risk
   E. yield

6. An estimator whose expected value equals the true value of the parameter being estimated is known as a(n) ____ estimator.
   A. accurate
   B. parameter
   C. unbiased
   D. biased
   E. naive

7. The extra amount that investors are willing to pay for short–term bonds is called the ____.
   A. risk premium
   B. liquidity premium
   C. spot premium
   D. forward rate
   E. ladder premium

8. The Market Segmentation Hypothesis argues that observed yield curve shapes are due to ____ in each segment of the bond market.
   A. biased estimates
   B. changes in spot rates
   C. changes in forward rates
   D. risk premiums
   E. supply and demand factors

9. The risk premium varies inversely with ____.
   A. maturity
   B. the business cycle
   C. the level of interest rates
   D. default risk
   E. the forward rate

10. A bond portfolio is ____ if its value is not sensitive to a change in interest rates.
    A. defaulted
    B. immunized
    C. forwarded
    D. forecast
    E. unbiased

11. The immunization strategy where the portfolio duration is set to match the investment horizon is known as the ____ strategy.
    A. trigger point
    B. bank immunization
    C. planning period
    D. dedicated portfolio
    E. contingent immunization

12. In contingent immunization, the ____ is the portfolio value that requires immunization to meet the minimum guaranteed return.
    A. trigger point
    B. bank immunization
    C. planning period
    D. dedicated portfolio
    E. liquidity premium

13. The strategy that matches cash inflows from coupon payments and maturing bonds to liability outflow streams is known as the ____ approach.
    A. trigger point
    B. bank immunization
    C. planning period
    D. dedicated portfolio
    E. contingent immunization

14. _____ rates of interest cover future time periods implied by currently available spot rates.
    A. Forward
    B. Implied
    C. Future
    D. Spot
    E. Forecast

15. The mathematical technique often employed to create a dedicated portfolio is known as a(n) ____.
    A. econometric model
    B. naive forecast
    C. immunization strategy
    D. contingent duration
    E. linear program

16. In the planning period strategy, increases in reinvestment rates offset ____.
    A. the automatic decrease in duration caused by the passage of time
    B. the transactions costs of rebalancing
    C. capital losses incurred on securities that have not matured at the end of the investment horizon
    D. the upward bias in forward rates caused by the liquidity premium
    E. the chance of missing the trigger point

17. Which of the following is *not* another name for the risk premium?
    A. yield differential
    B. risk differential
    C. yield spread
    D. yield required to compensate for the chance of default
    E. liquidity premium

18. A portfolio has been immunized correctly if ____.
    A. the liquidity premium equals the expected future spot rate
    B. the RCYTM equals the expected yield
    C. the dumbbell transactions costs equal the laddered transactions costs
    D. Macaulay's duration equals the alternative duration measure
    E. the trigger point equals the investment horizon

19. The immunization strategy that matches the duration of assets and liabilities is known as the ____ strategy.
    A. trigger point
    B. bank immunization
    C. planning period
    D. dedicated portfolio
    E. contingent immunization

20. The immunization strategy that guarantees a minimum return and includes active management is known as the ____ strategy.
    A. trigger point
    B. bank immunization
    C. planning period
    D. dedicated portfolio
    E. contingent immunization

21. If your planning period is six years and you must allocate a portfolio between investments that have durations of two years and eight years, ____ percent of your holdings must be invested in the shorter maturity security.
    A. 25
    B. 33
    C. 50
    D. 67
    E. 75

22. You have owned a $1,000 face value, 8 percent annual coupon bond for four years. It has just matured. If your reinvestment rate was 6 percent, your terminal wealth is $____.
    A.   254.69
    B.   259.71
    C. 1,350.00
    D. 1,334.69
    E. 1,339.71

23. The dumbbell strategy allocates a bond portfolio to ____.
    A. all maturities available in even amounts
    B. forward rates, ignoring liquidity premiums
    C. default risk classes on the basis of bond ratings
    D. the longest and shortest maturities available
    E. cover the yield curve

24. One advantage of a dumbbell strategy is that it ____.
    A. is easy to maintain
    B. is easy to alter the maturity structure of the portfolio
    C. relies on the ability to make accurate interest rate forecasts
    D. immunizes the portfolio against default risk
    E. avoids reliance on forward rates

25. If a two–year Treasury security yields 10.5 percent and a three–year Treasury security yields 11 percent, the one–year forward rate for two years in the future is ____ percent.
    A. 10.95
    B. 12.01
    C. 12.21
    D. 12.32
    E. 13.67

Review Problems

1. Use the following data on spot interest rates for Problems 1, 2, and 3.

Maturity (years)	Yield
1	.110
2	.115
3	.123
4	.125
5	.128

    a. What is the annual one–year forward rate for the period from year 1 to year 2?
    b. What is the annual two–year forward rate for the period from year 3 to year 5?
    c. What is the annual three–year forward rate for the period from year 1 to year 4?
    d. What is the annual one–year forward rate for the period from year 4 to year 5?
    e. If you believe the Pure Expectations Theory, what is your forecast of the spot rate on a two–year bond issued in three years?

2. From the information given, compute the one–year forward rates for each year in the term structure.

3. Assume a two year bond must pay a .30 percent greater annual yield than a series of one year bonds. Using the spot rates in Problem 1, compute the expected spot rate for one year from now, $r_{1,2}$. Compare this rate to the forward rate for this same period.

4. A bank has assets of $5,000 in loans with a duration of four years and a yield of 10 percent. It has $4,000 in deposit liabilities with a duration of two years and a yield of 10 percent. The remainder of the assets are financed by $1,000 in owner's equity.
    a. How much will owner's equity change by if interest rates fall by 1 percent?
    b. How much will owner's equity change by if interest rates rise by 1 percent?
    c. What is the danger in this mis–matched approach?

5. You have a four–year planning period and can choose between two bonds. Bond A has two years to maturity, an 8 percent annual coupon rate, a price of $965.29, a yield of 10 percent, and a duration of 1.925 years. Bond B has six years to maturity, a 12 percent annual coupon rate, a market price of $1,087.11, a yield of 10 percent, and a duration of 4.665 years.
    a. How must you allocate your portfolio so that its duration equals your investment horizon?
    b. How much must you invest to create the portfolio?
    c. Prove that your RCYTM is immunized against a 1 percent rise in interest rates.

    d.   Prove that your RCYTM is immunized against a 1 percent fall in interest rates.

6.   You have been asked to manage a $1,000,000 portfolio for five years. You can immunize today to earn 10 percent, but the investor chooses to allow you to actively manage the portfolio with contingent immunization at 8 percent.

    a.   Compute the second and third year trigger points.

    b.   What is the investor's opportunity loss if either of the trigger points is activated?

7.   Use the forward rates in the text to compute the alternative duration measure for a $1,000 face value, 12 percent annual coupon rate, 5–year bond priced at $931.34 to yield 14 percent.

Answers

Multiple–Choice Questions

1. B	10. B	19. B
2. A	11. C	20. E
3. A	12. A	21. B
4. E	13. D	22. C
5. E	14. A	23. D
6. C	15. E	24. B
7. B	16. C	25. B
8. E	17. E	
9. B	18. B	

Review Problems

1.   The general solution to forward rate problems is:

$$(1 + \text{long spot rate})^{\text{years}} =$$

$$(1 + \text{short spot rate})^{\text{years}} (1 + \text{short forward rate})^{\text{years}}$$

Knowing any two of the three rates lets you calculate the third by multiplying or dividing and taking the appropriate root.

    a.   The square of the two–year spot rate is equal to the product of the one–year spot rate and the one–year forward rate:

$$(1 + r_{0,2})^2 = (1 + r_{0,1})(1 + r_{1,2}), \text{ or}$$

$(1.115)^2 = (1.11)(1 + r1_{1,2})$, or

$(1 + r_{1,2}) = 1.243/1.11 = 1.12$, so $r_{1,2} = 12$ percent.

b.   The product of the cube of the three–year spot rate and the square of the two–year forward rate is equal to the five–year spot rate to the fifth power.

$(1 + r_{0,5})^5 = (1 + r_{0,3})^3 (1 + r_{3,5})^2$, so

$(1 + r_{3,5})^2 = (1.128)^5/(1.123)^3 = 1.2895$

$(1 + r_{3,5}) = (1.2895)^{1/2}$, or $r_{3,5} = 13.55$ percent.

c.   The four–year spot rate to the fourth power is equal to the product of the one–year spot rate and the cube of the three–year forward rate.

$(1 + r_{0,4})^4 = (1 + r_{0,1})(1 + r_{1,4})^3$, or

$(1 + r_{1,4})^3 = (1.125)^4/1.11 = 1.4431$

$(1 + r_{1,4}) = (1.4431)^{1/3}$, so $r_{1,4} = 13.00$ percent.

d.   The product of the four–year spot rate to the fourth power and the one–year forward rate is equal to the five–year spot rate to the fifth power.

$(1 + r_{0,5})^5 = (1 + r_{0,4})^4 (1 + r_{4,5})$, so

$(1 + r_{4,5}) = (1.128)^5/(1.125)^4 = 1.1401$, so

$r_{4,5} = 14.01$ percent.

e.   Your forecast would be the two–year forward rate from year three to year five, computed in Problem b as 13.55 percent.

2.   The one–year forward rate in one year is equal to the square of the two–year spot rate divided by the one–year spot rate:

$(1.115)^2/(1.11) = 1.12$, or 12.00 percent

The one–year forward rate in two years is equal to the cube of the three–year spot rate divided by the square of the two–year spot rate:

$(1.123)^3/(1.115)^2 = 1.1392$, or 13.92 percent.

The one–year forward rate in three years is equal to the four–year spot rate to the fourth power divided by the cube of the three–year spot rate:

$(1.125)^4/(1.123)^3 = 1.1310$, or 13.10 percent.

The one–year forward rate in four years is equal to the five–year spot rate to the fifth power divided by the four–year spot rate to the fourth power:

$(1.128)^5/(1.125)^4 = 1.1401$, or 14.01 percent.

3. If the two–year bond returns 11.5 percent annually over its life, a series of two one–year bonds must have an average annual return of 11.20 percent (11.5 – .30). Therefore, the expected spot rate in one year (according to the liquidity premium theory) is found by:

$$(1.112)^2 = (1.11)(1+r_{1,2})$$

$$r_{1,2} = 11.4 \text{ percent}$$

As found in Problem 2, the forward rate for one year from now using the unadjusted spot rate is 12 percent.

The forward rates or, expected spot rates, calculated from spot rates that have been adjusted for the liquidity premium are always less than those computed from unadjusted spot rates. This is precisely the argument of the liquidity premium hypothesis. If investors demand an extra return to hold long–term bonds instead of short–term bonds, the slope of the yield curve, and the forward rates computed from it, will always be biased upward by the amount of the premium.

4a. If interest rates fall by 1 percent, the value of the assets will rise by:

$[(-4)(-.01)/(1.1)]\$5,000 = \$181.82$.

The value of the liabilities will rise by:

$[(-2)(-.01)/(1.1)]\$4,000 = \$72.73$.

With assets worth \$5,181.82 and liabilities worth \$4,072.73, owner's equity must be worth:

$(\$5,181.82 - \$4,072.73) = \$1,109.09$.

Owner's equity has increased because the value of the higher duration assets rose more quickly than the value of the lower duration liabilities.

b. If interest rates rise by 1 percent, the value of the assets will fall by:

$[(-4)(.01)/(1.1)]\$5,000 = -181.82$ to \$4,818.18.

The value of the liabilities will fall by:

$[(-2)(.01)/(1.1)]\$4{,}000 = -\$72.72$ to $\$3{,}927.27$.

Owner's equity falls from $\$1{,}000$ to

$(\$4{,}818.18 - \$3{,}927.27) = \$890.91$, a loss of $\$109.09$.

c. This mis–matched approach is dangerous because there is a limited amount of owner's equity available to protect against further rises in interest rates. If owner's equity becomes negative, the bank is bankrupt.

5a. The portfolio must be allocated so that its duration is four years. Let X be the percentage invested in Bond A and $(1 - X)$ be the percentage invested in Bond B.

$X(1.925) + (1 - X)4.665 = 4$, or

$1.925X + 4.665 - 4.665X = 4$, or

$.665 = 2.74X$, or $X = .665/2.74 = 24.3$ percent.

Investing 24.3 percent of your funds in A requires investing:

$(1 - .243) = 75.7$ percent of your funds in B.

b. This portfolio costs:

$.243(\$965.29) + .757(\$1{,}087.11) = \$1.057.51$.

c. If rates immediately rise to 11 percent, Bond A contributes coupons and face value reinvested to the four–year horizon at 11 percent. The first coupon payment is reinvested for three years and the second coupon payment and the face value are reinvested for two years, for terminal wealth of:

$\$80(1.11)^3 + \$1{,}080(1.11)^2 = \$1{,}440.08$.

Now find the price of Bond B as a two–year, 12 percent bond with two years to maturity and an 11 percent yield:

$\$120/1.11 + \$1{,}120/(1.11)^2 = \$1{,}017.13$.

The value of the reinvested coupons from Bond B is:

$\$120(1.11)^3 + \$120(1.11)^2 + \$120(1.11) + 120 = \$565.17$.

Notice that the last coupon payment from Bond B has just been received, so it is not reinvested.

Bond B contributes a total of:

$565.17 + $1,017.13 = $1,582.30 to terminal wealth.

Your portfolio is worth:

.243($1,440.08) + .757($1,582.30) = $1,547.74.

Your RCYTM is $(\$1,547.74/\$1,057.51)^{1/4}$

= 1.0999, or 9.99 percent, or 10 percent ignoring the rounding error.

d. If rates fall immediately to 9 percent, Bond A contributes:

$80(1.09)^3 + \$1,080(1.09)^2 = \$1,386.75$.

The price of Bond B is: $\$120/(1.09) + \$1,120/(1.09)^2 = \$1,052.77$.

Reinvested coupons from Bond B are worth:

$\$120(1.09)^3 + \$120(1.09)^2 + \$120(1.09) + 120 = \$548.78$.

The total realized return on Bond B is: $1,052.77 + $548.78 = $1,601.55.

Your portfolio is worth: .243($1,386.75) + .757($1,601.55) = $1,549.35

for an RCYTM of: $(\$1,549.35/\$1,057.51)^{1/4} = 1.1002$, or 10.02 percent.

Once again, this is identical to the expected yield, except for the rounding error. Thus, your realized investment value does not change if there is an immediate change in interest rates in either direction.

6a. A $1,000,000 portfolio with a guaranteed 8 percent return will be worth:

$(\$1,000,000)(1.08)^5 = \$1,469,328$ in five years.

The trigger point in two years is the investment value needed to grow to $1,469,328 in three years at 8 percent, or:

$\$1,469,328/(1.08)^3 = \$1,166,400$.

The trigger point in three years is the investment value needed to grow to $1,469,328 in two years at 8 percent, or:

$1,469,328/(1.08)^2 = $1,259,712.

b. If the portfolio had been immunized throughout its entire life, it would have earned 10 percent, and been worth:

$1,000,000(1.10)^5 = $1,610,510.

If the trigger point is reached at any time in its life, it will be worth a total of $1,469,328 in five years, instead of $1,610,510, for an opportunity loss of:

$1,610,510 − $1,469,328 = $141,182.

The investor is willing to accept this opportunity loss in return for the chance that the terminal value of the portfolio will exceed $1,610,510 at the end of five years with active management by an expert.

7. In the alternative duration measure, the interest rates used to discount the time–weighted payments are the forward rates expected to hold across the relevant reinvestment period.

For the first time–weighted payment: $120(1)/(1.12) = $107.14.

For the second time–weighted payment: $120(2)/(1.12)(1.13) = $189.63.

For the third time–weighted payment:

$120(3)/(1.12)(1.13)(1.1401) = $249.50.

For the fourth time–weighted payment:

$120(4)/(1.12)(1.13)(1.1401)(1.1501) = $289.25.

For the fifth time–weighted payment:

$1120(5)/(1.12)(1.13)(1.1401)(1.1501)(1.1602) = $2,908.57.

Summing the time–weighted payments:

$107.14 + $189.63 + $249.50 + $289.25 + $2,908.57 = $3,744.09.

Dividing by the price gives a duration of:

$3,744.09/$931.34 = 4.02 years.

CHAPTER NINE

Preferred and Common Stock Valuation

Chapter Objectives

Upon completion of this chapter, you should be able to:
1. Compare and contrast the risks and rewards from investing in preferred or common stock.
2. Value a share of preferred stock.
3. Explain the Dividend Valuation Model and use its constant dividend, constant growth, and irregular dividend forms.
4. Explain how capital gains, irregular dividend streams, and dividends beginning in the future are incorporated into the Dividend Valuation model.
5. Explain the relationship between the Dividend Valuation Model and earnings under a constant payout policy and a complete payout policy.
6. Explain how the Dividend Valuation Model leads to an investment strategy.
7. Discuss the relative risks of investing in bonds, common stock, and preferred stock of the same firm.

Chapter Outline

I. Preferred Stock

A. Preferred stock is a hybrid security, sharing features of both bonds and common stock. It is usually issued with a stated par value, such as $100.

B. Payments made on preferred stock are called dividends and are usually expressed as a percentage of the par value.

C. There are important differences between preferred stock and corporate bonds.
   1. Preferred stock never matures.

2. The purchaser of preferred stock never receives a return of the par value.

3. Unlike the case of corporate bonds, if the firm misses a scheduled payment on preferred stock, the firm has not defaulted, and the preferred stockholder has no immediate legal remedy against the corporation.

D. Most preferred stock is cumulative. With **cumulative preferred stock**, any dividend payments that the firm misses must be paid later, as soon as the firm is able, and typically before common shareholders are paid.

E. The features of no maturity, no return of principal, and no default when a payment is missed combine to make preferred stock riskier than a corporate bond issued by the same corporation.

F. Like many bonds, some preferred stock is callable. The issuing firm can require the preferred stockholders to surrender their shares in exchange for a cash payment.

G. Usually, preferred stockholders, like bondholders, are not allowed to vote on matters of concern to the firm.

H. Financing with Preferred Stock
    1. Advantages.
        a. Preferred stock gives the issuer a great deal of flexibility because the issuer is not in default if it misses a preferred stock dividend.
        b. By issuing preferred stock, the corporation can secure financing without surrendering voting control in the firm.
    2. Disadvantages.
        a. Interest payments on bonds are made from the firm's before–tax income.
        b. Dividend payments to preferred stockholders are made from the firm's after–tax earnings.
    3. For the securities investor, preferred stock is similar to a **perpetuity**—a bond that makes interest payments of a fixed amount forever and never returns its principal.

II. The Valuation of Preferred Stock

A. The value or price of a share of preferred stock must equal the present value of all cash flows that will come from the stock.

B. Because preferred stock is scheduled to make payments forever, it is treated as a perpetuity for valuation purposes:

$$P = \frac{D_p}{k_p}$$

where:

P = the price of the preferred share
D_p = the dividend on the preferred share
k_p = the discount rate appropriate to the preferred share

III. Common Stock Valuation

A. Holders of common stock commit their funds and assume the last–place claim on the value of the firm in the hopes of securing a substantial profit.

B. While the stock is owned, the only cash flow from the shares is the cash dividend.

C. The timing and amounts of dividend payments are not as predictable as the cash flows of most bonds or preferred stocks.

D. Because of the greater speculative element in the amount and timing of dividend payments, risk assessment for equity securities is of great concern.

E. The perceived riskiness of shares is reflected in the rate of return required by stockholders, which is the discount rate applied to the firm's dividend stream.

F. The Dividend Valuation Model

1. The value of a share of common stock can be expressed by the **Dividend Valuation Model**:

$$P_0 = \sum_{t=1}^{n} \frac{D_t}{(1 + k)^t}$$

where:
P_0 = the price of the share today
D_t = the dividend expected at time t
k = the return the market requires on the share

2. This equation states that the current stock price equals the sum of the present values of all future expected dividends when those dividends are discounted at the stockholder's required rate of return.

3. This equation appears to neglect **capital gains**, which are profits generated by an increase in the price of an asset.

G. The Dividend Valuation Model and Capital Gains

1. According to the Dividend Valuation Model, the only cash flows that matter to an investor in common stock are the dividends that are expected to be paid to the shareholder. Yet, many investors buy stocks for the expected capital gains.

2. The Dividend Valuation Model does not ignore capital gains, but treats them indirectly, through their relationship to dividends.

3. The anticipated capital gain over the amount of time that the stock is to be held is due to the changing valuation of the future dividends. So even if capital gains are not *explicitly* shown in the Dividend Valuation Model, they are reflected *implicitly*.

4. Another way of seeing that the value of a share depends on the expected future dividends is to reflect upon the following question: How much is a share of stock worth, assuming that everyone knows it will absolutely never pay a dividend?

5. The hope of selling such a share for a capital gain is based on what is known as the *greater fool theory*—to pay something for a stock that promises never to pay a cent in dividends is very foolish.

H. The Indefinite Future of Dividends

Another apparent problem with the Dividend Valuation Model is the possibly indefinite number of dividends that populate the right side of the equation.

I. The Constant Growth Model

1. Even if dividends are not constant, there is still a way to apply the model and to avoid the pitfall of trying to add a potentially infinite number of dividends.

2. If the dividends grow at a regular rate, g, then the Dividend Valuation Model can be greatly simplified. In this case, the dividend in the second year equals the dividend in the first year plus the growth in dividends, or :

$$D_2 = D_1 (1 + g)$$

3. For a constant growth rate in dividends, the Dividend Valuation Model is mathematically equal to:

$$P_0 = \frac{D_1}{k - g}$$

4. This model is known as the **Constant Growth Model**.

5. There are several assumptions behind this simplification of the model.

   a. The dividends grow each year at the constant growth rate g.

   b. The dividends grow at the rate g forever.

   c. The growth rate g is less than the discount rate k.

J. The Dividend Valuation Model and Irregular Dividend Patterns

1. A final challenge for the Dividend Valuation Model is its applicability to stocks that pay no current dividends. For such a stock, the Dividend Valuation Model simply says that the future dividends are the pertinent cash flows. Their value, whenever they occur, is simply discounted back to the present.

2. As can be seen, the Dividend Valuation Model is very flexible. It can handle situations for those firms with initially irregular dividend streams, or for firms that pay no current dividends.

3. The model is not applicable to firms that will never have any regular growth in dividends, but in practice this is a minor problem.

K. The Dividend Valuation Model and Earnings

1. The earnings that a firm generates have three, and only three, outlets according to accounting convention.

   a. They must be paid in taxes.

   b. They must be paid as dividends.

   c. They must be retained for further investment in the firm.

2. Growing firms typically pay small dividends because it is often important to generate as much cash as possible for reinvestment in the firm.

3. Firms that pay a fixed percentage of their earnings follow a **constant payout policy**. For such firms, there is a lawlike relationship between earnings and dividends; that is, dividends are always a fixed fraction of earnings.

4. For firms with a constant payout policy, in a given year, t, the dividend is given by the expression:

$$D_t = (1 - b)E_t$$

where $(1 - b)$ is the percentage of earnings paid as a dividend.

L. The Dividend Valuation Model and the P–E Ratio

1. As you can see from the formulation above, earnings and earnings growth are intimately linked to the price of a firm's shares.

2. Stocks of firms that are expected to enjoy a rapid increase in earnings are known as **growth stocks**.

3. Another measure of the relationship between stock price and earnings is the **price–earnings ratio** or **P–E ratio**, calculated as:

$$\frac{\text{Stock Price}}{\text{Current Annual Earnings}}$$

4. A high P–E ratio usually indicates the expectation of rapid future growth in earnings.

M. The Dividend Valuation Model and Constant Payout Policies

1. Rearranging the Constant Growth Model allows further insights regarding firms which follow a constant payout policy:

$$k = \frac{D_1}{P_0} + g$$

2. Here, the term D_1/P_0 is the **dividend yield** and the equation says that the cost of equity capital for a firm equals the dividend yield plus the long–term growth rate in dividends.

3. For a firm with no growth prospects, the cost of equity capital equals the dividend yield.

4. For a firm with a zero growth rate and a policy of paying all earnings as dividends so that the retention ratio is zero, it must also be the case that:

$$k = \frac{E_1}{P_0}$$

In this special case $D_t = E_t$

IV. Dividends and Share Prices in the Economy

A. We can use real–world data to provide a broad understanding of the relationship among dividends, earnings, the retention ratio, the growth rate, and their effect on stock prices.

B. The difference between the discount rate and the growth rate must equal the dividend–price ratio:

$$\frac{D_1}{P_0} = k - g$$

C. A firm with a zero growth rate will have a discount rate equal to the dividend–price ratio, and as the growth rate increases, the discount rate increases as well.

D. In the long run, extremely high growth rates are impossible to sustain; a realistic long–term growth rate for most firms is in the 3–4 percent range.

E. The Dividend Valuation Model and Equity Investing
   1. By estimating the future flow of dividends and earnings, and the appropriate rate of discount to be applied to those dividends and earnings, it is possible to calculate a value for the stock using the dividend valuation model.
   2. This calculated value is known as the **intrinsic value** of the share, which may differ from the **market value** of the share.
   3. This suggests a trading strategy if the estimated intrinsic value differs from the market value of the share:
      a. If the intrinsic value exceeds the current market value, buy the shares.
      b. If the intrinsic value is less than the market value, sell the shares.
   4. While these rules are quite simple, their success depends upon the accuracy of the estimates used to calculate intrinsic value.
   5. In addition, the application of this rule depends on the belief that the market will eventually come to realize the intrinsic value of the stock.

F. The Dividend Valuation Model and Stock Analysis
   1. If all stock analysts correctly analyze the value of a given stock, they will all be willing to pay the same amount for it, and the intrinsic value will equal the market value of the stock.
   2. The greater the discrepancy between the intrinsic value and the market value of a share, the greater the opportunity for profit.
   3. The enormous potential reward of correct analysis continues to call forth the efforts of very intelligent people anxious to learn the techniques of analysis in the hope of applying them to generate spectacular wealth.

V. *Risk and the Required Rate of Return*

A. One of the major differences among the different financing vehicles we have discussed (bonds, preferred stock, and common stock) is the risk that the owner takes in giving money to the firm in exchange for promises of future cash flows from the company.

B. In general, all of the bondholders have a less risky position than all of the stockholders. Also, preferred stockholders bear less risk than common stockholders. The differences in risk levels are reflected in the different rates of return that these various securities earn.

C. The basic principle is clear: the greater the risk, the greater the expected return must be to encourage investors to commit their funds.

Key Terms and Concepts

callable preferred stock	preferred stock that can be redeemed at a fixed price by the issuer any time it chooses to
capital gains	a price increase in an asset that is owned
common stock	represents a residual ownership in a corporation which has a claim on all assets left over after debt and preferred equity claims have been satisfied
Constant Growth Model	a stock valuation model which assumes that a firm's dividends grow at a constant rate forever
constant payout policy	the policy of paying out a fixed percentage of earnings as dividends each period
cost of equity capital	the expected return investors demand to purchase the shares of a firm
cumulative preferred stock	a type of preferred stock requiring that any dividend payments that the firm misses be made up as soon as the firm is able, often before common stockholders receive any dividends
dividend payout ratio	the percentage of earnings paid out in dividends
Dividend Valuation Model	a stock valuation model which expresses the value of a share today as the present value of all expected future dividends

dividend yield	the dividends expected on a stock in the next period divided by its current price
growth rate	the annual rate at which a firm's dividends are expected to grow
growth stocks	stocks of firms expected to enjoy rapid increases in earnings in the future; typically trading at high P–E ratios today
intrinsic value	the true value of a stock according to the investor's estimates and the dividend growth model, which may not equal the market value
irregular dividends	dividends that are not constant in amount or growth rate over time
market value	the current price of a share in the market
perpetuity	a scheduled cash flow that occurs at regular intervals and never ends
preferred stock	represents an equity position in a firm, never matures, pays out fixed dividends (if dividends are paid) and stands between debt and common equity in strength of claim
price–earnings ratio	also P–E ratio; a stock's current price divided by its most recent annual earnings per share
zero growth firm	typically, a firm that pays all of its earnings out in dividends

Multiple–Choice Questions

1. For an investor, common stock is usually a riskier investment than preferred stock of the same company because ____.
    A. common stock dividends are paid out of after–tax earnings
    B. preferred stock dividends are deductible for income tax purposes
    C. preferred stock dividends are paid before common stock dividends
    D. preferred stock dividends are paid in nominal dollars
    E. preferred stock dividends are expected to grow

2. Which of the following is *not* required to value a share of preferred stock?
   A. a return the market requires
   B. the market price of the share
   C. the par value for the preferred
   D. the dividend rate of the preferred
   E. the dollar value of the preferred dividend

3. A constant cash flow with an infinite maturity is known as a ____.
   A. coupon
   B. cumulative payment
   C. perpetuity
   D. callable payment
   E. capital gain

4. A share of preferred stock with a par value of $100 pays a 10 percent annual dividend. If the discount rate is 8 percent, the preferred stock is worth _____.
   A. 20
   B. 125
   C. 100
   D. 60
   E. 70

5. A firm declared dividends of $1.10 last year and $1.32 this year. If it is a constant growth firm, the dividend expected next year is $____.
   A. 1.20
   B. 1.52
   C. 1.54
   D. 1.58
   E. 1.90

6. A constant dividend stock that is priced at $10 per share pays a dividend of $2. The required return is ____ percent.
   A. 2
   B. 5
   C. 10
   D. 20
   E. 50

7. If preferred stock dividends that have been skipped must be made up before common dividends are paid, the firm's preferred stock is ____ preferred.
   A. callable
   B. cumulative
   C. growth
   D. capital gain
   E. nominal

8. Other things equal, the price of a share of constant growth common stock falls as the ____.
   A. required return rises
   B. growth rate rises
   C. common dividend rises
   D. preferred dividend falls
   E. flotation cost falls

9. If preferred stock is redeemable at the option of the issuer, it is ____ preferred.
   A. cumulative
   B. nominal
   C. irregular
   D. callable
   E. payout

10. A constant dividend stock has a required return of 12.5 percent and a price of $64. The dividend is $____.
    A. 5.12
    B. 8.00
    C. 13.12
    D. 16.00
    E. 21.12

11. A firm has 1,000 shares of $100 par value, 8 percent preferred stock outstanding. If it is in a 40 percent tax bracket, before–tax earnings of $____ are needed to pay the preferred dividend.
    A. 4,000.00
    B. 6,000.00
    C. 8,000.00
    D. 13,333.33
    E. 20,000.00

12. For a zero–growth firm that pays all earnings as dividends, the dividend yield is equal to the ____.
    A. inverse of the P–E ratio
    B. required return on preferred stock
    C. dividend payout ratio
    D. intrinsic value of the share
    E. call price

13. In the term "P–E ratio," the initials stand for ____.
    A. paid/expected
    B. preferred/earned
    C. par/earnings
    D. price/earnings
    E. price/expected

14. An investor's estimate of the true value of a share of stock is known as the ____ value.
    A. market
    B. call
    C. cumulative
    D. dividend
    E. intrinsic

15. Which of the following group of investors has the weakest legal claim on a firm's assets?
    A. mortgage bond holders
    B. subordinated debenture holders
    C. callable preferred shareholders
    D. cumulative preferred shareholders
    E. common shareholders

16. A zero–growth firm that pays all earnings as dividends has annual earnings of $5 per share. If its shares are trading at $40, its cost of equity capital is ____ percent.
    A. 4.0
    B. 5.0
    C. 8.0
    D. 12.5
    E. 15.0

17. Shares in firms with high P–E ratios and strong earnings prospects are known as ____ stocks.
    A. common
    B. callable
    C. cost of capital
    D. growth
    E. intrinsic

18. Ksmart corporation is expected to pay a dividend of $1.80 at the end of the year. Based on the riskiness of this security, you require a return of 11 percent and expect that the long–term growth rate for the dividends of this company will be 5 percent. Based on this information, you would pay $____ for this stock.
    A. 30
    B. 20
    C. 180
    D. 90
    E. 80

19. The term D_1/P_0 is called the _____ yield.
   A. zero growth
   B. dividend
   C. market
   D. price/earnings
   E. cumulative

20. According to the investment rule resulting from the dividend valuation model, a share should be sold if its intrinsic value is less than its ____ value.
   A. zero growth
   B. dividend
   C. market
   D. price/earnings
   E. cumulative

21. A firm that pays all of its earnings in dividends has 100,000 shares outstanding and earned $250,000 after taxes. If its shares are trading at $20, its cost of equity capital is ____ percent.
   A. 5.0
   B. 8.0
   C. 12.5
   D. 20.0
   E. 25.0

22. You are confident that Never Prosper corporation will never pay a cent in dividends. The price you would expect to be able to sell this stock for is _____.
   A. the highest price the market will bare
   B. $0
   C. $100
   D. $1,000
   E. $200

23. If a firm pays out all of its earnings in dividends, the inverse of the P–E ratio is equal to the firm's ____.
   A. common stock price
   B. callable value
   C. cost of equity capital
   D. growth rate
   E. intrinsic value

24. According to the Dividend Valuation Model, the present value of a firm's expected future dividends discounted at a risk–adjusted rate is equal to the _____ of the shares.
    A. common value
    B. callable value
    C. cost of capital
    D. growth value
    E. intrinsic value

25. If a firm has $4,000,000 in earnings, 100,000 shares outstanding, and dividends of $12 per share, its payout ratio is _____ percent.
    A. 20
    B. 30
    C. 40
    D. 60
    E. 70

Review Problems

1. A share of preferred stock with a par value of $100 pays a 12 percent annual dividend. If the discount rate is 10 percent, how much would the preferred stock be worth?

2. A share of preferred stock with a par value of $100 pays a 14 percent annual dividend. If the discount rate were 8 percent, how much would the preferred stock be worth?

3. You are thinking about investing in Oberhardt Industries. You expect the stock to pay $1.60 in dividends at the end of the year. Based on your assessment of the riskiness of the industry, you believe that such an investment should pay a return of 18 percent, and that the long–term growth rate for the dividends of the company will be 5 percent. How much should the share be worth?

4. You are interested in investing in the Ding–Dong corporation and are not sure whether you are getting a good price for the shares. You do not expect Ding–Dong to pay a dividend for the next three years. In the fourth year you expect a dividend of $2 per share, and believe that dividends will then grow at a long–term rate of 10 percent. On an investment as risky as Ding–Dong, you demand a rate of return of 20 percent. How much is Ding–Dong worth, given these assumptions?

5. Show the expected dividend stream for Ding–Dong for the next six years.

6. A firm has a long–term constant growth rate of 6 percent and will pay a $1 dividend in one year. If the firm's cost of equity capital is 11 percent, is a share worth $25 today? Why or why not?

7. A firm with a cost of equity capital of 15 percent plans to make dividend payments for the next three years of $1.50, $1.80, and $2.05. After that, the dividends should grow at a rate of 3 percent. What should the firm's stock be worth today?

8. A firm with expected earnings for the next period of $1.50 per share pays out 60 percent of its earnings in dividends. Assuming constant earnings, what should the shares sell for if the firm's cost of equity capital is 13 percent?

9. A firm will pay $1.20 in dividends next period. The market expects an annual dividend growth rate of 4 percent. If the shares are trading for $15, what is the firm's cost of equity capital?

10. A firm's earnings for the next period are expected to be $2.50 per share. The firm follows a constant payout policy, retaining 60 percent of all earnings for future investment. This reinvestment should generate a 6 percent rate of growth in earnings. If the cost of equity capital for this firm is 11 percent, what share price should prevail?

Answers

Multiple–Choice Questions

1. C	10. B	19. B
2. B	11. D	20. C
3. C	12. A	21. C
4. B	13. D	22. B
5. D	14. E	23. C
6. D	15. E	24. E
7. B	16. D	25. B
8. A	17. D	
9. D	18. A	

Review Problems

1.
$$P = \frac{\$12}{.10} = \$120$$

2.
$$P = \frac{\$14}{.08} = \$175$$

3.
$$P_0 = \frac{D_1}{(k - g)} = \frac{\$1.60}{.18 - .05} = \$12.31$$

4. A two–step procedure is necessary.

    According to the Dividend Valuation Model, the value of the shares at time 3 is given by the following expression:

    $$P_3 = \frac{D_4}{(k - g)} = \frac{\$2}{(.20 - .10)} = \$20$$

    Now, the value of Ding–Dong at year 3 must be discounted back to the present at Ding–Dong's cost of capital.

    $$P_0 = \frac{P_3}{(1 + k)^3} = \$20/(1.20)^3 = \$11.57$$

    You should not pay more than $11.57 for Ding–Dong.

5. D_1 $0
    D_2 $0
    D_3 $0
    D_4 $2
    D_5 $2.20
    D_6 $2.42

6. No, if the required return is 11 percent and the annual dividend is expected to grow at 6 percent, a share that pays a dividend of $1 in one year is worth:

    $$P = \frac{\$1}{.11 - .06} = \$20$$

7. First divide the dividend stream into the period of irregular growth (the first three years) and the period of regular growth (year 4 and beyond). Then, compute the value of both parts of the dividend stream.

    For the regular part, the dividend in period 4 will be:

    $2.05(1.03) = $2.11. Therefore:

    $$P_3 = \frac{\$2.11}{.15 - .03} = \$17.60$$

The present value of P_3 today:

$$P_3 = \frac{\$17.60}{(1.15)^3} = \$11.57$$

In addition to the present value of the dividends in period 4 and beyond, we have the present value of the dividends in the first three years.

Present value of first three dividends:

$$= \frac{\$1.50}{1.15} + \frac{1.80}{1.15^2} + \frac{2.05}{1.15^3}$$

$$= 1.30 + 1.36 + 1.35 = \$4.01.$$

The price of the share equals the present value of all of the dividends:

$$P_0 = \$4.01 + \$11.57 = \$15.58.$$

8. For a firm paying 60 percent of its earnings as dividends:

$$P_0 = \frac{\$1.50(.6)}{.13} = \$6.92$$

9.

$$\$15 = \frac{\$1.20}{(k - .04)}$$

$$(k - .04) = \$1.20/\$15 = .08$$

$$k = 12 \text{ percent}$$

10. First, we must find the dividend for the next period. With a constant payout policy of paying 40 percent of earnings and projected earnings of $2.50, the dividend for the next period is:

$$D_1 = .4(\$2.50) = \$1.00$$

We now apply the Constant Growth Model to value the shares:

$$P_0 = \frac{\$1}{(.11 - .06)} = \$20$$

CHAPTER TEN

Economic Analysis and the Stock Market

Chapter Objectives

Upon completion of this chapter, you should be able to:

1. Explain the signs and strengths of the relationships between stock returns and: inflation and interest rates, the federal debt, monetary policy, and fiscal policy.
2. Explain the relationship between leading, lagging, and roughly coincident indicators and the business cycle.
3. Explain the problems inherent in using leading indicators to create a stock–investing strategy.
4. Compare and contrast the costs and benefits of using time series models, econometric models, judgmental forecasts, and technical forecasts.

Chapter Outline

I. Overview

A. As evidenced by the activities on Wall Street during October 1987, stocks tend to move together. In fact, stocks tend to act as a herd, moving up and down en masse.
B. There is a good reason for stock prices to move in unison, and the alert investor needs to know the basic relationships between broad economic movements in production, interest rates, and fiscal and monetary policy, on the one hand, and stock prices on the other.
C. If one could predict changes in broad economic measures correctly, then it might be possible to use those predictions to guide a successful trading strategy in the stock market.

II. Tidal Movements

A. It is a fact of economic life that there are cycles of boom and bust. Since there is a clear relationship between price movements in the stock market and the health of the economy as a whole, studying economic developments may help the stock investor to invest more wisely.

B. The Herd Instinct
   1. The tendency of stocks to rise and fall together is an important and pervasive factor in understanding the price movement of any stock.

C. The Business Cycle
   1. One of the most pervasive effects on the stock market is the **business cycle**, the periodic expansion and contraction of the economy.
   2. A **recession** is a sharp and significant reduction in overall business activity.
   3. Stock prices respond to the business cycle—recessions are often accompanied by extended bear markets, and expansionary periods are often heralded by a bull market. .
   4. Stocks that are particularly sensitive to the business cycle are called **cyclical stocks**.
   5. Examples of cyclical stocks are in heavy industry, such as shipping, oil services, and steel.
   6. Some firms are relatively immune to the business cycle. For example, supermarkets attract shoppers throughout both recessions and strong economic periods.

D. Interest Rates and Inflation
   1. Fisher's equation for nominal interest rates stresses the close relationship between expected inflation and interest rates.
   2. Evidence shows that recent experience gives reason to favor low–inflation environments rather than high–inflation environments. Thus, it seems that common stock investment does not provide a perfect protection against inflation.
   3. Whether the inflation is anticipated or unanticipated, there seems to be a strong negative impact on real and nominal stock returns. In general, inflation is one of the stock investors' worst enemies.

E. The Federal Debt
   1. One of the great social and political issues today is the growing federal debt. An excessively high debt level keeps interest rates high, running the risk of high inflation.
   2. High interest rates could result from the excessive demand for funds on the part of the government, for which the government would need to pay a very high rate of interest in order to attract the required volume of funds.
   3. If the government wishes to spend more than its income, it can borrow in the financial markets or increase the money supply.

4. Increasing the money supply too rapidly is likely to stimulate inflation, because there would be more money in circulation relative to the amount of goods available.

5. One of the factors that makes the level of debt so difficult to control is the fact that the federal government is obligated to make large payments under various entitlement programs, such as Social Security.

6. How the deficit is handled will have a profound effect on the stock market. Uncontrolled increases in deficits, or the general expectation of such deficits, are bound to adversely affect the stock market. By contrast, implementing effective policies to reduce the deficit should have a beneficial effect on the market.

F. Monetary Policy

1. In setting monetary policy, the Federal Reserve Board determines the rate at which the money supply will grow.

2. If the money supply grows too quickly, there will be too much money relative to the amount of goods available and inflation will likely result.

3. On the other hand, if the money supply grows too slowly, there will not be sufficient funds to support a robust economy.

4. The most useful tool the Federal Reserve Board uses for conducting monetary policy is an **open market operation**—the Federal Reserve Board can increase the money supply by buying government securities or decrease the money supply by selling government securities.

5. For an increase in the money supply to benefit stock prices, the market must not feel the increase is excessive.

6. If the market believes that the increase in the money supply will lead to higher inflation rates, stock prices may well fall in response to inflationary fears.

7. It is not even certain that monetary policy affects stock prices. If the stock market correctly anticipates a future change in monetary policy, the market may react in advance of the actual change in policy.

   a. If the change in policy is correctly anticipated, implementing the policy is unlikely to have any effect.

   b. By contrast, if a policy change is unanticipated, a definite effect is likely.

8. According to **rational expectations theory**, market participants form expectations of future Federal Reserve Board actions that are rational in the sense that they reflect all available information. In this environment, Fed actions may have little or no effect because they are too well anticipated.

9. Recent studies indicate that stock prices move before changes in the money supply when the changes are anticipated. Thus, the studies claim that stock prices reflect anticipated changes in the money supply before the changes actually occur.

10. For the investor, it is difficult to use changes in the money supply as a signal for a successful trading strategy.

G. Fiscal Policy
   1. The federal government establishes fiscal policy by setting tax and spending levels. Both policy actions have potentially profound effects on financial markets in general and on the stock market in particular.
   2. By taxation, the federal government withdraws money from the economy as a whole.
   3. In addition to collecting taxes, the federal government also spends. Spending may stimulate productivity and the economy or cause inflation.
   4. In order to turn a study of monetary and fiscal policy into usable strategic information for investing in the stock market, an investor needs earlier or better information than other investors.

III. Leading Indicators and the Business Cycle

A. While there are hundreds of economic variables related to the business cycle, some have proven more useful for forecasting than others, and these have been used to form composite indexes of economic performance.
B. Three composite indexes are followed most closely.
   1. The index of leading economic indicators tends to rise before increases in GNP and fall before decreases in GNP.
   2. The index of roughly coincident indicators tends to reach its peaks and troughs at about the same time as GNP.
   3. The index of lagging indicators tends to reach its peaks and troughs after GNP.
C. For the stock market investor, the main interest of the indicator series is in finding some indicator that leads the stock market.
D. There are four reasons why investors should be careful when using these indicators.
   1. The lead times before peaks are median lead times, so one does not know exactly how much one variable leads another in a particular economic cycle.
   2. It is difficult to determine that an economic variable has reached its peak at the time of the peak.
   3. The leading indicators occasionally give false signals, or fail to signal.
   4. The stock market itself has the greatest overall score as a leading indicator.
E. While the leading indicators give useful information about the future course of GNP, there is little reason to hope that this information could be used to guide an investment strategy.

IV. Professional Forecasting Techniques

A. Time Series Models

1. The last decade has witnessed the growing popularity of **time series models** as economic forecasting tools, stemming from the work of Box and Jenkins.
2. A time series model is a statistical model that relates the current value of a variable to some function of the history of that same variable.
3. A new battery of techniques known as **ARCH models** may allow for better forecasts of an economic variable based on past values of the same variable.
4. Another increasingly popular concept is the idea of **cointegration**, a statistical relationship that arises when changes in two variables can be combined to create a statistically stable third variable.

B. Econometric Models
   1. Econometric models are also statistically based models, but they are much more complicated in theory and design than time series models.
   2. The designer of the model builds economic relationships that are expected to hold into the model by expressing the relationships in mathematical equations.
   3. A complex econometric model may have hundreds of equations, all to be solved simultaneously.

C. Judgmental Forecasts
   1. A judgmental forecast emerges from the reflection of a group of people or a single individual.
   2. Judgmental means essentially non–mathematical, relying instead on the experience of the forecaster, who takes all of the relevant information into account.
   3. Often the judgmental forecast is superimposed upon some mechanical, or entirely non–judgmental, forecast.

D. Technical Forecasts
   1. Technical analysis uses previous values of economic variables to forecast future values. Traditionally, it has not used statistical techniques.
   2. The technical analyst attempting to predict future stock market movements would look at the historical performance of key variables in an attempt to identify recurring patterns.
   3. As a more concrete example of the kinds of information that technical analysts watch, consider a moving average.
   4. A **moving average** is the average of some variable over a certain period. Technical analysts might compare the moving average of the S&P 500 to the current level of the S&P itself.
   5. As another example of technical analysis, some market observers believe that the P–E ratio and the dividend yield also provide useful buy and sell indicators.
      a. A P–E ratio that is too high indicates that the investor should sell.
      b. A low P–E indicates a buying opportunity.
   6. As a final example of a technical indicator, we consider the activity of corporate insiders. Since the insiders presumably know more than the

rest of us about their stocks, technical analysts believe it is a good idea to buy when the insiders buy.

V. Some Recent Forecasting Results

A. Time Series Models vs. Econometric Models
  1. Since time series models use such a limited information set, forecasts of economic variables arrived at using time series techniques can be used as a minimal standard. A single individual could create a time series model forecast of GNP in one or two days. By contrast, a full–scale econometric model might take many person–years of effort to construct.
  2. To justify that additional effort and expense, the large econometric model should be able to out–perform the time series model.
  3. After his investigation illustrated difficulties with econometric models, researcher Nelson concluded that because time series models are simple and inexpensive, the value of using econometric models for forecasting should be re–evaluated.
B. Judgmental Forecasts vs. Econometric Models
  1. Each year, *Business Week* surveys a group of economists for forecasts of key economic variables.
  2. Thomas Fomby collected these forecasts for the years 1972–1981 and compared them to forecasts for econometric models.
  3. These forecasts, in terms of increasing complexity are as follows.
      a. The **no–change forecast** is the most naive and cheapest to produce.
      b. The next forecast is the **time series forecast**, which performs a little better than the no–change forecast.
      c. Next is the **consensus forecast**, the average of the economists polled by *Business Week*, which shows a marked improvement over the time series model.
      d. Finally, the errors of the econometric models, taken as a whole, are presented as well.
  4. *Institutional Investor* surveyed a number of economists for their interest rate predictions, and the results revealed a tremendous range of responses and errors.
      a. Unfortunately, there seems to be little consistency from one period to the next; that is, the best forecaster in one period is quite likely to be among the worst in the next period.
      b. There are some exceptions to this general rule and some individual forecasters have records worthy of envy.

Key Terms and Concepts

ARCH models	a new battery of techniques that may allow for better forecasts of an economic variable based on past values of the same variable
business cycle	the periodic expansion and contraction of the economy
cointegration	a statistical relationship that arises when changes in two variables can be combined to create a statistically stable third variable
consensus forecast	the average of the economists polled by *Business Week*
cyclical stocks	stocks that are particularly sensitive to the business cycle
deflation	a decrease, or negative rate of change, in the price level
econometric model	a complicated system of equations representing economic relationships
entitlements	automatic federal expenditures that indirectly add to the federal debt
federal debt	borrowing by the U.S. government or its agencies
fiscal policy	changes in government spending and/or taxation
Gross National Product	also GNP; the dollar value of all final goods and services produced by the economy in a given year
inflation	an increase, or positive rate of change, in the price level
judgmental forecast	an opinion based on the experience and feelings of an expert
lagging indicator	a variable whose trend follows changes in the economy

leading indicator	a variable whose trend precedes changes in the economy
monetary policy	the Fed's changing of the amount of money in the economy
moving average	the average of some variable over a certain period
no–change forecast	predicts that there will be no change and is the most naive and cheapest to produce
open market operations	the Fed's buying or selling of government securities to change the money supply
rational expectations theory	states that market participants form expectations of future Federal Reserve Board actions that are rational in the sense that they reflect all available information
recession	a sharp and significant reduction in overall business activity
roughly coincident indicator	a variable whose trend moves with changes in the economy
technical forecast	a forecast of future events based on recurring historical patterns in a variable
time series model	a statistical model that relates the current value of a variable to some function of the history of that same variable

Multiple–Choice Questions

1. The most naive and cheapest to produce forecast is the _____.
   A. time series forecast
   B. implementation forecast
   C. consensus forecast
   D. financial expectations forecast
   E. no–change forecast

2. Automatic federal expenditures that indirectly increase the federal debt are known as ____.
    A. fiscal policy
    B. monetary policy
    C. entitlements
    D. leading indicators
    E. econometrics

3. Non–statistical analysis that creates a forecast from recurring historical patterns is known as a(n) ____ model.
    A. technical
    B. judgmental
    C. econometric
    D. time series
    E. federal

4. Recurring expansions and contractions in the economy are known as ____.
    A. time series
    B. leadings
    C. deflations
    D. inflations
    E. business cycles

5. The total value of all final goods and services produced by an economy is known as the ____.
    A. federal debt
    B. fiscal policy
    C. gross national product
    D. roughly coincident product
    E. monetary production

6. The essentially nonmathematical recommendation of a professional investment advisor is a type of ____ forecast.
    A. time series
    B. judgmental
    C. naive
    D. technical
    E. econometric

7. One of the biggest problems inherent in attempting to use monetary policy to forecast future stock returns lies in distinguishing ____ changes.
    A. spot from forward
    B. current from expected
    C. inflationary from deflationary
    D. anticipated from unanticipated
    E. nominal from real

8. Which of the following is *not* fiscal policy?
    A. raising corporate tax rates
    B. buying government securities
    C. increasing government spending
    D. decreasing the scope of entitlement programs
    E. raising marginal tax rates

9. An econometric model is a(n) ____.
    A. set of interrelated equations describing the economy
    B. expert's opinion
    C. forecast based on historical patterns
    D. statistical relationship between the current and past values of a variable
    E. naive forecast of no change

10. Indicators which change with GNP are ____.
    A. coincident
    B. consensus
    C. current
    D. leading
    E. lagging

11. Stocks that are particularly sensitive to the business cycle are called _____ stocks.
    A. leading
    B. following
    C. cyclical
    D. sensitive
    E. lagging

12. Changes in government spending or taxation in an attempt to influence GNP is known as ____.
    A. fiscal policy
    B. monetary policy
    C. entitlements
    D. business cycles
    E. federal debt

13. When the Federal Reserve buys or sells government securities to the financial system, it is pursuing ____.
    A. fiscal policy
    B. monetary policy
    C. entitlements
    D. business cycles
    E. federal debt

14. Borrowing by the U.S. government or its agencies increases ____.
    A. fiscal policy
    B. monetary policy
    C. entitlements
    D. business cycles
    E. federal debt

15. The statistical relationship between the current value of a variable and one or more of its past values generates a ____.
    A. lagging indicator
    B. leading indicator
    C. judgment forecast
    D. naive forecast
    E. time series forecast

16. A non–statistical estimate based on recurring historical patterns in a variable is a ____.
    A. lagging indicator
    B. leading indicator
    C. judgment forecast
    D. technical forecast
    E. time series forecast

17. The historical relationship between stock market returns and GNP indicates that market returns often function well as a ____.
    A. lagging indicator
    B. leading indicator
    C. judgment forecast
    D. technical forecast
    E. time series forecast

18. A statistic whose trend tends to follow changes in GNP serves as a ____.
    A. lagging indicator
    B. leading indicator
    C. judgment forecast
    D. technical forecast
    E. time series forecast

19. An increase in the price level is known as ____.
    A. inflation
    B. an open market operation
    C. an entitlement
    D. a time series
    E. a trough

20. Indicators which change before GNP are ____ indicators.
    A. coincident
    B. lagging
    C. judgmental
    D. time series
    E. leading

21. An example of a firm relatively immune to the business cycle is a _____.
    A. steel firm
    B. supermarket
    C. real estate developer
    D. ship builder
    E. luxury car builder

22. A _____ is a sharp and significant reduction in overall business activity.
    A. boom
    B. upturn
    C. low economic phase
    D. repression
    E. recession

23. An opinion based on the experience and feeling of an expert is a ____.
    A. lagging indicator
    B. leading indicator
    C. judgment forecast
    D. technical forecast
    E. time series forecast

24. The Gross National Product is the total amount of ____.
    A. money in circulation
    B. borrowing by the U.S. government and its agencies
    C. personal, corporate, and municipal borrowing
    D. tax revenue received by the Federal government and state governments
    E. final goods and services produced in the economy

25. A set of inter–related equations describing the economy is ____.
    A. monetary policy
    B. fiscal policy
    C. an econometric model
    D. a roughly coincident indicator
    E. a naive forecast

Answers

Multiple–Choice Questions

1. E	10. A	19. A
2. C	11. C	20. E
3. A	12. A	21. B
4. E	13. B	22. E
5. C	14. E	23. C
6. B	15. E	24. E
7. D	16. D	25. C
8. B	17. B	
9. A	18. A	

CHAPTER ELEVEN

Industry Analysis

Chapter Objectives

Upon completion of this chapter, you should be able to:

1. Explain how demographic trends such as the aging of the population, the changes in income distribution, the industrial mix, and regional employment patterns can be expected to affect different industries.
2. Explain the industry life cycle.
3. Explain how possible changes in the various forms of government regulation, such as tariffs, quotas, subsidies, the income tax code, and deregulation efforts, can be expected to affect different industries.
4. Define and interpret the key financial ratios used in industry analysis.
5. Discuss the problems inherent in attempting to compare the ratios across industries at a point in time or within an industry over time.
6. Explain the problems that might arise in trying to decide which firms make up an industry that is to be analyzed.

Chapter Outline

I. Overview

A. In industry analysis, the analyst examines those features of the economic landscape that are particular to a given industry.
B. An industry analysis will focus on the "family resemblances" among the various firms in a given industry, which provides important economies of analysis, since the entire analysis need not be repeated for each company.
C. Company analysis interprets the effects of industry–wide factors on a particular firm.
D. Broad demographic factors and a changing society probably have the greatest impact on determining which industries will succeed.

E.   The industry life cycle describes the pattern of growth, maturity, and decay that is followed by many industries.

II. Differences in Growth and Investment Performance Across Industries

A.   Output, productivity, and profitability have differed greatly across major industries in the U.S. economy in recent years.
B.   Therefore, the investment performance of shares of the firms in these industries has differed as well.
C.   Investors attempting to apply the Dividend Valuation Model must be able to assess how economic trends affect an industry since all firms in the industry tend to experience similar effects.
D.   These trends affect the size of future dividends and the discount rate applied to the dividend to value the shares.

III. Demographic Factors and Social Change

A.   Aging America
   1.   The average age of Americans has been increasing and will continue to do so.
   2.   People of different ages have different interests and needs in life, which are reflected in their spending habits.
   3.   Firms that meet the needs of age groups that are increasing in size can look forward to correspondingly larger sales.
B.   Changing Income Distribution
   1.   Recent figures show a growing affluence in the population as a whole and, even more dramatically, an increasing variability of income.
   2.   For the fortunate upper–income group, there is more disposable income, allowing concentration on luxury and leisure goods.
   3.   Increasing affluence is good news to firms that cater to specialized and expensive tastes.
   4.   By the same token, there may be more interest in inexpensive, staple goods among those families in the lower income strata.
   5.   Being able to anticipate these changes could lead to better anticipation of dividend streams and to wiser stock selection.
   6.   It may be that a strategy of specializing in either the high or low end of the market may be more successful than the traditional middle–of–the–road approach represented by a firm like Sears.
C.   The Changing Industrial Mix in the United States
   1.   There is a strong movement away from smokestack industries and toward high–tech industries, away from manufacturing and toward service industries.
   2.   There is also a strong tendency for the movement to high–technology industries to carry over into the service sector, with some service industries even declining.

3. Generally, service industries requiring more skilled employees seem to be prospering relative to those service industries relying on low–skilled employees.

D. Regional Employment Patterns
  1. Another major social movement in the United States is the shifting of population and employment toward the Sun Belt and the West, and away from the industrial Northeast.
  2. The growth rates for high–technology employment are much more rapid for the western half of the country. Overall, higher growth rates are recorded in the West and the South.

E. A newcomer to the investment market is unlikely to achieve any benefit from investing on the basis of generally accepted information, because the market presumably already reflects this information.

F. To exploit the kinds of social and demographic analysis discussed here, investors must either get their information earlier than other market participants or interpret it more wisely.

IV. The Industry Life Cycle

A. The success of firms in establishing good growth records depends to a great extent on the growth opportunities in their industry.

B. These industry growth opportunities depend, in turn, on the point the industry as a whole occupies in the industry life cycle.

C. The **industry life cycle** refers to a regular pattern of growth, maturity, and decay experienced by many industries. Industry–wide sales begin at a zero level as the new industry is created, pass through a growth stage into a phase of maturity, and eventually go into a decline.
  1. The creation of a new industry is generally brought about by the introduction of some product, which may be the fruit of some technological leap.
  2. After the creation stage and initial acceptance of the new industry, new competitors enter. As a result, the competitive structure in the industry changes from a monopoly to an oligopoly.
  3. After an initial growth phase, the industry matures and competitive pressures increase.
  4. As industries begin to decline, profit margins are reduced and the emphasis turns to production efficiencies, with price competition continuing to be a major threat to profits.
  5. Once a decline has started, a new technological leap, or a replacement product, may cause the cycle to begin again.

D. As reflected in the dividend valuation model, investors should prefer growth industries, other factors being equal.

V. *The Federal Government and Industry Analysis*

A. Regulation
   1. The decades of the 1960s and 1970s witnessed broad penetration in all aspects of the U.S. economy by the federal government.
   2. Regulation during this period had a major impact on the financial services industry, automobiles, airlines and other forms of interstate commerce, and the pharmaceutical industry.
   3. The 1980s brought with it a strong trend toward deregulation, which has had a different impact on these same industries. Deregulation tends to increase competition, lower prices, and remove or penalize inefficient firms.
   4. In the early 1990s, federal regulation appears to be gaining strength.
   5. While many economists believe that government regulation often acts to shelter industries from competition, governmental regulation is often not helpful to industry earnings.
   6. When conducting an industry analysis, it is important to take into account the level of federal regulation present.
   7. In addition, as the level of regulation changes, one must also look at the likely future impact of regulation.
B. Taxation and Subsidies
   1. Federal taxation falls unevenly on different industries.
   2. Rules for depreciation, tax–loss carries, and reinvestment incentives are written in a way that gives benefits to some industries while denying those benefits to others.
   3. Clearly, firms that are highly capital intensive, such as electrical utilities, are helped more than those that are less capital intensive, such as a service industry, when the depreciation rules are liberalized.
   4. Perhaps the clearest instance of a subsidy by the federal government can be drawn from the agricultural industry with programs of federal price supports.
   5. Other forms of government subsidies are programs like Medicare, which has helped hospital and medical supply firms in the past. This subsidy is decreasing.
   6. Another way in which the government subsidizes certain industries at the expense of others is through tariffs and quotas, as they tend to protect U.S. industries from foreign competition.
   7. The federal government has such a large potential impact on firms in certain industries that firms in these industries employ staffs to follow and influence governmental policy.

VI. A Typical Industry Analysis

A. Industry Comparisons
1. The **return on assets** (ROA) and **return on equity** (ROE) measures are both gauges of accounting profitability.
2. ROA and ROE calculations reveal large differences across industries, and, in general, these kinds of measures of profitability are not comparable across industries.
3. ROA is defined as:

$$\frac{\text{Net Income}}{\text{Total Assets}}$$

    a. ROA is usually low for capital intensive industries that have large amounts of assets.
    b. Because of the different levels of capital intensity, ROA figures are difficult to compare across industries. This means that time series analysis of the figure within a given industry is likely to be more meaningful.
4. ROE is defined as:

$$\frac{\text{Net Income}}{\text{Total Equity}}$$

    a. The interpretation of the ROE figure across industries is hazardous because of the different capital structure employed in different industries.
    b. **Capital structure** measures the division of a firm's financing between debt and equity.
    c. Other things equal, the higher the proportion of debt, the greater will be the ROE, assuming that there is at least some net income.
5. Capital structure is often measured by the Debt–to–Equity ratio:

$$\frac{\text{Long-Term Debt}}{\text{Total Equity}}$$

6. Differences in debt levels characterize different industries, but within industries firms tend to have very similar capital structures.
7. In many respects, the P–E ratio may be interpreted as a measure of prospective growth rates in earnings and dividends.
8. Closely related to the P–E ratio is the payout ratio, which is the percentage of earnings paid by a firm in dividends:

$$\frac{\text{Cash Dividends}}{\text{Net Income}}$$

9. High–growth industries are normally characterized by low payout ratios.

10. High P–E ratios tend to go with low payout ratios, both being associated with higher growth rates.
11. In general, the higher the payout ratio in a given industry, the more important dividends are to shareholders. For a firm in a high–growth industry, a dividend cut might be regarded as bad news, but it is unlikely that it would have such a drastic effect.
12. The dividend yield is an important measure since it makes up one of the two components of the stock investor's return, the other being capital gain.
13. Dividend yield is given by:

$$\frac{\text{Dividends for the Year}}{\text{Stock Price at the Beginning of the Year}}$$

    a. The dividend yield varies significantly across industries.
    b. In general, the lower the dividend yield, the greater must be the anticipated price appreciation.
B. In interpreting industry ratios, it is important to remember the following.
  1. Most of the ratios vary across industries.
  2. Most of the ratios vary over time within a given industry.
  3. Most of the ratios are sensitive to the particular practices within a given industry, such as the use of debt.

VII. The Paper Industry

A. Industrial Classifications
  1. One of the first issues that must be addressed in any potential industry analysis is the proper definition of the industry.
    a. Using the Standard Industrial Classification (SIC) code, one can specify the industry loosely or more specifically, depending on the digits used.
    b. In making the number of firms studied manageable, the definition used may leave out many well–known firms.
    c. Another problem in industry definition comes from the fact that large firms almost always operate in two or more different industry areas, and these differences can be important when it comes to selecting firms to invest in.
B. Paper Industry Overview
  1. Paper is a commodity good, and the paper industry is in the mature phase of the industry life cycle.
  2. Paper is generally quite cyclical, so production will probably expand in line with general industrial production; further, paper prices are very elastic and respond dramatically to small shifts in capacity utilization.
  3. The ability to raise prices depends on a high capacity utilization rate, but excess capacity will probably continue to create difficulties.

C. Environmental Concerns
   1. Growing environmental awareness threatens the paper industry in two ways:
      a. First, we have already noted a growing willingness for consumers to recycle paper products.
      b. Second, the paper industry employs some highly toxic chemicals.
   2. New legislative initiatives aimed at curbing acid rain will have a significant impact on the paper industry.
   3. From an investment perspective; note the following.
      a. Firms that have already incurred substantial pollution control expenses may be positioned to perform better in the years ahead, to the extent that this early expenditure is not already fully reflected in share prices.
      b. Firms with operations in more tolerant jurisdictions may be able to avoid the full cost of their pollution.
D. The U.S.–Canada Connection
   1. Canada is a net exporter of paper to the United States, and U.S.–Canada trade in paper is critical to U.S. supplies.
   2. Many paper firms have significant Canadian operations.
E. Internationalization
   1. Beyond trade with Canada, the U.S. paper industry is moving toward even more complete internationalization.
   2. U.S. paper firms are moving to capture more of the global paper market, and appear to be well situated to capitalize on some inherent advantages.
      a. First, U.S. paper plants are the most modern and technologically advanced in the world.
      b. Second, compared to many countries that might compete in paper production, the United States is endowed with a very rich resource base.
      c. Third, the paper industry is capital intensive, not labor intensive. Therefore, the paper industry is not as subject to competition from low labor cost environments as some other industries would be.
   3. From an investment point of view, the movement to internationalization is potentially of great importance.
      a. From consumption figures, it is apparent that growth opportunities are likely to be better overseas.
      b. Environmental concerns in the United States are higher than elsewhere, so foreign operations may help firms to avoid environmental pressures at home.
      c. By obtaining rights to foreign pulp sources, firms may be able to diversify their resource base in a way that will protect them from fluctuating exchange rates.
F. Investment Prospects in the Paper Industry
   1. *Value Line Investment Survey* reviews industries and groups firms according to its own classification.

2.   *Value Line* ranks the paper industry 80th in attractiveness among the 97 industries that it follows. As substantiation, the publication notes the following.

     a.   The paper industry is highly cyclical.

     b.   The excess capacity in the industry is critical in the pricing of the final product.

     c.   Pollution abatement and other environmental concerns will adversely affect paper company profits.

Key Terms and Concepts

capital structure	the division of a firm's financing between debt and equity
debt–to–equity ratio	long–term debt/total equity
deregulation	removal of restrictions imposed by regulatory agencies
dividend yield	annual dividends per share/share price
industry analysis	an attempt to forecast trends that will affect firms in an industry to determine their investment prospects
industry life cycle	the regular pattern of creation, growth, maturity, and decline experienced by many industries
payout ratio	cash dividends/net income
price–earnings ratio	the price per share/earnings per share
regulation	government restriction on the actions of firms in an industry
return on assets	also ROA; net income/total assets
return on equity	also ROE; net income/total equity
standard industry code	also SIC; the classification system that attempts to separate firms into particular industries

Multiple–Choice Questions

1. The pattern of growth, maturity, and decay exhibited by many industries is known as the industry ____.
   A. mix
   B. ratio
   C. life cycle
   D. demographic
   E. payout

2. High industry P–E ratios often signal ____.
   A. a bear market
   B. a mature industry
   C. high dividend payout
   D. high debt–to–equity ratios for the firms in the industry
   E. good earnings growth prospects for the industry

3. The P–E ratio is determined by ____.
   A. dividing stock price per share by earnings per share.
   B. multiplying stock price per share by earnings per share.
   C. subtracting stock price per share from earnings per share.
   D. dividing stock price per share by equity per share.
   E. multiplying stock price per share by equity per share.

4. The government directly restricts the amount of a good imported through ____.
   A. tariffs
   B. subsidies
   C. taxation
   D. quotas
   E. deregulation

5. The payout ratio measures ____.
   A. the division between debt and equity financing
   B. price as a multiple of recent earnings
   C. the percentage of earnings paid out in dividends
   D. the stage of the industry life cycle that fits a particular industry
   E. an industry's capital structure

6. Which phase of the industry life cycle is characterized by the existence of a few dominant, profitable firms?
   A. creation
   B. growth
   C. maturity
   D. decline
   E. rebirth

7. Which of the following movements is *not* a major recent trend in U.S. life?
    A. an increase in women in the paid work force
    B. an increasing proportion of part–time workers
    C. a decrease in the median age of Americans
    D. a growing number of one–person families
    E. a population shift toward the Sunbelt

8. Which of the following is *not* typically considered a type of government regulation?
    A. tariffs
    B. quotas
    C. depreciation rules
    D. entitlement programs
    E. rules for tax–loss carries

9. If an industry is near peak capacity, an increase in demand will probably lead to a(n) ____.
    A. increase in prices
    B. increase in payout ratios
    C. increase in capital structure
    D. decrease in union domination
    E. decrease in P–E ratios

10. Which of the following demographic trends is true with respect to the recent history of the U.S. economy?
    A. a population shift away from sun belt
    B. an increase in population in the Northeast
    C. an increase in the number of women in the labor force
    D. a decrease in part–time employment
    E. a decrease in market share in the high–technology industries

11. A classification that sorts firms into industries is known as a(n) ____.
    A. standard industrial classification code
    B. capital structure
    C. deregulation
    D. industry life cycle
    E. bear market

12. The recent increase of women in the work force is an example of a(n) ____.
    A. standard industrial classification code
    B. capital structure
    C. demographic trend
    D. industry life cycle
    E. bear market

13. The division of a firm's financing between debt and equity is its ____.
    A. standard industrial classification code
    B. capital structure
    C. deregulation
    D. industry life cycle
    E. demographic trend

14. Which of the following ratios is calculated by dividing net income by the total value of common equity?
    A. return on equity
    B. price/earnings
    C. dividend yield
    D. payout ratio
    E. return on assets

15. Which of the following ratios gives a firm's share price as a multiple of its most recent annual accounting earnings?
    A. return on equity
    B. price/earnings
    C. dividend yield
    D. payout ratio
    E. return on assets

16. Which of the following ratios is calculated by dividing the cash dividend per share by earnings per share?
    A. return on equity
    B. price/earnings
    C. dividend yield
    D. payout ratio
    E. return on assets

17. Dividing net income by the value of a firm's assets creates the ____ ratio.
    A. return on equity
    B. price/earnings
    C. dividend yield
    D. payout
    E. return on assets

18. Dividing the dividend per share by the price per share measures the ____.
    A. return on equity
    B. price/earnings
    C. dividend yield
    D. payout ratio
    E. return on assets

19. A limit placed by the government on the amount of a specific good imported is known as a ____.
    A. tariff
    B. quota
    C. subsidy
    D. bull market
    E. deregulation

20. A tax by the government that artificially raises the price of an imported good is known as a ____.
    A. tariff
    B. quota
    C. subsidy
    D. bull market
    E. deregulation

21. The removal of government restrictions on an industry's practices is known as a ____.
    A. tariff
    B. quota
    C. subsidy
    D. bull market
    E. deregulation

22. A government regulation that supports prices or income in a particular industry is known as a ____.
    A. tariff
    B. quota
    C. subsidy
    D. bull market
    E. deregulation

23. Other things equal, firms that show positive profits and have a large amount of debt will show ____.
    A. high returns on equity
    B. high standard industry codes
    C. low returns on assets
    D. low dividend yields
    E. low capital structure

24. Firms with strong earnings prospects tend to have ____.
    A. high dividend payout ratios
    B. high P/E ratios
    C. low returns on assets
    D. low standard industry codes
    E. low capital structure

25. Other things equal, firms with low P/E ratios tend to have ____.
    A. high payout ratios
    B. high tariffs
    C. low subsidies
    D. related dividend yields
    E. low capital structure

Answers

Multiple–Choice Questions

1. C	10. C	19. B
2. E	11. A	20. A
3. A	12. C	21. E
4. D	13. B	22. C
5. C	14. A	23. A
6. B	15. B	24. B
7. C	16. D	25. A
8. D	17. E	
9. A	18. C	

CHAPTER TWELVE

Company Analysis

Chapter Objectives

Upon completion of this chapter, you should be able to:
1. Explain the Fundamental Analyst's Model and the trading strategy that it implies.
2. Explain the three requirements necessary to apply the model successfully.
3. Describe and comment on the three popular techniques for forecasting earnings: percentage of revenue forecasting, trend analysis, and judgmental forecasts.
4. Discuss how accounting earnings, dividend policy, financial leverage, and notes to financial statements can affect the justified P–E ratio.
5. Explain the difference between accounting earnings and economic earnings.
6. Explain how the five components of management style and special firm characteristics can have an impact on the justified P–E ratio.

Chapter Outline

I. The Fundamental Analyst's Model

A. The model is a straightforward technique for gauging the intrinsic value of a share of stock. It states:

Stock Value = (Expected Earnings)(Justified P–E Ratio)

B. The model simply states that the intrinsic value of a share of stock equals the expected earnings for the firm in the next period, multiplied by the justified P–E ratio for the firm's shares.

C. The **justified P–E ratio** is the correct ratio of share price to current earnings that reflects both the firm's future growth prospects in earnings and the level of risk associated with future earnings.

    D. Price versus Value
       1. The model makes a distinction between price and value because it is a technique designed to find discrepancies between the two.
       2. The analyst is estimating stock values to find situations in which the market pricing mechanism has made a mistake and has allowed the stock's price to diverge from its true value.
       3. Investment rules are as follows.
          a. If the estimated value > market price, **buy** the stock.
          b. If the estimated value < market price, **sell** the stock.
    E. Three Requirements for Applying the Model
       1. To profit by following this strategy requires three conditions:
          a. The estimate of the true value of a share must be correct.
          b. The true value must be estimated before the rest of the market discovers the true value.
          c. The other participants in the market must come to recognize that the share is worth its estimated value.
       2. Since any estimate is only as good as its inputs, attention must focus on the two key inputs to the fundamental analyst's model—the expected earnings and the justified P–E ratio.

II. Earnings Growth

    A. The growth rate and pattern of earnings and dividends are crucial for both the justified P–E ratio and the expected earnings estimate.
    B. If the investor knew the present level of earnings and the growth rate to be experienced over the next period, the earnings for the next period could be estimated with total accuracy.

III. Forecasting Earnings

    A. While it is important to be able to measure historical earnings growth, the main emphasis should be on future growth in earnings. Future growth determines future earnings figures, and this helps determine the justified P–E ratio.
    B. The Percentage of Revenue Technique
       1. This technique assumes that a firm will continue to earn the same percentage on each dollar of sales as it has done in the past.
       2. If one can forecast sales for the next period, it is possible to derive a forecast of earnings.
       3. The method converts the problem of forecasting earnings to the problem of forecasting sales in the hope that the latter amount is easier to estimate accurately.
       4. The technique is easy to apply and calculate. However, one needs to have reliable estimates of profitability and revenue.

5. Thus, the main weakness of this approach to forecasting earnings is that it substitutes the problem of forecasting revenues and profit margins for the original problem of forecasting earnings.

C. Trend Analysis

1. Trend analysis is a common mathematical tool used to forecast future earnings for a firm by extrapolating a linear trend from past earnings to the future.

2. Many statisticians believe that time series analysis, which forecasts a variable as a function of one or more of its past values, offers better forecasts of some types of variables than simple trend analysis does.

3. All of these methods hazardously assume that the growth rate characterized by the sample period will continue in the future.

4. Thus, in general, the longer into the future the forecast is made, the greater will be the size of the probable errors.

D. Judgmental Forecasts

1. This forecast relies on the informed judgment of the forecaster and considers a number of factors in addition to the past data on earnings and revenues.

2. While the judgmental forecaster will certainly be interested in recent performance, he or she will also be sure to concentrate on the future prospects of the company.

IV. The Justified P–E Ratio

A. After obtaining the best estimate of the expected earnings, the investor must include the justified P–E ratio in the fundamental analyst's model.

B. Justified P–E Ratios and Firm Financial Characteristics

1. Financial characteristics both reflect and help to determine the justified P–E ratio of particular firms.

   a. **Accounting earnings** may be thought of as the results of applying a set of accounting rules to the operations of the firm. Accounting earnings are not the same as economic earnings.

   b. **Economic earnings** reflect the change in purchasing power a firm has earned during a given period.

   c. Since economic earnings truly measure the operating results of the firm, the fundamental analyst must be careful to reconcile any discrepancy between the accounting earnings and the estimated economic earnings.

   d. Accepted accounting rules make it possible for firms with identical operations to show widely different earnings.

      (1) For example, inventory accounting under the **FIFO method** (first in, first out) understates the cost of sales, overstating earnings in times of rising costs. The **LIFO method** (last in, first out) is more conservative.

e. The fact that firms can manage their earnings means that it is sometimes possible to fabricate an amazing growth record in earnings even when there is no real improvement in cash flow.

f. For the analyst, the different accounting strategies mean that the reported earnings must be adjusted to reveal the true economic earnings more accurately.

2. **Dividend policy** affects the future earnings growth of the firm because funds paid to shareholders as dividends cannot be retained in the firm for reinvestment.

   a. In the fundamental analyst's model, the importance of a dividend policy lies in its implications for future earnings growth and the justified P–E ratio that depends so heavily on future earnings growth.

   b. Managers may try to signal information regarding their firm's growth prospects by the dividend policy.

      (1) An increasing dividend payout ratio may signal an end to a period of rapid growth and internal expansion.

      (2) A decrease in the dividend payout ratio may signal the beginning of a period of growth and expansion, or management's fear that it will not be able to sustain a high dividend in the future.

   c. In general, firms with high dividend payout ratios tend to have low P–E ratios.

3. When firms use debt as a source of financing, the fixed payments that must be made on the debt gives rise to **financial leverage.**

   a. The use of debt has two important effects on the justified P–E ratio.

      (1) The first effect arises from the tax deductibility of interest payments, which may convey a real advantage to a firm with some debt in its capital structure.

      (2) The second effect arises from the fact that a firm may use debt to increase its EPS, assuming that it has positive earnings.

   b. Financial leverage may convey real benefits to shareholders if the tax savings outweigh the increase in risk.

   c. Other things equal, if two firms are alike except that one has no debt, the no–debt firm should have a higher P–E ratio since it has unused debt capacity that it could tap to increase assets and earnings later.

   d. **Debt capacity** refers to the amount of debt financing a firm can safely use.

   e. These considerations mean that the justified P–E ratio depends to some extent on the amount of leverage that is being used.

4. **Notes to the financial statements** contain much relevant information for the financial analyst. For example, pending litigation and unfunded pension fund liabilities are disclosed in note form.

   a. As a result of prior abuses, firms must now report their EPS figures on a **fully diluted basis**, which is calculated by assuming that all securities that could be converted into common stock are already converted.

    b. **Unfunded pension liabilities** can be quite large for some firms and thus have an impact on their earnings growth and their justified P–E ratios.

C. Justified P–E Ratios and Managerial Style

    1. Public Perception and Investment Value

        a. Overall investor perceptions about the admirability of firms will clearly have an impact on their investment decision.

        b. General perception of firms is tied to more specific factors, such as management quality.

    2. Management Quality

        a. Managers of corporations are important because they make all of the key decisions about the way in which the assets of a corporation are to be deployed, about the lines of business that will be pursued and abandoned, about the financial structure of the firm, and about the utilization and development of personnel.

        b. Management quality is hard to assess, particularly for the outside investor.

        c. Readers of the financial press can at least become acquainted with the personalities and major plans of major corporate leaders, but the situation is more difficult for smaller firms.

        d. For professional analysts, one of the key means of assessing management quality is attending company presentations and visiting the facilities of the corporation.

        e. The larger brokerage houses assign analysts to research and visit particular companies to acquire information.

        f. The separation between ownership and management can lead to **agency problems**—a situation that arises when the agent (corporate manager) does not act in the interest of the principal (shareholders).

            (1) The CEO of a corporation may pack the board of directors with cronies and arrange outlandish compensation.

            (2) Also, top executives might arrange tremendous perquisites for themselves to the detriment of the shareholders.

    3. Reputation for Quality of Products or Services
Corporate reputations for the quality of their products and services can also be an important influence on the investment prospects of a particular firm.

    4. Innovation—Research and Development

        a. Firms may view a changing environment as providing an opportunity or as posing a threat.

        b. In terms of the industry life cycle, the best opportunities are likely to be found in emerging industries.

    5. Social Responsibility

        a. In recent years, the social responsibility of corporations has also become increasingly important for investors.

      b. Socially responsible firms are concerned about the health of their customers and the well–being of the environment. This improves reputation and may avoid expensive litigation in the future.

  D. Justified P–E Ratios and Special Firm Characteristics

      1. There are a number of essentially financial factors that influence the firm and its justified P–E ratio that are not within the direct control of management, or that cannot be altered within a short period of time.

      2. These factors are often associated with the point occupied by the firm and industry in the life cycle and also depend on the nature of the business in which the firm is engaged.

      3. Small Capitalization Firms

         a. Smaller firms tend to have greater rates of earnings growth than do larger firms because small firms tend to be in new industries where the growth opportunities are naturally greater.

         b. As firms get larger, they tend to diversify into other product lines in addition to those that made them successful. One result is limited growth since the growth of the whole firm will depend on the growth of the parts and the relationship among the success rates for the different sectors.

      4. Merger Potential

         a. Firms that are acquired tend to experience statistically significant price increases, which become very large if two or more buyers begin to compete to acquire a given firm.

         b. Attributes that make a company attractive as a takeover target include a large pool of liquid assets or a large pool of temporarily undervalued assets.

Key Terms and Concepts

accounting earnings	earnings measured according to generally accepted accounting rules
agency problems	a situation that arises when the agent (corporate manager) does not act in the interest of the principal (shareholders)
convertible debt	bonds that may be turned in for stock at the option of the holder
debt capacity	the amount of debt a firm may safely use
dividend policy	the managerial decision regarding how to split each year's earnings between dividends paid to shareholders and earnings retained for investment in the firm

earnings per share	also EPS; net income/number of shares
economic earnings	the change in purchasing power earned by a firm in a given period
financial leverage	a product of the use of debt financing and its fixed payments
first in, first out	also FIFO; an inventory valuation method that assumes the oldest units in inventory are used first, which may understate the cost of production and overstate earnings in times of rising prices
fully diluted EPS	calculating earnings per share assuming that all securities that could be converted into common equity have been converted
Fundamental Analyst's Model	a stock valuation model that argues that the true, intrinsic, value of a share is equal to the expected earnings multiplied by the justified P–E ratio
justified P–E ratio	the correct ratio of share price to current earnings that reflects both the firm's future growth prospects and the level of risk associated with future earnings
last in, first out	also LIFO; an inventory valuation model which assumes that the latest units purchased are used in production, and provides a conservative estimate of accounting earnings in times of rising prices
management quality	the intelligence, foresight, and people skills exhibited by a firm's managers
merger potential	the chance that a firm will be acquired by another firm
notes to financial statements	additional information relevant to the firm's future that is disclosed in written form in the annual report
percentage of revenue technique	an earnings forecasting technique that assumes that earnings will remain at the historical percentage of sales

small firms

new firms, often in growth industries, that have tended to outperform larger firms

trend analysis

an earnings forecasting technique that extrapolates past growth linearly into the future

unfunded pension liabilities

pension fund obligations that have not yet been contributed by the firm

Multiple-Choice Questions

1. _____ assumes that historical growth rates can be extrapolated into the future.
   A. Judgmental forecasts
   B. Trend analysis
   C. Ratio analysis
   D. Full dilution
   E. The Fundamental Analyst's Model

2. The Fundamental Analyst's Model makes a distinction between _____ because it is a technique designed to find discrepancies between the two.
   A. revenue and earnings
   B. profit and revenue
   C. price and intrinsic value
   D. accounting and economic earnings
   E. nominal and real earnings

3. Unfunded pension fund liabilities and pending litigation are often disclosed in the _____.
   A. earnings per share calculation
   B. income statement
   C. balance sheet
   D. notes to financial statements
   E. fed regulation reports

4. The inventory valuation model that overstates earnings if prices are rising is _____.
   A. first in, first out
   B. intrinsic valuation
   C. economic valuation
   D. justified valuation
   E. last in, first out

5. The change in purchasing power earned by the firm in a given period represents its ____ earnings.
   A. accounting
   B. economic
   C. statistical
   D. monetary
   E. nominal

6. The amount of borrowing a firm can safely undertake is its ____.
   A. debt capacity
   B. intrinsic value
   C. economic leverage
   D. unfunded liability
   E. merger potential

7. If a firm has $250,000 in earnings, 100,000 common shares outstanding, convertible bonds that can be turned in for 20,000 shares, and convertible preferred that can be turned in for 5,000 shares, its fully diluted earnings per share is $____.
   A.   2.00
   B.   2.08
   C.   2.38
   D.   2.50
   E.   10.00

8. Financial leverage may benefit shareholders because it ____.
   A. smooths the earnings stream when sales are volatile
   B. increases the payout ratio
   C. lowers the P–E ratio
   D. insures that all possible equity sources are included in the earnings per share calculation
   E. is subsidized by the Federal government through the Internal Revenue Code

9. Which of the following statements regarding small firms is *false*?
   A. They tend to dominate mature industries.
   B. They tend to outperform larger firms.
   C. They tend to concentrate in one industry.
   D. They tend to have more volatile earnings growth than larger firms.
   E. They tend to be riskier than large firms.

20. The chance that one firm will be acquired by another firm is reflected in its ____.
    A. percentage of revenue forecast
    B. trend analysis forecast
    C. management quality
    D. unfunded pension liabilities
    E. merger potential

21. Which of the following is *not* required for the successful application of the Fundamental Analyst's Model?
    A. an estimate of the justified P/E ratio
    B. an estimate of the firm's expected earnings
    C. a share price equal to its intrinsic value
    D. assessing the intrinsic value before the rest of the market does
    E. market recognition of the intrinsic value calculated

22. Which of the following is *not* a component of managerial style?
    A. leverage
    B. public perception
    C. innovation—R&D
    D. reputation
    E. social responsibility

23. Which of the following statements about merger potential is *false*?
    A. Prices paid for acquired firms tend to increase as the number of bidders rises.
    B. Acquired firms tend to exhibit statistically significant price increases.
    C. Firms with large liquid asset balances are seldom targets.
    D. Merger activity has industry–specific characteristics.
    E. Merger potential is greater for small firms, because they are easier to acquire.

24. In general, if the estimated value _____ the market price, buy the stock.
    A. is less than
    B. is comparable to
    C. is greater than
    D. is analogous to
    E. compensates for

25. If a firm raises its dividend payout ratio, this suggests that _____.
    A. it is in a growth industry
    B. its earnings per share have been fully diluted
    C. its management is not socially responsible
    D. its managers possibly foresee slower growth
    E. its economic earnings are low

Answers

Multiple–Choice Questions

1. B	10. C	19. D
2. C	11. D	20. E
3. D	12. E	21. C
4. A	13. B	22. A
5. B	14. E	23. C
6. A	15. C	24. C
7. A	16. A	25. D
8. E	17. D	
9. A	18. C	

CHAPTER THIRTEEN

Diversification and Portfolio Formation

Chapter Objectives

Upon completion of this chapter, you should be able to:

1. Explain the simplifying assumptions that underlie portfolio theory.
2. Explain and give examples of dominance.
3. Calculate the covariance and the correlation between the returns on two assets.
4. Calculate the expected return, variance, and standard deviation of a two–asset or three–asset portfolio.
5. Discuss the effect of positive or negative correlation across security returns.
6. Find the proper allocation of funds between two assets to create a zero–risk portfolio when the returns on the assets are perfectly negatively correlated.
7. Explain how the efficient set and the efficient frontier are created through portfolio diversification.
8. Discuss how the number of securities in the portfolio affects portfolio risk under naive diversification.
9. Discuss how investors' preferences, represented by the slope of their indifference curves, determine the optimal point on the efficient frontier.
10. Distinguish between, and draw indifference curves for, risk tolerant, risk averse, risk neutral, and risk abhorrent investors.

Chapter Outline

I. Overview

A. A **portfolio** is a collection of securities held by a single investor, whether an individual or institution.
B. One of the main incentives for forming portfolios is **diversification**, which is the allocation of investable funds to a variety of assets.

    C. By diversifying, investors reduce the risk that they would otherwise bear.

II. Assumptions of the Analysis

    A. A **perfect market** is a market without any impediments to trading, such as transaction costs or costly information.

    B. The Assumptions
        1. Securities markets operate with no transaction costs.
        2. All investors have free access to the complete body of information about securities and everything relevant to the pricing of securities.
        3. All investors appraise this information in a similar way; that is, they have **homogeneous expectations**—they expect the same risk and return for securities.
        4. Investors are interested only in the risk and expected return characteristics of securities. They seek securities with higher expected returns and try to avoid risk.
        5. All investors in the marketplace have the same one–period time horizon.

    C. The Role of the Assumptions
        1. While most of the assumptions are not literally true, they serve as a close approximation of the truth, and greatly simplify analysis.
        2. The strictness of the assumptions is necessary mainly to allow mathematical precision; relaxing the assumptions has the principal effect of making the mathematics much more complicated, but the basic ideas do not change.

III. Risk/Expected Return Space

    A. Risk/Expected Return Axes
        1. An investor considering Security B (low–risk, low expected return) and Security A (high–risk, high expected return) faces a "risk/expected return trade–off."
        2. This trade–off stems from the fact that the expected return of A is greater than that of B, but to get the higher expected return, the investor must also be willing to accept the greater risk of Security A. Therefore, one must sacrifice higher expected return to obtain lower risk, or vice versa.

    B. The Concept of Dominance
        1. When an investor has investment opportunities in which this risk/return trade–off is not confronted, one investment opportunity "dominates" the other.
        2. In establishing a definition of **dominance**, one security dominates another if it meets at least one of the following three conditions.
            a. If one security offers greater expected return, but the same risk as another security, the first security dominates the second.

      b. If one security offers the same expected return, but lower risk than another security, the first security dominates the second.

      c. If one security offers greater expected return and lower risk than another security, the first security dominates the second.

3. Sometimes, it is not possible to say in advance that all investors would prefer one security to another. Their preferences would depend on their willingness to accept additional risk in order to capture additional expected returns.

IV. *Two–Asset Risky Portfolios*

A. A two–asset risky portfolio is just that—a portfolio made up of two risky assets.

B. Expected Return of a Two–Asset Risky Portfolio

    1. The expected return on a two–asset portfolio depends on the expected returns of the individual assets and their relative weight or percentage of funds invested in each.

    2. The expected return of a two–asset portfolio is given by the following, where the two assets are Asset i and Asset j:

$$E(R_p) = W_i E(R_i) + W_j E(R_j)$$

    3. The expected return is a simple weighted average of the expected returns of the individual assets. The individual weights must sum to one because the two assets make up the entire portfolio.

C. The Risk of a Two–Asset Portfolio

    1. The risk of a portfolio can be measured by the variance or standard deviation of returns. The riskiness of a portfolio depends on the tendency of the returns of the assets in the portfolio to move together. Mathematically, this tendency can be measured by the covariance of returns.

    2. Definition of Variance

$$\sigma_p^2 = W_i^2 \sigma_i^2 + W_j^2 \sigma_j^2 + 2W_i W_j \sigma_{i,j}$$

      a. To calculate the variance of a two–asset portfolio, we need to know the proportion of funds committed to each asset, the variance or standard deviation of each asset, and the covariance between the returns of the two assets.

    3. Definition of Covariance

$$\sigma_{i,j} = \frac{\displaystyle\sum_{t=1}^{T} [R_{i,t} - E(R_i)][R_{j,t} - E(R_j)]}{T}$$

4. Calculating the Covariance
   The covariance between the returns of two assets is calculated by summing the products of the differences of the actual return from the expected return for each security at each point in time over all time periods and dividing the sum by the number of time periods.

5. Calculating the Standard Deviation
   To find the Standard Deviation, take the square root of the variance:

$$\sigma_p = \sqrt{\sigma_p^2}$$

6. The Correlation Coefficient
   a. The risk measures for portfolios can also be expressed using the correlation coefficient instead of the covariance.
   b. The correlation coefficient is calculated by the following formula:

$$\rho_{a,b} = \frac{\sigma_{a,b}}{\sigma_a \sigma_b}$$

   c. The correlation is essentially a scaled covariance measure. The correlation coefficient should fall between -1 and $+1$.
   d. A correlation coefficient that exceeds 0 indicates that the returns on the two assets tend to move together over time.
   e. A correlation coefficient that is less than 0 indicates that the returns on the two assets tend to move in opposite directions over time.
   f. A correlation coefficient of 0 indicates that the returns on the securities move independently of one another over time.

V. Risk, Covariance, and Correlation

A. In portfolio building, one of the greatest factors affecting the risk of any portfolio is the covariance or correlation among the individual assets comprising the portfolio.

B. Correlation = $+1.0$
   1. The formula for the variance of a two–asset portfolio using the correlation coefficient is:

$$\sigma_p^2 = W_i^2 \sigma_i^2 + W_j^2 \sigma_j^2 + 2W_i W_j \rho_{i,j} \sigma_i \sigma_j$$

   2. From this formula, if the correlation coefficient equals 1, the last term can be simplified, and the expression for the variance becomes a perfect square which we can take the square root of to obtain the formula:

$$\sigma_p = W_i \sigma_i + W_j \sigma_j$$

   3. In the special case of the correlation equaling 1, the risk of the portfolio depends only on the risk of the individual assets and on the weight that they represent in the portfolio.

C. Correlation = –1.0
   1. If the correlation coefficient equals –1, the last term can again be simplified, creating an expression for variance that is a perfect square. We take the square root of the variance formula to obtain almost the same standard deviation formula as when correlation equalled 1.0, except now the second term has a negative sign:

$$\sigma_p = W_i\sigma_i - W_j\sigma_j$$

   2. As the text illustrates, whenever two assets have a perfectly negative correlation, it is possible to form a riskless portfolio.
D. Correlation Between –1 and +1
   1. Because the correlation must lie within the –1 to +1 range, these two extremes define the entire realm of possibilities for risk/return combinations that can be formed for two securities.
   2. Typical Correlations Between Securities
      a. For the vast majority of security pairs, the correlation of returns between them lies at neither extreme of +1 or –1.
      b. Most securities are positively correlated with each other.
      c. The lower the correlation between securities, the greater the amount of curvature in the line indicating the portfolio possibilities. As such, any decrease in correlation benefits the investor.

VI. An Intuitive Approach to Multiple Risky Assets

A. Treating Portfolios as Single Assets
   For purposes of analyzing risk and expected return characteristics, we can treat a portfolio as a single asset.
B. How Portfolios Dominate Single Assets
   1. The process of creating new portfolios out of individual assets and other portfolios that were previously created has two interesting results (see Figure 13.9 in the text).
      a. First, some of the new portfolios can dominate the individual assets and some other portfolios.
      b. Also, this process does not go on forever, but stops when the curved line from Asset 1 to Asset 3 is reached.
C. The Minimum Risk Portfolio
   Given the initial set of only three assets, there are limits to what can be achieved through diversification.

VII. Risk and Expected Return of Multiple–Asset Portfolios

A. All of the basic ideas introduced in the context of two–asset portfolios hold when investors are allowed to construct portfolios of many assets.
B. Computing Risk and Expected Return for Multi–Asset Portfolios
   1. In general, the expected return for a multiple–asset risky portfolio is:

$$E(R_p) = \sum_{i=1}^{n} W_i E(R_i)$$

2. The variance of a multi–asset portfolio is given by:

$$\sigma_p^2 = \sum_{i=1}^{n} \sum_{j=1}^{n} W_i W_j \sigma_{i,j}$$

C. A Sample Calculation
1. The correlation and variance–covariance matrices show the correlation between all possible pairs of assets in a given set.
    a. The correlation of each asset with itself is 1.0.
    b. The returns of assets are perfectly correlated with themselves.
    c. In the variance–covariance matrix, the variance terms lie on the **main diagonal**—the diagonal running from the northwest to southeast.
2. Computing the Expected Return
    The expected return of a three–asset portfolio is:

$$E(R_p) = W_i E(R_i) + W_j E(R_j) + W_k E(R_k)$$

VIII. The Efficient Set and the Efficient Frontier

A. Within the risk/return space, the **efficient set** is the set of all assets and portfolios that are not dominated.
B. The **efficient frontier** is the graphical representation of the elements of the efficient set.
C. Investors who desire higher expected returns and wish to avoid risk will want to invest in portfolios that are members of the efficient set.

IX. The Dramatic Effects of Diversification

A. To examine the effects of diversification, a study considered the risk of portfolios with increasing numbers of randomly selected securities, starting with one–stock portfolios and observing the change in the risk level of the portfolios as additional stocks were added, one stock at a time.
B. Portfolios with the highest average risk level were the one–stock portfolios. The two–stock portfolios had lower risk, and so on to the twenty–stock portfolios, which had the lowest average risk.
C. A twenty–stock portfolio had about 40 percent less risk than a one–stock portfolio.
D. The process of choosing stocks at random to construct a portfolio is called **naive diversification**. This was the technique used in the Wagner and Lau study.

E. A more sophisticated technique of diversification (utilizing certain mathematical programming techniques) is called **Markowitz diversification**, after its creator. Markowitz diversification is designed to find portfolios on the efficient frontier.

X. International Diversification

A. Solnik found that the U.S. investor can diversify away about 60 percent of the risk in a typical single stock by holding a portfolio of about 30 stocks. By contrast, a Belgian investor can diversify away about 73 percent of risk.
B. In terms of diversifying internationally, the benefits differ from one country to another.
  1. Because so many large U.S. corporations have extensive foreign operations, the U.S. market is already internationally diversified in many ways.
  2. However, an investor in a small country with a stock market that is not very well diversified can achieve even greater benefits by diversifying internationally.

XI. Investors' Preferences

A. Although we have assumed investors prefer higher expected returns and wish to avoid risk, the desire for returns and the abhorrence of risk differ from investor to investor.
B. Because investor psychology differs from person to person, we must consider the individual investor's preferences to know what kind of portfolio he or she would like to have.
C. Each investor may have his or her own special preferences regarding risk and return—yet he or she will always prefer one of the portfolios on the efficient frontier.
D. Indifference Curves
  1. For each investor, there is a set of curves representing different levels of satisfaction or utility.
  2. These **indifference curves** express the trade–off between risk and expected return for a particular investor.
  3. The investor is indifferent among all of the points that lie on a particular indifference curve.
E. Combining Investors' Preferences with the Opportunity Set
  1. Investors always want to attain the highest possible indifference curve available in a set.
  2. This occurs where an investor's indifference curve is just tangent to the efficient frontier.
  3. The steeper the slope of an investor's indifference curve, the greater his or her risk aversion. The flatter the slope, the more risk tolerance the investor exhibits.

    F. The Range of Investors' Preferences
        1. A horizontal indifference curve indicates that an investor is risk neutral (complete concern with expected return), while a vertical indifference curve reflects total concern with risk.
        2. As long as the indifference curve is curved, there is some trade–off between risk and return.

Key Terms and Concepts

correlation coefficient	a mathematical representation of the degree to which returns on two securities vary together over time, with a maximum value of +1 (perfect positive correlation) and a minimum value of –1 (perfect negative correlation)
covariance	a mathematical representation of the degree to which the returns on two assets move together over time; because this measure is not bounded, it may turn out to be any number, however large or small
diversification	the allocation of investable funds to a variety of securities with different risk/expected return characteristics
dominance	the absolute superiority of one portfolio over another in the risk/expected return space
efficient frontier	the graphical representation of the elements of the efficient set
efficient set	the set of all assets and portfolios that are not dominated in the risk/expected return space
homogeneous expectations	the assumption that in securities markets, all investors appraise relevant information in a similar way
indifference curve	the set of all points in the risk/expected return space that give an individual investor the same level of satisfaction
main diagonal	in the variance/covariance matrix, the elements that lie on the diagonal line running from northwest to southeast

Markowitz diversification	selecting a portfolio on the efficient frontier through mathematical programming techniques
naive diversification	diversification by the random selection of securities
perfect market	a market without any impediments to trading, such as transaction costs or costly information
portfolio	a collection of securities held by a single investor
risk abhorrence	reflects a total concern with risk, evidenced by a vertical indifference curve
risk aversion	requiring an increase in expected return to accept an increase in risk, represented by an indifference curve whose slope is steeper than horizontal
risk/expected return space	a graph with risk on the horizontal axis and expected return on the vertical axis where the efficient frontier and an individual investor's indifference curves are plotted
risk neutrality	represents an indifference to risk and total concern with expected return, evidenced by a horizontal indifference curve
risk tolerance	the willingness to accept a large increase in risk for a small increase in expected return, evidenced by a relatively flat indifference curve

Multiple–Choice Questions

1. Naive diversification ____.
   A. allocates investable funds randomly to a variety of securities
   B. increases risk and expected return
   C. uses mathematical programming techniques to create portfolios on the efficient frontier
   D. allocates funds to a variety of securities with the same risk/expected return characteristics
   E. increases the level of risk that investors bear

2. Portfolio theory makes certain simplifying assumptions about the way in which markets operate. Which of the following is *not* one of those assumptions?
    A. All investors prefer greater expected return and less risk.
    B. All investors have free access to the complete body of information relevant to the pricing of securities.
    C. All investors appraise the available information in a similar way.
    D. Investors are interested only in the risk and expected return characteristics of securities.
    E. Transactions costs are negatively related to the size of the portfolio.

3. An investor with a horizontal indifference curve is risk ____.
    A. averse
    B. neutral
    C. diversified
    D. tolerant
    E. abhorrent

4. Dominance occurs when one security has ____ another security.
    A. higher risk and a higher expected return than
    B. the same risk and the same expected return as
    C. the same expected return and less risk than
    D. lower risk and a higher expected return than
    E. C & D

5. In a two–asset portfolio, the correlation coefficient measures the ____.
    A. size of the potential benefits from diversifying between the two assets
    B. degree of risk aversion exhibited by the average investor
    C. increase in expected return available from using Markowitz diversification instead of naive diversification
    D. impact of adding another randomly selected stock to the portfolio
    E. dominance of one security over the other

6. A risk tolerant investor is ____.
    A. not interested in the benefits of diversification
    B. willing to accept a large increase in risk for a small increase in expected return
    C. concerned only with risk
    D. concerned only with expected return
    E. an investor with a vertical indifference curve

7. If the returns on two stocks are perfectly negatively correlated, ____.
    A. diversification will not increase expected return or lower risk
    B. Markowitz diversification will outperform naive diversification
    C. the efficient frontier is horizontal
    D. it is possible to construct a portfolio with zero risk
    E. the indifference curve of the average investor is horizontal

8. Which of the following is *not* required to compute the standard deviation of a two–asset portfolio?
   A. the amount invested in each stock
   B. the expected return on a risk–free asset
   C. the standard deviation of the returns on each stock
   D. the correlation between the returns on each stock
   E. the variance in returns on each stock

9. If you invest 20 percent of your holdings in a security with an expected return of 10 percent and the remainder in a security with an expected return of 16 percent, the expected return on your portfolio is ____ percent.
   A. 2.0
   B. 8.0
   C. 11.2
   D. 12.8
   E. 14.8

10. If Security A has an expected return of 10 percent and Security B has an expected return of 15 percent, how should you weight your holdings to get an expected return of 12 percent?
   A. 20 percent in A, 80 percent in B
   B. 40 percent in A, 60 percent in B
   C. 50 percent in A, 50 percent in B
   D. 60 percent in A, 40 percent in B
   E. 80 percent in A, 20 percent in B

11. What is the correlation coefficient between the returns on Assets A and B if the standard deviation of returns for Asset A is .08, the standard deviation of returns for Asset B is .12, and the covariance between the returns on Assets A and B is .004?
   A. .020
   B. .033
   C. .417
   D. .050
   E. .072

12. Covariance and the correlation coefficient differ in that the correlation coefficient ____.
   A. depends on the expected return
   B. can never be negative
   C. is calculated at a point in time based on historical data
   D. is essentially a scaled covariance that must lie between +1 and −1
   E. increases exponentially as the number of assets in the portfolio increases

13. The standard deviation of Assets A and B are 15 percent and 17 percent respectively. If the correlation coefficient between the two assets is .8, the covariance is ____.
   A. .1024
   B. .2358
   C. .0204
   D. +1
   E. −1

14. You have a portfolio of two assets that are perfectly negatively correlated. You have 70 percent of your funds invested in Asset A, which has a standard deviation of .05. Asset B has a standard deviation of .02. What is the standard deviation of the portfolio?
   A. .0205
   B. .0290
   C. .0410
   D. .0820
   E. .4300

15. From the information in Question 14, you must invest ____ percent of your funds in Asset A to create a risk–free portfolio.
   A. 20.0
   B. 28.6
   C. 40.0
   D. 60.0
   E. 71.4

16. The allocation of funds to securities with different risk/expected return characteristics is known as ____.
   A. the correlation coefficient
   B. diversification
   C. dominance
   D. the efficient frontier
   E. the indifference curve

17. The scaled statistic which represents the degree to which returns on two securities vary together over time is known as ____.
   A. the correlation coefficient
   B. diversification
   C. dominance
   D. the efficient frontier
   E. the indifference curve

18. The trade–off between risk and expected return exhibited by a particular investor appears in ____.
    A. the correlation coefficient
    B. diversification
    C. dominance
    D. the efficient frontier
    E. the indifference curve

19. All non–dominated portfolios in the risk/expected return space rest on the ____.
    A. correlation coefficient
    B. diversification quotient
    C. dominance coefficient
    D. efficient frontier
    E. indifference curve

20. Selecting a portfolio on the efficient frontier by using mathematical programming techniques is a technique of ____ diversification.
    A. naive
    B. Markowitz
    C. risk abhorrent
    D. utility
    E. risk neutrality

21. The satisfaction an investor derives from an investment with a given set of risk/expected return characteristics is known as ____.
    A. indifference
    B. Markowitz pleasure
    C. risk abhorrence
    D. utility
    E. risk neutrality

22. Investors with vertical indifference curves exhibit ____.
    A. naivety
    B. Markowitz pleasure
    C. total concern with risk
    D. utility
    E. risk neutrality

23. Investors with relatively flat indifference curves exhibit ____.
    A. naive diversification
    B. Markowitz pleasure
    C. risk abhorrence
    D. utility
    E. risk tolerance

24. If you invest 40 percent of your holdings in a security with an expected return of 8 percent and the remainder in a security with a expected return of 12 percent, the expected return on your portfolio is ___ percent.
    A.   3.2
    B.   4.8
    C.   7.2
    D.   9.6
    E.   10.4

25. If Security A has an expected return of 5 percent and Security B has an expected return of 10 percent, how should you weight your holdings to create a portfolio with an expected return of 8 percent?
    A.   20 percent in A, 80 percent in B
    B.   40 percent in A, 60 percent in B
    C.   50 percent in A, 50 percent in B
    D.   60 percent in A, 40 percent in B
    E.   80 percent in A, 20 percent in B

Review Problems

1. You are trading in a market that has only two securities available. Security A has an expected return of 8 percent and a standard deviation of 40 percent. Security B has an expected return of 20 percent and a standard deviation of 120 percent.
    a. If you place half of your money in each stock, what is your expected return?
    b. If you place 40 percent of your money in A and the remaining 60 percent in B, what is your expected return?
    c. How should you weight your holdings to get an expected return of 10 percent?
2. If the correlation between the returns of Securities A and B (in Problem 1) is .8, what is the variance and the standard deviation of the returns of each of the three portfolios you found in Problem 1?
3. Do any of the three portfolios in Problem 1 dominate each other, or the investment of holding either security in isolation? Why or why not?
4. You are trading in a market that has only two securities. Security C has an expected return of 6 percent and a standard deviation of 2.5 percent. Security D has an expected return of 15 percent and a standard deviation of 8 percent. The correlation between the returns on the two securities is –1.
    a. How would you weight the holdings of the two securities to develop a portfolio that has zero risk?
    b. What is this portfolio's expected return?
    c. Does this portfolio dominate holding either of the securities alone? Why or why not?

5. You are considering investing in two securities and have accumulated the following information:

Year	Actual Return on Security E	Actual Return on Security F
1991	13%	1%
1992	–6%	4%
1993	2%	1%

    a. Does the historical return pattern exhibited by these two securities conform to the risk/expected return trade–off? Why or why not?

    b. Calculate the correlation between the two security returns and the variance and standard deviation of a portfolio that invests 40 percent of its funds in Security E and 60 percent of its funds in Security F.

    c. Show mathematically that diversification benefits the investor in this portfolio.

Answers

Multiple–Choice Questions

1. A	10. D	19. D
2. E	11. C	20. B
3. B	12. D	21. D
4. E	13. C	22. C
5. A	14. B	23. E
6. B	15. B	24. E
7. D	16. B	25. B
8. B	17. A	
9. E	18. E	

Review Problems

1. The expected return on any portfolio depends on the percentage invested in each stock and the expected return of the stock:

    a. $.5(.08) + .5(.20) = .04 + .10 = .14$ or 14 percent.

    b. $.4(.08) + .6(.20) = .032 + .12 = .152$ or 15.2 percent.

    Notice that the weights add to 1 since these two securities are the only two choices. Also, the expected return increases as the percentage invested in the security with the higher expected return increases.

c.   Given that the weights must add to 1, we want to find x such that:

$$xE(R_A) + (1 - x)E(R_B) = \text{Desired Return, or}$$

$$x(.08) + (1 - x)(.20) = .10. \text{ Simplifying,}$$

$$.08x + .20 - .20x = .10, \text{ or } -.12x = -.10, \text{ so}$$

$$x = .10/.12 = .83 \text{ in Security A and the remaining } .17 \text{ in Security B.}$$

2.   The problem provides almost all of the information necessary to solve the formula for the variance of a portfolio of imperfectly correlated assets:

$$\sigma^2_p = W_A^2\sigma^2_A + W_B^2\sigma^2_B + 2W_AW_B\sigma_A\sigma_B CORR_{A,B}$$

You must remember that the variance of a security's return is the square of the standard deviation, so:

$$\sigma^2_A = (.4)^2 = .16 \text{ and } \sigma^2_B = (1.2)^2 = 1.44$$

For the equally weighted portfolio:

$$\sigma^2_p = (.5)^2(.16) + (.5)^2(1.44) + 2(.5)(.5)(.4)(1.2)(.8)$$

$$= (.25)(.16) + (.25)(1.44) + 2(.5)(.5)(.4)(1.2)(.8)$$

$$= .04 + .36 + .192 = .592$$

$$\sigma_p = (.592)^{.5} = .769 = 76.9 \text{ percent.}$$

Calculating the variances for the other portfolios merely requires changing the weights.

For the 40 percent, 60 percent portfolio:

$$\sigma^2_p = (.4)^2(.16) + (.6)^2(1.44) + 2(.4)(.6)(.4)(1.2)(.8)$$

$$= .0256 + .5184 + .1843 = .7283$$

$$\sigma_p = (.7283)^{1/2} = .853 = 85.3 \text{ percent.}$$

For the 83 percent, 17 percent portfolio:

$$\sigma_p^2 = (.83)^2(.16) + (.17)^2(1.44) + 2(.83)(.17)(.4)(1.2)(.8)$$

$$= .1102 + .0416 + .1084 = .2602$$

$$\sigma_p = (.2602)^{1/2} = .51 = 51 \text{ percent.}$$

3. To determine dominance, list the five possible portfolios in order of their expected return:

Portfolio % in A, % in B	Expected Return	Standard Deviation
100, 0	8.0%	40.0%
83, 17	10.0%	51.0%
50, 50	14.0%	76.9%
40, 60	15.2%	85.3%
0, 100	20.0%	120.0%

The table shows that the standard deviation (the risk measure) increases as the expected return increases. None of the portfolios offers higher expected returns for the same risk, the same expected return for lower risk, or higher expected return and lower risk, so none of the portfolios dominates any of the other portfolios. The choice a particular individual makes among these portfolios, or any of the other infinite number of ways to combine the two stocks, depends upon personal risk/expected return preferences.

4. a. When the returns on two securities are perfectly negatively correlated, the standard deviation of a portfolio composed of the two securities is equal to:

$$\sigma_P = W_C\sigma_C - W_D\sigma_D$$

so we want to find x such that:

$$x(.025) - (1 - x)(.08) = 0, \text{ or } .025x - .08 + .08x = 0.$$

Simplifying:

$$.105x = .08 \text{ or } x = (.08/.105) = .76.$$

Invest 76 percent of the holdings in Security C and the remaining 24 percent in Security D.

b. The expected return on this portfolio is:

$$ER_P = .76(.06) + .24(.15) = 8.16 \text{ percent.}$$

c. The portfolio has a higher return and lower risk than an investment in Security C alone, so it dominates this investment. The portfolio has a lower expected return and lower risk than an investment in Security D alone, so the portfolio does not dominate D.

5. a. To determine if the historical returns on these securities conform to the risk/expected return trade–off, calculate the arithmetic mean return and the standard deviation of the return over the three–year holding period:

Mean Return on E = $(.13 - .06 + .02)/3 = .09/3 = .03$

Mean Return on F = $(.01 + .04 + .01)/3 = .06/3 = .02$

$$\sigma_E^2 = (.13 - .03)^2 + (-.06 - .03)^2 + (.02 - .03)^2$$

$$= (.10)^2 + (-.09)^2 + (-.01)^2$$

$$=.01 + .0081 + .0001 = .0182/3 = .006067$$

$$\sigma_E^2 = (.006067)^{1/2} = .07789$$

$$\sigma_F^2 = (.01 - .02)^2 + (.04 - .02)^2 + (.01 - .02)^2$$

$$= (-.01)^2 + (.02)^2 + (-.01)^2$$

$$= .0001 + .0004 + .0001 =.0006/3 = .0002$$

$$\sigma_F = (.0002)^{1/2} = .014142$$

The historical returns of the two securities conform to the risk/expected re-turn trade–off because E has a larger arithmetic return and a larger standard deviation than F. It is important to remember that the theoretical trade–off is based on expected returns, not actual returns. In this case, however, reality conforms to theory.

b. Computation of the correlation (CORR) requires computation of the covariance, which is a three–step procedure. First, compute the deviation from the mean for each return for each security. If the mathematics are correct, the deviations should sum to 1.

E	F
(.13 − .03) = .10	(.01 − .02) = −.01
(−.06 − .03) = −.09	(.04 − .02) = .02
(.02 − .03) = −.01	(.01 − .02) = −.01
.00	.00

Now, multiply the deviations at each point in time, and sum the products:

$$(.10)(-.01) + (-.09)(.02) + (-.01)(-.01)$$

$$= -.001 - .0018 + .0001 = -.0027$$

Finally, divide the sum by the number of returns to get the covariance:

$$COV_{E,F} = -.0027/3 = -.0009$$

The correlation is equal to the covariance divided by the product of the standard deviations:

$$CORR_{E,F} = (COV_{E,F})/[(\sigma_E)(\sigma_F)], \text{ or}$$

$$-.0009/[(.07789)(.014142)] = -.0009/.001102 = -.8167$$

Then, using the formulas for a portfolio that invests 40 percent in E and 60 percent in F:

$$E(R_P) = .4(.03) + .6(.02) = .012 + .012 = .024$$

$$\sigma_P^2 = (.4)^2(.07789)^2 + (.6)^2(.014142)^2 + 2(.4)(.6)(.07789)(.014142)(-.8167)$$

$$= .00097 + .000072 - .00043 = .000612$$

$$\sigma_P = (.000612)^{1/2} = .02474$$

c. If the returns on the two securities were perfectly positively correlated, the standard deviation of the portfolio would be the weighted average of the two security standard deviations:

$$\sigma_P = .4(.07789) + .6(.014142) = .03116 + .0085 = .04$$

Because the actual correlation is less than one, diversification has reduced the risk associated with a 2.4 percent expected return by $(.04 - .02474) = .015 = 1.5$ percent, benefitting any risk averse investor.

CHAPTER FOURTEEN

The Market Price of Risk

Chapter Objectives

Upon completion of this chapter, you should be able to:

1. Explain the impact of the existence of a risk–free asset on portfolio theory.
2. Explain how an individual investor chooses the best risky portfolio given the ability to borrow and lend at the risk–free rate.
3. Explain how the market portfolio is determined.
4. Explain how the existence of a risk–free asset leads to the separation theorem, and why all investors who choose to hold risky assets will hold the same portfolio of risky assets.
5. Explain how the existence of a risk–free asset expands the portfolio choices of most, but not all, investors.
6. Explain, compare, and contrast the Capital Market Line, the characteristic line, and the Security Market Line.
7. Calculate expected return and risk measures, for portfolios and securities, if the Capital Asset Pricing Model holds and a risk–free asset exists.
8. Explain the concept of partitioning the risk inherent in an individual security.
9. Distinguish between systematic and unsystematic risk and explain how the Capital Asset Pricing Model suggests that investors are compensated for bearing each type of risk.
10. Compare domestic and world market portfolios, and discuss risk measures for foreign markets.
11. Explain the distribution tendencies of beta over time.

Chapter Outline

I. Overview

A. In the idealized world under investigation, this chapter shows how the presence of the risk–free asset greatly increases the investor's opportunities and how it makes virtually all investors better off than they would be in a market with only risky assets.

B. This chapter also shows how the introduction of the risk–free asset gives rise to a market standard against which other investment opportunities can be compared.

C. In addition, we will also examine the **Separation Theorem**, which states that all investors should hold the same portfolio of risky assets, no matter how risk tolerant or risk averse they may be.

D. Finally, the chapter leads to an exposition of the **Capital Asset Pricing Model** (CAPM), a general model that expresses the equilibrium rate of expected return for an asset as a function of its inherent risk characteristics.

II. Introduction of the Risk–Free Asset

A. The risk–free asset has three important features:
 1. It has no default risk.
 2. Its expected return is certain.
 3. The variance of returns for the risk–free asset is zero.

B. Two–Asset Portfolios: A Brief Review
 1. The expected return of a two–asset portfolio is given by:

$$E(R_p) = W_i E(R_i) + W_j E(R_j)$$

 2. Likewise, the original equation for the variance of a two–asset portfolio still holds, and is given by:

$$\sigma_p^2 = W_i^2 \sigma_i^2 + W_j^2 \sigma_j^2 + 2 W_i W_j \sigma_{i,j}$$

C. Expected Return of a Two–Asset Portfolio with a Risk–Free Asset
 The expected return on a two–asset portfolio when one of the assets is risk–free is:

$$E(R_p) = W_f(R_f) + W_j E(R_j)$$

D. Variance of a Two–Asset Portfolio with a Risk–Free Asset
 1. The risk of a two–asset portfolio including R_f will be:

$$\sigma_p^2 = W_j^2 \, \sigma_j^2$$

 2. The standard deviation of the portfolio will be:

$$\sigma_p = W_j \, \sigma_j$$

III. Choosing the Best Risky Portfolio

A. All rational investors will choose the same particular risky portfolio to combine with the risk–free asset.

B. The risk–free asset enriches the investor's choices by creating the opportunity to borrow or lend at the risk–free rate.

C. The effecient frontier will change by the introduction of the risk–free asset.

D. The straight line that slopes upward from the risk–free rate and is just tangent to the efficient frontier dominates all other points on the efficient frontier, including the minimum–risk portfolio, (MR).

E. The point of tangency between the straight line and the efficient frontier is the market portfolio (M).

F. Lending Portfolios

1. Portfolios on the straight line from the risk–free rate to M imply that the investor places some funds in Portfolio M and some funds in the risk–free asset (i.e., lending to the government via the purchase of Treasury bills).

2. Investing in Treasury bills is simply lending to the government, so we may say that portfolios lying between R_f and M are **lending portfolios**, because they involve holding some stock and lending some funds to the government.

G. Borrowing Portfolios

1. The idea of a lending portfolio raises the possibility that there could also be a **borrowing portfolio**, one constructed by borrowing funds and investing the borrowed funds, in addition to the investor's original capital, in some risky portfolio.

2. Due to the assumption of perfect markets, it must be possible to both borrow and lend at the risk–free rate R_f.

3. Not only does borrowing at R_f to invest in a risky portfolio increase the expected return, it also increases the risk.

H. The Effect of Leverage on Risk and Expected Return
The use of borrowing, or **leverage**, increases both the expected returns and the variability of returns.

I. The Efficient Frontier with Borrowing and Lending

1. With the possibility of borrowing and lending added to the picture, some portfolios that were in the efficient set are now dominated.

2. There is only one risky portfolio that is not dominated, Portfolio M.

IV. Investor Utility and the Risk–Free Asset

A. The introduction of the risk–free asset means that virtually every investor in the marketplace can improve his or her position, and investors will be able to reach a higher utility curve than would be possible without the existence of the risk–free asset.

B. The Market Portfolio
 1. All investors who commit any funds to risky securities will invest in Portfolio M.
 2. Portfolio M must be the **market portfolio,** a **value–weighted** combination of every risky security available in the marketplace.
 3. Portfolio M must be the market portfolio because of the following.
  a. Investors hold M as their risky portfolio because they will be better off by doing so.
  b. All securities must be owned by someone.
  c. The only way that all securities can have an owner and all investors can have the same risky portfolio is for each investor to hold the market portfolio of risky securities.
C. The Separation Theorem
 If all investors who hold risky assets hold M, this choice is independent of the chosen position on the line from the risk–free rate to M and beyond. This argument, known as the **separation theorem,** suggests that the investment decision of which risky portfolio to hold is independent of the method (borrowing or lending) chosen to finance that investment.

V. The Capital Market Line

A. The line from the risk–free rate to M and beyond represents the trade–off between risk and expected return available in the market. Hence, it is known as the **Capital Market Line,** (CML).
B. The slope of the CML is the rate of exchange between expected return and risk, and is given by the equation:

$$\text{CML Slope} = \frac{E(R_m) - R_f}{\sigma_m}$$

C. Since the location of any point on a straight line can be determined by adding the line's intercept to the product of the line's slope times the quantity on the x–axis, the expected return on any security (j) that has a standard deviation of returns of SD_j is:

$$E(R_j) = R_f + \sigma_j \left(\frac{E(R_m) - R_f}{\sigma_m} \right)$$

VI. Risk and Expected Returns for Portfolios and Individual Securities

A. The most important feature of the CML is the relationship it expresses between the riskiness of a portfolio and its expected return.

B. One limitation of the CML is that it pertains only to well–diversified portfolios, and it has very little to say about what returns should be expected for individual securities.

C. The **security market line** (SML) expresses a relationship between the expected returns of an individual security (or portfolio) and its level of relevant risk.

D. Investors will be concerned with the risk level of individual securities only to the extent that the individual security contributes to the risk of the market portfolio.

E. The relevant risk of an individual security is that which remains after diversification and is left in the market portfolio. It will be that unavoidable portion of the risk that will be compensated in the market.

F. This measure of risk is called the beta of a security or a portfolio. **Beta** is a measure of the nondiversifiable risk inherent in a security or portfolio.

VII. Beta and the Risk of Individual Securities

A. Beta measures the riskiness of a security or portfolio by examining the correlation between the security or portfolio, on the one hand, and the market portfolio, on the other.

B. For a security or portfolio j, and the market portfolio m, the beta of Security j, β_j, is given by the expression:

$$B_j = \frac{\sigma_{j,m}}{\sigma_m^2} = \frac{\sigma_j}{\sigma_m} \rho_{j,m}$$

C. Beta and the Characteristic Line
   1. The relationship between the returns of an individual security and the returns of the market, which is measured by β, can also be shown graphically.
   2. The **characteristic line** is a line chosen by regression analysis to fit the pattern of dots in the graph in the best way.
   3. The Equation of the Characteristic Line
      The regression equation, or the equation for the characteristic line, is given by the following equation for some security i:

$$R_{i,t} = \alpha_i + \beta_i R_{m,t} + \varepsilon_{i,t}$$

D. Beta as a Measure of Relative Risk
   1. The beta of a security or portfolio is a relative risk measure because it measures risk relative to the market portfolio.
   2. Because the beta of the market portfolio must always be +1, by definition, it provides a standard against which to measure other securities or portfolios.
      a. A security or portfolio that has a beta greater than 1 is **aggressive** because it involves more risk than the market portfolio.

    b. A security or portfolio with a beta less than 1 is **defensive** because it has less risk than the market portfolio.

E. The Partition of Risk
1. The total risk of a security can be divided into two parts.
   a. The portion that depends on movements with the market is known as **market risk, systematic risk,** or **nondiversifiable risk.**
   b. The remainder, which is specific to a security or a portfolio that is not fully diversified, is known as **nonmarket risk, unsystematic risk,** or **diversifiable risk.**
2. Market risk is nondiversifiable risk because this element of risk associated with fluctuations in the market portfolio makes it impossible to eliminate or reduce by diversification.
3. By contrast, nonmarket risk is associated with the unique or special features of a particular security or portfolio that is not fully diversified. Consequently, its risk is nonsystematic—it is not tied to the performance of the market as a whole, and it therefore can be eliminated by proper diversification.
4. The risk level of a portfolio will only be as low as the market risk level when the portfolio is perfectly diversified, and this happens only when it is itself the market portfolio.
5. Portfolios that are not well diversified have nonmarket risk which can be eliminated through diversification.

VIII. *The Expected Return of a Security*

A. One difference between a single security and the fully diversified portfolios lying on the capital market line is the fact that the single security still has diversifiable risk, while the fully diversified portfolio on the CML is free of diversifiable risk. Consequently, the question is whether the nonsystematic diversifiable risk of a single security is compensated for in the marketplace by a greater expected return.
B. In the market described by the capital market theory, additional risk is compensated for by additional expected return; however, only nondiversifiable risk is compensated for because there is no need to reward investors for bearing unnecessary risks.
C. For an individual security, the expected return includes compensation for the passage of time, which is the risk–free rate, plus a reward for bearing systematic risk. The measure of the amount of systematic risk that is undertaken is beta. So, the expected return of an individual security should equal the risk–free rate, plus an additional amount for the bearing of risk.
D. This relationship is expressed by the security market line.

IX. *The Security Market Line*

A. The security market line (SML) expresses the central idea of the Capital Asset Pricing Model (CAPM):

> The expected return of a security depends on the risk–free rate, plus additional compensation for the bearing of systematic risk, as measured by beta.

B. In equalibrium, the expected return of each security or portfolio lies on the SML.

C. The expected return of a Security i can also be expressed as the equation of the SML, which is the basic equation of the CAPM:

$$E(R_i) = R_f + \beta_i [E(R_m) - R_f]$$

D. This equation gives the market risk premium by the term:

$$[E(R_m) - R_f]$$

E. The Capital Market Line and the Security Market Line

    1. The major points of difference between the CML and the SML are as follows.

        a. The risk measure for the CML is the standard deviation, a measure of total risk, while the risk measure for the SML is beta, a measure of systematic risk.

        b. In equilibrium, only fully diversified portfolios lie on the CML, while individual securities plot below the CML. For the SML, all securities and all portfolios fall exactly on the SML in equilibrium.

X. *International Capital Asset Pricing*

A. Domestic versus World Market Portfolios

    1. In theory, it appears that the real market portfolio is a world market portfolio in which all risky assets in the world would be included in proportion to their contribution to total world wealth.

    2. Using only stocks tends to neglect the two greatest categories of world wealth—human capital and real estate.

    3. Part of the reason for restricting attention to just the U.S. stock market has been the belief that capital markets across international boundaries are segmented.

        a. A **segmented market** is a market in which capital cannot move freely from one part of the market to another. This has important implications for investors' abilities to diversify fully.

        b. With segmented markets, the expected return of a security would depend only on the beta of that security when it is measured against the market portfolio from the same country.

    4. If capital markets are strictly segmented, it will be impossible to diversify abroad. However, if capital markets are weakly segmented,

there may be even greater potential gains to international diversification.

B. Risk Measures for Foreign Stock Markets
1. The risk equivalent world portfolio is a portfolio constructed of the world equity portfolio and the risk–free asset in proportions to match the risk of the domestic portfolio.
2. For each of the countries that Lessard studied, there would have been a gain in expected return by holding the world portfolio rather than just the domestic portfolio.
3. There are substantial advantages to be gained from international diversification, and the magnitude of these advantages depends upon the investor's home country.
4. Even though the benefits to the U.S. investor from international diversification are small, they are still significant, as evidenced by a recent strong trend in the U.S. toward international diversification.
5. Both the investor who holds a portfolio of only a few stocks and the investor who diversifies only in the domestic market are earning a lower rate of return than they could achieve by holding the world market portfolio.

XI. Characteristics of Betas

A. Three important conclusions about the distribution of security betas over time can be drawn:
1. Betas tend to change in particular ways over time.
2. Despite this tendency, the distribution of betas is remarkably stationary.
3. Therefore, one can draw conclusions about the way a particular beta may change over time.
B. Specifically:
1. Betas tend to move closer to the mean of all betas, namely, 1.0.
2. Betas that are close to 1.0 at a point in time tend to move away from 1.0 at the next point in time.

Key Terms and Concepts

aggressive portfolio	a portfolio whose beta exceeds 1, indicating a higher risk level than the market portfolio
alpha	the vertical intercept of a line
beta	a measure of the volatility of a security's returns relative to that of the market portfolio, or the measure of a security's systematic risk

borrowing portfolio	a portfolio created by borrowing at the risk–free rate and investing the borrowed funds and the original endowment in the market portfolio
Capital Asset Pricing Model (CAPM)	a general model that expresses the equilibrium rate of expected return for an asset as a function of its inherent risk characteristics
Capital Market Line	a straight, upward–sloping line that expresses the risk/expected return trade–off available in the capital market, when risk is measured as standard deviation
characteristic line	a line chosen by regression analysis to fit the pattern of dots in the graph the best way
defensive portfolio	a portfolio whose beta is less than 1, indicating a lower risk level than the market portfolio
lending portfolio	a portfolio created by investing some funds in the market portfolio and lending some funds to the government by investing in the risk–free asset
leverage	increasing a portfolio's expected return and risk by investing borrowed funds and one's initial funds
market portfolio	the portfolio of risky assets that includes every risky security in the marketplace
market risk	also known as systematic, or nondiversifiable risk; the portion of a security's risk that cannot be avoided by holding a properly diversified portfolio—investors are compensated for bearing market risk via increases in expected return
market risk premium	expressed as the expected return on the market portfolio minus the risk–free rate, or the additional return an investor expects to earn by investing in the market portfolio instead of the risk–free asset
nonmarket risk	also known as nonsystematic, or diversifiable risk; the portion of a security's risk that does not depend on the market because it can be removed by holding a diversified portfolio—investors are not compensated for bearing nonsystematic risk

regression analysis

a statistical method that determines the best linear relationship between two or more variables

risk–free asset

an asset that has no default risk and no variance in returns over a one–period horizon

Security Market Line

a straight, upward–sloping line that displays the relationship between the expected returns on securities and the systematic risk of those securities

separation theorem

states that all investors should hold the same portfolio of risky assets, no matter how risk tolerant or risk averse they may be

slope of a line

the change in the vertical distance divided by the change in the horizontal distance

value–weighted portfolio

a portfolio where the percentage of funds invested in each asset is determined by the ratio of the market value of the asset to the value of all assets in the market

Multiple–Choice Questions

1. The argument that all investors who hold risky assets will hold the market portfolio, no matter whether they are borrowers or lenders, is known as the ____ theorem.
   A. diversification
   B. zero beta
   C. separation
   D. naive
   E. aggressive portfolio

2. If the risk–free rate is 12 percent and the expected return on a risky security is 22 percent, the expected return on a two–asset portfolio that holds 20 percent of its funds in the risk–free asset is ____ percent.
   A. 2.4
   B. 4.4
   C. 9.6
   D. 17.6
   E. 20.0

3. If the standard deviation of the risky security's returns is 35 percent, the standard deviation of the portfolio returns in Question 2 is ____ percent.
   A. 7
   B. 14
   C. 21
   D. 28
   E. 35

4. The statistical, linear relationship between the returns on a specific security and the returns on the market portfolio is known as the security's ____.
   A. beta
   B. alpha
   C. correlation coefficient
   D. diversification coefficient
   E. standard deviation

5. The Security Market Line graphs the relationship between the ____.
   A. expected return on a security and the expected return on the market portfolio
   B. expected return on the market portfolio and its standard deviation
   C. expected return on securities and their systematic risk
   D. risk–free rate and the expected return on the market portfolio
   E. risk–free rate and the efficient set

6. If a security has a beta of 1.2 when the risk–free rate is 6 percent and the expected return on the market portfolio is 18 percent, the expected return on the security is ____ percent.
   A. 14.4
   B. 20.4
   C. 21.6
   D. 25.2
   E. 27.6

7. An important difference between the Capital Market Line and the Security Market Line lies in the ____.
   A. direction that the lines slope
   B. units measured on the vertical axis
   C. treatment of the risk–free asset
   D. treatment of stocks with negative betas
   E. risk measure each considers

8. Market risk is also known as _____ risk.
   A. nonsystematic
   B. nondiversifiable
   C. covariance
   D. correlation
   E. defensive

9. If a two–asset portfolio contains investment in the risk–free asset, its standard deviation is equal to the _____.
   A. percentage of funds invested in the risk–free asset times the standard deviation of the returns of the risk–free asset
   B. percentage of funds invested in the risk–free asset times the beta of the risk–free asset
   C. percentage of funds invested in the risky asset times the beta of the risky asset
   D. percentage of funds invested in the risky asset times the standard deviation of the risky asset
   E. percentage of funds invested in the risky asset times the beta of the market portfolio

10. The correlation between the returns on the risk–free asset and the returns on a risky asset is always _____.
    A. 0
    B. –1
    C. +1
    D. the expected return on the market
    E. the standard deviation of the market return

11. An aggressive portfolio would have a beta of _____.
    A. .8
    B. 1
    C. 2
    D. .5
    E. –2

12. The existence of a risk–free asset provides a risk–averse investor with richer portfolio possibilities unless the investor's indifference curve is tangent to the efficient frontier at the _____.
    A. minimum risk portfolio
    B. risk–free asset
    C. origin of the risk/expected return space
    D. market portfolio
    E. beta of the highest return portfolio

13. The slope of the Capital Market Line is equal to the ____.
    A. expected return on the risk–free asset minus the expected return on the market, divided by the standard deviation of the market return
    B. expected return on the market minus the risk–free rate, divided by the standard deviation of the market return
    C. expected return on the market times the standard deviation of the market return, divided by the risk–free rate
    D. expected return on the market times the beta of the market portfolio, divided by the standard deviation of the market return
    E. expected return on the market times the standard deviation of the return on the market, divided by the beta of the market portfolio

14. If the risk–free rate is 10 percent, the expected return on the market is 20 percent, the standard deviation of the market return is 12 percent, and the standard deviation of a portfolio's return is 15 percent, the expected return on the portfolio is ____ percent.
    A. 8.0
    B. 10.0
    C. 12.5
    D. 18.0
    E. 22.5

15. The portfolio in Question 14 is aggressive because ____.
    A. its expected return exceeds the risk–free rate
    B. its expected return exceeds the expected return on the market
    C. the standard deviation of the portfolio return is less than the standard deviation of the market return
    D. the standard deviation of the portfolio return is greater than the risk–free rate
    E. the standard deviation of the portfolio return is greater than the expected return on the market portfolio

16. The use of leverage ____.
    A. increases the expected return and the variability of returns
    B. decreases the expected return and increases the variability of returns
    C. increases the expected return and decreases the variability of returns
    D. decreases the expected return as well as the variability of returns
    E. does not affect expected returns or the variability of returns

17. The portfolio of risky assets that includes every risky security in the market-place weighted proportionally to its market value is known as the ____ portfolio.
   A. utility maximizing
   B. value–weighted
   C. efficient
   D. market
   E. risk neutral

18. The intercept and the slope of the characteristic line are known, respectively, as the ____.
   A. regression point and the alpha
   B. beta and the alpha
   C. alpha and the beta
   D. beta and the gamma
   E. gamma and the beta

19. A security or portfolio with a beta less than 1 is ____.
   A. risk tolerant
   B. risk neutral
   C. risk seeking
   D. aggressive
   E. defensive

20. Portfolios that do not have unsystematic risk lie on the ____.
   A. Financial Market Line
   B. Security Characteristic Line
   C. Risk–Free Rate
   D. Capital Market Line
   E. Diversification Line

The next five questions are based on the following data:

Consider a portfolio that is to be made up of the risk–free asset, R_f, and a risky portfolio, j, where the data for R_f and j are as follows:

	R_f	j
Expected Return	.20	.28
Standard Deviation		.24
Portfolio Weight	.36	

21. What is the standard deviation of the risk–free asset?
    A. .00
    B. .12
    C. .24
    D. .76
    E. 1.00

22. What is the portfolio weight for Portfolio j?
    A. .00
    B. .64
    C. .50
    D. .24
    E. 1.00

23. What is the covariance between R_f and Portfolio j?
    A. .00
    B. .24
    C. .36
    D. .50
    E. 1.00

24. The expected return for the portfolio is _____ percent.
    A. 25.12
    B. 20.45
    C. 23.67
    D. 25.00
    E. 34.98

25. The standard deviation of the portfolio is _____.
    A. .1155
    B. .1234
    C. .1536
    D. .1787
    E. .1975

Review Problems

1. The risk–free rate is 6 percent, the expected return on Security j is 15 percent, and the standard deviation of the return on Security j is 12 percent. Calculate the expected return and the standard deviation of return for a portfolio that is split evenly between Asset j and the risk–free asset.
2. How would you construct a portfolio based on the information in Problem 1 to acquire an expected return of 13 percent? Why does this portfolio require placing more than 50 percent of your money in Security j?
3. Calculate the standard deviation of the portfolio you constructed in Problem 2.

4. The risk–free rate is 14 percent and the expected return on the market is 24 percent. You have an initial endowment of $1,000. Calculate your expected return if you plan to borrow an additional $500, and if you plan to borrow an additional $1,000. In economic terms, why does your expected return increase with the amount you borrow?

5. Calculate your actual return from the information in Problem 4 if the actual return on the market deviates from its expected value by plus or minus 3 percent. Explain how these results confirm the explanation capital market theory would provide for your results in Problem 4.

6. The risk–free rate is 8 percent and the expected return on the market is 16 percent. How would you construct a portfolio to generate an expected return of 20 percent?

7. A security has a beta of 1.5 when the risk–free rate is 4 percent and the expected return on the market is 12 percent. Calculate the expected return on the security.

8. If the beta on the security in Problem 7 increases to 2, what is the new expected return? Why does the expected return increase as the beta rises?

9. The risk–free rate is 7 percent and the expected return on the market portfolio is 15 percent with a standard deviation of 20 percent. What is the expected return on a portfolio that has a standard deviation of returns of 18 percent?

10. Other things equal, what is the new risk–free rate if the expected return on the security in Problem 9 rises to 14.4 percent? Economically, why has the expected return on the security risen as the risk–free rate has risen?

Answers

Multiple–Choice Questions

1. C	10. A	19. E
2. E	11. C	20. D
3. D	12. D	21. A
4. A	13. B	22. B
5. C	14. E	23. A
6. B	15. B	24. A
7. E	16. A	25. C
8. B	17. D	
9. D	18. C	

Review Problems

1. The expected return on the portfolio is:

$$.5(.06) + .5(.15) = 10.5 \text{ percent.}$$

The standard deviation of the portfolio's returns is:

$$.5(.12) = 6 \text{ percent.}$$

2. The expected return on the portfolio must be 13 percent:

$$x(.06) + (1 - x)(.15) = .13, \text{ or}$$

$$.06x + .15 - .15x = .13, \text{ or } .02 = .09x, \text{ so}$$

the percentage invested in the risk–free asset must be .02/.09 = 22.2 percent and the percentage invested in Security j must be (1–.222) = 77.8 percent. The desired return exceeds the average of the risk–free rate and the expected market return so the investor must allocate more than half of the funds to the risky asset.

3. The standard deviation of the new portfolio is .778(.12) = 9.33 percent, which is also higher than that of the equally weighted portfolio. This must be the case to justify the increased expected return.

4. Borrowing $500 lets you invest $1,500 in the market with an eventual debt of (1.14)($500) = $570. Your expected return is:

$$\$1,500(1.24) - \$570 = \$1,290, \text{ for an expected return of 29 percent.}$$

Borrowing $1,000 lets you invest $2,000 in the market with an eventual debt of (1.14)($1,000) = $1,140. Your expected return now is:

$$\$2,000(1.24) - \$1,140 = \$1,340, \text{ for an expected return of 34 percent.}$$

Borrowing at 14 percent to earn 24 percent increases the expected return on your investment because of positive expected leverage.

5. If the actual market return is .24 – .03 = .21, and you borrow $500, your actual return is:

$$\$1,500(1.21) - \$570 = \$1,245, \text{ or, 24.5 percent.}$$

If you borrow $1,000, your actual return is:

$$\$2,000(1.21) - \$1,140 = \$1,280, \text{ or, 28 percent.}$$

If the actual return on the market is .24 + .03 = .27, and you borrow $500, your actual return is:

$$\$1,500(1.27) - \$570 = \$1,335, \text{ or, 33.5 percent.}$$

If you borrow $1,000, your actual return is:

$$\$2,000(1.27) - \$1.140 = \$1,400, \text{ or, } 40 \text{ percent.}$$

If you borrow $500, deviations of plus or minus 3 percent in the market return change your terminal wealth by plus or minus $45. If you borrow $1,000, the same deviations in the market return change your terminal wealth by plus or minus $60. Borrowing more increases the volatility of your terminal wealth. It is this increase in risk that justifies the increased expected return created by leveraging the portfolio.

6. To generate an expected return of 20 percent:

$$(x).08 + (1 - x).16 = .20, \text{ or}$$

$$.08x + .16 - .16x = .20, \text{ or } -.08x = .04, \text{ so}$$

the percentage of funds invested in the risk–free asset must be $(-.04/.08) = -50$ percent. The negative value implies that you borrow an additional 50 percent of your initial endowment and invest all of your funds in the market portfolio. For example, if you borrow $500 against an initial endowment of $1,000 you will be obligated to repay $(1.08)\$500 = \$540$. Your market investment will return $(\$1,500)(1.16) = \$1,740$, for a net of $\$1,740 - \$540 = \$1,200$, a 20 percent return on your initial $1,000 endowment.

7. The expected return on the security is:

$$.04 + 1.5(.12 - .04) = .16.$$

8. The new expected return is:

$$.04 + 2(.12 - .04) = .20.$$

A security's beta measures risk relative to the market (systematic risk). Since investors are compensated for bearing systematic risk, the expected return on a security must increase as its beta increases.

9. The expected return on the portfolio is:

$$.07 + (.18/.20)(.15 - .07) = 14.2 \text{ percent}$$

10. The new risk–free rate, x, is determined as follows:

$$x + (.18/.20)(.15 - x) = .144 \text{ , or}$$

$$x + .135 - .9x = .144, \text{ or } .1x = .009, \text{ so}$$

the new risk–free rate is: .009/.1 = .09 or 9 percent.

As the return on risk–free assets rises, the expected return on risky assets must rise as well.

CHAPTER FIFTEEN

Efficient Markets and the Capital Asset Pricing Model

Chapter Objectives

Upon completion of this chapter, you should be able to:
1. Compare and contrast operationally and informationally efficient markets.
2. Discuss the three forms of the Efficient Markets Hypothesis and the inter–relationships among the three forms.
3. Explain the interdependency between the Efficient Markets Hypothesis and the Capital Asset Pricing Model, and discuss the theoretical and practical problems created in testing the relationships.
4. Explain the features of the Random Walk Hypothesis and how it relates to market efficiency.
5. Discuss the Arbitrage Pricing Theory and its characteristics.
6. Discuss the results of previous empirical tests of the Efficient Markets Hypothesis and the Capital Asset Pricing Model.
7. Discuss the anomalies that have been developed to challenge the joint EMH/CAPM hypothesis and explain how each anomaly contradicts a form of the EMH.
8. Explain the theoretical challenges to the Capital Asset Pricing Model that have been developed.
9. Discuss both mean reversion and noise trading in securities markets.

Chapter Outline

I. Overview

A. An **efficient market** is a market in which prices fully reflect a specified information set.

B. In briefest terms, an efficient market is one that responds well and quickly to new information.

C. The rapid adjustment of market prices to new information is the mechanism by which the market moves toward equilibrium. If market prices do not respond to new information in a way that moves the market toward equilibrium, there is no reason to think that actual markets behave as implied by the CAPM. Therefore, there is an intimate theoretical and practical connection between the CAPM and the **efficient markets hypothesis** (EMH).

II. The Efficient Markets Hypothesis

A. An **operationally efficient** market works smoothly, with limited delays. This type of market is one in which trades are accomplished quickly and correctly. A market may be operationally efficient, however, without being informationally efficient.

B. For our discussion, the key concept of efficiency is **informational efficiency**, which is defined as:

> A market is efficient with respect to some set of information, if prices in the market, at all times, fully reflect all information in the information set.

C. If market prices fully reflect a set of information, it means that prices have already completely adjusted to levels consistent with the new information, and there is no way to use that information to one's advantage in trading.

D. Weak Form Efficiency

A market is **weak form efficient** if security prices reflect all historical information. The weak form implies that all forms of technical analysis of past price movements are useless, at least when trying to make money.

E. Semi–Strong Form Efficiency

A market is **semi–strong efficient** if security prices reflect all public information, including published reports, announcements, and market data.

F. Strong Form Efficiency

A market is **strong form efficient** if its prices reflect all public and private information.

G. Relationships Among the Three Forms of Market Efficiency

The three forms are strongly interrelated. Violation of weak form efficiency implies that the semi–strong and strong forms are also violated, but violation of the strong form does not imply that the weak form or the semi–strong form is incorrect.

H. The Practical Consequences of the Efficient Markets Hypothesis

1. The Efficient Markets Hypothesis is important because it is not just an academic theory. If the EMH in its different versions is true, it has important implications for actual market conduct.

2. If the weak form is true, the sale of charts (a form of technical analysis designed to predict future price movements from the pattern in past prices) is not worthwhile, despite the millions of dollars spent each year for charting services.

3. If the semi–strong form is true, fundamental analysis of the economy, an industry, or a firm (of the sort discussed in Chapters 12–14) is not worthwhile.

4. If the strong form is true, the various laws regarding the appropriate use of privileged information are unnecessary.

III. The CAPM and the Efficient Markets Hypothesis

A. There is an intimate connection between the Efficient Markets Hypothesis and the Capital Asset Pricing Model.

B. The CAPM specifies the market standard for the relationship between risk and expected return, and tests of the EMH seek violations of that specified relationship.

1. Consider a security that trades on two different exchanges and carries different prices on the two exchanges.

2. An informed trader could buy the share where its price is low and contract immediately to sell it where its price is high.

3. This transaction which is riskless and requires no capital from the trader is known as an **arbitrage transaction**.

C. Arbitrage opportunities directly contradict the Capital Asset Pricing Model, which argues that a riskless transaction should earn the risk–free rate of return which correlates to the length of the investment. Therefore, if the trade is immediate and requires no investment, the profit should be zero.

D. The presence of arbitrage opportunities is also inconsistent with equilibrium pricing.

E. If we were faced with frequent arbitrage opportunities, we would have to admit that the market was not efficient, even in the weak sense, and that the CAPM was false.

F. In well–developed markets, one expects never to find arbitrage opportunities. Once found, the problem could lie either with the CAPM, the EMH, or both.

G. Attempts to test the EMH or the CAPM turn out to be tests of both theories, and determining the source of the discrepancy may be impossible.

IV. Performance Measurement and "Beating the Market"

A. Within a CAPM framework, beating the market means that the investor finds securities that lie off the SML.

B. High returns on a portfolio do not necessarily indicate successful performance, because although a security offers high returns, the returns may not be sufficient to justify the security's risk.

C. We should always want to know both how much risk was involved in a portfolio and how consistently an analyst turned in a good performance.

D. In order for us to believe that any analyst is truly successful, his or her track record must be sufficiently good and sufficiently long to rule out the possibility that he or she produced such a record by chance.

V. The Random Walk Hypothesis and Market Efficiency

A. The concept of market efficiency is often linked to the **random walk hypothesis**, a very strong statistical hypothesis that might be applied to any variable for which observations over time are possible.

B. The random walk hypothesis consists of two sub–hypotheses:
   1. First, it asserts that successive returns are statistically independent, implying that the correlation between one period's return and the next is zero.
   2. Second, it asserts that the distribution of returns in all periods is identical.

C. Robert's experiment illustrated that purely random price changes can generate changes in price levels that appear to have important trends.

D. Security prices do not follow a random walk, strictly speaking; tests indicate that there are small, but statistically significant, departures from randomness in most price change series.

E. The random walk hypothesis is a statistical hypothesis, while the efficient markets hypothesis is an economic hypothesis. To refute the efficient markets hypothesis, there must be rules for trading to beat the market. Refuting the random walk hypothesis, albeit a very strong statistical hypothesis, does not show that markets are inefficient.

VI. Challenges to the Capital Asset Pricing Model

A. Roll's Critique
   1. In theory, the market portfolio used in the CAPM should include all assets in the world in proportion to their value.
   2. In practice, most tests use a stock index limited to U.S. firms. This neglects human capital, real estate, and different countries. It appears there is no hope of being able to construct an adequate index of the true market portfolio.
   3. Since we cannot observe the market portfolio, there is no way to test its efficiency, which means that all other tests of the CAPM must have uncertain results.
   4. Further, even if the index used in practice is quite good, there can still be problems. For example, even if two indexes have a .95 correlation, they could give different answers in issues of performance evaluation.
   5. Roll has concluded that the only legitimate empirical test of the CAPM would test whether the market portfolio is efficient.

6. Roll has shown the disastrous consequences his conclusions have for measuring performance within a CAPM framework.
7. Whether the index is efficient or not does not matter too much because both lead to disastrous results.
   a. If the index is efficient, the performance of every security examined will lie exactly on the security market line as a matter of mathematical necessity.
   b. If the index is not efficient, any ranking of performance is possible, and the particular ranking that a test gives will depend only on the way in which the index is inefficient.
8. Therefore, the CAPM provides a meaningless benchmark of performance. Either every security lies on the SML or can diverge in unpredictable ways from the risk/expected return relationship expressed by the CAPM.

B. Arbitrage Pricing Theory
   The **arbitrage pricing theory** by Stephen Ross maintains that there can be a number of risk factors that are priced in the market. If these factors do not affect the expected return of a security, there will be arbitrage opportunities.

C. The Arbitrage Pricing Model
1. The APT relies on four key assumptions:
   a. Capital markets are perfect.
   b. Investors have homogeneous expectations about the structure of security returns and the identity of factors affecting security returns.
   c. There is some undetermined number (K) of factors common to all securities.
   d. The number of securities (N) exceeds the number of common factors (K) determining security returns.
2. Given these assumptions, Ross is able to prove mathematically that the expected return on any security will depend on the risk–free rate of interest and K factors, each multiplied by the market determined price for each unit of that type of risk.

VII. Tests of Efficient Markets and Pricing Models

A. The Joint Nature of Efficiency Tests
1. Tests for market efficiency amount to determining whether price behavior in a market meets a given standard. However, the standards provided by a theory of pricing such as the CAPM or the APT are not cast in stone, and are themselves subject to debate.
2. Because we can achieve consistency by rejecting either the efficient markets hypothesis or the CAPM, we effectively have a joint test of market efficiency and the CAPM.
3. Prices not behaving as theory suggests they should can mean that either the market is inefficient or the theory is no good.

B. Tests of the Weak Form of Market Efficiency
   1. In its purest form, technical analysis focuses on patterns of securities prices and measures of market mood or investor behavior.
   2. The strategies that focus on market mood consider matters such as the level of insider trading activity and the behavior of the odd lot trader.
   3. The idea is to follow the knowledgeable investors.
      a. Active net buying by corporate insiders would be a **buy signal**.
      b. The odd–lot theory suggests that one should do exactly the opposite of the odd–lot traders.
   4. The technical trading techniques that focus on price patterns have received more attention from researchers than strategies focusing on market mood, probably because they are more specific in their prescriptions for trading behavior.
   5. Three different techniques have been employed to test for the existence of price patterns in stock prices.
      a. Serial Correlation Tests
         (1) Serial Correlation holds that if price changes behaved in regular ways from one day to the next, an investor could learn the regular rules for their behavior and use that information to earn fantastic returns.
         (2) One way to test for this possibility is to examine stock returns to determine whether such a rule persists.
         (3) Graphing clearly indicates that there is little tendency toward any correlation in the returns from one period to the next.
         (4) Studies have determined that the random walk hypothesis is probably false, but the results do not provide evidence against the market efficiency hypothesis.
      b. Runs Tests
         (1) While tests for serial correlation reflect the size of returns, a **runs test** examines the tendencies for losses or gains to be followed by further losses or gains.
         (2) Runs tests are often performed by examining a time series of returns for a security and testing whether the number of consecutive price gains or price drops shows a pattern.
         (3) Any sequence uncovered is subject to a runs test to determine whether the gains and losses are similar to those generated by chance.
         (4) Studies have revealed statistically significant departures from randomness in runs of stock prices. In particular, gains tended to follow gains and losses tended to follow losses.
         (5) However, while these departures from randomness may be statistically significant, that does not mean that they are economically significant. That is, they do not show the market to be inefficient.
         (6) To take advantage of runs, one must be able to trade on the information. Yet, even when the lowest feasible transaction

        costs are taken into account, the prospective advantage from trading to take advantage of the runs disappears.

  c. Filter Tests

    (1) A **filter rule** has the following form:

        If the daily closing price of a security rises at least x%, buy the security and hold it until its price moves down at least x% from a subsequent high. At that point sell the security short and maintain the short position until the price rises at least x% above a subsequent low.

    (2) Filter rules have been found to generate positive returns on a consistent basis if transaction costs are ignored.

    (3) Filter strategies generate frequent trading, and even if transaction costs are low, the high volume of trading means that apparent profits are almost always turned to losses.

  6. In general, researchers have been unable to find any compelling evidence that technical analysis works.

  7. Further, the continued absence of evidence in favor of technical trading rules justifies a skepticism about the value of technical analysis.

C. Tests of the Semi–Strong Form of Market Efficiency

  1. The semi–strong form of the market efficiency hypothesis maintains that security prices always reflect all publicly available information.

  2. Therefore, the semi–strong version implies it is impossible to use any public information to direct a trading strategy earning more than the equilibrium risk–adjusted rate of return.

  3. Stock Splits—The Fama, Fisher, Jensen, Roll Study

    a. One implication of the semi–strong version of the EMH is that it should be impossible to earn supernormal returns by responding very quickly to new public information; the public announcement should be so well anticipated by the market that security prices will already have adjusted to their new equilibrium level.

    b. Research shows that, with regard to stock splits, and to the extent that the split was good news, the market had anticipated the good news and gave no reaction to the announcement itself.

    c. Stock splits are important in that they tend to accompany announcements of changing cash dividends.

    d. For firms that announced a stock split, but had a dividend decrease, stock price performance was well under the market norm.

    e. While the market appears to be efficient with respect to the public information embodied in the stock split announcement, it does appear that superior returns could be earned if the investor could find out in advance about the stock split.

    f. The early detection of cash dividend increases would be very useful. However, evidence suggests such predictions cannot be made on a consistently successful basis.

4. The Sharpe–Cooper Study
   a. Sharpe and Cooper tested the central claim of the CAPM—that stocks with higher betas are expected to have higher returns.
   b. In evaluating the results of their test, it is important to remember that the CAPM focuses on expected returns, and because of this focus on the future it expresses an **ex ante** theory—one that deals with expectations.
   c. However, in actuality, results can be measured only **ex post**, or after the fact.
   d. Sharpe and Cooper's results revealed a fairly close congruence between the ex ante theory and the ex post results.
   e. Their results generally have been interpreted as supporting the CAPM and the EMH.

5. Interpretation of Early Tests
   a. In general, early testing generally supported the joint hypothesis of the CAPM and EMH.
   b. Through approximately 1985, scholars generally believed that the empirical evidence strongly favored the CAPM and the EMH.
   c. With the bulk of evidence favoring the semi–strong EMH, most scholars believed that fundamental analysis was essentially a waste of time. As more recent evidence surfaces, however, the semi–strong version of the EMH has been called into very serious question.

D. Tests of the Strong Form of Market Efficiency
   1. If the strong form of the EMH is true, no information is valuable for directing a securities investment program, because security prices already reflect all information.
   2. The best evidence clearly indicates that the strong form of the EMH is false.
   3. Corporate Insiders
      a. There is considerable anecdotal evidence that insiders are able to make money by trading on their privileged information.
      b. Corporate insiders are required to report their trading activity to the SEC within two weeks of the trade, and the SEC publishes this information in its "Official Summary of Insider Trading."
      c. Studies of this information reveal that insiders consistently earn more than would be expected in an efficient market.
   4. Market Specialists
      a. The stock exchange specialist holds a book showing the orders awaiting execution at different prices.
      b. The specialist also holds an inventory in the stocks for which he or she is the specialist, and the specialist may increase or decrease this inventory at will.
      c. Specialists appear to average returns of about 100 percent on their invested capital—clearly more than the risk–adjusted norm.

5. A Thought Experiment
   In the strictest sense, the strong–form EMH claims that no person has inside information that would help develop a trading strategy, but a simple thought experiment reveals that some individuals do indeed possess very valuable information.

VIII. Recent Evidence on Market Efficiency and the CAPM

A. Market Anomalies
   1. A **market anomaly** is a well–established empirical fact that does not fit accepted theories.
   2. The Weekend Effect
      a. A great deal of evidence now exists to show that returns are different depending on the day of the week.
      b. Specifically, Friday returns are generally larger than those for other days. By contrast, returns from the Friday close to the Monday close are generally negative.
      c. The day–of–the–week effect suggests that either the semi–strong EMH is not true, the CAPM is not true, or both.
   3. The January Effect
      a. The peculiar behavior in security returns in the month of January has become known as the **January effect**, or the **turn–of–the–year–effect**.
      b. Returns in January are very large relative to other months, both in the United States and abroad.
      c. Large firms by themselves do not exhibit this effect, so the January effect is concentrated mainly among small firms.
      d. The January effect is probably large enough to cover transaction costs of low–cost traders, and may give all traders reason to alter timing decisions.
   4. Earnings Reports
      a. By buying those stocks with especially favorable announcements and selling those with unfavorable announcements, several studies have shown that it is possible to beat the market, even when including transactions costs.
      b. If the market is efficient with respect to these announcements and the CAPM gives the correct pricing relationship for risk and return, it would be impossible to react to these announcements in a way that gave a supernormal return.
      c. Therefore, this evidence from earnings reports presents a strong and still poorly understood challenge to the CAPM and the EMH.
   5. The Small Firm Effect
      The **small firm effect** is the empirically observed regularity that small capitalization firms earn a rate of return that is higher than the risk–adjusted market standard implies.

B. Anomalies in the Japanese Stock Market
  1. Kato and Schallheim studied the January effect and the small firm effect for the Tokyo Stock Exchange over the period 1964–1981. They concluded that the Japanese markets exhibit the same anomalies that the U.S. markets experience.
  2. They found that small firms tend to earn higher returns than one would expect from the CAPM and returns in January tend to be higher than for other months.
  3. Jaffe and Westerfield also found evidence of a day–of–the–week effect. However, the Japanese markets have horrible weekends, from which they tend not to recover until Wednesday.
C. Excess Volatility
  1. Shiller tested the volatility of prices against the volatility of the fundamental factors of the expected dividend, the discount rate, or the growth rate.
  2. He concluded that price volatility was so high that the market price of stocks could not be reacting efficiently to new information about fundamentals of expected dividends, growth rates, or discount rates.
D. Mean Reversion and Overreaction in Security Prices
  1. **Mean Reversion** is a statistical term that refers to the tendency of a variable to return to its average values. If stock prices are mean reverting, this means that they are predictable.
  2. Mean reversion opens the door to stock price prediction that would beat the market. Strong mean reversion also implies that the market is not efficient, because it suggests a trading strategy that would earn a return greater than the risk–adjusted return.
  3. Some scholars think that human psychology is such that investors may overreact to both good news and bad news. DeBondt and Thaler showed strong mean reversion in stock prices: the stock market overreacted to bad news and good news, but the overreaction to bad news was even more extreme.
  4. DeBondt and Thaler concluded that if the CAPM beta adequately measures risk, then the differences in winner/loser returns that they found cannot be attributed to differences in risk.
E. Noise Trading
  1. Some researchers have abandoned the efficient markets hypothesis and instead are concentrating on developing theories that accord with the presence of at least some irrational investors in the marketplace.
  2. A **noise trader** is an investor whose demand for financial assets is affected by beliefs or sentiments that are not fully justified by the fundamentals. Noise traders contrast with rational speculators or arbitrageurs.
  3. Arbitrageurs face risk factors that prevent them from conducting their arbitrage with perfect efficiency and allow noise traders to move prices away from their fundamentally justified levels.

4. The noise trader approach to finance suggests that prices can diverge from fundamentals in dramatic ways and for extended periods. Some scholars believe that this approach may help to bring financial theory new power in explaining the actual behavior of security prices.

Key Terms and Concepts

abnormal profits	actual returns, net of transactions costs, that are consistently and significantly higher than those justified by the systematic risk of a trading strategy
arbitrage	a trade that generates a certain return with no investment
Arbitrage Pricing Theory	an economic theory that argues that security returns are a function of several risk factors, not just systematic risk
arbitrage transaction	a transaction that earns an immediate, riskless profit
beating the market	consistently earning abnormally high profits on a risk–adjusted basis when transactions costs are considered
day–of–the–week effect	the market anomaly which argues that security returns are dependent on the day of the week; specifically, Friday returns are significantly larger than those for other days, and returns from the Friday close to the Monday close are generally negative
efficient market	a market in which prices fully reflect a specified information set
efficient markets hypothesis	states that a market is efficient with respect to some body of information; this means that different versions of the EMH can be developed by specifying different information sets; see weak form, semi–strong form, and strong form efficiency
ex ante theory	a theory that deals with expectations, such as the CAPM
ex post	after the fact

filter rule	a technical trading strategy which argues that the size and sign of past price changes can be used to predict future price movements
fundamental analysis	the search for securities that lie above (to buy) or below (to short) the Security Market Line by studying public information about the company or the economy
informational efficiency	a market which fully reflects all information in the information set
January effect	a market anomaly which argues that returns in January are very large relative to other months
market anomaly	an observed market behavior that is not consistent with the Capital Asset Pricing Model/Efficient Markets Hypothesis theories
mean reversion	a statistical term referring to the tendency of a variable to return to its average values
noise trader	an investor whose demand for financial assets is affected by beliefs or sentiments that are not fully justified by the fundamentals
operational efficiency	a market where trades are executed quickly and correctly
random walk hypothesis	a strong statistical hypothesis that stock returns from different periods are not correlated and that the distribution of stock returns is identical for all periods
runs test	a technical trading rule which argues that the historical pattern of the signs of price changes can be used to predict future security prices
semi–strong form efficiency	the argument that stock prices reflect all publicly available information
serial correlation	a statistical relationship between price changes measured over a constant time interval, such as a day

strong form efficiency	the argument that stock prices reflect all public and private information
technical analysis	the process of predicting future price movements by analyzing patterns in historical price changes
weak form efficiency	the argument that stock prices reflect all historical information

Multiple–Choice Questions

1. The ability to earn a certain return without investment is known as an ____ transaction.
    A. abnormal
    B. efficient
    C. operational
    D. informational
    E. arbitrage

2. A market where trades are made quickly, correctly, and smoothly is known as a(n) ____ efficient market.
    A. informationally
    B. correlationally
    C. operationally
    D. abnormally
    E. serially

3. Weak form efficiency implies that security prices reflect all ____ price information.
    A. private
    B. public
    C. Internal Revenue Code
    D. historical
    E. specialist

4. The existence of arbitrage opportunities violates the ____ form of the efficient markets hypothesis.
    A. anomaly
    B. semi–strong
    C. serial
    D. specialist
    E. arbitrage

5. According to the random walk hypothesis, the correlation between current and future security returns is _____.
   A. positively related to the security's beta
   B. positive
   C. negative
   D. negatively related to the risk–free rate
   E. zero

6. If a high government official uses information that has not yet been made public to obtain trading profits, this breaks the _____ form of market efficiency.
   A. random
   B. weak
   C. semi–strong
   D. quasi
   E. strong

7. If one is able to use technical analysis to beat the market, this breaks the _____ form of market efficiency.
   A. strong
   B. weak
   C. semi–strong
   D. quasi
   E. A, B, and C

8. The world's two largest asset categories are _____ and _____.
   A. government spending; government securities
   B. debt; equity
   C. real estate; equity
   D. human capital; equity
   E. human capital; real estate

9. Generally, according to technical analysis, active net buying by corporate insiders provides a _____ signal.
   A. buy
   B. sell
   C. wait and see
   D. high risk
   E. loss

10. Violations of the capital asset pricing model and the efficient markets hypothesis are known as ____.
    A. anomalies
    B. arbitrage profits
    C. correlation profits
    D. filters
    E. trading systems

11. Roll argued that the capital asset pricing model cannot be defended as the correct description of market equilibrium until ____.
    A. one can test the efficiency of the market portfolio
    B. arbitrage trading strategies consider transactions costs
    C. securities markets are open twenty–four hours a day around the world
    D. there is a single, global securities exchange
    E. tax laws are identical across countries

12. Tests of the size and sign of past price changes are combined in ____ rules.
    A. runs
    B. size
    C. day–of–the week
    D. January
    E. filter

13. If market specialists earn abnormal risk–adjusted profits, the ____ form of the efficient markets hypothesis is violated.
    A. weak
    B. semi–strong
    C. strong
    D. random walk
    E. filter

14. Which of the following is recognized as a market anomaly?
    A. the day–of–the–week effect
    B. all significant positive serial correlations between security price movements
    C. abnormal profits earned by corporate insiders
    D. abnormal profits earned by market specialists
    E. price declines after stock splits

15. The performance evaluation standards advocated by a joint belief in the CAPM and the EMH argue that ____.
    A. investors with homogenous expectations must ignore transactions costs
    B. returns must be measured over time on a risk–adjusted basis
    C. high beta portfolios should perform well in bear markets
    D. superior analysts must incorporate all of the appropriate arbitrage factors in their valuation models
    E. an investor must choose one form of the efficient markets hypothesis to develop a standard with which to measure superior performance

16. From the finance perspective, the key concept of efficiency is ____ efficiency.
    A. informational
    B. relative
    C. operational
    D. infinite
    E. mutual

17. If prices in a market fully reflect all information in the information set at all times, the market is ____.
    A. efficient
    B. constant
    C. variable
    D. strong
    E. full

18. If prices in a particular market at all times fully reflect all public information, the market is ____ efficient.
    A. weak form
    B. hard form
    C. semi–strong form
    D. strong form
    E. super–strong form

19. If prices in a particular market fully reflect all public and private information, the market is ____ efficient.
    A. weak form
    B. hard form
    C. semi–strong form
    D. strong form
    E. super–strong form

20. The presence of _____ opportunities means that there are investments that generate positive profits with no risk.
    A. arbitrage
    B. leverage
    C. diversification
    D. mortgage
    E. efficient

21. The capital asset pricing model expresses the equilibrium level of expected returns for a given level of systematic risk graphically by the _____.
    A. capital market line
    B. efficient frontier
    C. indifference curve
    D. security market line
    E. risk–free rate

22. "Beating the market" requires consistently finding securities that lie _____.
    A. above the risk–free rate
    B. above the indifference curve
    C. off the security market line
    D. below the efficient frontier
    E. below the beta

23. According to technical analysis, _____ are the least sophisticated traders in the market.
    A. insiders
    B. institutional traders
    C. odd–lot traders
    D. round lot traders
    E. brokers

24. Corporate insiders are required to report their trading activity to the _____.
    A. president of the firm
    B. state government
    C. Securities and Exchange Commission
    D. New York Stock Exchange
    E. Arbitrage Pricing Board

25. The alternative theory that has emerged to challenge the capital asset pricing model is known as the _____.
    A. Capital Pricing Theory
    B. Leverage Pricing Model
    C. Marginal Pricing Theory
    D. Arbitrage Pricing Theory
    E. Risk/Return Pricing Model

Answers

Multiple-Choice Questions

1.	E	10.	A	19.	D
2.	C	11.	A	20.	A
3.	D	12.	E	21.	D
4.	B	13.	C	22.	C
5.	E	14.	A	23.	C
6.	E	15.	B	24.	C
7.	E	16.	A	25.	D
8.	E	17.	A		
9.	A	18.	C		

CHAPTER SIXTEEN

Investment Companies and Performance Evaluation

Chapter Objectives

Upon completion of this chapter, you should be able to:

1. Compare and contrast closed–end investment companies and mutual funds.
2. Explain the types of transactions costs an investor might face in purchasing investment company and fund shares and the typical expenses incurred in operating a fund.
3. Explain the regulation and taxation of mutual and closed–end investment companies.
4. Explain the practical reasons why mutual funds may benefit the small investor.
5. Explain, calculate, and compare the three performance measures typically used to evaluate the investment performance of managed portfolios.
6. Comment on the existing empirical evidence regarding the ability of mutual funds to "beat the market."

Chapter Outline

I. Overview

A. Prospective investors will find a great deal of information when faced with the task of portfolio formation.
B. One possible answer for many investors is to place funds with an **investment company** that collects funds from a wide group of investors and invests them in a portfolio of securities.
C. Each of the investors in the fund has title to a fractional share of all of the investments in the portfolio.

D. A **closed–end company** accepts funds only at its creation, and the funds contributed at that point form the investment base that the company has to invest throughout its life.
E. A **mutual fund**, by contrast, is always ready to receive money from new investors.

II. General Features of Investment Companies

A. Mutual funds have had a larger growth than closed–end companies.
B. The preference for mutual funds must be due to their ability to continue to receive funds at any point, making growth easier.
C. Closed–end companies, once established, can grow in asset size only through successful investment of the originally contributed funds.
D. All investment companies must provide a prospectus to prospective investors.
E. Investors in the investment company purchase shares, which are titles to fractions of the assets of the investment company.
F. The total assets of the company, minus the liabilities, constitute the **net asset value**.
G. The **net asset value per share** is simply the total net asset value of the company, divided by the number of shares outstanding.
H. The investment company must keep accurate records of ownership of shares in the company and provide reports and payments to the shareholders.
I. The management of an investment company takes on the function of the investment advisor by making all of the decisions about which securities will be held in the firm's portfolio.
J. Advantages of Investment Companies
   1. Diversification
       Investment companies provide a ready–made portfolio for the investor.
   2. Clerical Function
       The investment company achieves important economies of scale in clerical and management functions which can benefit the investor.
   3. Professional Management
       The investment company offers professional investment advice by choosing the portfolio based on its research. However, the value of this portfolio selection is questionable.

III. Closed–End Investment Companies

A. These companies refuse to accept new funds for investment during their lives. Once the original shares are issued, no more shares can ever come into existence.

B. The investment company itself will not redeem shares for their owners. Instead, shares of closed–end companies are traded in the market for whatever price the laws of supply and demand allow.

C. Intrinsic Value of Closed–End Funds

1. Since closed–end shareholders cannot redeem the shares for their net asset value, the price of the shares is free to wander away from the net asset value.

2. If the share price exceeds the net asset value, it is said to be at a **premium**, while a share price below the net asset value is at a **discount**.

D. Discounts and Premiums on Closed–End Funds

1. Shares of closed–end funds often sell at a discount to their net asset value.

2. In recent times, however, the closed–end funds have actually sold at a premium to their net asset values.

3. The presence and size of closed–end fund discounts may be related to past investment performance and taxes.

4. Lee, Shleifer, and Thaler suggest that smart money traders have limited opportunities to trade to exploit departures from net asset value.

a. First, there is little way to arbitrage the differential.

b. Second, the supply of investors willing to make long–term bets against prices that depart from net asset values is quite limited.

5. These factors allow persistent and wide divergences between net asset values and the prices of closed–end fund shares.

IV. Mutual Funds: Growth and Diversity

A. The size and diversity of mutual funds has increased dramatically since their introduction in the 1940s. Today, there are also different types of mutual funds. For example, some focus on international securities, while others focus on stocks of emerging companies or other specialties.

B. From their inception in 1974, money market mutual funds—funds that hold money market securities—have come to dominate the market.

C. Ownership of Mutual Fund Shares

While mutual funds have traditionally been regarded as investment vehicles particularly well suited to small investors, institutional investors have become very active in money market funds.

D. Load vs. No–Load Mutual Funds

1. A **load fund** imposes a sales charge to invest in the fund. For example, if the firm has a 10 percent sales charge, a $100 investment will yield a net asset value of only $90.

2. A **no–load fund** does not impose a sales charge.

3. No–load funds operate only by mail and have no sales force to provide compensation for.

E. Costs of Investing in Mutual Funds
1. In addition to a load, mutual funds also charge other fees for the services they offer.
2. Expenses for managerial services must ultimately be borne by the investors in the fund.
3. Also, there are other expenses such as commissions, which are not normally part of the percentage levied against each account for expenses.
F. Mutual Fund Quotations
1. The quotations, reported daily in *The Wall Street Journal*, give the name of the mutual fund, the net asset value per share, and the offering price.
2. If the offering price differs from the net asset value, the difference is the load charge.
G. Mutual Fund Families
1. Families are companies that offer a number of different types of mutual funds to span the range of possible investor needs.
2. Through families, an investor in one fund can switch investments from one fund in the family to another to take advantage of whatever beliefs they have about the direction of the market.

V. Regulation and Taxation of Investment Companies

A. Regulation
1. The Investment Company Act of 1940 gave the SEC control over both types of investment companies.
2. The act has two main purposes.
    a. The act requires disclosure of information in a prospectus to prospective investors.
    b. The act also attempts to curb potential abuse on the part of the management of the investment company.
3. For example, in order to protect investors from collusion between brokers or underwriters and fund managers, the act does not allow underwriters or brokers more than a minority interest in investment companies.
B. Taxation of Investment Company Returns
1. Many investment companies, both closed-end companies and mutual funds, are exempt from federal income taxation.
2. Instead, the individuals are taxed on the proceeds they receive from the fund.
3. To qualify for this treatment, the fund must distribute at least 90 percent of its taxable investment income to its shareholders each year.

VI. Mutual Fund Performance

A. We must consider whether mutual funds are able to outperform the market by earning a return that is higher than the market rate of return for the fund's level of risk.

B. The principal issue is to find the mutual fund with the best performance prospects having the kind of portfolio appropriate to the investor.

C. Most research shows that there is very little consistency between rankings from one year to the next, making it difficult to evaluate the performance of mutual funds.

D. In general, mutual funds do not outperform stock market indexes of comparable risk. Risk adjustment is a necessary part of correct performance comparison, especially in those cases where performance is not consistent.

E. The important performance question concerning mutual funds is: How well does a mutual fund perform in achieving a level of return, given its level of risk?

F. The idea that performance can only be evaluated accurately when the risk level is taken into account is a central tenet of the CAPM, so this application of the theory is extremely important.

VII. Methods of Performance Evaluation

A. There are three well–accepted methods for evaluating the performance of mutual funds or other managed portfolios, and all stem directly from capital market theory.

B. The Sharpe Index (SI):
   1. This index is based on an historical, or ex–post version, of the Capital Market Line.

$$SI_p = \frac{R_p - R_f}{\sigma_p}$$

   2. If the Sharpe Index for a portfolio exceeds the Sharpe Index value for the market, then the portfolio has beaten the market.
   3. Graphically, the portfolio that beats the market lies above the Capital Market Line.

C. The Treynor Index (TI):
   1. This index is based on the ex–post Security Market Line relationship.
   2. Following the same mathematical reasoning as the Sharpe Index:

$$TI_p = \frac{R_p - R_f}{B_p}$$

   3. The Treynor Index for the market portfolio is the market risk premium, because the market portfolio always has a beta of one.

4. A Treynor Index value that is greater than the market risk premium means that such a portfolio will lie above the SML.

D. Jensen's Alpha:
1. Jensen restated the Security Market Line on an ex–post basis over time:

$$(R_j - R_f)_t = \alpha_j + \beta_j(R_m - R_f)_t + \varepsilon_{jt}$$

2. If the Security Market Line relationship holds, the constant term, alpha, should not be different from zero.
    a. An alpha greater than zero indicates that the portfolio has outperformed the market during the period in question.
    b. An alpha less than zero means that the portfolio has not performed as well as the market on a risk–adjusted basis.

E. Risk–Adjusted Mutual Fund Performance
1. Mutual funds have professional management and a great deal of funds available to develop diversified portfolios. Therefore, they should be the most likely vehicles to outperform the market.
2. If mutual funds underperform a portfolio made up of the risk–free asset and the market portfolio, then this would be a strong piece of evidence consistent with the semi–strong form of the Efficient Markets Hypothesis.
3. A classic study by Jensen reviewed the risk–adjusted performance of mutual funds through comparisons to a benchmark portfolio, made up of the market portfolio and the risk–free asset in proportions that made the risk of the mutual fund and the constructed portfolio equal.
4. Ignoring the management and sales fees, the benchmark portfolio slightly outperformed the mutual funds.
5. When management fees are considered, the benchmark portfolio beat the mutual funds by an average of 1.1 percent.
6. Some funds do beat the benchmark, and this might be due to skill, although this is difficult to prove statistically. The number of mutual funds that beat the market is about what one would expect to happen by chance, with no real skill being involved.
7. True ability should lead to consistently good performance, but there appears to be very little correlation between good performance in one year by a mutual fund and its performance in the next year.
8. While mutual funds apparently do not have the ability to beat the market, they may provide useful diversification services to many investors in a cost–effective way.

VIII. International Investment Companies

A. U.S.–Based Investment Companies
1. In the United States, there is a wide variety of both investment companies and mutual funds specializing in non–U.S. securities.
2. International mutual funds provide a form of ready–made international diversification.

B. Foreign Mutual Funds
1. Foreign countries also have their own mutual funds that may either specialize in their own domestic markets or are international as well.
2. Funds in some foreign countries have experienced phenomenal growth.
C. Investment Performance of International Mutual Funds
1. Cumby and Glen explored the performance of 15 international mutual funds based in the United States using both a U.S. index and a world index of stock market performance as proxies for the market portfolio.
2. Consistent with Jensen's classic study for domestic U.S. mutual funds, they found that international mutual funds did not earn a superior risk–adjusted return.

Key Terms and Concepts

capital gains distribution	a bookkeeping technique for keeping track of the tax liability of the share owners
closed–end fund	an investment company that accepts funds from investors only at its creation
discount fund	a closed–end investment company whose shares are trading for less than net asset value
investment company	a firm that pools funds from diverse investors and invests the money in a collection of securities
Investment Company Act	1940 legislation that gave the Securities and Exchange Commission control over closed–end investment companies and mutual funds
Jensen's Alpha	a time series performance measure based on risk–adjusted returns relative to the Security Market Line
load fund	a mutual fund that charges investors a sales commission to purchase shares
mutual fund	an investment company that grows and contracts as investors purchase new shares or redeem existing shares
mutual fund families	a group of funds with different objectives managed by a single firm

net asset value	the total assets of the company, minus the liabilities
net asset value per share	the total net asset value of a fund, divided by the number of shares outstanding
no–load fund	a mutual fund that allows investors to purchase shares with no sales charge
open–ended fund	a mutual fund that accepts new investors through the creation of new shares
premium fund	a closed–end investment company whose shares are trading for more than net asset value per share
prospectus	a legal document stating a fund's investment objectives that is distributed to prospective shareholders
redemption fee	a charge to sell mutual fund shares back to the investment company
Sharpe Index	a performance measure based on returns relative to the Capital Market Line at a point in time
Treynor Index	a performance measure based on returns relative to the Security Market Line at a point in time

Multiple–Choice Questions

1. A company that collects funds from a wide group of investors in order to invest those funds in a portfolio of securities is known as a(n) _____ company.
   A. redemption
   B. investment
   C. funding
   D. dividend
   E. capital gain

2. A(n) _____ company is always ready to receive money from new investors.
   A. closed–end
   B. discount
   C. premium
   D. diversified
   E. open–end

3. Which of the following is *not* an advantage of investing in a mutual fund family?
   A. access to a diversified portfolio
   B. record–keeping expertise
   C. professional portfolio management
   D. the earning of risk–adjusted abnormal profits
   E. easy switching to other funds in the family

4. The total assets of a fund minus its liabilities, divided by the number of shares in the fund, is known as the _____ value per share.
   A. redemption
   B. open–end
   C. net asset
   D. load
   E. premium

5. _____ funds tend to aim for an increase in share value rather than a steady stream of dividend income.
   A. Preservation
   B. Corporate
   C. Growth
   D. Municipal
   E. Money market

6. If a mutual fund owns securities with a market value of $100,000, has 25,000 shares outstanding, owes its advisors $5,000, and has a 2% load charge, its net asset value per share is $_____.
   A. 3.72
   B. 3.80
   C. 3.92
   D. 4.00
   E. 4.20

7. Despite the fact that mutual funds as a group have not demonstrated the ability to "beat the market," one could argue that specific funds offer superior performance if _____.
   A. mutual funds did not have to pay taxes
   B. some funds consistently outperformed the market on a risk–adjusted basis
   C. closed–end funds were allowed to create new shares
   D. funds did not have to charge sales commissions or redemption fees
   E. the capital asset pricing model market portfolio included foreign securities

8. An existing closed–end investment company can only grow by ____.
   A. investing in a mutual fund
   B. reinvesting accumulated profits and originally contributed funds
   C. collecting its trading premium from its shareholders
   D. accruing of management fees
   E. beating the market on a risk–adjusted basis

9. A ____ fund imposes a sales charge to invest in the fund.
   A. redemption
   B. premium
   C. discount
   D. load
   E. portfolio

10. A $10,000 investment in a load fund with an 8 percent sales charge will yield
    a net asset value of $____.
    A. 9,000
    B. 9,100
    C. 9,150
    D. 9,200
    E. 10,100

11. Mutual funds have a natural advantage in growth because they are _____.
    A. open–ended
    B. closed–ended
    C. not taxed twice
    D. highly leveraged
    E. none of the above

12. One of the most important features in the development of mutual funds in the
    recent past has been the emergence of the _____.
    A. new tax laws
    B. money market mutual fund
    C. higher returns available in the market
    D. lower risk in the market
    E. income fund market

13. Which of the following statements about investment company performance is
    true when the market is performing well?
    A. The load charge declines on load funds.
    B. The redemption fee declines on no–load funds.
    C. The net asset value of closed–end fund shares declines.
    D. The discount on closed–end fund shares declines.
    E. Jensen's Alpha falls.

14. Investment companies are not liable for federal income taxes if they _____.
    A. usually invest in municipal securities
    B. do not earn capital gains
    C. distribute at least 90 percent of their taxable income to shareholders
    D. do not redeem shares
    E. charge a load fee

15. Which of the following is *not* one of the performance measures discussed in the text?
    A. Jensen's Alpha
    B. Sharpe Index
    C. Treynor Index
    D. A, B, and C
    E. Arbitrage Performance Theory

16. The _____ gave the SEC control over investment companies.
    A. Securities Act of 1933
    B. Rule 144a
    C. Investment Company Act of 1940
    D. Glass–Steagall Act
    E. none of the above

17. An investment fund that accepts funds from investors only at its creation is known as a(n) _____.
    A. open–ended fund
    B. fund family
    C. load fund
    D. no–load fund
    E. closed–end fund

18. Generally, if you purchase shares in a fund at net asset value, you have bought into a(n) _____.
    A. open–ended fund
    B. fund family
    C. load fund
    D. high–load fund
    E. closed–end fund

19. If you are charged a sales charge to purchase shares, you have bought into a(n) _____.
    A. open–ended fund
    B. fund family
    C. load fund
    D. no–load fund
    E. closed–end fund

20. A group of mutual funds with different investment objectives managed by a single firm is known as a(n) ____.
    A. open–ended fund
    B. fund family
    C. load fund
    D. no–load fund
    E. closed–end fund

21. A fund that accepts new investors by creating new shares is known as a(n) ____.
    A. open–ended fund
    B. fund family
    C. load fund
    D. no–load fund
    E. closed–end fund

22. If the shares of a closed–end investment company are trading below net asset value, the fund is trading at a(n) ____.
    A. open–ended position
    B. premium
    C. load
    D. no–load fund
    E. discount

23. A firm that pools funds from different investors and invests the funds in a collection of securities is known as a(n) ____.
    A. investment company
    B. portfolio family
    C. premium fund
    D. prospectus
    E. discount fund

24. The value of a fund's assets minus its liabilities is known as the fund's ____.
    A. load
    B. discount
    C. premium
    D. net asset value
    E. redemption value

25. Which of the following statements about investing in shares of investment companies is true?
    A. Closed–end funds offer statistically higher risk–adjusted returns than open–end funds.
    B. The professional management skills of fund managers have been shown to consistently generate abnormal risk–adjusted returns.
    C. Investment companies provide a ready–made portfolio for the investor.
    D. Investment companies cannot achieve significant economies of scale in clerical and management functions.
    E. Mutual funds are prohibited from charging redemption fees but closed–end funds are not.

Answers

Multiple–Choice Questions

1. B	10. D	19. C
2. E	11. A	20. B
3. D	12. B	21. A
4. C	13. D	22. E
5. C	14. C	23. A
6. B	15. E	24. D
7. B	16. C	25. C
8. B	17. E	
9. D	18. A	

CHAPTER SEVENTEEN

The Futures Market

Chapter Objectives

Upon completion of this chapter, you should be able to:
1. Compare and contrast futures contracts and forward contracts.
2. Explain the institutional details of futures trading.
3. Explain the role of the clearinghouse.
4. Explain how the cost–of–carry model determines the price of futures contracts.
5. Discuss the social functions of futures markets.
6. Discuss the types of speculators and the economic role of speculation.
7. Design and calculate the returns on intercommodity and intracommodity spreads.
8. Explain the relationship between interest rate futures yields and the spot market yield curve.
9. Discuss stock index futures and the theories relating them to stock market volatility.

Chapter Outline

I. Overview

A. Futures markets arose in the mid–1800s in Chicago and institutionalized an ancient form of contracting, called forward contracting.
B. A **forward contract** is an agreement reached at one point in time calling for the delivery of some commodity at a specified later date at a price established at the time of contracting.

II. *Forward Contracts*

A. In a typical forward contract, calling for the delivery of a commodity at a future time for a payment to be made upon delivery, two parties come together and agree to terms that they believe to be mutually beneficial.
B. The price for immediate delivery of a good is the cash or **spot price**.
C. There are some problems with forward contracting that have restricted forward markets in size and scope:
1. Strong incentives to default on a contract may exist, and this is known in advance to both parties.
2. The conditions surrounding the contract may be quite restrictive and may leave many potential traders unable to consummate their desired trades.
3. There may be difficulty in fulfilling an obligation without actually completing delivery.

III. *The Futures Exchange*

A. A futures exchange is a nonprofit organization composed of members holding seats on the exchange. These seats are traded on an open market, so an individual wishing to become a member of the exchange can do so by buying an existing seat from a member and by meeting other exchange criteria for financial soundness and ethical reputation.
B. Each exchange determines the kinds of goods that it will trade and the contract specifications for each of the goods. There is a great variety of goods traded, and some exchanges tend to specialize in certain segments of the industry.

IV. *Futures Contracts and Futures Trading*

A. Typical Contract Terms
The standardization of the contract terms means that all of the traders will immediately know the exact characteristics of the good being traded, with no need for negotiation or long discussion.
B. Order Flow
1. Futures contracts are created when an order is executed on the floor of the exchange by either a member or an outsider who enters the order through a broker.
2. A trading **pit** is a particular area of the exchange floor designated for the trading of a particular commodity.
3. The rules of the exchange require that any offer to buy or sell must be made by **open–outcry** to all other traders in the pit.

C. The Clearinghouse and its Functions
1. To resolve the uncertainty about performance in accordance with the contract terms, each futures exchange has a **clearinghouse**—a well—capitalized financial institution that guarantees contract performance to both parties.
2. As soon as the trade is consummated, the clearinghouse interposes itself between the buyer and seller—acting as buyer to the seller and seller to the buyer.
3. The traders only need to trust the clearinghouse, instead of each other, and the clearinghouse has a large supply of capital, so there is little need for concern.
4. After all the transactions are completed, the clearinghouse will have neither funds nor goods. It only acts to guarantee performance to both parties.

D. The Clearinghouse and the Trader
1. While the clearinghouse guarantees performance on all futures contracts, it now has its own risk exposure.
2. To protect the clearinghouse and the exchange, traders must deposit funds with their brokers in order to trade futures contracts. This deposit, known as **margin**, must be in the form of cash or short–term U.S. Treasury securities.
3. If a trader defaults on his or her obligations, the broker may seize the margin deposit to cover the trading losses.
4. The margin deposit is normally quite small relative to the value of the goods being traded.
5. Because losses on a futures contract could be much larger than the margin deposit, the clearinghouse needs other protection from potential default by the trader.
6. To give this protection, futures exchanges have adopted a system known as **daily resettlement** or **marking–to–market**. The policy of daily settlement means that futures traders realize their paper gains and losses in cash on the results of each day's trading.

E. Fulfillment of Futures Contracts
1. After executing a futures contract, both the buyer and seller have undertaken specific obligations to the clearinghouse. Fulfillment of those obligations can be accomplished in two basic ways.
   a. First, the trader may actually make or take delivery as contemplated in the original contract.
   b. Second, if a trader does not wish to make or take delivery, the trader can fulfill all obligations by entering a reversing or offsetting trade.
2. Delivery
   a. After the clearinghouse interposes itself between the original buyer and seller, each of the trading partners has no obligation to any other trader. As delivery approaches, the clearinghouse supervises the arrangements for delivery.

       (1) First, the clearinghouse will pair buyers and sellers for the delivery and will identify the two parties to each other. Prior to this time, the two traders had no obligations to each other.

       (2) Second, the buyer and seller will communicate the relevant information concerning the delivery process to the opposite trading partner and to the clearinghouse. Usually, the seller has the choice of exactly what features the delivered goods will have.

       (3) The seller must also tell the buyer the name of the bank account to which the funds are to be transmitted.

       (4) Once the funds have been transmitted to the seller's account and this transaction has been confirmed by the seller's bank, the seller will deliver title to the goods to the buyer. Title is usually in the form of a warehouse receipt.

  3. Reversing Trades

     a. Since the type of goods and the location of the delivery warehouse are decided by the seller, the buyer may be inconvenienced by the actual delivery process. In that case, one, or both, parties may decide to execute a **reversing trade**.

     b. A reversing trade brings a party's futures obligations to zero by offsetting existing contracts.

     c. The purchase of a futures contract is offset by the sale of that identical contract, and vice–versa.

     d. Reversing trades allow a trader to realize a gain or loss on a futures contract without having to actually handle the physical good.

     e. The vast majority of futures positions are completed by reversing trades instead of by delivery.

     f. Reversing trades may be undertaken at any time prior to contract expiration, but they must be for exactly the same futures contract as originally traded.

F. Futures Price Quotations

  1. *The Wall Street Journal* contains a great deal of information regarding futures trading.

  2. The quotations are grouped by commodities and fall into four major groups.

     a. Agricultural and Metallurgical Commodities

     b. Interest Rate Futures

     c. Foreign Exchange Futures

     d. Stock Index Futures

  3. Each set of entries corresponds to a specific contract and displays the name of the exchange the contract is traded on, the name of the commodity, and the number of units traded in each contract.

  4. Each maturity date has a separate line. The contract closest to maturity is known as the **nearby contract**, while the others are referred to as **distant** or **deferred contracts**.

5. The **settlement price** is usually the price of the last trade before the market closed. If there were no trades toward the end of the day, a settlement committee establishes a settlement price. The settlement price governs the gains and losses incurred in marking–to–market.

6. The **open interest** is the number of contracts currently obligated for delivery. If a buyer and seller each trade one contract, and neither is reversing a previous trade, the open interest increases by one contract.

7. Open interest typically increases over a contract's life until just prior to maturity. Then, reversing trades reduce the open interest until the few remaining contracts are closed by delivery.

8. The final line of the quotations shows the number of contracts that were estimated to have traded on the day being reported and the actual volume for the preceding day's trading. This line also shows the total open interest, and the change in the open interest since the preceding day.

V. Futures Pricing

A. The Basis

1. The difference between the cash price and the futures price is known as the **basis**, and is defined as:

$$\text{Basis} = \text{Cash Price} - \text{Futures Price}$$

2. The basis of a contract must be zero at the delivery date to prevent arbitrage opportunities from occurring.

3. Equivalently, the cash price of a good must equal the futures price for the same good at the time of delivery.

B. The Cost–of–Carry Relationship for Futures Prices

1. Arbitrage also governs the relationship between spot prices and futures prices during the life of the contract by the **cost–of–carry relationship**:

$$\text{Futures Price} \leq \text{Cash Price} + \underbrace{\frac{\text{Storage Costs} + \text{Financing Costs}}{}}_{\text{Cost-of-Carry}}$$

2. If this relationship did not hold, traders could lock in a sure profit with no investment.

3. With unrestricted short selling, in order to avoid arbitrage opportunities, the following rule must also hold:

$$\text{Futures Price} \geq \text{Cash Price} + \text{Interest}$$

4. Having assumed the same borrowing and investment rates, we can put the above relationships together and obtain the following rule given unrestricted short selling:

$$\text{Cash Price} + \text{Interest} \leq \text{Futures Price}$$
$$\leq \text{Cash Price} + \text{Storage} + \text{Financing Costs}$$

5. For some commodities, such as corn, it is virtually impossible to enter a short sale. For financial assets, it is possible, but there are charges to be incurred. This means that the cost–of–carry relationship implies the following:

$$\text{Futures Price} \cong \text{Cash Price} + \text{Storage Costs} + \text{Financing Costs}$$

C. Spreads and the Cost–of–Carry
   1. For a single commodity, a **spread** is the difference in price between two futures contracts of differing maturities.
   2. The cost–of–carry relationship also implies a price relationship between futures prices for contracts with differing maturities. With unrestricted short selling, it must be the case that the distant futures price approximately equals the nearby futures price plus storage and financing costs.
   3. To rule out arbitrage, prices must adjust so that it is impossible to sell a distant futures contract, accept delivery on a nearby futures contract, carry the delivered good to delivery on the distant contract, and make a profit.
   4. Ultimately, the cost–of–carry relationship, with the assumption of unrestricted short selling, determines the relationship between the cash price and any futures price, and it also determines the price relationship among all futures contracts.
D. Observed Futures Prices and the Cost–of–Carry Relationship
   1. While the futures price generally exceeds the cash price for storable commodities, as the cost–of–carry relationship with unrestricted short selling implies, that is not always true.
   2. More distant futures contract prices do not always exceed the nearby prices.
   3. To see how normal price relationships can be dramatically upset by unexpected shifts in supply or demand, consider the effect of the Iraqi invasion of Kuwait on world oil markets.
      a. In the pre–invasion period, there was a **normal market** with more distant contract prices being greater than the nearby prices.
      b. The pattern of crude oil prices after the invasion—with prices on deferred contracts lying below the nearby contract price—is known as an **inverted market**.
   4. In the post–invasion period, if unrestricted short selling were possible in the oil market, an arbitrageur could have made a fortune trading at these prices.
   5. From the price patterns in the post–invasion period, we are able to see two things.
      a. A trader's ability to sell a good short depends on being able to borrow the good from someone else. After the invasion of Kuwait, oil was not available. If oil had been available, arbitrageurs would have driven oil prices into line with the cost–of–carry relationship.
      b. Also, in markets where unrestricted short selling is not possible, as was the case in the oil market after the invasion of Kuwait, the

cost–of–carry relationship does not tell the whole story of futures prices. We need to account for shortages and the role of price expectations in the establishment of futures prices.

E. Futures Prices and Expected Future Spot Prices
1. Traders' expectations in futures markets about the future cash prices for various commodities affect futures prices.
2. If futures prices diverge from traders' expectations about future cash prices, they will take speculative positions to profit from the difference.
3. If there were unrestricted short selling, the prices would have to exhibit a strictly increasing pattern. On the other hand, if short selling were totally impossible in a given market, the futures prices should equal the expected future spot price of the commodity in question in order to eliminate any opportunities to earn excessive speculative profits.

VI. The Social Function of Futures Markets

A. Price Discovery
1. Futures markets provide society with a mechanism for estimating the expected future price of a commodity, quickly and cheaply, on a timely basis.
2. Some researchers regard price discovery as the most important social function that the market serves.
B. Risk Transference
1. In addition, futures markets allow the transference of risk from individuals who are unwilling to bear risk to individuals who are willing to bear it.
2. Transacting in the futures market can also allow parties to reduce their risk.
3. A **hedge** is a transaction that is designed to offset some risk.

VII. Speculation with Futures

A. There are many cases where there will not be opportunities for mutual risk reduction in the futures market. In such cases, risk that is transferred away from the hedger must be borne by a speculator.
B. There are three main types of speculators:
1. The **scalper** has the shortest time horizon of all of the futures market speculators. The scalper is hoping to make a profit out of a one or two–tick fluctuation in a futures contract price, and generally has a round trip transaction cost of less than $1.
    a. A **tick** is the minimum price movement on a contract that is permitted by the exchange, usually $25 or less.
    b. A **round trip** is the purchase and sale of the contract.
2. **Day traders**, who may hold futures positions for two to three hours, never maintain a position overnight.

3. The speculator with the longest time horizon is the **position trader**, whose position may last for weeks or months. Position trades may be either outright positions or spreads.
    a. An **outright position** is simply buying or selling a given futures contract of a single maturity; it is probably the riskiest of all futures strategies.
    b. With a spread, the position trader takes a position in two or more related contracts in a way that reduces the risk below the level which would be encountered in an outright position.
        (1) If the spreads are for different contract maturities within a single commodity, they are called **time spreads** or **intracommodity spreads**.
        (2) If the position is in two related, but different commodities, the trade is called an **intercommodity** spread.
4. Any spread trader feels that the alignment between futures contract prices is being violated in some sense.

C. The Role of the Speculator
    1. Speculators benefit society in two important ways.
        a. They provide liquidity for the futures markets by buying and selling contracts. This allows hedgers to transact quickly, with low bid/asked spreads.
        b. In addition, speculators perform an extremely important function by bearing risk for hedgers.

D. Speculation and the Behavior of Futures Prices
    1. Speculators do not bear risk out of the goodness of their hearts; they trade expecting to earn a profit that compensates them for the risk of their position.
    2. Keynes and Hicks maintain that the hedger's needs usually require speculators to be buyers of futures contracts. Speculators take on long positions by buying futures contracts at prices that are less than the expected future spot price of the commodity. This implies that futures prices should rise over time as the low futures price rises to meet the expected future spot price at the maturity of the futures contract. This phenomenon is known as **normal backwardation**.
    3. If the hedgers' needs require speculators to be short in the aggregate, the futures price must lie above the expected future spot price if speculators are to be rewarded for their risk–bearing services. In this situation, the futures price must fall over time, in order for the futures price to equal the lower spot price at the maturity of the contract. This phenomenon is known as a **contango**.
    4. In spite of considerable research, neither of these hypotheses has been validated. Many studies continue to show that the futures price is normally equal to the observed cash price at maturity. If this is the case, there is little opportunity for speculators to make a profit on a consistent basis.

5. One study explains the small returns to speculators by arguing that they are not bearing systematic risk. Thus, in a Capital Asset Pricing Model context, they do not deserve a significant reward.

VIII. Interest Rate Futures

A. Interest Rate Futures and the Yield Curve
   1. In the interest rate futures markets, the exchanges have made a conscious effort to offer interest–rate futures that cover the yield curve.
   2. Essentially, interest rate futures yields may be interpreted as forward rates of interest.
   3. Strong pricing relationships prevent arbitrage across spot and futures market financial instruments. Hence, futures contract yields correspond closely to forward rates calculated from the yield curve.
   4. A comprehensive study of divergences from the cost–of–carry relationship in the Treasury bill market found that deviations did not suggest trades whose profits were large enough to compensate for transaction costs and the cost of short selling.

IX. Stock Index Futures

A. The most important stock index futures contracts are based on the S&P 500 stock index and on the Major Market Index (MMI).
B. Stock Index Arbitrage
   1. Efforts to exploit discrepancies between stock index futures prices and the prices of the underlying stocks are known as **stock index arbitrage**.
   2. Traders use computers to monitor futures prices and stock prices constantly, always searching for arbitrage opportunities. Exploiting any arbitrage opportunity depends critically on speed in responding to a momentary opportunity.
   3. **Program trading** is the use of computer programs to initiate orders to buy or sell stocks, and program trading plays a key role in stock index arbitrage.
C. Program Trading and Stock Market Volatility
   1. General Stock Market Volatility
      Most studies of stock market volatility conclude that volatility in the 1980s (the period of stock index futures trading) was not more noticeable than in other periods.

2. Episodic Volatility
   a. Temporary episodes of extremely high volatility are known as **episodic volatility** or **jump volatility**.
   b. The bulk of evidence suggests a connection between stock index futures trading and jump volatility. However, the evidence does not suggest that the temporary increase in volatility associated with futures trading impairs the functioning of the stock market.

Key Terms and Concepts

arbitrage	the chance to earn a certain riskless profit with no investment
basis	the cash price minus the futures price
clearinghouse	a well–capitalized financial institution that guarantees contract performance to both parties
contango	the condition of futures prices falling to meet expected future spot prices over the life of a futures contract; occurs if hedgers are typically buyers and speculators are typically sellers
contract maturity	in futures markets, the time at which a futures contract is due for delivery
cost–of–carry relationship	a pricing formula which relates the futures price to the cash price of a commodity by specifying conditions which must hold to prevent cash market/futures market arbitrage opportunities
daily settlement	or marking–to–market, the practice, required by the futures exchanges, of realizing trading gains and losses each day through additions to, or subtractions from, the margin account
day trader	a futures market speculator who attempts to anticipate price changes that will occur during a single trading day
distant contract	also deferred contract; a futures contract whose maturity date is later than that of the nearby contract

episodic volatility	also jump volatility; temporary episodes of extremely high volatility
forward contract	a contract for the trade of a good in the future at a price specified today
futures contract	a forward contract traded on an organized exchange with standardized terms
hedger	an individual who trades in the futures market to reduce the risk of a cash market position
intercommodity spread	a position in two different, but related, futures contracts
intracommodity spread	also time spread; a position in futures contracts for the same commodity with different delivery dates
inverted market	a condition where the prices on deferred contracts lie below the nearby contract price
margin	the good faith deposit required of traders by the exchange as security for the fulfillment of futures obligations
nearby contract	the futures contract closest to maturity
normal backwardation	the pattern of futures prices rising to meet expected future spot prices over the life of a futures contract; this occurs if hedgers are typically sellers and speculators are typically buyers
normal market	a market with deferred contract prices being greater than the nearby prices
open interest	the number of futures contracts currently obligated for future delivery
open outcry	the method of trading in the futures market where traders shout their offers so that all other traders may hear and participate
outright position	a position in a single futures contract
pit	an area of the exchange floor where specific futures contracts are traded

position trader	a futures market speculator who tries to anticipate price changes that will occur over time intervals longer than one trading day
price discovery	using futures market prices to estimate the future cash market price of a commodity
program trading	the use of computer programs to initiate orders to buy or sell stocks; plays a key role in stock index arbitrage
reversing trade	trading to bring a futures position to zero (offsetting a buy with a sell in the same contract, or vice–versa)
round trip	the purchase and sale of a contract
scalper	a futures market speculator with the shortest time horizon
settlement committee	a committee of exchange members who determines the settlement price for marking–to– market if the contract has not traded immediately prior to the close
settlement price	the price of the last trade during a day, or a settlement committee's estimate of the closing price, used to determine gains and losses for marking–to–market
spot price	the price for immediate delivery of a good
spread	the difference in price between two futures contracts
stock index arbitrage	efforts to exploit discrepancies between stock index futures prices and the prices of the underlying stocks
tick	the minimum price fluctuation on a contract that is permitted by the exchange

Multiple–Choice Questions

1. Forward contracts differ from futures contracts because forward contracts _____.
   A. are traded in a centralized location
   B. do not require trust between the parties
   C. do not require direct negotiation between the parties
   D. do not provide a means for erasing the contract before maturity
   E. do not provide a means for reducing risk

2. Which of the following is *not* required by the futures exchanges?
   A. marking to market
   B. daily settlement
   C. margin deposits
   D. delivery on contracts
   E. trading only between members or through an exchange member

3. The _____ determines the kinds of goods that it will trade and the contract specifications for each of the goods.
   A. exchange
   B. buyer
   C. seller
   D. speculator
   E. hedger

4. Futures trading is accomplished by _____.
   A. hedging
   B. open–outcry
   C. speculating
   D. over–the–counter dealers
   E. market makers

5. The clearinghouse rule that daily gains and losses are reflected in a trader's margin account is known as _____.
   A. scalping
   B. hedging
   C. marking–to–market
   D. pitting
   E. clearing

6. A reversing trade _____.
   A. offsets a trader's position in a futures contract
   B. is a trade between a hedger and a speculator
   C. signals that a seller is ready to deliver
   D. occurs only in financial futures markets
   E. requires the short sale of the cash market asset

7. Traders who attempt to profit from minute–to–minute changes in futures prices are known as ____.
   A. hedgers
   B. basers
   C. day traders
   D. position traders
   E. scalpers

8. The number of futures contracts currently obligated for delivery is known as the ____ interest.
   A. settlement
   B. daily
   C. margin
   D. open
   E. nearby

9. A farmer who wants to lock in a price for next year's harvest would ____ a futures contract.
   A. sell
   B. buy
   C. scalp
   D. reverse
   E. day trade

10. The argument that most hedgers are sellers, so that futures prices rise to meet expected future spot prices, is known as ____.
    A. risk transference
    B. normal backwardation
    C. open interest
    D. contango
    E. systematic expectations

11. The physical area in which futures trading is conducted is known as the ____.
    A. exchange
    B. clearinghouse
    C. pit
    D. seat
    E. scalp

12. The clearinghouse protects buyers and sellers by ____.
    A. storing goods until delivery
    B. collecting the purchase price from buyers in advance
    C. determining the minimum price fluctuation allowed on contracts
    D. preserving the relationship between cash prices and spot prices
    E. acting as a party to every trade

13. The _____ price is the price for immediate delivery of a good.
   A. forward
   B. future
   C. spot
   D. primary
   E. negotiated

14. A contango occurs when ____.
   A. futures prices fall to meet expected future spot prices
   B. speculators buy futures contracts
   C. interest rate futures cover the yield curve
   D. speculators earn positive profits
   E. futures prices and forward prices diverge

15. Forward contracts and futures contracts are similar in that they ____.
   A. are traded on organized exchanges
   B. require direct contact between buyers and sellers
   C. allow hedgers to lock in prices before future trades occur
   D. provide a means for removing obligations before maturity
   E. are traded on agricultural commodities, but not financial commodities

16. Opposite positions in two futures contracts for the same commodity with different maturities are known as ____ spreads.
   A. basis
   B. intercommodity
   C. time
   D. contango
   E. normal backwardation

17. A _____ is the minimum price movement on a contract that is permitted by the exchange.
   A. basis
   B. divergence
   C. variance
   D. spread
   E. tick

18. If there are restrictions on the short sale of a commodity, then ____.
   A. a negative basis may appear
   B. futures prices may indicate an upward–sloping yield curve
   C. speculators may be forced to take outright positions
   D. an inverted market may develop
   E. hedgers may be forced to bear systematic risk

19. An opposite position in two different, but related, commodities is known as a(n) ____ spread.
    A. basis
    B. intercommodity
    C. time
    D. contango
    E. normal backwardation

20. The basis is defined as ____.
    A. cash price / futures price
    B. futures price + cash price
    C. futures price – cash price
    D. spread – futures price
    E. cash price – futures price

21. A _____ is a transaction that is designed to offset some existing or anticipated risk.
    A. short sale
    B. hedge
    C. bridge
    D. basis
    E. speculation

22. The ____ is used frequently in futures markets and is a legal document representing title to a commodity.
    A. tick
    B. indenture
    C. warehouse receipt
    D. settlement receipt
    E. spot contract

23. Which of the following is *not* a major grouping used in commodities quotations?
    A. Agricultural and Metallurgical Commodities
    B. Interest Rate Futures
    C. Foreign Exchange Futures
    D. Fortune 500 Futures
    E. Stock Index Futures

24. Many experts feel that ____ is the most important social function of futures markets.
    A. risk transference
    B. price discovery
    C. speculation
    D. hedging
    E. contracting

25. The _____ committee determines the price for marking–to–market if the contract has not traded for some time prior to the close.
   A. settlement
   B. scalping
   C. estimating
   D. spot price
   E. margin

Review Problems

1. You purchase a 5,000 bushel corn contract at $2.22 per bushel. Your margin deposit is $2,000. Three days later, the contract settles at $2.03 per bushel. Three days after that, the contract settles at $2.10 per bushel. Two weeks after that, you sell the contract at $2.33 per bushel. Show the pattern of the values in your margin account.

2. Cash market wheat is priced at $4.53 per bushel, and a futures contract for 5,000 bushels that matures in six months closes at $4.97 per bushel. You can borrow or lend at an annual rate of 6 percent per year, and it costs $.03 per month to store a bushel of wheat (assume storage costs are paid at delivery date). Design an arbitrage strategy that will generate a riskless profit from the prices above, and determine the amount of your profit. Explain how the cash and futures prices will adjust to remove the arbitrage opportunity.

3. Cash market corn is priced at $1.85 per bushel, and a futures contract for 5,000 bushels that matures in one year closes at $1.92 per bushel. You can borrow and lend at an annual rate of 12 percent, and it costs $.01 per month to store a bushel of corn. Design an arbitrage strategy that will generate a riskless profit from the prices above, and determine the amount of your profit. Explain how the cash and futures prices will adjust to remove the arbitrage opportunity.

4. A wheat farmer expects to harvest 100,000 bushels in six months. The cash price today is $4.17 per bushel, and a 5,000 bushel wheat contract that matures in six months is priced at $4.43. What is the basis? How would the farmer trade to hedge his harvest? Six months later, the cash price is $4.47 per bushel. How much has the farmer made or lost on hedging? Is he better off for having hedged? Why or why not ?

5. Heating oil for March delivery is priced at $30 per barrel for a 42,000 barrel contract. The June contract is priced at $27.50 per barrel. You believe that the price spread is to narrow. One month later, the March contract is priced at $32.50 per barrel and the June contract is priced at $28 per barrel. Design a spread trade that will be profitable if the normal price alignment returns during the month you will hold the contract. What type of spread is this? Calculate your net gain or loss if you hold the spread position for one month. Did the price movement conform to your expectations? Why or why not?

6. March corn is priced at $2.22 per bushel for a 5,000 bushel contract. March oats are priced at $1.83 per bushel for the same size contract. You believe that the normal price spread is $.25 per bushel. Two months later, March corn is priced at $2.03 and March oats are priced at $1.59. Design a spread trade that will be profitable if the normal price alignment returns during the two months you will hold the contract. What type of spread is this? Calculate your net gain or loss if you hold the spread position for two months. Did the price movement conform to your expectations? Why or why not?

Answers

Multiple–Choice Questions

1. D	10. B	19. B
2. D	11. C	20. E
3. A	12. E	21. B
4. B	13. C	22. C
5. C	14. A	23. D
6. A	15. C	24. B
7. E	16. C	25. A
8. D	17. E	
9. A	18. D	

Review Problems

1. You purchased the futures contract so price increases lead to profits and price decreases lead to losses.

   During the first three days, you lost ($2.22 − $2.03) = $.19 per bushel, or 5,000($.19) = $950. Your margin account falls to $2,000 − $950 = $1,050.

   During the next three days, you gained ($2.10 − $2.03) = $.07 per bushel, or 5,000($.07) = $350. Your margin account rises to $1,050 + $350 = $1,400.

   During the next two weeks, you gained (2.33 − $2.10) = $.23 per bushel, or 5,000($.23) = $1,150. Your margin account rises to $1,400 + $1,150 = $2,550.

   Your net gain of ($2,550 − $2,000) = $550 is also equal to the net price change over the life of your trade:

   ($2.33 − $2.22)5,000 = $550.

2. Shorting the cash good and investing the proceeds for six months at $1/2$ percent per month (6 percent per year) implies a futures price of:

    $4.53(1.005)^6 = 4.67, which is less than the current futures price of $4.97, so there is no arbitrage in that direction.

    Borrowing the money to buy and store the cash good implies a futures price of:

    $[$4.53(1.005)^6 + 6($.03)] = 4.85, which is less than the current futures price. This situation implies arbitrage profits as follows:

    The futures price is too high, so sell the contract. To cover delivery on the contract, buy and store the cash market good today. You will earn:

$$\text{Price received in 6 months} = $4.97(5,000) = $24,850$$

$$\text{Cost to purchase today} = $4.53(5,000) = $22,650$$

$$\text{Storage for 6 months} = 5,000($.03)(6) = $900$$

$$\text{Repayment on borrowing} = $22,650(1.005)^6 + $900$$

$$= $24,238.05$$

$$\text{Arbitrage profit} = ($24,850 - $24,238.05)$$

$$= $611.95$$

Everyone will buy the cash market good, increasing its price, and sell the futures contract, decreasing its price. These transactions will continue until the future price/cash price relationship once again conforms to the cost–of–carry relationship.

3. Borrowing to buy and store the cash good for one year implies a futures price of: $[$1.85(1.01)^{12} + 12(.01)] = 2.20, which exceeds the current futures price so there is no arbitrage in this direction.

    Shorting the cash good and investing the proceeds until delivery implies a futures price of:

    $($1.85)(1.01)^{12} = 2.08, which exceeds the current futures price of $1.92. This situation implies arbitrage profits as follows:

The current futures price is too low, so you should buy the contract. Then, short the cash market good and invest the proceeds. Taking delivery on the futures contract will provide the goods to cover your short sale. You will earn:

Short Sale Proceeds = $1.85(5,000) = $9,250

Return from Investing = ($9,250)(1.01)^{12} = $10,423

Obligation from Buying Contract = $1.92(5,000) = $9,600

Arbitrage Profit = ($10,423 − $9,600) = $823.

Everyone will buy the futures contract, sending its price up, and short sell the cash good, sending its price down, until the two prices are far enough apart to remove the arbitrage opportunity from the violation of the cost–of–carry relationship.

4. The basis is (the cash price − the futures price)

$$= \$4.17 − \$4.43 = −\$.26.$$

The farmer is concerned that the cash market price will fall before he can harvest and sell, so he should sell futures now.

Selling (100,000/5,000) = 20 contracts creates a position worth:

$$\$4.43(5,000)(20) = \$443,000.$$

Six months later, the position is worth:

$$\$4.47(5,000)(20) = \$447,000, \text{ for a loss of:}$$

$443,000 − $447,000 = −$4,000 since the price of a contract the farmer sold rose after he sold it. The farmer is still better off hedging than not hedging because he has reduced the risk of his farming operations. The $4,000 loss is the price he paid to reduce this risk. A safer position justifies the lower return.

5. The current price spread is ($30.00 − $27.50) = $2.50, narrower than the relationship that you think should hold. A widening price spread implies that the price of the March contract will rise and the price of the June contract will fall. Therefore, you should buy the March contract and sell the June contract. These trades will create opposite positions in contracts for the same commodity for different maturities, an intracommodity spread, or a time spread.

One month later, the price of the March contract, which you bought, has risen. You have a gain of:

($32.50 − $30.00)42,000 = $105,000 on one contract.

The price of the June contract, which you sold, has also risen, creating a loss of:

($28.00 − $27.50)42,000 = $21,000 for one contract.

Your net gain is $105,000 − $21,000 = $84,000.

The new price spread is ($32.50 − $28.00) = $4.50, wider than the $2.50 spread in place when you created the position.

Notice that your net gain could have been computed as the favorable change in the price spread using the number of gallons traded:

($4.50 − $2.50)42,000 = $84,000.

As long as the price spread widens, your net position will be profitable, no matter what direction the prices of the individual contracts move.

6. The actual price spread is ($2.22 − $1.83) = $.39, wider than your opinion of the normal alignment. A narrowing spread implies that the price of the corn contract will fall and the price of the oat contract will rise. Therefore, you should sell the corn contract and buy the oats contract. This would mean taking opposite positions in two different, but related, contracts, an intercommodity spread.

Two months later, the corn contract, which you sold, is priced at $2.03. Its price has fallen so you show a gain of:

($2.22 − $2.03)5,000 = $950 for one contract.

The price of the oats contract, which you bought, has fallen to $1.59, for a loss of:

(1.59 − $1.83)5,000 = −$1,200 for one contract.

Your net loss is:

$950 − $1,200 = −$250.

The new price spread is ($2.03 − $1.59) = $.44, wider than the spread in place when you initiated your trades, despite the fact that you thought the price spread would narrow. Therefore, you have a loss that can be calculated directly as the net, unfavorable–spread change, times the number of bushels:

($.39 − $.44) = −$.05; −$.05(5,000) = −$250.

CHAPTER EIGHTEEN

The Options Market

Chapter Objectives

Upon completion of this chapter, you should be able to:
1. Distinguish between put and call options.
2. Understand the terminology of options and option price quotations.
3. Value put and call options at expiration.
4. Determine option profits/losses at expiration.
5. Understand the relationships between the values of call options with different strike prices or different maturities.
6. Explain how the risk–free rate and the volatility of the underlying stock price impact call option values.
7. Explain and employ the Black–Scholes option pricing model.
8. Explain and use the put–call parity relationship.
9. Explain hedging and speculating with options.

Chapter Outline

I. Overview

A. An **option** is the right to buy or sell, for a limited time, a particular good at a specified price.
B. In 1973, the Chicago Board Options Exchange (CBOE) began trading options on individual stocks. Since that time, the options market has experienced rapid growth.
C. As in the futures market, much option speculation relies on techniques of **spreading**, which involves trading two or more related options to create a single position.
D. Options are also very useful for hedging.

E. The successful option trader must have a firm grasp of the institutional details and terminology employed in the market, as well as the pricing relationships that prevail there.

II. Call and Put Options

A. Ownership of a **call option** gives the owner the right to buy a particular good at a certain price, with that right lasting until a particular date. With a call option, the seller receives a payment from the buyer and gives the buyer the option to buy.

B. Ownership of a **put option** gives the owner the right to sell a particular good at a specified price, with that right lasting until a particular date. With a put option, the seller receives a payment from the buyer, and the buyer may then sell a good to the seller at a certain price.

C. In all cases, ownership of an option involves the right, but not the obligation, to make a certain transaction. However, option sellers have no such discretion; they are obligated to perform in certain ways if the owners of the options so desire.

III. Option Terminology

A. The seller of an option is known as the **writer** of an option, and the act of selling is called **writing an option**.

B. If the owner of the call takes advantage of the option, he or she is said to **exercise** the option.

C. Each option contract stipulates a price that will be paid if the option is exercised, and this price is known as the **exercise price**, **strike price**, or the **striking price**.

D. The price of the option is the option **premium**. The option has no validity after its **expiration date**, or **maturity**.

IV. Option Exchanges

A. As with the futures market, there is a seller for every buyer, and both markets allow offsetting trades.

B. To buy an option, one pays for the option at the time of the trade and simply transacts through a brokerage firm that is a member of the options exchange.

C. In selling a call option, the seller may need large financial resources to fulfill his or her obligations. Accordingly, the broker, who is representing the trader to the exchange, is obligated to be sure that the trader has the necessary financial resources to fulfill all obligations.

D. Writing call options against stock that the writer owns is called writing a **covered call**.

E. If the writer of a call does not own the underlying stocks, he or she has written a **naked option**, in this case a **naked call**.

F. The Option Clearing Corporation (OCC) oversees the conduct of the market and assists in making an orderly market.

V. Option Quotations

A. Quotations pertain to the close of trading on the previous trading day. They list the closing price and the various strike, or exercise, prices available for an option.

B. The striking, or exercise, prices are kept fairly near the prevailing price of the stock. As the stock price fluctuates, new striking prices are opened for trading at $5 intervals. As a consequence, volatile stocks are likely to have a greater range of striking prices available for trading at any one time.

C. Each contract is written on 100 shares, but the prices quoted are on a per–share basis.

D. For any given expiration, the lower the striking price for a call, the greater the price will be. Similarly, the longer the time to expiration, the higher the price will be.

VI. Option Pricing

A. Prices of options on stocks without cash dividends depend upon five factors.
  1. Stock price (S)
  2. Exercise price (E)
  3. Time until expiration (T)
  4. The volatility of the underlying stock (σ)
  5. The risk–free interest rate (r_f)

B. For a call option, we can express the call price as a function of the stock price, the exercise price, and the time until expiration using the notation:

$$C(S, E, T) = \text{Price}$$

VII. The Pricing of Call Options at Expiration

A. The term **at expiration** refers to the moment just prior to expiration.

B. If the stock price is less than or equal to the exercise price ($S \leq E$), the call option will have no value.

C. If the stock price exceeds the exercise price ($S > E$), the call option must have a price equal to the difference between the stock price and the exercise price.
  1. This occurs because the owner of the option may buy the stock through the option at the exercise price and immediately sell it in the market at the market price, making a profit equal to the price differential.

2. If this relationship did not hold, there would be arbitrage opportunities.
D. Combining the two relationships discussed allows us to state the first basic principle of option pricing:

$$C(S, E, 0) = \max(0, S - E)$$

E. The options market is a **zero–sum game**. That is, the buyer's gains are the seller's losses and vise versa. If we add up all of the gains and losses in the options market, ignoring transaction costs, the total will equal zero.
F. The reverse of each of the above relationships holds true for put options.
   1. At expiration, the put option is worthless if its strike price is less than the market price because the shares would generate a higher price if sold in the stock market.
   2. The put is worth the exercise price minus the stock price if this amount is positive.
G. An option may have value at expiration while the trader of that option nets a loss. Traders profit on buying options only if the difference between the market price and the exercise at expiration exceeds the price paid for the option.

VIII. The Pricing of a Call Option with a Zero Exercise Price and Infinite Time until Expiration

A. A call option with an exercise price of zero and an infinite time to maturity can be surrendered at any time for the stock at no cost. Since such an option can be transformed into the stock without cost, it must have a value as great as the stock itself.
B. An option on an asset can never be worth more than the underlying asset itself. This allows us to state another principle of option pricing:

$$C(S, 0, \infty) = S$$

C. Although zero–exercise price, infinite–maturity options are not traded, this kind of option represents an extreme situation, and, as such, it can be used to set boundaries on possible option prices.

IX. Relationships Between Option Prices

A. If two call options are alike, except that the exercise price of the first is less than that of the second, then the option with the lower exercise price must have a price that is equal to or greater than the price of the option with the higher exercise price.
B. If there are two options that are otherwise alike, the option with the longer time to expiration must sell for an amount equal to or greater than the option that expires earlier.

C. Call options whose exercise prices are below the market price of the stock (and put options whose exercise prices are above the market price of the stock) are **in–the–money**. Call options whose exercise prices are above the market price of the stock (and put options whose exercise prices are below the market price of the stock) are **out–of–the–money**. If the market price of the stock equals the exercise price of the option, the option is **at–the–money**.

D. Prior to expiration, an in–the–money option will normally be worth more than S – E. This difference (S – E) is the **intrinsic value** of the option, which is simply the value of the option if it were exercised immediately.

X. Call Option Prices and Interest Rates

A. A call option is always worth at least as much as the quantity:
   Current Stock Price – Present Value of the Exercise Price.
   1. The present value of the exercise price is determined by discounting at the risk–free rate.
   2. Therefore, call option values increase as the risk–free rate of interest rises.

XI. Prices of Call Options and the Riskiness of Stocks

A. The riskier the stock on which an option is written, the greater will be the value of the call option.

B. Therefore, other things being equal, a call option on a riskier good will be worth at least as much as a call option on a less risky good.

XII. Call Options as Insurance Policies

A. Options provide insurance because they create a floor on the value of a bond/option portfolio that can be purchased instead of buying the underlying shares.

B. Paying more for an option than its maximum payoff can make sense if it is included in a bond/option portfolio, because part of the benefit from holding the option portfolio is the insurance that the minimum total payoff from the portfolio is known.

C. Therefore, holding the bond/option portfolio is less risky than holding the stock.

D. Taking the value of the insurance policy inherent in the option into account, we can say that:

$$C(S, E, T, R_f, \sigma) = S - \text{Present Value}(E) + I$$

E. However, we have no way, thus far, of putting a numerical value on the insurance policy denoted by I. This task requires an examination of the option pricing model.

XIII. The Option Pricing Model

    A. Previous arguments have shown that the value of a call option should be a function of the current price of the underlying stock and its volatility, the exercise price, the risk–free rate, and the time to expiration.

    B. Black and Scholes developed a complicated mathematical formula for the value of a call option that includes all of the above arguments and specifies the movement in the underlying stock price as being continuous over time and normally distributed.

    C. This model applies to European options on non–dividend paying stocks, though adjustments can be made to the model to deal with other cases.

    D. A **stochastic process** is simply a mathematical description of the change in the value of some variable through time.

    E. The stochastic process adopted by the Black–Scholes model is known as a **Wiener process**. The key features of this process are that the variable changes continuously through time and that the changes it might make over any given time interval are distributed normally.

    F. The formula for the Black–Scholes OPM is given by:

$$C = SN(d_1) - Ee^{-R^fT}N(d_2)$$

    G. An important ingredient in the Black–Scholes model is the use of a cumulative normal distribution function to incorporate the probability distribution of the future stock price.

    H. The terms involving the cumulative probability function are the terms that take account of risk.

    I. The Black–Scholes model price is usually very close to the market price of an option, and as such, its acceptance is widespread.

XIV. The Valuation of Put Options

    A. Although the OPM pertains specifically to call options, it can also be used to price put options, through the principle of **put–call parity**.

    B. The portfolio of one share of stock, one put, and short one call (with the put and call options being on the same stock and having the same exercise price and expiration) can be used to synthesize a risk–free instrument that will pay the exercise price when the options expire.

    C. Therefore, we can say:

$$S - C + P = E / (1 + r_f)^T$$

    D. Since it is possible to know all of the values except for the price of the put, P, we can use this put–call parity relationship to calculate P by simply rearranging the terms.

XV. Speculating with Options

    A. Options offer exciting speculative opportunities because they are investments which have a much greater degree of leverage than stocks. For example, a given percentage change in the stock price will cause a much greater percentage change in the price of the option.

    B. While options can be risky investments, they need not be. In fact, options can be used to take very low risk speculative positions by using them in combinations. The possibilities for these combinations are virtually endless.

XVI. Hedging with Options

    A. Lastly, it is also possible to hedge with options. Part of the Black–Scholes option pricing formula gives a hedge ratio, which is used to determine the number of options to trade to immunize the total portfolio value against changes in the stock price.

    B. As with duration–based hedging, option pricing hedging holds only for small changes in price. Therefore, the hedge must be adjusted periodically as the stock price changes.

XVII. Foreign Currency Options

    A. The text considers a two–option portfolio and a futures contract.

Key Terms and Concepts

at–the–money option	an option whose exercise price is equal to the current price of the underlying stock
call option	gives the owner the right to buy a particular good at a fixed price for a fixed period of time
covered call option	a call option written against shares that are owned
exercising an option	taking advantage of the right embodied in an option (buying the good for a call option and selling the good for a put option)
expiration date	the time at which an option expires and must be exercised or allowed to expire unexercised
in–the–money option	a call option whose exercise price is below the underlying stock price, or a put option whose exercise price is above the underlying stock price

intrinsic value	for a call option, the market price of the stock minus the exercise price or the value of the option if it were exercised immediately
naked option	an option written on shares that one does not own
option	the right to trade a good at a fixed price for a limited period of time
option premium	the price of an option
out–of–the–money option	a call option whose exercise price is above the market price of the underlying stock or a put option whose exercise price is below the market price of the underlying stock
put–call parity	the relationship between a put, call, stock, and bond, where the options have the same exercise price and expiration
put option	gives the owner the right to sell a particular good at a fixed price for a stated amount of time
stochastic process	a mathematical description of the way a variable changes over time
strike price	also exercise price; the price that must be paid for the good when an option is exercised
Wiener process	a mathematical stochastic process where the value of a variable changes continuously through time with the changes being normally distributed
writer	the seller of an option
writing an option	selling an option
zero–sum game	a market where every trader's profit is exactly equal to another trader's loss

Multiple–Choice Questions

1. Options differ from futures contracts in that options ____.
   A. do not allow hedging
   B. do not allow speculating
   C. cannot be used to acquire a cash market commodity
   D. do not require margin deposits
   E. are not traded on stocks

2. Selling an option is known as ____.
   A. putting
   B. calling
   C. writing
   D. spreading
   E. straddling

3. When the underlying stock is trading at $63, you buy a call with a $60 exercise price for $5. The stock price at expiration needed to break even on the option trade is $____.
   A. 60
   B. 62
   C. 63
   D. 65
   E. 68

4. When the underlying stock is trading at $92, you buy a call with an exercise price of $85 for $10. The option premium is $____.
   A. 3
   B. 7
   C. 10
   D. 15
   E. 17

5. When the underlying stock is trading at $92, you buy a call with an exercise price of $85 for $10. The intrinsic value of the option is $____.
   A. 3
   B. 7
   C. 10
   D. 15
   E. 17

6. The value of a call option is negatively related to the ____.
   A. strike price
   B. time to maturity
   C. market price of the stock
   D. option premium
   E. intrinsic value

7. Taking advantage of the right embodied in an option is known as ____.
   A. straddling
   B. exercising
   C. spreading
   D. discounting
   E. striking

8. The price of a call option with an exercise price of zero and an infinite time to maturity must be equal to the ____.
   A. value of a similar put option
   B. value of the underlying stock
   C. exercise price
   D. value of the strike price discounted at the risk–free rate
   E. none of the above

9. If you write a call option against shares of stock that you do not own, you have created a(n) ____ option.
   A. naked
   B. out–of–the–money
   C. in–the–money
   D. premium
   E. covered

10. Options trading is a zero–sum game because ____.
    A. the intrinsic value of an option must be zero when it expires
    B. an in–the–money option must be exercised at maturity
    C. an option buyer's profit is an option writer's loss, and vice–versa
    D. any option can expire worthless
    E. option prices move to prevent the existence of arbitrage profits

11. A call option whose exercise price is equal to the market value of the underlying stock is ____–the–money.
    A. in
    B. out–of
    C. at
    D. across
    E. behind

12. The Black–Scholes option pricing model assumes that price changes in the underlying stock are ____.
    A. normally distributed
    B. discrete over time
    C. negatively related to the volatility of the stock
    D. negatively related to the risk–free rate
    E. positively related to the age of the company

13. Trading two or more related options to create a single position is known as ____.
    A. spreading
    B. waiving
    C. arbitrage
    D. hedging
    E. covering

14. A call option with an exercise price of $100 was priced at $10. At expiration, the underlying stock is selling for $120. If you purchased this call for the $10, your profit/loss at expiration would be _____.
    A. $20
    B. $15
    C. $10
    D. –$5
    E. $0

15. If the underlying stock is priced at $32, the value of an expiring call with an exercise price of $35 is $ _____.
    A. 0.00
    B. 2.00
    C. 3.00
    D. 3.50
    E. 5.00

16. If the underlying stock is priced at $32, the value of an expiring put with an exercise price of $35 is $____.
    A. 0.00
    B. 2.00
    C. 3.00
    D. 3.50
    E. 5.00

17. If you buy a call option, the worst thing that can happen to you is that ____.
    A. the stock is exercised away
    B. you recover the price you paid at expiration
    C. the option expires worthless
    D. you get to keep the option premium
    E. you earn the risk–free rate on your investment

18. The put–call parity relationship argues that the stock price plus the put value minus the call value is equal to the ____.
    A. risk–free rate
    B. stock volatility
    C. present value of the exercise price
    D. option premium
    E. intrinsic value

19. The value of a call option is greater than the difference between the stock price and the present value of the exercise price by the amount of the ____.
    A. insurance policy value
    B. put–call parity premium
    C. intrinsic value
    D. writer's premium
    E. straddle value

20. Options have a greater speculative potential than stock shares because ____.
    A. investors can buy or sell calls
    B. options have a minimum value at expiration
    C. a given percentage change in the value of a stock causes a much greater percentage change in the value of an option
    D. put and call options trade against the same stock
    E. option prices tend to be less volatile than the prices for the underlying shares

21. An option has no validity after its _____ date.
    A. horizon
    B. expiration
    C. calling
    D. stop
    E. redemption

22. A stock is trading at $73; you buy a call with an exercise price of $70 for $8. The option premium is $____.
    A. 3
    B. 5
    C. 8
    D. 11
    E. 14

23. Ownership of a _____ option gives the owner the right to sell a particular good at a specified price.
    A. call
    B. forward
    C. stop
    D. put
    E. straddle

24. If a stock is trading at $66, and you buy a call with an exercise price of $64 for $12, the intrinsic value of the option is $____.
    A. 2
    B. 4
    C. 12
    D. 64
    E. 66

25. If an investor has the option to buy a share of a company at $100, when it is selling in the market at $140, the exercise price would be $____.
    A. 0
    B. 40
    C. 100
    D. 140
    E. 240

Review Problems

1. When the underlying stock trades at $40, a call with an exercise price of $40 is priced at $5. Assume that you buy this call. Calculate your profits/losses for stock prices at expiration of $20, $30, $40, $50, and $60.
2. For the problem above, calculate your profits/losses for the same stock prices at expiration, if you were the writer of the call.
3. Use the Black–Scholes option pricing model to value a call option with an exercise price of $75 when the underlying stock is selling at $78, the risk–free rate is 8 percent per year, the standard deviation of the stock's return is 15 percent, and the option has 9 months to expiration (T = three–quarters of a year = .75).
4. At expiration, a call with an exercise price of $100 has a price of $5. If the underlying stock is currently selling for $110, how would you take advantage of this pricing? At what price must the call sell for to prevent arbitrage opportunities?
5. For Problem 4, what transactions would you make if the call had a price of $15?
6. A stock is selling for $100, and a call option selling for $10 has a strike price of $100. Find the price of a put if the call and put have the same exercise price,

E, and the same expiration date of one year. Assume a risk–free rate of 8 percent.

Answers

Multiple–Choice Questions

1. D	10. C	19. A
2. C	11. C	20. C
3. D	12. A	21. B
4. C	13. A	22. C
5. B	14. C	23. D
6. A	15. A	24. A
7. B	16. C	25. C
8. B	17. C	
9. A	18. C	

Review Problems

1.

Price at Expiration	Value of Call	Profit/Loss
$20	$0	−$5
$30	$0	−$5
$40	$0	−$5
$50	$10	$5
$60	$20	$15

2. Remember that the writer of an option keeps the option premium if the option expires worthless. The gain or loss from writing an option is the premium (in this case, $5 from each option) minus the current value of the option.

Price at Expiration	Value of Call	Profit/Loss
$20	$0	$5
$30	$0	$5
$40	$0	$5
$50	$10	−$5
$60	$20	−$15

Notice that the writer's profits/losses are exactly the opposite of the buyer's profits/losses, which highlights the point that option trading is a zero–sum game. One trader's gains are always another trader's losses.

3.

$$d1 = \frac{\ln(\$78/\$75) + [.08 + (.5)(.15)^2](.75)}{.15 \sqrt{.75}}$$

$$= .8288$$

$$d2 = .8288 - .15 \sqrt{.75} = .6988$$

Referring to the table for standardized Z–scores in the text,

$$N(d1) = N(.83) = .7967 \text{ and } N(d2) = N(.70) = .7580.$$

Thus, the value of the call option is:

$$\$78(.7967) - \$75e^{-.08(.75)}(.7580) = \$8.60$$

4.   Due to the fact that the call is underpriced, you would:

Transaction	Cash Flow
Buy 1 call	–$5
Exercise the call	–$100
Sell the share	$110
Net Cash Flow	+$5

These transactions would cause tremendous demand for the call and tremendous supply of the share. These supply and demand forces would subside only after the call and share price adjust to prevent arbitrage.

The call price of $10 would have prevented any arbitrage opportunities.

5.   Due to the fact that the call is overpriced, you would:

Transaction	Cash Flow
Sell 1 call	+$15
Buy the share	–$110
Initial Cash Flow	–$95

The owner of this call must then immediately exercise the option or allow it to expire. If the option is exercised, the seller has these additional transactions:

Transaction	Cash Flow
Deliver share	0
Collect exercise price	+$100
Total Net Cash Flow	+$5

6. Using the put–call parity relationship, we can find the value of a put.

By simply manipulating this relationship to solve for the value of the put, we get:

$$P = C - S + Ee^{-rt} \text{ or,}$$

$$P = \$10 - \$100 + \$92.31$$

$$P = \$2.31$$

CHAPTER NINETEEN

The Swap Market

Chapter Objectives

Upon completion of this chapter, you should be able to:
1. Discuss the characteristics of the swap market.
2. Explain plain vanilla swaps, including interest rate swaps and foreign currency swaps.
3. Define the motivations for swaps, including commercial needs and comparative advantage.
4. Explain the respective roles of swap facilitators as swap brokers and swap dealers.
5. List and explain the factors that affect swap pricing.
6. Discuss the factors surrounding risk management with swap portfolios.

Chapter Outline

I. Overview

    A. A **swap** is an agreement between two or more parties to exchange sets of cash flows over a period in the future.

    B. The parties that agree to the swap are known as **counterparties**.

    C. The cash flows that the counterparties make are generally tied to the value of debt instruments or to the value of foreign currencies. Therefore, the two basic kinds of swaps are **interest rate swaps** and **currency swaps**.

    D. The swap market has grown rapidly in the last few years, because it provides firms that face financial risks with a flexible way to manage risk.

    E. **Swap facilitators** are economic agents who help counterparties identify each other and help the counterparties consummate swap transactions.

    F. Because swap facilitators often expose themselves to the risk that counterparties are trying to avoid, they must do two things.

     1.   Price the swap to provide a reward for their services in bearing risk.

     2.   Effectively manage their swap portfolio.

II. The Swap Market

A. Review of Futures and Options Market Features

    1.   The futures and options markets are regulated markets and are dominated by the exchanges where trading takes place.

    2.   Their contracts are highly standardized, limited to relatively few goods, and have a few fixed expirations per year.

    3.   The horizon over which they trade is often much shorter than the risk horizon that businesses face.

B. Characteristics of the Swap Market

    1.   Swaps are custom tailored to the needs of the counterparties.

    2.   Thus, swap agreements are more likely to meet the specific needs of the counterparties than exchange–traded instruments. Counterparties can select the dollar amount they wish to swap and choose the exact maturity they need.

    3.   The Commodity Futures Trading Commission has formally announced that it will not seek jurisdiction over the swap market, which means that the swap market should remain free of federal regulation for the foreseeable future.

    4.   The swap market has some inherent limitations:

        a. To consummate a swap transaction, one potential counterparty must find a counterparty that is willing to take the opposite side of a transaction.

        b. Because a swap agreement is a contract between two counterparties, the swap cannot be altered or terminated early without the agreement of both parties.

        c. The swap market has no guarantor, and parties to the swap must be certain of the creditworthiness of their counterparties. This problem of potential default is perhaps the most important.

    5.   The swap market is virtually limited to firms and financial institutions.

C. The Emergence of the Swap Market

Currency traders developed currency swaps in the late 1970s, and the first interest rate swap was in 1981. Since then, the market has grown rapidly.

III. Plain Vanilla Swaps

A. A **plain vanilla swap** is the simplest kind of swap that can be initiated. These swaps can be interest rate swaps or foreign currency swaps.

B. Interest Rate Swaps

    1.   In a plain vanilla interest rate swap, one counterparty has an initial position in a fixed rate debt instrument, while the other counterparty has an initial position in a floating rate obligation. By swapping the

floating rate obligation, one counterparty eliminates exposure to changing interest rates. For the party with the fixed rate obligation, the swap increases the interest rate sensitivity.

2. For example, Party A will agree to pay Party B a fixed rate, while in return Party B agrees to pay Party A a floating rate of LIBOR + x percent.

3. Because the principal is not actually exchanged, it is called a **notational principal**, an amount used as a base for computations.

4. Generally, only the **net payment**, the difference between the two obligations, takes place. So, if Party A's obligation for year one is $120,000, and Party B's obligation is $130,000, then Party B will simply pay Party A the sum of $10,000.

C. Foreign Currency Swaps

1. In a currency swap, a party holds one currency and desires a different currency. The swap arises when one party provides a certain principal in one currency to its counterparty in exchange for an equivalent amount of a different currency.

2. A plain vanilla currency swap involves three different sets of cash flows.

    a. First, at the initiation of the swap, the two parties actually do exchange cash.

    b. Second, the parties make periodic interest payments to each other during the life of the swap. In actual practice, the parties will make only net payments.

    c. Third, at the termination of the swap, the parties again exchange the principal.

D. Summary

1. The essential feature of the interest rate swap is the transformation of a fixed rate obligation to a floating rate obligation for one party, and a complementary transformation of a floating rate obligation to a fixed rate obligation for the other party.

2. In a currency swap, the two parties exchange currencies to obtain access to a foreign currency that better meets their business needs.

IV. Motivations for Swaps

A. Commercial Needs

1. As an example of a prime candidate for an interest rate swap, consider a savings and loan association and its vulnerability to rising rates. If rates rise, the savings and loan will be forced to increase the rate it pays on deposits, but it cannot increase the interest rate it charges on the mortgages that have already been issued.

2. To escape this interest rate risk, the savings and loan might use the swap market to transform its fixed rate assets into floating rate assets or transform its floating rate liabilities into fixed rate liabilities.

3.   For example, in exchange for a fixed rate mortgage it holds, the savings and loan wishes to pay a fixed rate of interest and receive a floating rate of interest.

4.   From the very nature of the savings and loan industry, the association finds itself with a risk exposure to rising interest rates. However, by engaging in an interest rate swap, the association can secure a fixed rate position.

B. Comparative Advantage

1.   In many situations, one firm may have better access to the capital market than another firm. For example, a U.S. firm may be able to borrow easily in the United States, but it might not have such favorable access to the capital market in Germany. Similarly, a German firm may have good borrowing opportunities domestically but poor opportunities in the U.S.

2.   This situation raises the possibility that each firm can exploit its comparative advantage and share the gains by reducing overall borrowing costs.

3.   In a currency swap, the two parties can make independent borrowings and then exchange the proceeds. For this reason, currency swaps are also known as an **exchange of borrowings**.

4.   By using the swap, both parties achieve an effective borrowing rate that is much lower than they could have obtained by borrowing the currency they needed directly. Both parties can use the comparative advantage of the other to reduce their borrowing costs.

V. Swap Facilitators

A. A swap facilitator is a third party who assists in the completion of a swap. When a swap facilitator acts strictly as an agent, without taking any financial position in the swap transaction, the facilitator acts as a **swap broker**.

B. In some instances, swap facilitators may actually transact for their own accounts to help complete the swap. In this case, the swap facilitator acts as a **swap dealer**.

C. Both swap brokers and swap dealers are known as **swap banks**, so a swap bank is equivalent to a swap facilitator.

D. Swap Brokers

1.   For a potential swap participant with a specific need, finding a counterparty can be very difficult, and this difficulty creates an opportunity for a swap broker.

2.   A swap broker has a number of firms in her client base and stands ready to search for swap counterparties upon demand. After a party solicits the assistance of a swap broker, the broker contacts potential counterparties.

3.   After finding a suitable counterparty, the broker brings the two parties together and helps to negotiate and complete the swap contract.

4. The swap broker receives a fee from each counterparty and does not bear any financial risk.

E. Swap Dealers
   1. A swap dealer fulfills all of the functions of a broker, but also takes a risk position in the swap transaction by becoming an actual party to the transaction. The swap dealer accepts the risk position in order to complete the transaction for the initial counterparty.
   2. If completing a swap results in a risk position for the swap dealer, the dealer will then try to minimize that risk by his own further transactions.

F. Swap Dealers as Financial Intermediaries
   1. Often, a swap dealer assumes a risk in the pursuit of profit. The dealer could take this position as a speculation on interest rates.
   2. However, the swap dealer prefers to act as a financial intermediary, making a profit by providing informational services.
   3. If a swap dealer acts as a financial intermediary, and is not able to escape all risk exposure he encounters, he will try to find another swap partner.
   4. In actuality, when the swap dealer acts as a counterparty, the dealer intends to be only a temporary substitute for an unavailable counterparty.

VI. Pricing of Swaps

A. Factors that Affect Swap Pricing
   1. Creditworthiness
      a. The swap dealer must appraise the creditworthiness of the swap partner. If the swap dealer suffers a default by one of its counterparties, the dealer must either absorb the loss or institute a lawsuit to seek recovery on the defaulted obligation.
      b. In swaps, because only the net amount is actually exchanged, default could seldom involve failure to pay the notional amount or even an entire periodic payment.
      c. Instead, a swap default would generally imply a loss of the change in value due to shifting interest rates.
      d. While this amount can be quite significant, such a default would not be as catastrophic as a bond default in which the entire principal could be lost.
      e. When a swap dealer suffers a default, the elaborate structure of offsetting risks can be upset. Because of the potential costs associated with default, the swap dealer will adjust the pricing on swaps to reflect the risk of default.
   2. Availability of Additional Counterparties
      a. Because we are assuming that the swap dealer wishes to act only as a financial intermediary, the swap dealer will be very concerned

about how the risk involved in a prospective swap can be offset by participating in other swaps.

   b. The swap dealer will be very pleased to create a structure of swaps that leaves no interest rate risk and still provides a decent profit.

3. The Term Structure of Interest Rates

   a. The market for interest rate swaps must reflect the term structure that prevails in the bond market.

   b. If the swap market did not reflect the term structure, traders would find ready arbitrage opportunities, and they could quickly discipline traders to pay attention to the term structure.

B. The Indication Swap Pricing Schedule

1. In the early to mid–1980s, swap banks were often able to charge a **front–end** fee for arranging a swap. As the market has matured, that ability has been competed away.

2. Therefore, the swap dealer today generally receives his total compensation by charging a spread between the rates he is willing to pay and the rate he demands on swap transactions.

3. A typical pricing schedule for an interest rate swap occurs as follows.

   a. First, the rate the swap bank pays or receives increases with the maturity in question.

   b. Second, the swap bank makes a gross profit that equals the spread between what the bank pays and what it receives.

VII. Swap Portfolios

A. Risks in Managing a Swap Portfolio

1. There is the risk that one of the counterparties might default.

2. The bank faces **basis risk**—the risk that the normal relationship between two prices might change.

3. The swap dealer also faces mis–match risk.

   a. When acting as a counterparty in a swap, the swap dealer accepts a risk position that he is anxious to offset by engaging in other swaps.

   b. Mis–match risk refers to the risk that the swap dealer will be left in a position that he cannot offset easily through another swap.

4. One of the most serious risks that swap dealers face is interest rate risk.

B. Managing Mis–Match and Interest Rate Risk in a Swap

1. Mis–match risk occurs when a dealer is unable to offset the risks associated with a swap.

2. Dealers can also suffer a loss if they must pay out a higher interest rate than they are receiving.

3. When dealers face these kinds of risks, they can use the futures market as a temporary means of offsetting the risk.

   a. While Eurodollar futures may be a close substitute for the unavailable swap, they are unlikely to prove a perfect substitute.

b. Because of the imperfections in substituting for the unavailable swap, swap dealers are likely to continue to seek a swap that meets their risk needs exactly.

Key Terms and Concepts

basis risk	the risk that the normal relationship between two prices might change
counterparties	the parties that agree to a swap
currency swaps	occurs when two parties exchange currencies to obtain access to a foreign currency that better meets their business needs
exchange of borrowings	also currency swaps; given because the two parties have made independent borrowings and then exchanged the proceeds
front–end fee	was charged by swap banks for arranging a swap but has subsequently been competed out of existence (except for some complicated swaps)
interest rate swaps	an agreement between two counterparties to exchange fixed–rate interest cash flows for floating–rate interest cash flows
net payment	the cash flow that actually takes place in a plain vanilla interest rate swap and is found by the difference between the two obligations
notional principal	the amount used as a base for computations in a plain vanilla interest rate swap but is not actually transferred from one party to another
plain vanilla swap	the simplest type of swap; can be an interest rate or foreign currency swap
swap	an agreement between two or more parties to exchange sets of cash flows over a period in the future
swap banks	another name for both swap brokers and swap dealers

swap broker   when a swap facilitator acts strictly as an agent, without taking any financial position in the swap transaction

swap dealer   when a swap facilitator transacts for his own account to help complete the swap

swap facilitators   economic agents who help counterparties identify each other and help the counterparties consummate swap transactions

Multiple–Choice Questions

1. The parties that agree to a swap are known as ____.
   A. facilitators
   B. counterparties
   C. speculators
   D. interparties
   E. brokers

2. Swap ____ expose themselves to risk that ____ are trying to avoid.
   A. counterparties; facilitators
   B. dealers; counterparties
   C. facilitators; brokers
   D. brokers; facilitators
   E. traders; brokers

3. Which of the following statements is *incorrect*?
   A. Swaps are for dollar amounts specified by the counterparties.
   B. Currency traders developed currency swaps in the late 1970s.
   C. Swap agreements are more likely to meet the needs of the counterparties than exchange–traded instruments.
   D. The swap market has no guarantor.
   E. Individual transactors dominate the swap market.

4. Swap agreements can be altered or terminated early ____.
   A. if a swap bank holds the contract
   B. upon one of the counterparties request
   C. only if both counterparties agree
   D. if interest rates move by more than 5 percent
   E. if interest rates move by more than 3 percent

5. The simplest type of swap is called a(n) _____ swap.
    A. ordinary
    B. run of the mill
    C. simple
    D. plain vanilla
    E. routine

6. In the swap market, the problem of _____ is perhaps most important.
    A. regulation
    B. potential default
    C. con artists
    D. competition from other markets
    E. government intervention

7. In effect, the swap market is virtually limited to _____ and _____.
    A. individuals; firms
    B. groups; individuals
    C. government institutions; individuals
    D. foreigners; individuals
    E. firms; financial institutions

8. A plain vanilla swap can be either an _____ or a _____ swap.
    A. governmental; institutional
    B. private; public
    C. insured; uninsured
    D. interest rate; foreign currency
    E. none of the above

9. A _____ principal is generally not exchanged but is used only as a base for payment computations.
    A. notional
    B. net
    C. simple
    D. compound
    E. fixed

10. The essential feature of the _____ swap is the transformation of a fixed rate obligation to a floating rate obligation for one party, and a complementary transformation of a floating rate obligation to a fixed rate obligation for another party.
    A. plain vanilla
    B. currency
    C. interest rate
    D. notional
    E. compound

11. A plain vanilla currency swap involves ____ different sets of cash flows.
    A. zero
    B. one
    C. two
    D. three
    E. four

12. In a(n) ____ swap, the two parties exchange currencies to obtain access to a foreign currency that better meets their business needs.
    A. money–rate
    B. currency
    C. international money
    D. fixed rate
    E. dollar deposit

13. The savings and loan industry is a good example of an industry with ____ as a motivation for swap transactions.
    A. governmental regulation
    B. rising interest rate risk
    C. mortgage default risk
    D. depositor default risk
    E. limited commercial market access

14. Currency swaps are also known as ____.
    A. an exchange of borrowings
    B. effective borrowing plans
    C. comparative advantage loans
    D. gain sharing plans
    E. interest rate swaps

15. A swap ____ is a third party who assists in the completion of a swap.
    A. expediter
    B. mediator
    C. arbitrator
    D. facilitator
    E. assistant

16. Both swap brokers and swap dealers are known as swap ____.
    A. houses
    B. banks
    C. facilities
    D. tellers
    E. depositories

17. Swap facilitators act as swap ____ when they transact for their own account to help complete a swap.
    A. tellers
    B. dealers
    C. brokers
    D. managers
    E. shoppers

18. The swap ____ receives a fee from each counterparty and does not bear any financial risk.
    A. dealer
    B. broker
    C. teller
    D. banker
    E. facilitator

19. Which of the following statements is *incorrect*?
    A. Often, a swap dealer assumes a risk in the pursuit of profit.
    B. If completing a swap results in a risk position for swap dealers, the dealers will then try to minimize that risk by their own further transactions.
    C. In actuality, when a swap dealer acts as a counterparty, the dealer intends to be only a temporary substitute for an unavailable counterparty.
    D. If the swap dealer suffers a default by one of his counterparties, the dealer must always absorb the loss.
    E. There is no clearinghouse in the swap market to guarantee performance on a contract if one of the counterparties defaults.

20. When a swap dealer acts as a financial intermediary, he or she is attempting to make a profit by ____.
    A. speculating on interest rates
    B. speculating on exchange rates
    C. providing informational services
    D. holding a note for one counterparty
    E. holding a note for both counterparties

21. Which of the following statements is *incorrect*?
    A. Because of the potential costs associated with default, the swap dealer will adjust the pricing on swaps to reflect the risk of default.
    B. The swap dealer will be very pleased to create a structure of swaps that leaves no interest rate risk and still provides a decent profit.
    C. The market for interest rate swaps is risky because it does not clearly reflect the term structure that prevails in the bond market.
    D. When a swap dealer suffers a default, the elaborate structure of offsetting risks can be upset.
    E. The swap dealer must appraise the creditworthiness of the swap partner.

22. The ____ fee, which was prevalent in the early 1980s, has been almost completely competed away.
   A. front–end
   B. up–front
   C. compensatory
   D. initiating
   E. instigating

23. ____ risk is the risk that the normal relationship between two prices might change.
   A. Mis–match
   B. Basis
   C. Interest rate risk
   D. Arbitrage
   E. Fluctuating

24. ____ risk refers to the risk that the swap dealer will be left in a position that he cannot offset easily through another swap.
   A. Mis–match
   B. Basis
   C. Interest rate
   D. Arbitrage
   E. Fluctuating

25. In managing the risk that swap dealers face, ____ may be a close substitute for the unavailable swap.
   A. Eurodollar futures
   B. stocks
   C. gold
   D. repos
   E. real estate

Review Problems

1. Explain the difference between a swap dealer and a swap broker.
2. For a plain vanilla interest rate swap, explain the rights and obligations of the two parties, with particular emphasis on their contractual cash flows.
3. Explain the role of the **notional principal** in an interest rate swap.
4. Explain why the swap market employs the practice of making only net payments.
5. Explain why an actual exchange of principal normally occurs in a foreign currency swap but not in an interest rate swap.

6. Assume that a swap dealer wants to perform strictly as a financial intermediary, and that the dealer expects rising interest rates. What risk position would the swap dealer want to take in an interest rate swap, to receive or to pay the floating rate?

7. Assume that you are a swap dealer and that you prepare your indication swap pricing schedule as a band around LIBOR. How would you adjust your pricing if you come to expect greater interest rate volatility?

8. Assume that you are a swap dealer and that you prepare your indication swap pricing schedule as a band around LIBOR. How would you adjust your pricing if you expect interest rates to rise more than other market participants do?

Use the following information to answer the next five problems. Assume that you are a swap dealer and have just acted as a counterparty in an interest rate swap. The notional principal for the swap was $10,000,000, and you are now obligated to make seven annual payments of 9 percent interest, or $900,000 per year. The floating rate that you will receive is 9.2 percent, and the floating payments to you are annual as well.

9. If interest rates do not change over the horizon, what will your net payments be?

10. Continuing with Problem 9, assuming a discount rate of 9 percent, what is the NPV of your swap agreement?

11. If LIBOR is unchanged for three years, and then falls by 2 percent, what are your net payments over the seven years?

12. In the interest rate environment of Problem 11, what will the NPV of the swap be assuming a discount rate of 9 percent?

13. Assuming that you have just consummated the swap described above and you want to function strictly as a financial intermediary, how would you transact to mitigate the interest rate risk that you face?

Use the following information for Problem 14. Two counterparties agree to enter a foreign currency swap between British pounds and Swiss francs. The current exchange rate is 3.2 francs per pound. The British firm needs 16 million francs and the Swiss firm needs 5 million pounds.

Firm	British Rate (%)	Swiss Rate(%)
British Firm	9	8
Swiss Firm	10	7

14. How would these two firms form a swap to meet their respective currency needs? What will be both firms' effective borrowing rates?

Answers

Multiple-Choice Questions

1. B	10. C	19. D
2. B	11. D	20. C
3. E	12. B	21. C
4. C	13. B	22. A
5. D	14. A	23. B
6. B	15. D	24. A
7. E	16. B	25. A
8. D	17. B	
9. A	18. B	

Review Problems

1. A swap broker acts purely as a middleman in bringing together the counter-parties to a swap. By contrast, the swap dealer takes a risk position in the swap by acting as a counterparty to facilitate the swap transaction.

2. One party undertakes to make a series of fixed payments over the life of the swap. The amount of these payments is known in advance and never change. The other party promises to make a series of payments, the value of which depends on the movement of a reference interest rate, usually the LIBOR rate.

3. The notional principal is the amount of principal on which an interest rate swap agreement is based. While never actually being exchanged, it is used for computing the interest payments that the counterparties must make to each other.

4. Making only net payments simplifies the transactions between two counter-parties, because only one party will have to make a payment. In addition, the practice of making net payments reduces the risk exposure inherent in a swap. If both parties made payments, each would suffer the risk that the counterparty would not pay as promised. Because the net payment is only the difference, there is a reduced risk of default.

5. One of the key motivations for a foreign currency swap is the desire to obtain the actual use of the foreign currency.

6. Functioning strictly as an intermediary, the swap dealer prefers to avoid any position. However, dealers may take positions to help complete the swap. If such a dealer takes a position, he or she would immediately seek another swap partner that would help avoid that risk exposure. If the swap dealer must take a position in the circumstances described, the dealer would prefer to receive the floating rate. Then, if interest rates rise as anticipated, the receipts will increase.

7. A typical response would be to increase the size of the band around LIBOR. In essence, the band of quoted rates is the dealer's bid–asked spread, and it is normal for bid–asked spreads to increase as market volatility increases.

8. Your expectation would offer an incentive for shading your price schedule to attract more floating rate payers, particularly if you were willing to act as a counterparty. For example, assume at the outset that LIBOR is 9.00 and that you usually are willing to receive LIBOR + 20 basis points and pay 9.00 fixed. Given your expectations, you might be willing to receive LIBOR + 15 basis points and pay 9.00 fixed. This would attract more floating rate payers and would benefit you if your interest rate expectations are correct.

9. You will pay $900,000 fixed and receive $920,000 floating, for a net inflow of $20,000 per year.

10. Under these assumptions, you have an annuity of seven years with a payment of $20,000, discounted at 9 percent. The present value factor for an annuity is:

$$PVIFA_{.09,7} = \frac{1 - (1.09)^{-7}}{.09} = 5.033$$

Therefore, the present value will be:

$$PV = 5.0330(\$20,000) = \$100,659.$$

11. For the first three years, you will pay $900,000 and receive $920,000, for a net inflow of $20,000 in each of the first three years. In the remaining years, you will continue to pay $900,000, but your new inflow will be $720,000. Therefore, for years 4–7 you will make a net payment of $180,000.

12.

$$PV = \frac{20{,}000}{1.09} + \frac{20{,}000}{1.09^2} + \frac{20{,}000}{1.09^3} - \frac{180{,}000}{1.09^4} -$$

$$\frac{180{,}000}{1.09^5} - \frac{180{,}000}{1.09^6} - \frac{180{,}000}{1.09^7}$$

$$= 18{,}349 + 16{,}834 + 15{,}444 - 127{,}517 -$$

$$116{,}988 - 107{,}328 - 98{,}466$$

$$= -\$399{,}672$$

13. Because you committed to pay fixed rate and receive floating rate payments, you need to transact so that you both receive and pay the floating rate, or so that you both receive and pay the fixed rate. Thus, you can mitigate your interest rate risk by entering another swap to receive a fixed rate and pay a floating rate. In this case, you would be both receiving and paying a fixed rate and you would be both receiving and paying a floating rate. Assuming that the notional principal and rates were appropriate, this transaction could leave you with no interest rate risk.

14. The British firm will borrow 5 million pounds from a third party lender at 9 percent, while the Swiss firm will borrow 16 million francs from a fourth party at 7 percent.

At this point each party has the ability to engage in a plain vanilla currency swap. To initiate this swap, the British firm forwards the 5 million pounds to the Swiss firm, and the Swiss firm forwards the 16 million francs to the British firm.

Each year the British firm will pay 450,000 pounds in interest for its borrowings of pounds but will receive 500,000 pounds from the Swiss. Also, the British firm will be paying 1,280,000 francs to the Swiss firm for its borrowing. The Swiss firm will be paying 1,120,000 francs on its own borrowing of the 16 million it borrowed to lend to the British firm.

The effective borrowing rate for the British firm borrowing francs is 7 percent. This is calculated as follows:

British firm collects 500,000 pounds and pays 450,000 pounds for a net profit of 50,000 pounds or 160,000 francs. On the other side of this swap, the British firm pays 1,280,000 francs to the Swiss. The net payout of the British firm is 1,280,000 − 160,000 = 1,120,000 francs. This gives an effective rate of 1,120,000/16,000,000 = .07 or 7 percent.

The effective rate of the Swiss firm borrowing pounds is 9 percent.

CHAPTER TWENTY

Financial Engineering

Chapter Objectives

Upon completion of this chapter, you should be able to:
1. Discuss the concept of financial engineering and how it extends the basic ideas of risk management.
2. Discuss the payoff distributions for straddles, strangles, bull spreads, bear spreads, and butterfly spreads.
3. Discuss synthetic instruments and their relationship with put–call parity.
4. Explain how to create synthetic equity, synthetic puts, synthetic call options, and synthetic T–bills.
5. Discuss the concept of a swap as a portfolio of forwards.
6. Explain the concept of portfolio insurance.

Chapter Outline

I. Overview

A. The idea of financial engineering is fairly new, and its concepts extend the basic ideas of risk management in finance.
B. This chapter has three main purposes.
   1. An exploration of techniques for combining options to generate profit profiles that are not available with positions in single options.
   2. An analysis of the relationship among underlying securities, futures, forwards, swaps, and options. Each of these building blocks can be simulated by a combination of the others, which leads to an exploration of how to create a **synthetic instrument**—a financial structure that has the same value as another identifiable instrument.
   3. An explanation of how to alter the risk and return characteristics of an existing position by using derivative instruments.

C. With financial engineering, the investment manager can tailor a given risk position in a variety of ways. Thus, given some initial position, financial engineering can create a less risky position, a riskier position, or a position with a very specialized risk exposure.

II. Option Combinations

A. Straddles
  1. A **straddle** is an option position involving a put and a call option on the same stock.
    a. To buy a straddle, an investor will buy both a put and a call that have the same expiration and the same striking price.
    b. To sell a straddle, a trader sells both the call and the put.
B. Strangles
  A long position in a **strangle** consists of a long position in a call and a long position in a put on the same underlying good with the same term to expiration, with the call having a higher exercise price than the put.
C. Bull and Bear Spreads
  1. A **bull spread** in the options market is a combination of call options designed to profit if the price of the underlying good rises.
  2. The buyer of a bull spread buys a call with an exercise price below the stock price and sells a call option with an exercise price above the stock price.
  3. The spread is a "bull" spread because the trader hopes to profit from a price rise in the stock. The trade is a "spread" because it involves buying one option and selling a related option.
  4. A **bear spread** is a combination of options designed to profit from a drop in the stock price. Actually, the bear spread is just the short position that matches the bull spread.
D. Butterfly Spreads
  1. To buy a **butterfly spread**, a trader buys one call with a low exercise price and buys one call with a high exercise price, while selling two calls with a medium exercise price.
  2. The spread profits most when the stock price is near the medium exercise price at expiration.
  3. In essence, the butterfly spread gives a payoff similar to a straddle but offers lower risk at the expense of reduced profit potential.

III. Synthetic Instruments

A. Put–Call Parity and Synthetic Instruments
  1. The put–call relationship provides the basic blueprint for creating synthetic securities. By rearranging the equation to isolate individual instruments, we see what combination of other instruments will simulate a particular instrument of interest.

2. Remember, to apply put–call parity, we need a call option with the same striking price and the same term to expiration as the put we are attempting to price.

B. Synthetic Equity

1. After rearranging the put–call parity equation, we can show that a position in the stock is equivalent to a long call plus a short put, coupled with an investment at the risk–free rate:

$$S = C - P + \frac{E}{(1 + R_f)^T}$$

2. Thus, **synthetic equity** consists of a long call, short put, and an investment of the present value of the exercise price in the risk–free rate.

C. Synthetic Put Options

The put–call parity relationship shows that a **synthetic put** consists of a long call and short stock position, coupled with investing the present value of the exercise price in a risk–free investment.

D. Synthetic Call Options

1. As the put–call parity relationship indicates, a **synthetic call** consists of a long position in both the stock and the put option, and a short position in a risk–free bond that will pay the exercise price at the expiration of the option.

2. To create a synthetic call, a trader would borrow the present value of the exercise price and use these funds to help finance the purchase of the put and the stock.

E. Synthetic T–Bills

A synthetic T–bill can also be created by the proper combination of a long put, short call, and a long position in the stock. The resulting position is a synthetic T–bill, because the synthetic instrument will pay the exercise price at the expiration date of the options no matter what the stock price might be.

F. Synthetic Futures and Forwards and Put–Call Parity

1. Most financial futures closely approximate the assumptions that the cost–of–carry relationship holds exactly and that the cost–of–carry equals the risk–free rate. Under these assumptions, the futures price will equal the spot price multiplied by one plus the cost of carry:

$$F = S(1 + R_f)$$

2. If we combine the above model with the put–call parity relationship and with the analysis of synthetic securities, we obtain the relationship:

$$C - P = \frac{F - E}{(1 + R_f)^T}$$

3. Now, the difference between the call and put price equals the present value of the difference between the futures price and the exercise price of the options.
4. For the special case in which the current futures price equals the exercise price, then the quantity F − E equals zero. This implies that C − P also equals zero, which means that the call and put must have the same price.
5. If the futures price is less than the exercise price, the quantity F − E is negative. This implies that the put will be more valuable than the call.

IV. The Swap as a Portfolio of Forwards

A. An interest rate swap generally includes a series of payments. Each of these payments can be analyzed as an interest rate forward contract. Because the swap agreement includes a sequence of a number of such arrangements, the swap is a portfolio of forward contracts.
B. Portfolio Insurance
    In **portfolio insurance**, a trader transacts to ensure that the value of a portfolio cannot fall below a given amount.
C. Synthetic Portfolio Insurance and Put–Call Parity
    1. Applying the put–call parity equation to the index example in the text, we have:

$$C = INDEX + P - \frac{E}{(1 + R_f)^T}$$

    2. An insured portfolio is the long put/long index position that has the same profits and losses as a call. From put–call parity, we can hold a long call plus invest the present value of the exercise price in the risk–free asset. From the put–call parity relationship, we see:

$$C + E(1 + R_f)^T = P + INDEX$$

    3. The long call plus investment in the risk–free asset creates the same insured portfolio as the long index plus the long put. Both positions have the same value and the same profits and losses at expiration.
D. Tailoring Risk and Return Characteristics with Futures and Options
    1. From the examples in the text, we can see that traders can use futures and options to tailor the risk characteristics of the portfolio to individual taste. With the variety of futures and option instruments available, the financial engineer can create almost any feasible combination of risk and return.
    2. In comparing the fully and partially insured portfolios with the uninsured portfolio, we have seen that portfolio insurance reduces risk. However, there must be a reduction in expected return that accompanies the reduction in risk.

E. Risk and Return in Insured Portfolios
    1. Terminal Values for Portfolios A–C
        Given the portfolios in the text: concentrating only on terminal values, and neglecting the different investments required to obtain each portfolio, the fully insured portfolio is the most desirable, followed by the half–insured portfolio, and then the uninsured portfolio.
    2. Returns on Portfolios A–C
        a. Because the portfolios in the text have different costs, we need to compare the returns on each portfolio to make them more directly comparable.
        b. When factoring in the possible returns, the risk/expected return trade–off implied by portfolio strategies is apparent.
        c. Portfolio insurance protects against large losses by sacrificing the change for large gains.

Key Terms and Concepts

bear spread	a combination of options designed to profit from a drop in stock prices; this spread is just the short position that matches the bull spread
bull spread	a combination of call options with different strikes designed to show a profit from a price rise in the stock; the buyer of a bull spread buys a call with an exercise price below the stock price and sells a call with an exercise price above the stock price
butterfly spread	occurs when the trader buys one call with a low exercise price and buys one call with a high exercise price, while selling two calls with a medium exercise price
portfolio insurance	transacting to ensure that the value of a portfolio cannot fall below a given amount
straddle	an option position involving a put and a call option on the same stock; to buy a straddle, an investor will buy both a put and a call that have the same expiration and the same striking price
strangle	consists of a long position in a call and a long position in a put on the same underlying good with the same term to expiration, with the call having a higher exercise price than the put

synthetic call	consists of a long position in both the stock and the put option, and a short position in a risk–free bond that will pay the exercise price at the expiration of the option
synthetic equity	consists of a long call, short put, and an investment of the present value of the exercise price in the risk–free rate
synthetic instrument	is a financial structure that has the same value as another identifiable instrument
synthetic put	consists of a long call and short stock position, coupled with investing the present value of the exercise price in a risk–free instrument

Multiple–Choice Questions

1. Which of the following statements is *incorrect*?
   A. Given some initial position, financial engineering can create a less risky position.
   B. Given some initial position, financial engineering can create a riskier position.
   C. Given some initial position, financial engineering can create a position with very specialized risk exposure.
   D. Financial engineering is an extension of the basic ideas of risk management in finance.
   E. Although the concept of financial engineering originated over four decades ago, it is only now gaining acceptance.

2. In essence, the butterfly spread gives a payoff similar to a ____, but offers lower risk at the expense of a reduced profit potential.
   A. straddle
   B. strangle
   C. bull spread
   D. bear spread
   E. synthetic put

3. A ____ instrument is a financial structure that has the same value as another identifiable instrument.
   A. formulated
   B. synthetic
   C. compounded
   D. manufactured
   E. transparent

4. A ____ is an option position involving a put and a call option on the same stock.
   A. straddle
   B. synthetic option
   C. bull spread
   D. bear spread
   E. butterfly spread

5. A butterfly spread profits most when the stock price is near the ____ exercise price at expiration.
   A. low
   B. medium
   C. high
   D. risk–free
   E. market

6. A long position in a ____ consists of a long position in a call and a long position in a put on the same underlying good with the same term to expiration, with the call having a higher exercise price than the put.
   A. straddle
   B. strangle
   C. bull spread
   D. bear spread
   E. butterfly spread

7. A ____ in the options market is a combination of call options designed to profit if the price of the underlying good rises.
   A. straddle
   B. strangle
   C. bull spread
   D. bear spread
   E. none of the above

8. The buyer of a bull spread buys a call with an exercise price ____ the stock price, and sells a call option with an exercise price ____ the stock price.
   A. above; below
   B. below; above
   C. above; above
   D. below; below
   E. at; above

9. A ____ is a combination of options designed to profit from a drop in the stock price.
    A. straddle
    B. strangle
    C. bull spread
    D. bear spread
    E. butterfly spread

10. A ____ consists of a long call and a short stock position, coupled with investing the present value of the exercise price in a risk–free investment.
    A. straddle
    B. strangle
    C. bull spread
    D. synthetic call
    E. synthetic put

11. The bear spread is just the short positions that match the ____.
    A. straddle
    B. strangle
    C. bull spread
    D. options market
    E. futures market

12. To buy a ____, a trader buys one call with a low exercise price and buys one call with a high exercise price, while selling two calls with a medium exercise price.
    A. straddle
    B. strangle
    C. bull spread
    D. bear spread
    E. butterfly spread

13. The ____ relationship provides the basic blueprint for creating synthetic securities.
    A. put–call
    B. CAPM
    C. futures market
    D. ratio spread
    E. risk–return

14. ____ consists of a long call, short put and an investment of the present value of the exercise price in the risk–free rate.
    A. Put–call parity
    B. A strangle
    C. Synthetic equity
    D. A bear spread
    E. A butterfly spread

15. A ____ consists of a long position in both the stock and the put option, and a short position in a risk–free bond that will pay the exercise price at the expiration of the option.
    A. straddle
    B. strangle
    C. synthetic T–bill
    D. synthetic call
    E. synthetic put

16. A synthetic T–bill will pay the exercise price at the expiration date of the options ____.
    A. no matter what the stock price may be
    B. if the stock price is below the exercise price
    C. if the stock price is above the exercise price
    D. only on rare occasions
    E. if the options are callable

17. An interest rate swap can generally be examined as a ____.
    A. portfolio of bonds
    B. portfolio of forward contracts
    C. series of option contracts
    D. series of call options
    E. series of put options

18. In portfolio ____, a trader transacts to ensure that the value of a portfolio cannot fall below a given amount.
    A. parity
    B. insurance
    C. swaps
    D. contracts
    E. T–bills

19. Which of the following statements is *incorrect*?
    A. Traders can use futures and options to tailor the risk characteristics of the portfolio to individual taste.
    B. In portfolio insurance, a trader transacts to ensure that the value of a portfolio cannot fall below a given amount.
    C. The long call plus investment in the risk–free asset creates the same insured portfolio as the long index plus the long put.
    D. Portfolio insurance reduces risk.
    E. Portfolio insurance defies the risk/return trade–off.

20. A stock is trading at $95 when a call with an exercise price of $90 costs $6 and a call with an exercise price of $100 costs $2. The break–even stock price at expiration for a bull spread is $____.
    A. 74.00
    B. 94.00
    C. 78.00
    D. 88.00
    E. 92.00

21. A call and a put both have exercise prices of $100. The call sells for $5 and the put sells for $4. The profit of a long straddle at expiration if the stock price is 110 is $_____.
    A. 2.00
    B. 1.00
    C. 3.00
    D. –1.00
    E. –45.00

22. A call has an exercise prices of $110 and a put has an exercise price of $90. The call sells for $5 and the put sells for $4. The profit of a long strangle at expiration if the stock price is 135 is $_____.
    A. 10.00
    B. 12.00
    C. 14.00
    D. 16.00
    E. 20.00

Review Problems

1. Consider a long straddle on a stock with an exercise price of $100.00. Complete the following table.

Terminal Stock Value	Terminal Call Value	Terminal Put Value	Terminal Straddle Value
90.00			
95.00			
100.00			
105.00			
110.00			

2. Consider a long straddle on a stock with an exercise price of $100.00. Assuming the put costs $4.00 and the call costs $5.00, complete the following table.

Terminal Stock Value	Terminal Call Profit/Loss	Terminal Put Profit/Loss	Terminal Straddle Profit/Loss
90.00			
95.00			
100.00			
105.00			
110.00			

Use the following information to answer the following questions. Consider a stock index that is currently trading at $75.00. A call on the index has a strike price of $75.00 and costs $10.00. A put with a strike of $75.00 costs $2.00. The put and call both expire in one year. A trader is considering Portfolio A, which consists of one long unit of the index, one short call, and one long put.

3. What is the cost of Portfolio A?

4. Complete the following table using the information provided:

Terminal Value of Index	Value of Portfolio A
70.00	
75.00	
80.00	
85.00	
90.00	

5. What is the risk–free rate of interest?
6. What portfolio would synthetically replicate the stock index? Explain in detail.
7. How would you trade to synthetically replicate a short put contract? Explain in detail.
8. Assume that you use a put option to ensure a long position in the stock index. Explain in detail exactly how you would trade.
9. What is the total cost of the insured portfolio (index plus options)?
10. For the insured portfolio, complete the following table.

Terminal Index Value	Value of Insured Portfolio	Return on the Stock Index	Return on the Insured Portfolio
70.00			
75.00			
80.00			
85.00			
90.00			

Answers

Multiple–Choice Questions

1. E	10. E	19. E
2. A	11. C	20. B
3. B	12. E	21. B
4. A	13. A	22. D
5. B	14. C	
6. B	15. D	
7. C	16. A	
8. B	17. B	
9. D	18. B	

Review Problems

1.

Terminal Stock Value	Terminal Call Value	Terminal Put Value	Terminal Straddle Value
90.00	0.0	10.0	10.0
95.00	0.0	5.0	5.0
100.00	0.0	0.0	0.0
105.00	5.0	0.0	5.0
110.00	10.0	0.0	10.0

2.

Terminal Stock Value	Terminal Call Profit/Loss	Terminal Put Profit/Loss	Terminal Straddle Profit/Loss
90.00	−5	6	1
95.00	−5	1	−4
100.00	−5	−4	−9
105.00	0	−4	⁻4
110.00	5	−4	1

3. The cost is $75.00 for the index itself, minus $10.00 for selling the call, plus $2.00 for the put, giving a total cost of $67.00.

4.

Terminal Value of Index	Value of Portfolio A
70.00	70.00 + 0.00 + 5.00 = 75.00
75.00	75.00 + 0.00 + 0.00 = 75.00
80.00	80.00 − 5.00 + 0.00 = 75.00
85.00	85.00 − 10.00 + 0.00 = 75.00
90.00	90.00 − 15.00 + 0.00 = 75.00

Under the column for the value of Portfolio A, the expressions give the value of the stock index plus the value of the call, plus the value of the put equaling the total value of Portfolio A. Thus, the value of Portfolio A is $75.00, no matter what the terminal value of the index might be.

5. From the preceding problem, we see that an investment in Portfolio A costs $67.00 and pays off $75.00 in one year. Therefore, the annual interest rate is $75.00/67.00 − 1 = 11.94$ percent.

6. The put–call parity relationship is:

$$S = C - P + \frac{E}{(1 + r)^t}$$

From put–call parity, we see that buying the call, selling the put, and holding an investment in the risk–free asset will replicate the stock index. Specifically, buying the call for $10.00, selling the put for $2.00, and investing $67.00 in the risk–free bond would synthetically replicate the stock index. This portfolio will have exactly the same cost and the same payoffs in one year as the stock index itself.

We can see this from the following considerations. First, the risk–free investment will be worth 67.00(1.1194) = 75.00. Notice that this amount equals the exercise price of the call or the put. Thus, we invest the present value of the exercise price in the risk–free asset. If the terminal value of the index exceeds $75.00, we can exercise our call and pay the exercise price with the $75.00 proceeds from our risk–free investment. The result will be that we hold the stock index itself. If the terminal value of the stock index is less than $75.00, the put that we sold will be exercised against us, and we will be forced to pay $75.00 for the stock index that is put to us. The result again is that we possess the stock index and nothing else. Finally, if the stock index is worth $75.00 at expiration, we hold $75.00 from our maturing risk–free investment, so our portfolio has the same value as the stock index.

7. From put–call parity, we see that a put can be replicated by buying a call, investing the present value of the exercise price in the risk–free bond, and selling the stock short. Keep in mind that this represents a synthetic long put contract, and we are trying to replicate a short put contract. In order to form this portfolio, we simply adapt the put–call relationship to replicate the short put position. This portfolio will include a short call, a short position in a risk–free bond, and a long position in the stock.

8. This form of portfolio insurance requires that we buy a put option on the entire stock index. In our example, we would buy the put with a strike of $75.00 for a price of $2.00.

9. The insured portfolio costs $2.00 for the put, plus $75.00 for the stock index itself, for a total outlay of $77.00.

10.

Terminal Index Value	Value of Insured Portfolio	Return on the Stock Index	Return on the Insured Portfolio
70.00	70.00 + 5 = 75.00	−6.67	−2.60
75.00	75.00 + 0 = 75.00	0.00	−2.60
80.00	80.00 + 0 = 80.00	6.67	3.90
85.00	85.00 + 0 = 85.00	13.33	10.39
90.00	90.00 + 0 = 90.00	20.00	16.88

From the table we can see that the insured portfolio offers protection against particularly adverse outcomes, but it sacrifices the chance for extremely good outcomes.

Software Installation

Why Do I Need to Install the Software?

The three programs that accompany *Investments*, STUDY!, Investmaster, and REALDATA, are included on a single disk in a highly compressed form. By following these installation instructions, you decompress the programs and data on the distribution diskette and prepare the individual programs for use. **Before any of these programs can be used, they must be installed according to the instructions presented here.**

Installation Instructions

This section describes the simple steps necessary to install the software and prepare the programs for use. You may install these program to a choice of four media or installation targets:

> hard drive
> 5.25" 1.2 meg diskette
> 3.5" 720k diskette
> 3.5" 1.44 meg diskette

To install the programs, you will need to have the correct number of blank formatted diskettes of the type that you have chosen as the installation target. Complete installation of all files requires one of the following amounts of space:

> 3.2 megabytes of hard disk space
> 3 5.25" 1.2 meg diskettes
> 5 3.5" 720k diskettes
> 3 3.5" 1.44 meg diskettes

Installation to a hard drive is best, because it is much more convenient than installation to a floppy, and access to the data is much faster.

Throughout these instructions, we assume that you plan to install from floppy drive A. The installation process is virtually identical if you wish to install from floppy drive B. If you plan to install from drive B, merely substitute "B" for "A" as the drive designation in the instructions that follow.

1. If you are installing to floppy diskettes, prepare the correct number of formatted diskettes based on the type of diskette you have chosen and the requirements shown above.
2. To start the installation program, place a distribution diskette in floppy drive A.
3. From the DOS prompt, type "A:" and press the ENTER key.
4. Type "INSTALL" and press the ENTER key.

The screen will now appear as shown in Figure 1, and the program asks for your choice of installation target, which can be either to a hard drive or to a floppy drive. Notice in Figure 1 that the screen indicates the number of each type of floppy disk that is required to complete the installation from the distribution diskette.

Figure 1

```
                    INSTALLATION PROGRAM

                    KOLB PUBLISHING COMPANY
             Copyright 1994 by Kolb Publishing Company

                    Installation Program for:
             INVESTMENTS: FOURTH EDITION by Robert W. Kolb

     Before you can use the programs that accompany this book, they must
     first be installed with this installation program. You can use this
     program to install the files to a hard disk or to floppy disks. The
     installed files require the following hard disk space or number of
     floppy disks:

     Press the corresponding number to choose an installation target:


         1        Hard disk space of 3.2 megabytes
         2        Three double-sided, high density 5.25" 1.2 meg diskette
         3        Five double-sided, double density 3.5" 720k diskettes
         4        Three double-sided, high density 3.5" 1.44 meg diskette
         ESC      Exit the installation program


     Choose one of the installation methods shown above, or press ESC to exit.
```

5. Choose a number 1–4 that corresponds to the installation strategy that you have chosen. Alternatively, you may press the escape key (ESC) to terminate the installation.

A. If you have chosen to install to a hard drive (choice number 1), the installation program presents the screen shown in Figure 2. The installation program now asks you to confirm the installation source and target. The program assumes that you will be installing from the A: floppy drive to C:\INV04, meaning hard drive C and directory INV04. If that is correct, merely press ENTER. If you wish to install to a different hard drive, you can use this screen to specify the exact name of the target path for the installation. Once the source and target are correct, press ENTER.

Figure 2

```
                    INSTALLATION PROGRAM

                  Kolb Publishing Company


The default method of installation is to install FROM floppy disk A:
TO the specified sub-directory of your hard disk C:. If the FROM and
TO destinations are correct, press function key F1 to install.

If the FROM and TO destinations are not correct, change them in the
spaces below, and press function key F1 to install.

Use ENTER OR RETURN to change fields.  Use ESC to abort installation.




        Installing FROM floppy drive   A:

        Installing TO directory        C:\INV04
```

B. If you have chosen to install to a floppy drive (choice numbers 2-4), the installation program presents the screen shown in Figure 3. The installation program now asks you to confirm the installation source and target. The program assumes that you will be installing from floppy drive A: to B:. If that is correct, merely press ENTER. If you wish to install from or to a different floppy drive, you can use this screen to specify your chosen source and target floppy drives. Once the source and target are correct, press ENTER.

6. If you have chosen to install to a hard drive, the installation program will now complete the installation for you. If you are installing to floppy diskettes, the installation program will complete the first target diskette and

prompt you to place fresh diskettes in the target drive that you have selected.

Following steps 1-6 completes the installation of all programs. After completing the installation, store the distribution diskette in a safe place.

Figure 3

```
                        INSTALLATION PROGRAM

                    Kolb Publishing Company


        The default method of installation is to install FROM floppy disk A:
        TO floppy disk B:. If the FROM and TO destinations are correct, be
        sure that diskettes are loaded and press function key F1 to install.

        If the FROM and TO destinations are not correct, change them in the
        spaces below, and press function key F1 to install.

        Use ENTER OR RETURN to change fields.   Use ESC to abort installation.




                    Installing FROM floppy drive  A:

                    Installing TO floppy drive     B:
```

STUDY!

What STUDY! Does

STUDY! is a program designed to help you review your understanding of the chapters in *Investments*. You can also use it for self–testing. In addition, your instructor may give you assignments to turn in using STUDY! **Before you can use the program, you must install the software according to the preceding installation instructions in the section entitled Software Installation.**

The program is essentially a tutorial on a disk. It allows you to select any combination of chapters from *Investments* that you want to study. After you select the chapters you want to study, the program loads all of the questions for those chapters in a random order. Thus, all of the questions are mixed, and each time you study the same set of chapters, the questions will appear in a different order. For each chapter, there are about 25 questions. Therefore, if you select five chapters to study, you will have about 125 questions available that will be presented to you in a random order.

STUDY! presents each question and waits for your answer. If you answer correctly, STUDY! acknowledges that fact, records your success, and updates your score, which appears on screen. If you give an incorrect answer, STUDY! gives the correct answer and updates your score.

How to Run STUDY!

After you have installed the software according to the preceding installation instructions, you are ready to run STUDY! for the first time. Depending on the way you installed the software, STUDY! will either be on the hard drive of your computer or on a floppy diskette.

Running STUDY! from a Hard Drive

If you installed the software to the hard disk, change to the directory where you installed the software. If you followed the default option during installation, the programs will be in the directory C:\INV04. To change to this directory, issue the following DOS command:

CD C:\INV04

To run STUDY!, issue the following DOS command:

STUDY!

Running STUDY! from a Floppy Drive

If you installed the software to a floppy disk, insert the floppy disk in the disk drive, which we presume is drive A:. To run STUDY!, change to the floppy disk by issuing the following DOS command:

A:

Then run STUDY! by issuing the following DOS command:

STUDY!

Registering as the Owner of STUDY!

The first time you run STUDY!, you will be asked to register as the owner of the program. The registration screen shown in Figure 1 will appear, and you will be asked to give your name and social security number. This is important so that your instructor will know that you have done your own work. Figure 2 shows the completed installation screen for a student named Mozart. If you are not as well known, you may wish to give your first and last name. Your name must fit in the space provided.

The program now shows your name and social security number as you have entered them. This screen is shown in Figure 3. If this information is correct, press **ENTER**. If it is not correct, press the **ESC** key, and you can re–enter the data. Pressing the **ENTER** key makes the name and social security number shown a permanent part of your program. Once you have completed the installation routine, the screens we have discussed will not appear again.

Figure 1
The Blank Registration Screen

```
            Tutorial to Accompany Investments Fourth Edition

                         Installation Screen

  Use this screen to identify yourself as a registered user of STUDY!. The
  information you provide here becomes a permanent part of the program.
  Each time you use the program, your name and social security number will
  appear. Also, your name and social security number will appear on every
  report you produce.

  Enter your name as you wish it to appear in the space provided. When
  it is correct, press RETURN.

        Name:    ████████████████

  Enter your social security number in the space provided, including dashes
  between the parts, (e.g., 123-45-6789). When it is correct, press RETURN.

  Social Security Number:    ██████████
```

Figure 2
Mozart's Completed Registration Screen

```
            Tutorial to Accompany Investments Fourth Edition

                         Installation Screen

  Use this screen to identify yourself as a registered user of STUDY!. The
  information you provide here becomes a permanent part of the program.
  Each time you use the program, your name and social security number will
  appear. Also, your name and social security number will appear on every
  report you produce.

  Enter your name as you wish it to appear in the space provided. When
  it is correct, press RETURN.

        Name:    MOZART███████████

  Enter your social security number in the space provided, including dashes
  between the parts, (e.g., 123-45-6789). When it is correct, press RETURN.

  Social Security Number:    123-45-6789
```

Figure 3
The Registration Confirmation Screen

```
You have selected the following information:


                    Name:  MOZART
Social Security Number:  123-45-6789


To accept this as permanent information, press RETURN now. To make changes
press ESC now.
```

Figure 4
The Chapter Selection Screen

```
              Tutorial to Accompany Investments Fourth Edition
                            by Robert W. Kolb

           Use this screen to select chapters that you wish to study.


  [X]  1. Introduction              [ ] 11. Industry Analysis
  [X]  2. The Debt Market           [ ] 12. Company Analysis
  [X]  3. The Stock Market          [ ] 13. Diversification
  [ ]  4. The Primary Market        [ ] 14. Market Price of Risk
  [X]  5. Sources of Information    [ ] 15. Efficient Capital Markets
  [ ]  6. Regulation and Taxation   [ ] 16. Investment Companies
  [ ]  7. Bond Pricing Principles   [ ] 17. The Future Market
  [ ]  8. Bond Portfolio Management [ ] 18. The Options Market
  [ ]  9. Stock Valuation           [ ] 19. The Swaps Market
  [ ] 10. Economic Analysis         [ ] 20. Financial Engineering


  Registered User:  MOZART          Number of chapters selected:    4
  Identification:   123-45-6789     Number of questions selected:  107

ARROWS to navigate; TAB to mark chapter; RETURN to begin answers; ESC to exit.
```

Using STUDY!

After installing the program, the chapter outline for *Investments* shown in Figure 4 will appear. This is also the first screen that will appear every time you run the program after the initial installation. Notice that the registered user is Mozart and his social security number also appears.

You may use this screen to select the chapters that you want to study. In Figure 4, Mozart has chosen chapters 1, 2, 3, and 5. You select the chapters by using **TAB** to select or deselect a chapter. (You may also type an **X**). The screen also shows the number of chapters selected and the total number of questions available from the selected chapters. In this case, four chapters are selected with a total of 107 questions available.

After selecting the chapters you want to study, press **ENTER**. STUDY! then begins to present questions as shown in Figure 5. Here Mozart has already answered the first question correctly. To select an answer, use the arrow keys to move the highlighted bar to the correct answer in the bottom left corner of the screen. Then press **ENTER**. You may also simply type the corresponding letter, **A–E**, to make your selection. Notice that the program also shows the user name and social security number, along with the time and date.

Figure 5
Mozart's First Question

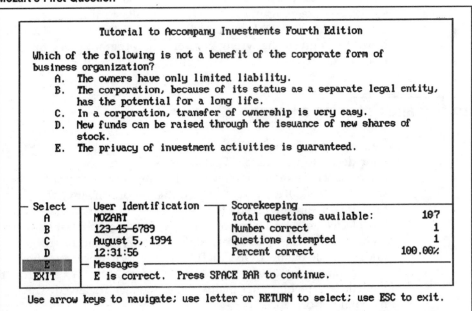

Figure 6
Mozart's Second Question

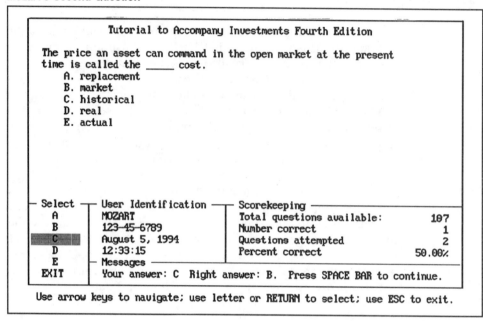

```
              Tutorial to Accompany Investments Fourth Edition

    The price an asset can command in the open market at the present
    time is called the _____ cost.
          A. replacement
          B. market
          C. historical
          D. real
          E. actual




  ─ Select ──┬─ User Identification ──┬─ Scorekeeping ─────────────────
      A      │  MOZART                │  Total questions available:    107
      B      │  123-45-6789           │  Number correct                  1
      C      │  August 5, 1994        │  Questions attempted             2
      D      │  12:33:15              │  Percent correct            50.00%
      E      ├─ Messages ─────────────┴────────────────────────────────
     EXIT    │  Your answer: C  Right answer: B.  Press SPACE BAR to continue.

    Use arrow keys to navigate; use letter or RETURN to select; use ESC to exit.
```

In Figure 5, Mozart has just answered correctly. The Messages block reads: "E is correct. Press **SPACE BAR** to continue." Also, this is the first question attempted, so the Scorekeeping block shows the results to this point. When you press the **SPACE BAR**, STUDY! presents the next question, as shown in Figure 6. Here Mozart has given the wrong answer. The program gives the correct answer and updates the score.

Exiting and Obtaining a Report

You may exit from the program at any time, by pressing **ESC**. After confirming your desire to terminate, STUDY! offers you the chance to have a report of your performance, as shown in Figure 7. This report can be printed directly, or it can be saved to a disk. If you want to print the report directly, you must ensure that the printer is on–line and ready to receive print commands. As Figure 7 shows, Mozart has elected to save his report to disk. The program asks for the name of a file where the report is to be recorded. In Figure 7, Mozart has chosen to save his report under the file name "CONCERTO." The report appears as shown in Figure 8. The report summarizes the results obtained before Mozart exited from the program. As you can see, he quit after the two questions we reviewed. The report summarizes his total performance.

Figure 7
The Report Selection Screen

```
              Tutorial to Accompany Investments Fourth Edition

                          by Robert W. Kolb



You may create a report that summarizes your work and save it to a file
or print the report, if the printer is on line.

Would you like a report? [Y/N] Y

Would you like to save a report to disk? [Y/N] Y

Please enter the name of the file where the report should be written in
the space provided. Then press return.

CONCERTO
```

Figure 8
Report of Mozart's Performance

```
           Tutorial to Accompany Investments Fourth Edition

                          by Robert W. Kolb




       Mozart
       123-45-6789
       August 5, 1994
       12:34:45




       Chapters selected      :   1 2 3 5

       Questions available    :   107
       Questions correct      :     1
       Questions attempted    :     2
       Percentage correct     :   50.00%
```

Investmaster

Introduction

This section gives a quick introduction to the ideas behind Investmaster so you can start using the program right away. Investmaster consists of ten modules geared to different functional areas of investments. Many of the chapters in *Investments* explain and utilize the concepts and techniques covered by Investmaster.

How to Run Investmaster

After you have installed the software according to the installation instructions in the Software Installation section of this manual, you are ready to run Investmaster for the first time. Depending on the way you installed the software, Investmaster will either be on the hard drive of your computer or on a floppy diskette.

Running Investmaster from a Hard Drive

If you installed the software to the hard disk, change to the directory where you installed the software. If you followed the default option during installation, the programs will be in the directory C:\INV04. To change to this directory, issue the following DOS command:

    CD C:\INV04

To run Investmaster, issue the following DOS command:

    IM

Running Investmaster from a Floppy Drive

If you installed the software to a floppy disk, insert the floppy disk in the disk drive, which we presume is drive A:. To run Investmaster, change to the floppy disk by issuing the following DOS command:

    A:

Then run Investmaster by issuing the following DOS command:

    IM

A Quick Start Example

After installing the software for *Investments*, start Investmaster by issuing the DOS command **IM** as described above. Then the main menu for Investmaster will appear as shown in Figure 1. To select a module, type its number and Investmaster starts the selected module.

Notice the very bottom line of the main menu screens. It says, "To exit Investmaster, press **ESC**." As you use Investmaster, observe this bottom line of the screen for special help that corresponds to the screen you are using. Pressing **ESC** while in the main menu terminates Investmaster and returns you to your operating system.

To show how to operate Investmaster, we will solve a sample problem, assuming that you now have Investmaster in operation. Let us assume that the main menu is on the screen. Let us assume also that you wish to use Investmaster to find how much a $1,000 bank account will be worth in one year if you invest the $1,000 at a rate of 10 percent. (Investmaster can solve much more complicated problems, but this is a good one for our present purposes.) This is a time value of money problem, so we type "2" to select the Time Value of Money module, and Investmaster presents the first screen of the module. This screen is itself a menu as Figure 2 shows.

Notice in Figure 2 that you can press **ESC** to return to the main menu of Investmaster. We want to deal with a problem using a single cash flow, so we press "1," and the solution screen shown in Figure 3 will appear. This is the screen we actually use to solve our problem.

The instruction on the screen says, "Enter any 3 of the following 4 values, then press **F1** to solve:" We want to find a future value, the value of our present $1,000 one year from now. Therefore, we enter data for the present value ($1,000), the number of periods (1), and the discount rate (.10). When the solution screen first appears, the cursor is on the present value variable, so we begin by entering "1000" at that point. We then need to move the cursor to the other fields on the screen. To do this, we use the up and down arrow keys. If you make a mistake in entering data, use the **DEL** key to erase the most recently entered character. After we enter

Figure 1
The Main Menu for Investmaster

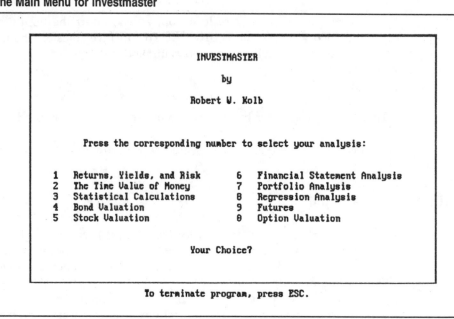

```
                        INVESTMASTER

                            by

                     Robert W. Kolb




      Press the corresponding number to select your analysis:


      1  Returns, Yields, and Risk    6  Financial Statement Analysis
      2  The Time Value of Money       7  Portfolio Analysis
      3  Statistical Calculations      8  Regression Analysis
      4  Bond Valuation                9  Futures
      5  Stock Valuation               0  Option Valuation


                       Your Choice?




              To terminate program, press ESC.
```

Figure 2
The Time Value of Money Menu

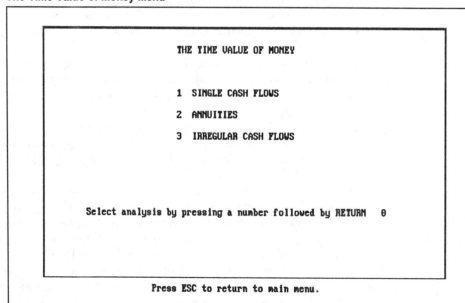

```
                   THE TIME VALUE OF MONEY



          1  SINGLE CASH FLOWS

          2  ANNUITIES

          3  IRREGULAR CASH FLOWS




    Select analysis by pressing a number followed by RETURN   0




              Press ESC to return to main menu.
```

Figure 3
The Solution Screen for the Time Value of Single Payments

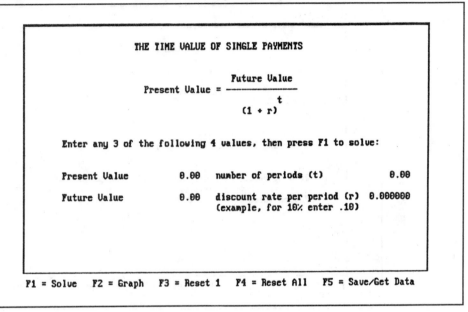

the three pieces of data, the screen appears as shown in Figure 4. We can now calculate the solution.

Notice the bottom line of the screen, which says:

F1=Solve F2=Graph F3=Reset 1 F4=Reset All F5=Save/Get Data

Watch this line for help in using the current screen. In this case, we see that we need to press **F1** to solve. If we press **ESC**, we leave this screen and find ourselves back in the time value menu. If we press **F3**, we reset the value at the location of the cursor to its original zero value. If we press **F4**, we reset all of the values on the screen to their original values. We discuss the use of **F2** for graphing below. At this point we want to solve our problem, so we press **F1**. The screen then appears as shown in Figure 5, with the solution to our future value problem of $1,100.

Let's review the steps to achieving this solution, starting from the main Investmaster menu:

1. Press "2" to select the time value module.

2. Press "1" to select the solution screen for single payments.

3. Enter the three pieces of data.

4. Press **F1** to solve.

Figure 4
The Solution Screen with Data in Place

```
                     THE TIME VALUE OF SINGLE PAYMENTS


                                        Future Value
                      Present Value = ----------------
                                              t
                                          (1 + r)


            Enter any 3 of the following 4 values, then press F1 to solve:


            Present Value        1000.00    number of periods (t)          1.00

            Future Value            0.00    discount rate per period (r)  0.100000
                                            (example, for 10% enter .10)




        F1 = Solve    F2 = Graph    F3 = Reset 1    F4 = Reset All    F5 = Save/Get Data
```

Figure 5
The Completed Solution

```
                     THE TIME VALUE OF SINGLE PAYMENTS


                                        Future Value
                      Present Value = ----------------
                                              t
                                          (1 + r)


            Enter any 3 of the following 4 values, then press F1 to solve:


            Present Value        1000.00    number of periods (t)          1.00

            Future Value         1100.00    discount rate per period (r)  0.100000
                                            (example, for 10% enter .10)




        F1 = Solve    F2 = Graph    F3 = Reset 1    F4 = Reset All    F5 = Save/Get Data
```

Saving and Retrieving Data

Investmaster also allows you to save or recall data. To explore this option, we continue with our sample problem. To save the data and solution for a current module, press **F5**. Investmaster then prints a menu on the bottom line of the screen asking whether you wish to save, recall, or abort. To save the current data, choose the save option. Investmaster then prompts for a filename, which you supply. Then press RETURN to save your data in the file specified.

You can recall data only if the data were originally saved by Investmaster. You then press **F5** and select the recall data option. At the prompt, supply the filename, and Investmaster will read the saved data into the current module. Notice that recalling data means that any current information on the screen will be written over and lost.

Graphing with Investmaster

Many of the modules in Investmaster offer a graphics feature. The bottom line of the screen indicates when graphics are available. When you enter the graphics phase of the analysis, the program uses the data from your most recent solution. To ensure that the data are valid, Investmaster requires that you follow these steps to use the graphics.

1. Achieve a valid solution by pressing **F1**. (If the solution is not valid, the computer will write an error message on the bottom line of the screen.)

2. Next press **F2**.

When you follow this procedure, the graphics menu appears. Figure 6 shows the graphics menu for the time value of single payments.

The graphics menus differ according to solution screen, but they all have the same structure. To leave the graphics part of the module, press "0". Otherwise, select any of the other listed alternatives. Following our sample problem, we press "1" to graph the future value as a function of the time the funds are invested. Investmaster then draws the graph shown in Figure 7. As the middle of the graph shows, with an investment period of one year, the future value is $1,100. If we keep our money invested for a longer period, the future value will be greater.

Saving Graphs to Disk

Investmaster also allows you to save a graph to the disk. To save a graph that is currently displayed, press **F7**. Investmaster will save the file on the currently logged directory. Investmaster assigns sequential file names to the graphs you save in a

Figure 6
The Graphics Menu for the Time Value of Single Payments

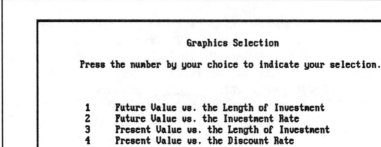

```
                        Graphics Selection

        Press the number by your choice to indicate your selection.


        1      Future Value vs. the Length of Investment
        2      Future Value vs. the Investment Rate
        3      Present Value vs. the Length of Investment
        4      Present Value vs. the Discount Rate




    When the graph is displayed, press F7 to save the graph or ESC to exit.

                        Your choice please?


                        Press ESC to exit.
```

particular directory. The first graph saved in a directory has the name
"FMGRF001.PCX". As you save more graphs on a given directory, new files will
be created with higher numbers.

Investmaster uses the familiar "PCX" format for saving graphs. This means that
any program that can manipulate PCX files can read the Investmaster files you
save. For example, WordPerfect and Microsoft Word can read, display, and print
these Investmaster graphic files. Many other programs can also handle PCX files,
such as PC Paintbrush.

Leaving Investmaster

When a graph is on the screen, we are in the innermost layer of Investmaster. To
exit from Investmaster to DOS, follow these steps.

1. Press any key (except the graph saving key **F7**) to erase the graph. The
    graphics menu will appear.

2. Press "0" to exit the graphics menu—the solution screen will appear.

3. Press **ESC** to leave the solution screen—the time value menu will appear.

Figure 7
The Future Value as a Function of the Length of Investment

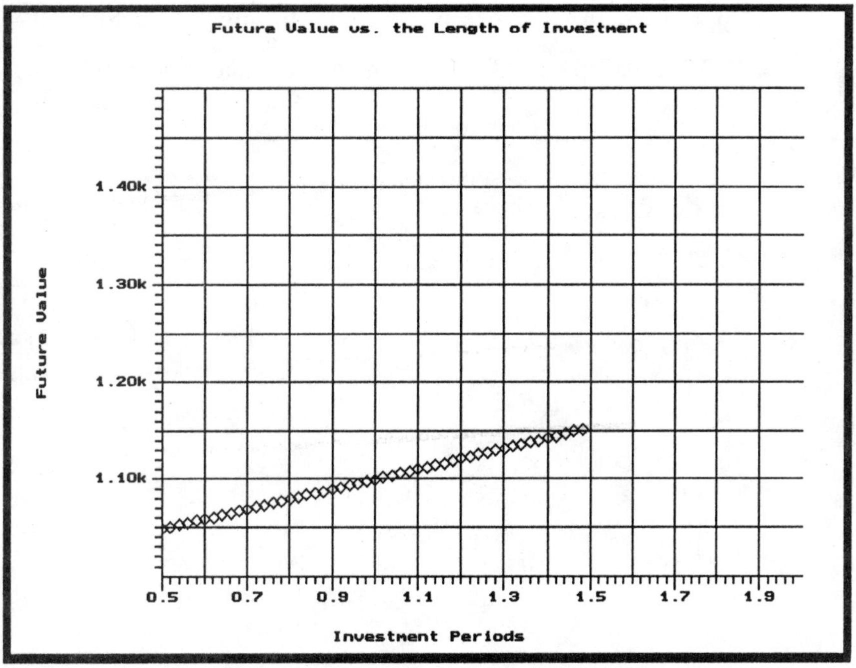

4.   Press **ESC** to leave the time value module—the main menu of Investmaster will appear.

5.   Press **ESC** to leave Investmaster—the DOS prompt will appear.

Command Summary

F1 = solve

F2 = graph

F3 = reset the 1 value at the cursor

F4 = reset all values on the screen

F5 = save/recall data

F7 = save a displayed graph to a file on the current directory

ESC = leave the current screen

DEL = remove most recently entered character

Up and Down Arrows = move cursor from one field to another

F8, F9, F10, PgUp, PgDn = commands to change screens

REALDATA

Introduction

What is REALDATA?

REALDATA provides real–world data in a convenient and consistent format to support the study of finance and economics. *REALDATA* includes almost 700 monthly and quarterly financial and economic time series covering the post World War II period. This manual describe these data completely.

All of the data series in *REALDATA* are contained in WK1 format spreadsheets for consistency of presentation and ease of access. All data files can be used by all major spreadsheet products including Lotus 123, Quattro Pro, Excel, and many others. Any program that can read a WK1 format file has full access to *REALDATA* information. **Accessing the data contained in REALDATA requires a spreadsheet program.**

This manual also contains more than 100 exercises that can be completed using the data contained in *REALDATA*. The exercises are designed so that they can be solved completely using a typical spreadsheet program. These exercises differ widely in the kinds of activity that they require. Some simply require that the user find certain information in the *REALDATA* files, while others have solutions that result from fairly elaborate computations. Still others call for the creation and interpretation of a graph, and some exercises demand all of these activities.

The following discussion provides a more detailed overview of *REALDATA*. It explains how to install the *REALDATA* files and discusses the standardized format of the files. The discussion concludes with pointers on how to solve the exercises using a typical spreadsheet program.

Types of Data in REALDATA

Data for the financial sector include information on the Federal Reserve, federal financing, the stock and bond markets, stock market activity and trends, the money markets, the money supply, deposit institution lending, federal credit agencies, finance companies, mortgage markets, the primary market, stock market activity, foreign stock, money, and bond markets, foreign exchange, inflation in the United States and many other countries. In addition, *REALDATA* offers coverage of individual mutual funds and contains monthly price and dividend information for 30 individual stocks.

For the real sector, *REALDATA* features data on federal taxation and expenditures, indicators of the business cycle, national income and product accounts, inventories, industrial production, wages and incomes, corporate profits, the automotive, construction, and energy sectors, manufacturing, trade balances between the United states and many other countries, employment, consumer credit, and foreign industrial production and investment.

REALDATA Spreadsheet Formats and Conventions

All *REALDATA* spreadsheets are organized in a similar manner. The first row of every spreadsheet contains a name that identifies the particular variable. The first column (column A) of each spreadsheet indicates the year of the data, with each row of column A indicating the specific year for all data points on that row. The second column (column B) holds an identifier for either the month or the quarter. Each row of column B holds a number 1–12 if the data in that spreadsheet are monthly data, or it holds a number 1–4 if the data in that spreadsheet are quarterly data. For spreadsheets with monthly data, the number in column B indicates the month of the data, with 1 for January, 2 for February, and so on. For spreadsheets with quarterly data, the number in column B indicates whether the data are for the first, second, third, or fourth quarter. The actual data begin in the third column (column C).

The descriptions of the data give full information about the spreadsheets and the data they contain. As an example, consider the following example:

Figure 1

Money Supply Measures
    Spreadsheet: MONEYSUP.WK1 Monthly Data.
    A   Year of the observation **Code:** MSYR
    B   Month of the observation (1 = January; 2 = February; etc.) **Code: MSMO**
    C   M1: Sum of currency, demand deposits, travelers checks, and other checkable deposits; averages of daily figures; billions of dollars; seasonally adjusted; from January 1970. **Source:** Board of Governors of the Federal Reserve System, *Statistical Release: Money Stock Measures and Liquid Assets*, H.6, various issues. **Code:** MS001

The heading (Money Supply Measures) indicates the topic area covered by a particular spreadsheet. In general, the spreadsheets are organized topically—they contain data on related variables pertaining to a topic area. The next line gives the name of the spreadsheet. In this example, the spreadsheet is named "MONEYSUP.-WK1," and the same line indicates whether the data are monthly or quarterly. For MONEYSUP.WK1, the data are monthly. (A particular spreadsheet holds either monthly data or quarterly data; the two are never mixed.)

Subsequent lines describe the contents of each column in the spreadsheet. As already mentioned, column A indicates the year of the observation, and column B indicates the month or quarter of the year for an observation. For each variable, the first row holds an alphanumeric code or variable identifier. For column A of MONEYSUP.WK1, the codes is "MSYR." For columns that hold actual data, like column C in our example, the entry describes the data, indicates the source from which the data are drawn, and specifies the code for the particular variable.

The data description also specifies the first period for which data are available. As the example indicates, column C of MONEYSUP.WK1 holds data on the M1 measure of the money supply and the data begin in January 1970. Some variables have missing values, a problem that plagues all data sources. Throughout the *REALDATA* spreadsheets, missing values are indicated by a –99.99 value.

Solution Techniques and Hints for REALDATA Exercises

The exercises in this text typically specify a starting and ending date for the data to be used in the exercise. Follow this specification closely to get the correct answer. Similarly, the exercises that require a graph specify the range for the horizontal and vertical axes. Create your graph using the same axes ranges as specified in the text.

Many exercises require the computation of statistical measures such as the variance or standard deviation of some observations. All solutions to *REALDATA* exercises should use the population measures for the variance and standard deviation, unless your instructor indicates otherwise. For example, the population variance is computed by dividing the sum of squared deviations by the full number of observations. By contrast, sample variances are computed by dividing the sum of square deviations by the number of observations minus one. Most spreadsheets provide functions for computing both the population and sample measures of variances and standard deviations. Generally, the population measures are named "@VAR" and "@STD" for the variance and standard deviation, respectively. The sample measures are typically named "@VARS" and "@STDS." Solutions to *REALDATA* exercises should use the @VAR and @STD functions.

Some exercises ask you to compute the correlation between two variables. Unfortunately, most spreadsheets do not include a correlation function. Nonetheless, correlations can be computed fairly easily by using the spreadsheet's regression feature. To compute a correlation between variables X and Y, follow these steps. First, regress X on Y or regress Y on X. (For our limited purpose, the two are equivalent.) Second, compute the square root of the R^2 provided as part of the regression output. The result is the absolute value of the correlation between variables X and Y. Thus, it still remains to determine whether the correlation is positive or negative, as correlations can be as small as –1.0 or as large as +1.0.

Third, the sign of the correlation is the same as the sign of the slope coefficient that is computed as part of the regression.

Most *REALDATA* spreadsheets contain several variables. It is generally easier to solve an exercise if the working spreadsheet is free of extraneous data. To solve a particular exercise, begin by identifying the necessary spreadsheet with the data for the exercise, and copy it to a temporary file, such as TEMP.WK1. Working on spreadsheet TEMP, delete the columns containing variables that are not of interest and delete rows for periods outside the time period of interest. You can then make the computations that the exercise requires. Be sure not to delete portions of the original spreadsheet, or it will be necessary to re–install from the *REALDATA* distribution diskettes.

The Financial Sector

Monetary Measures and Federal Finance

Money Supply Measures
Spreadsheet: MONEYSUP.WK1   Monthly Data
- A   Year of the observation **Code:** MSYR
- B   Month of the observation (1 = January; 2 = February; etc.) **Code:** MSMO
- C   M1: Sum of currency, demand deposits, travelers checks, and other checkable deposits; averages of daily figures; billions of dollars; seasonally adjusted; from January 1970. **Source:** Board of Governors of the Federal Reserve System, *Statistical Release: Money Stock Measures and Liquid Assets*, H.6, various issues. **Code:** MS001
- D   M2: M1 plus overnight RP's and Eurodollars, MMMF balances, MMDA's, and savings and small time deposits; averages of daily figures; billions of dollars; seasonally adjusted; from January 1970. **Source:** Board of Governors of the Federal Reserve System, *Statistical Release: Money Stock Measures and Liquid Assets*, H.6, various issues. **Code:** MS002
- E   M3: M2 plus large time deposits, term RP's, term Eurodollars, and institution–only MMMF balances; averages of daily figures; billions of dollars; seasonally adjusted; from January 1970. **Source:** Board of Governors of the Federal Reserve System, *Statistical Release: Money Stock Measures and Liquid Assets*, H.6, various issues. **Code:** MS003
- F   L: M3 plus other liquid assets; averages of daily figures; billions of dollars; seasonally adjusted; from January 1970. **Source:** Board of Governors of the Federal Reserve System, *Statistical Release: Money Stock Measures and Liquid Assets*, H.6, various issues. **Code:** MS004
- G   Components of money stock measures and liquid assets: Currency; average of daily figures; billions of dollars; seasonally adjusted; from January 1970. **Source:** Board of Governors of the Federal Reserve System, *Statistical Release: Money Stock Measures and Liquid Assets*, H.6, various issues. **Code:** MS005

H   Components of money stock measures and liquid assets: Travelers checks; average of daily figures; billions of dollars; seasonally adjusted; from January 1970. **Source:** Board of Governors of the Federal Reserve System, *Statistical Release: Money Stock Measures and Liquid Assets*, H.6, various issues. **Code:** MS006

I   Components of money stock measures and liquid assets: Demand deposits; average of daily figures; billions of dollars; seasonally adjusted; from January 1970. **Source:** Board of Governors of the Federal Reserve System, *Statistical Release: Money Stock Measures and Liquid Assets*, H.6, various issues. **Code:** MS007

J   Components of money stock measures and liquid assets: Other checkable deposits; average of daily figures; billions of dollars; seasonally adjusted; from January 1970. **Source:** Board of Governors of the Federal Reserve System, *Statistical Release: Money Stock Measures and Liquid Assets*, H.6, various issues. **Code:** MS008

K   Components of money stock measures and liquid assets: Overnight repurchase agreements, general purpose and broker/dealer; average of daily figures; billions of dollars; from January 1970. **Source:** Board of Governors of the Federal Reserve System, *Statistical Release: Money Stock Measures and Liquid Assets*, H.6, various issues. **Code:** MS009

L   Components of money stock measures and liquid assets: Overnight Eurodollars, general purpose and broker/dealer; average of daily figures; billions of dollars; from January 1977. **Source:** Board of Governors of the Federal Reserve System, *Statistical Release: Money Stock Measures and Liquid Assets*, H.6, various issues. **Code:** MS010

M   Components of money stock measures and liquid assets: Money market mutual fund balances, general purpose and broker/dealer; average of daily figures; billions of dollars; from January 1974. **Source:** Board of Governors of the Federal Reserve System, *Statistical Release: Money Stock Measures and Liquid Assets*, H.6, various issues. **Code:** MS011

N   Components of money stock measures and liquid assets: Savings deposits including money market deposit accounts; average of daily figures; billions of dollars; seasonally adjusted; from January 1970. **Source:** Board of Governors of the Federal Reserve System, *Statistical Release: Money Stock Measures and Liquid Assets*, H.6, various issues. **Code:** MS012

O   Components of money stock measures and liquid assets: Small denomination time deposits (less than $100,000); average of daily figures; billions of dollars; seasonally adjusted; from January 1970. **Source:** Board of Governors of the Federal Reserve System, *Statistical Release: Money Stock Measures and Liquid Assets*, H.6, various issues. **Code:** MS013

P   Components of money stock measures and liquid assets: Large denomination time deposits (greater than $100,000); average of daily figures; billions of dollars; seasonally adjusted; from January 1970. **Source:** Board of Governors of the Federal Reserve System, *Statistical Release: Money Stock Measures and Liquid Assets*, H.6, various issues. **Code:** MS014

Q   Components of money stock measures and liquid assets: Term repurchase agreements at commercial banks; average of daily figures; billions of dollars; from January 1970. **Source:** Board of Governors of the Federal Reserve System, *Statistical Release: Money Stock Measures and Liquid Assets,* H.6, various issues. **Code:** MS015

R   Components of money stock measures and liquid assets: Term repurchase agreements at thrift institutions; average of daily figures; billions of dollars; from January 1971. **Source:** Board of Governors of the Federal Reserve System, *Statistical Release: Money Stock Measures and Liquid Assets,* H.6, various issues. **Code:** MS016

S   Components of money stock measures and liquid assets: Term Eurodollars; average of daily figures; billions of dollars; from January 1970. **Source:** Board of Governors of the Federal Reserve System, *Statistical Release: Money Stock Measures and Liquid Assets,* H.6, various issues. **Code:** MS017

T   Components of money stock measures and liquid assets: Money market mutual fund balances; (institution only); average of daily figures; billions of dollars; from January 1974. **Source:** Board of Governors of the Federal Reserve System, *Statistical Release: Money Stock Measures and Liquid Assets,* H.6, various issues. **Code:** MS018

U   Components of money stock measures and liquid assets: Bankers' Acceptances; average of daily figures; billions of dollars; seasonally adjusted; from January 1970. **Source:** Board of Governors of the Federal Reserve System, *Statistical Release: Money Stock Measures and Liquid Assets,* H.6, various issues. **Code:** MS019

V   Components of money stock measures and liquid assets: Commercial paper; average of daily figures; billions of dollars; seasonally adjusted; from January 1970. **Source:** Board of Governors of the Federal Reserve System, *Statistical Release: Money Stock Measures and Liquid Assets,* H.6, various issues. **Code:** MS020

W   Components of money stock measures and liquid assets: Short–term Treasury securities (held by other than depository institutions, money market mutual funds, and foreign entities) average of daily figures; billions of dollars; seasonally adjusted; from January 1970. **Source:** Board of Governors of the Federal Reserve System, *Statistical Release: Money Stock Measures and Liquid Assets,* H.6, various issues. **Code:** MS021

Depository Institution Reserves
Spreadsheet: RESERVES.WK1   Monthly Data

A   Year of the observation **Code:** RESYR

B   Month of the observation (1 = January; 2 = February; etc.) **Code:** RESMO

C   Reserves of Depository Institutions: Total; adjusted for changes in reserve requirements; average of daily figures; millions of dollars; seasonally adjusted; from January 1970.
Source: *Federal Reserve Bulletin,* Table 1.20, various issues. **Code:** RES001

D   Reserves of Depository Institutions: Nonborrowed; adjusted for changes in reserve requirements; average of daily figures; millions of dollars; seasonally adjusted; from January 1970. **Source:** *Federal Reserve Bulletin*, Table 1.20, various issues. **Code:** RES002

E   Reserves of Depository Institutions: Nonborrowed plus extended credit; adjusted for changes in reserve requirements; average of daily figures; millions of dollars; seasonally adjusted; from January 1970. **Source:** *Federal Reserve Bulletin*, Table 1.20, various issues. **Code:** RES003

F   Reserves of Depository Institutions: Required; adjusted for changes in reserve requirements; average of daily figures; millions of dollars; seasonally adjusted; from January 1970. **Source:** *Federal Reserve Bulletin*, Table 1.20, various issues. **Code:** RES004

G   Reserves of Depository Institutions: Excess; average of daily figures; millions of dollars; from January 1970. **Source:** *Federal Reserve Bulletin*, Table 1.20, various issues. **Code:** RES005

H   Monetary Base: Adjusted for changes in reserve requirements; average daily figures; millions of dollars; seasonally adjusted; from January 1970. **Source:** *Federal Reserve Bulletin*, Table 1.20, various issues. **Code:** RES006

I   Total Vault Cash: Average daily figures; millions of dollars; from January 1970. **Source:** *Federal Reserve Bulletin*, Table 1.20, various issues. **Code:** RES007

Federal Credit Agencies
Spreadsheet: FEDCRED.WK1   Monthly Data

A   Year of the observation **Code:** FCYR

B   Month of the observation (1 = January; 2 = February; etc.) **Code:** FCMO

C   Debt of Federal and Federally Sponsored Agencies: Total; millions of dollars; from January 1970. **Source:** *Federal Reserve Bulletin*, Table 1.44; various issues. **Code:** FC001

D   Debt of Federally Sponsored Agencies: Federal Home Loan Mortgage Corporation; millions of dollars; from January 1970. **Source:** *Federal Reserve Bulletin*, Table 1.44; various issues. **Code:** FC002

E   Debt of Federally Sponsored Agencies: Federal National Mortgage Association; millions of dollars; from January 1970. **Source:** *Federal Reserve Bulletin*, Table 1.44; various issues. **Code:** FC003

Inflation
Spreadsheet: INFLATE.WK1   Monthly Data

A   Year of the observation **Code:** INFYR

B   Month of the observation (1 = January; 2 = February; etc.) **Code:** INFMO

C   Consumer Price Index: All Items, (1982–84=100) seasonally adjusted; from January 1970. **Source:** U.S. Department of Labor, Bureau of Labor Statistics, *The Consumer Price Index*, various issues. **Code:** INF001

D   Consumer Price Index: Food and Beverages, (1982–84=100) seasonally adjusted; from January 1970. **Source:** U.S. Department of Labor, Bureau of Labor Statistics, *The Consumer Price Index*, various issues. **Code:** INF002

E   Consumer Price Index: Housing, (1982–84=100) seasonally adjusted; from January 1970. **Source:** U.S. Department of Labor, Bureau of Labor Statistics, *The Consumer Price Index*, various issues. **Code:** INF003

F   Consumer Price Index: Commodities, (1982–84=100) seasonally adjusted; from January 1970. **Source:** U.S. Department of Labor, Bureau of Labor Statistics, *The Consumer Price Index*, various issues. **Code:** INF004

G   Consumer Price Index: Services, (1982–84=100) seasonally adjusted; from January 1970. **Source:** U.S. Department of Labor, Bureau of Labor Statistics, *The Consumer Price Index*, various issues. **Code:** INF005

H   Producer Price Index: Finished Goods, (1982–84=100) seasonally adjusted; from January 1970. **Source:** U.S. Department of Labor, Bureau of Labor Statistics, *The Producer Price Index*, various issues. **Code:** INF006

I   Producer Price Index: Intermediate Materials, Supplies, & Components (1982–84=100) seasonally adjusted; from January 1970. **Source:** U.S. Department of Labor, Bureau of Labor Statistics, *The Producer Price Index*, various issues. **Code:** INF007

J   Producer Price Index: Crude Materials for Further Processing (1982–84=100) seasonally adjusted; from January 1970. **Source:** U.S. Department of Labor, Bureau of Labor Statistics, *The Producer Price Index*, various issues. **Code:** INF008

K   Producer Price Index: All Commodities (1982–84=100); from January 1970. **Source:** U.S. Department of Labor, Bureau of Labor Statistics, *The Producer Price Index*, various issues. **Code:** INF009

L   Producer Price Index: Farm Products, Processed Foods, and Feeds (1982–84=100); from January 1970. **Source:** U.S. Department of Labor, Bureau of Labor Statistics, *The Producer Price Index*, various issues. **Code:** INF010

M   Producer Price Index: Industrial Commodities (1982–84=100); from January 1970. **Source:** U.S. Department of Labor, Bureau of Labor Statistics, *The Producer Price Index*, various issues. **Code:** INF011

N   Consumer Price Indexes (1982–84=100); United States; from January 1970. **Source:** *Survey of Current Business*, various issues. **Code:** INF012

Foreign Inflation
Spreadsheet: FORINFLA.WK1   Monthly Data

A   Year of the observation **Code:** FINFYR

B   Month of the observation (1 = January; 2 = February; etc.) **Code:** FINFMO

C   Consumer Price Indexes (1982–84=100); United States; from January 1970. **Source:** *Survey of Current Business*, various issues. **Code:** FINF001

D   Consumer Price Indexes (1982–84=100); Japan; from January 1970. **Source:** *Survey of Current Business*, Table 15, various issues. **Code:** FINF002

E   Consumer Price Indexes (1982–84=100); Federal Republic of Germany; from January 1970. **Source:** *Survey of Current Business*, Table 15, various issues. **Code:** FINF003

F   Consumer Price Indexes (1982–84=100); France; from January 1970. **Source:** *Survey of Current Business*, Table 15, various issues. **Code:** FINF004

G   Consumer Price Indexes (1982–84=100); United Kingdom; from January 1970. **Source:** *Survey of Current Business*, Table 15, various issues. **Code:** FINF005

H   Consumer Price Indexes (1982–84=100); Italy; from January 1970. **Source:** *Survey of Current Business*, Table 15, various issues. **Code:** FINF006

I   Consumer Price Indexes (1982–84=100); Canada; from January 1970. **Source:** *Survey of Current Business*, Table 15, various issues. **Code:** FINF007

Financial Institutions

Depository Institutions
Spreadsheet: DEPOSINS.WK1   Monthly Data

A   Year of the observation **Code:** DEPYR

B   Month of the observation (1 = January; 2 = February; etc.) **Code:** DEPMO

C   Loans and Securities at all Commercial Banks: Total; billions of dollars; seasonally adjusted; from January 1973. **Source:** *Federal Reserve Bulletin*, Table 1.23, various issues. **Code:** DEPO01

D   Loans and Securities at all Commercial Banks: U.S. government securities; billions of dollars; seasonally adjusted; from January 1973. **Source:** *Federal Reserve Bulletin*, Table 1.23, various issues. **Code:** DEPO02

E   Loans and Securities at all Commercial Banks: Total loans and leases; billions of dollars; seasonally adjusted; from January 1973. **Source:** *Federal Reserve Bulletin*, Table 1.23, various issues. **Code:** DEPO03

F   Loans and Securities at all Commercial Banks: Commercial and industrial loans outstanding plus nonfinancial commercial paper; seasonally adjusted; millions of dollars; from January 1970. **Source:** *Survey of Current Business*, various issues. **Code:** DEPO04

G   Assets and Liabilities of Commercial Banks: Loans and investments excluding interbank: billions of dollars; from January 1980. **Source:** *Federal Reserve Bulletin*, various issues. **Code:** DEPO05

H   Assets and Liabilities of Commercial Banks: Total cash assets; billions of dollars; from January 1980. **Source:** *Federal Reserve Bulletin*, various issues. **Code:** DEPO06

I   Assets and Liabilities of Commercial Banks: Total deposits; billions of dollars; from January 1980. **Source:** *Federal Reserve Bulletin*, various issues. **Code:** DEPO07

J   Assets and Liabilities of Commercial Banks: Transaction accounts (1980–1983 series listed as Demand Accounts); total; billions of dollars; from January 1980. **Source:** *Federal Reserve Bulletin*, various issues. **Code:** DEPO08

Consumer Credit
Spreadsheet: CONSUMCR.WK1   Monthly Data

A   Year of the observation **Code:** CCRYR

B   Month of the observation (1 = January; 2 = February; etc.) **Code:** CCRMO

C   Consumer Installment Credit Outstanding; total; not seasonally adjusted; millions of dollars; from January 1975. **Source:** Federal Reserve Bulletin, various issues. **Code:** CCR001

D   Consumer Installment Credit Outstanding; total; Commercial Banks; millions of dollars; not seasonally adjusted; from January 1970. **Source:** Federal Reserve Bulletin, various issues. **Code:** CCR002

E   Consumer Installment Credit Outstanding; automobile; millions of dollars; not seasonally adjusted; from January 1975. **Source:** Federal Reserve Bulletin, various issues. **Code:** CCR003

F   Consumer Installment Credit Outstanding; revolving; millions of dollars; not seasonally adjusted; from January 1980. **Source:** Federal Reserve Bulletin, various issues. **Code:** CCR004

G   Consumer Installment Credit Outstanding; revolving; commercial banks; millions of dollars; not seasonally adjusted; from January 1970. **Source:** Federal Reserve Bulletin, various issues. **Code:** CCR005

H   Consumer Installment Credit Outstanding; revolving; retailers; millions of dollars; not seasonally adjusted; from January 1977. **Source:** Federal Reserve Bulletin, various issues. **Code:** CCR006

I   Consumer Installment Credit Outstanding; revolving; gasoline companies; millions of dollars; not seasonally adjusted; from January 1971. **Source:** Federal Reserve Bulletin, various issues. **Code:** CCR007

Mutual Funds Indexes
Spreadsheet: LIPPER.WK1   Monthly Data

A   Year of the observation **Code:** LIPYR

B   Month of the observation (1 = January; 2 = February; etc.) **Code:** LIPMO

C   Lipper Mutual Fund Index: Capital Appreciation; net asset value weighted index of the 30 largest Capital Appreciation funds; adjusted for dividends and capital gains distributions as of the ex–dividend dates; December 31, 1980=100; from December 1986. **Source:** Lipper Analytical Services. **Code:** LIP001

D   Lipper Mutual Fund Index: Balanced; net asset value weighted index of the 30 largest funds within the Balanced Fund investment objective; adjusted for income dividends and capital gains distributions as of the ex–dividend dates; December 31, 1960=100; from December 1986. **Source:** Lipper Analytical Services. **Code:** LIP002

E   Lipper Mutual Fund Index: Equity Income; net asset value weighted index of the 30 largest Equity Income mutual funds; adjusted for income dividends and capital gains distributions as of the ex–dividend dates; December 31, 1978=100; from January 1990. **Source:** Lipper Analytical Services. **Code:** LIP003

F   Lipper Mutual Fund Index: Gold; net asset value weighted index of the 10 largest funds within the Gold fund category; adjusted for income dividends and capital gains distributions as of the ex–dividend dates; December 31, 1984=100; from December 1986. **Source:** Lipper Analytical Services. **Code:** LIP004

G   Lipper Mutual Fund Index: Growth; net asset value weighted index of the 30 largest Growth mutual funds; adjusted for income dividends and capital gains distributions as of the ex–dividend dates; December 31, 1968=100; from December 1986. **Source:** Lipper Analytical Services. **Code:** LIP005

H   Lipper Mutual Fund Index: Growth and Income; net asset value weighted index of the 30 largest funds within the Growth and Income objective; adjusted for income dividends and capital gains distributions as of the ex–dividend dates; December 31, 1968=100; from December 1986. **Source:** Lipper Analytical Services. **Code:** LIP006

I   Lipper Mutual Fund Index: International; net asset value weighted index of the 30 largest funds within the International Funds category; adjusted for income dividends and capital gains distributions as of the ex–dividend dates; December 31, 1968=100; from December 1984. **Source:** Lipper Analytical Services. **Code:** LIP007

J   Lipper Mutual Fund Index: Science & Technology; net asset value weighted index of the 10 largest funds within the Science & Technology investment objective; adjusted for income dividends and capital gains distributions as of the ex–dividend dates; December 31, 1984=100; from December 1984. **Source:** Lipper Analytical Services. **Code:** LIP008

K   Lipper Mutual Fund Index: Small Company Growth; net asset value weighted index of the 30 largest Small Company Growth funds; adjusted for income dividends and capital gains distributions as of the ex–dividend dates; December 31, 1980=100; from December 1984. **Source:** Lipper Analytical Services. **Code:** LIP009

Individual Mutual Funds
Spreadsheet: MUTUFUND.WK1   Monthly Data
A   Year of the observation **Code:** MUTYR
B   Month of the observation (1 = January; 2 = February; etc.) **Code:** MUTMO
C   Mutual Fund Net Asset Values: Fidelity Funds: Capital Appreciation Fund; end of month closing; from January 1987. **Source:** Fidelity Investments. **Code:** MUT001
D   Mutual Fund Net Asset Values: Fidelity Funds: Global Bond Fund; end of month closing; from April 1989. **Source:** Fidelity Investments. **Code:** MUT002
E   Mutual Fund Net Asset Values: Fidelity Funds: Growth and Income Fund; end of month closing; from January 1987. **Source:** Fidelity Investments. **Code:** MUT003
F   Mutual Fund Net Asset Values: Fidelity Funds: High Yield Fund; end of month closing; from December 1986. **Source:** Fidelity Investments. **Code:** MUT004
G   Mutual Fund Net Asset Values: Fidelity Funds: Magellan Fund; end of month closing; from January 1986. **Source:** Fidelity Investments. **Code:** MUT005

H   Mutual Fund Net Asset Values: Fidelity Funds: Municipal Bond Fund; end of month closing; from December 1986. **Source:** Fidelity Investments. **Code:** MUT006

I   Mutual Fund Net Asset Values: Fidelity Funds: Mortgage Security Fund; end of month closing; from March 1991. **Source:** Fidelity Investments. **Code:** MUT007

J   Mutual Fund Net Asset Values: Fidelity Funds: Puritan Fund; end of month closing; from January 1987. **Source:** Fidelity Investments. **Code:** MUT008

Financial Markets

The Primary Market
Spreadsheet: PRIMMKT.WK1   Monthly Data

A   Year of the observation **Code:** PMKTYR

B   Month of the observation (1 = January; 2 = February; etc.) **Code:** PMKTMO

C   New Security Issues; U.S. Corporations; all issues; millions of dollars; from January 1970. **Source:** *Federal Reserve Bulletin*, Table 1.46, various issues. **Code:** PMKT001

D   New Security Issues; U.S. Corporations; stocks: (only public offerings); millions of dollars; from January 1977. **Source:** *Federal Reserve Bulletin*, Table 1.46, various issues. **Code:** PMKT002

E   New Security Issues; U.S. Corporations; Stocks: by type of offering: Public preferred; millions of dollars; from January 1977. **Source:** *Federal Reserve Bulletin*, Table 1.46, various issues. **Code:** PMKT003

F   New Security Issues; U.S. Corporations; Stocks: by type of offering: Common; millions of dollars; from January 1970. **Source:** *Federal Reserve Bulletin*, Table 1.46, various issues. **Code:** PMKT004

G   New Security Issues; Tax–Exempt State and Local Governments; General Obligation; millions of dollars; from January 1970. **Source:** *Federal Reserve Bulletin*, Table 1.45, various issues. **Code:** PMKT005

H   New Security Issues; Tax–Exempt State and Local Governments; Revenue; millions of dollars; from January 1970. **Source:** *Federal Reserve Bulletin*, Table 1.45, various issues. **Code:** PMKT006

I   New Security Issues; U.S. Corporations; Bonds; millions of dollars; from January 1970. **Source:** *Federal Reserve Bulletin*, Table 1.46, various issues. **Code:** PMKT007

J   New Security Issues; U.S. Corporations; Bonds: by type of offering: Public; domestic; millions of dollars; from January 1970. **Source:** *Federal Reserve Bulletin*, Table 1.46, various issues. **Code:** PMKT008

K   New Security Issues; U.S. Corporations; Bonds: by type of offering: Sold abroad; millions of dollars; from January 1983. **Source:** *Federal Reserve Bulletin*, Table 1.46, various issues. **Code:** PMKT009

Stock Market Prices and Yields
Spreadsheet: STKINDEX.WK1   Monthly Data

A   Year of the observation **Code:** STKINYR

B   Month of the observation (1 = January; 2 = February; etc.) **Code:** STKINMO

C   Common Stock Prices: Dow Jones 30 Industrial Stocks; Average of Daily Closing Prices; from January 1970. **Source:** Dow Jones & Company, *The Wall Street Journal*, various issues. **Code:** STKIN001

D   Common Stock Prices: New York Stock Exchange: Composite (1965=50); monthly averages of daily closing rates; from January 1970. **Source:** *Federal Reserve Bulletin*, Table 1.36, various issues. **Code:** STKIN002

E   Common Stock Prices: New York Stock Exchange: Industrial (1965=50); monthly averages of daily closing rates; from January 1970. **Source:** *Federal Reserve Bulletin*, Table 1.36, various issues. **Code:** STKIN003

F   Common Stock Prices: New York Stock Exchange: Transportation (1965=50); monthly averages of daily closing rates; from January 1970. **Source:** *Federal Reserve Bulletin*, Table 1.36, various issues. **Code:** STKIN004

G   Common Stock Prices: New York Stock Exchange: Utility (1965=50); monthly averages of daily closing rates; from January 1970. **Source:** *Federal Reserve Bulletin*, Table 1.36, various issues. **Code:** STKIN005

H   Common Stock Prices: New York Stock Exchange: Finance (1965=50); monthly averages of daily closing rates; from January 1970. **Source:** *Federal Reserve Bulletin*, Table 1.36, various issues. **Code:** STKIN006

I   Common Stock Prices: Standard and Poor's Corporation: Composite (S&P's 500) 1941–43=10: monthly average of daily prices; from January 1970. **Source:** Standard and Poor's Corporation, *The Outlook*, various issues. **Code:** STKIN007

J   Common Stock Prices: Standard and Poor's Corporation: Industrial, 1941–43=10: monthly average of daily prices; from January 1970. **Source:** Standard and Poor's Corporation, *The Outlook*, various issues. **Code:** STKIN008

K   Common Stock Prices: Standard and Poor's Corporation: Capital Goods, 1941–43=10: monthly average of daily prices; from January 1970. **Source:** Standard and Poor's Corporation, *The Outlook*, various issues. **Code:** STKIN009

L   Common Stock Prices: Standard and Poor's Corporation: Transportation, 1970=10: monthly average of daily prices; from January 1970. **Source:** Standard and Poor's Corporation, *The Outlook*, various issues. **Code:** STKIN010

M   Common Stock Prices: Standard and Poor's Corporation: Public Utilities, 1941–43=10: monthly average of daily prices; from January 1970. **Source:** Standard and Poor's Corporation, *The Outlook*, various issues. **Code:** STKIN011

N   Common Stock Prices: Standard and Poor's Corporation: Finance, 1970=10: monthly average of daily prices; from January 1970. **Source:**

Standard and Poor's Corporation, *The Outlook*, various issues. **Code:** STKIN012

O   NASDAQ over–the–counter price indexes: Composite (2/5/71=100); from January 1971. **Source:** *Survey of Current Business*, Table 6 of Current Business Statistics, various issues. **Code:** STKIN013

P   NASDAQ over–the–counter price indexes: industrial (2/5/71=100); from January 1971. **Source:** *Survey of Current Business*, Table 6 of Current Business Statistics, various issues. **Code:** STKIN014

Q   NASDAQ over–the–counter price indexes: insurance (2/5/71=100); from January 1971. **Source:** *Survey of Current Business*, Table 6 of Current Business Statistics, various issues. **Code:** STKIN015

R   NASDAQ over–the–counter price indexes: bank (2/5/71=100); from January 1971. **Source:** *Survey of Current Business*, Table 6 of Current Business Statistics, various issues. **Code:** STKIN016

S   Common Stock Prices: Wilshire Associates, Wilshire 5000 Stock Index, from October 1990. **Source:** Commodity Services, Inc. **Code:** STKIN017

T   Common Stock Prices: Frank Russel Corporation, Russell 2000 Stock Index, from September 1992. **Source:** Frank Russell Corporation. **Code:** STKIN018

U   Yields (Standard and Poor's Corp.), percent: composite (500 stocks); from January 1977. **Source:** *Survey of Current Business*, Table 6 of Current Business Statistics, various issues. **Code:** STKIN019

V   Yields (Standard and Poor's Corp.), percent: industrials (400 stocks); from January 1977. **Source:** *Survey of Current Business*, Table 6 of Current Business Statistics, various issues. **Code:** STKIN020

W   Yields (Standard and Poor's Corp.), percent: utilities (40 stocks); from January 1977. **Source:** *Survey of Current Business*, Table 6 of Current Business Statistics, various issues. **Code:** STKIN021

X   Yields (Standard and Poor's Corp.), percent: transportation (20 stocks); from January 1977. **Source:** *Survey of Current Business*, Table 6 of Current Business Statistics, various issues. **Code:** STKIN022

Y   Yields (Standard and Poor's Corp.), percent: financial (40 stocks); from January 1977. **Source:** *Survey of Current Business*, Table 6 of Current Business Statistics, various issues. **Code:** STKIN023

Z   Yields (Standard and Poor's Corp.), percent: preferred (10 stocks, high–grade); from January 1977. **Source:** *Survey of Current Business*, Table 6 of Current Business Statistics, various issues. **Code:** STKIN024

AA   Dividend Yield: Standard and Poor's Common Stock Composite; monthly; percent per annum; from January 1970. **Source:** Standard and Poor's Corporation, *The Outlook*, various issues. **Code:** STKIN025

AB   Dividend Yield: Standard and Poor's Preferred Stock Yield; monthly; percent per annum; from January 1970. **Source:** Standard and Poor's Corporation, *The Outlook*, various issues. **Code:** STKIN026

Stock Market Activity
Spreadsheet: STKACTIV.WK1   Monthly Data
   A   Year of the observation **Code:** STKACYR
   B   Month of the observation (1 = January; 2 = February; etc.) **Code:** STKACMO
   C   Sales: Total on all registered exchanges (SEC); market value; millions of dollars; from January 1977. **Source:** *Survey of Current Business,* Table 6 of Current Business Statistics, various issues. **Code:** STKAC001
   D   Sales: Total on all registered exchanges (SEC); shares sold; millions; from January 1977. **Source:** *Survey of Current Business,* Table 6 of Current Business Statistics, various issues. **Code:** STKAC002
   E   Sales: Total on New York Stock Exchange; market value; millions of dollars; from January 1977. **Source:** *Survey of Current Business,* Table 6 of Current Business Statistics, various issues. **Code:** STKAC003
   F   Sales: Total on New York Stock Exchange; shares sold; (cleared or settled) millions; from January 1977. **Source:** *Survey of Current Business,* Table 6 of Current Business Statistics, various issues. **Code:** STKAC004
   G   Sales: Total on NASDAQ over–the–counter; market value; millions of dollars; from January 1983. **Source:** *Survey of Current Business,* Table 6 of Current Business Statistics, various issues. **Code:** STKAC005
   H   Sales: Total on NASDAQ over–the–counter; shares sold; millions; from November 1971. **Source:** *Survey of Current Business,* Table 6 of Current Business Statistics, various issues. **Code:** STKAC006
   I   Volume Traded on the New York Stock Exchange; millions of shares; monthly average; from January 1970. **Source:** New York Stock Exchange. **Code:** STKAC007
   J   Stock Market Composition; reported share volume by size; (at 5000 shares and over); monthly; percent; from January 1970. **Source:** New York Stock Exchange; *Statistical Highlights,* various issues. **Code:** STKAC008
   K   Stock Market: Customers' Stock Margin Debt; millions of dollars; from May 1970. **Source:** New York Stock Exchange, *Statistical Highlights,* various issues. **Code:** STKAC009

International Stock Indexes
Spreadsheet: FORSTOCK.WK1   Monthly Data
   A   Year of the observation **Code:** FSTKYR
   B   Month of the observation (1 = January; 2 = February; etc.) **Code:** FSTKMO
   C   Stock Price Indexes (1967=100); United States; from January 1970. **Source:** *Survey of Current Business,* Table 15 of Current Business Statistics, various issues. **Code:** FSTK001
   D   Stock Price Indexes (1967=100); Japan; from January 1970. **Source:** *Survey of Current Business,* Table 15 of Current Business Statistics, various issues. **Code:** FSTK002
   E   Stock Price Indexes (1967=100); Federal Republic of Germany; from January 1970. **Source:** *Survey of Current Business,* Table 15 of Current Business Statistics, various issues. **Code:** FSTK003

F   Stock Price Indexes (1967=100); France; from January 1970. **Source:** *Survey of Current Business*, Table 15 of Current Business Statistics, various issues. **Code:** FSTK004

G   Stock Price Indexes (1967=100); United Kingdom; from January 1970. **Source:** *Survey of Current Business*, Table 15 of Current Business Statistics, various issues. **Code:** FSTK005

H   Stock Price Indexes (1967=100); Italy; from January 1970. **Source:** *Survey of Current Business*, Table 15 of Current Business Statistics, various issues. **Code:** FSTK006

I   Stock Price Indexes (1967=100); Canada; from January 1970. **Source:** *Survey of Current Business*, Table 15 of Current Business Statistics, various issues. **Code:** FSTK007

Individual Stock Data
Spreadsheet: STOCKS.WK1   Monthly Data

A   Year of the observation **Code:** STOCKYR

B   Month of the observation (1 = January; 2 = February; etc.) **Code:** STOCKMO

C   Common Stock Prices: American Express; end of month closing price; adjusted for stock splits; from July 1988. **Source:** Commodity Systems, Inc. **Code:** STOCK01

D   Common Stock Dividends: American Express; from July 1988. **Source:** Commodity Systems, Inc. **Code:** STOCK02

E   Common Stock Prices: Anheuser–Busch; end of month closing price; adjusted for stock splits; from July 1988. **Source:** Commodity Systems, Inc. **Code:** STOCK03

F   Common Stock Dividends: Anheuser–Busch; from July 1988. **Source:** Commodity Systems, Inc. **Code:** STOCK04

G   Common Stock Prices: Apple Computer; end of month closing price; adjusted for stock splits; from July 1988. **Source:** Commodity Systems, Inc. **Code:** STOCK05

H   Common Stock Dividends: Apple Computer; from July 1988. **Source:** Commodity Systems, Inc. **Code:** STOCK06

I   Common Stock Prices: American Telephone and Telegraph; end of month closing price; adjusted for stock splits; from July 1988. **Source:** Commodity Systems, Inc. **Code:** STOCK07

J   Common Stock Dividends: American Telephone and Telegraph; from July 1988. **Source:** Commodity Systems, Inc. **Code:** STOCK08

K   Common Stock Prices: Boeing end of month closing price; adjusted for stock splits; from July 1988. **Source:** Commodity Systems, Inc. **Code:** STOCK09

L   Common Stock Dividends: Boeing from July 1988. **Source:** Commodity Systems, Inc. **Code:** STOCK10

M   Common Stock Prices: Chevron; end of month closing price; adjusted for stock splits; from July 1988. **Source:** Commodity Systems, Inc. **Code:** STOCK11

N   Common Stock Dividends: Chevron; from July 1988. **Source:** Commodity Systems, Inc. **Code:** STOCK12

O   Common Stock Prices: Citicorp; end of month closing price; adjusted for stock splits; from July 1988. **Source:** Commodity Systems, Inc. **Code:** STOCK13P

P   Common Stock Dividends: Citicorp; from July 1988. **Source:** Commodity Systems, Inc. **Code:** STOCK14

Q   Common Stock Prices: Coca–Cola; end of month closing price; adjusted for stock splits; from July 1988. **Source:** Commodity Systems, Inc. **Code:** STOCK15

R   Common Stock Dividends: Coca–Cola; from July 1988. **Source:** Commodity Systems, Inc. **Code:** STOCK16

S   Common Stock Prices: Disney; end of month closing price; adjusted for stock splits; from July 1988. **Source:** Commodity Systems, Inc. **Code:** STOCK17

T   Common Stock Dividends: Disney; from July 1988. **Source:** Commodity Systems, Inc. **Code:** STOCK18

U   Common Stock Prices: Dow Chemical; end of month closing price; adjusted for stock splits; from July 1988. **Source:** Commodity Systems, Inc. **Code:** STOCK19

V   Common Stock Dividends: Dow Chemical; from July 1988. **Source:** Commodity Systems, Inc. **Code:** STOCK20

W   Common Stock Prices: Exxon; end of month closing price; adjusted for stock splits; from July 1988. **Source:** Commodity Systems, Inc. **Code:** STOCK21

X   Common Stock Dividends: Exxon; from July 1988. **Source:** Commodity Systems, Inc. **Code:** STOCK22

Y   Common Stock Prices: Florida Power and Light; end of month closing price; adjusted for stock splits; from July 1988. **Source:** Commodity Systems, Inc. **Code:** STOCK23

Z   Common Stock Dividends: Florida Power and Light; from July 1988. **Source:** Commodity Systems, Inc. **Code:** STOCK24

AA   Common Stock Prices: Genentech; end of month closing price; adjusted for stock splits; from July 1988. **Source:** Commodity Systems, Inc. **Code:** STOCK25

AB   Common Stock Dividends: Genentech; from July 1988. **Source:** Commodity Systems, Inc. **Code:** STOCK26

AC   Common Stock Prices: General Motors; end of month closing price; adjusted for stock splits; from July 1988. **Source:** Commodity Systems, Inc. **Code:** STOCK27

AD   Common Stock Dividends: General Motors; from July 1988. **Source:** Commodity Systems, Inc. **Code:** STOCK28

AE   Common Stock Prices: Hewlett–Packard; end of month closing price; adjusted for stock splits; from July 1988. **Source:** Commodity Systems, Inc. **Code:** STOCK29

AF   Common Stock Dividends: Hewlett–Packard; from July 1988. **Source:** Commodity Systems, Inc. **Code:** STOCK30

AG   Common Stock Prices: Homestake Mining; end of month closing price; adjusted for stock splits; from July 1988. **Source:** Commodity Systems, Inc. **Code:** STOCK31

AH   Common Stock Dividends: Homestake Mining; from July 1988. **Source:** Commodity Systems, Inc. **Code:** STOCK32

AI   Common Stock Prices: International Business Machines; end of month closing price; adjusted for stock splits; from July 1988. **Source:** Commodity Systems, Inc. **Code:** STOCK33

AJ   Common Stock Dividends: International Business Machines; from July 1988. **Source:** Commodity Systems, Inc. **Code:** STOCK34

AK   Common Stock Prices: International Paper; end of month closing price; adjusted for stock splits; from July 1988. **Source:** Commodity Systems, Inc. **Code:** STOCK35

AL   Common Stock Dividends: International Paper; from July 1988. **Source:** Commodity Systems, Inc. **Code:** STOCK36

AM   Common Stock Prices: J. P. Morgan; end of month closing price; adjusted for stock splits; from July 1988. **Source:** Commodity Systems, Inc. **Code:** STOCK37

AN   Common Stock Dividends: J. P. Morgan; from July 1988. **Source:** Commodity Systems, Inc. **Code:** STOCK38

AO   Common Stock Prices: Eastman Kodak; end of month closing price; adjusted for stock splits; from July 1988. **Source:** Commodity Systems, Inc. **Code:** STOCK39

AP   Common Stock Dividends: Eastman Kodak; from July 1988. **Source:** Commodity Systems, Inc. **Code:** STOCK40

AQ   Common Stock Prices: McDonald's; end of month closing price; adjusted for stock splits; from July 1988. **Source:** Commodity Systems, Inc. **Code:** STOCK41

AR   Common Stock Dividends: McDonald's; from July 1988. **Source:** Commodity Systems, Inc. **Code:** STOCK42

AS   Common Stock Prices: Microsoft; end of month closing price; adjusted for stock splits; from July 1988. **Source:** Commodity Systems, Inc. **Code:** STOCK43

AT   Common Stock Dividends: Microsoft; from July 1988. **Source:** Commodity Systems, Inc. **Code:** STOCK44

AU   Common Stock Prices: Minnesota Mining and Manufacturing; end of month closing price; adjusted for stock splits; from July 1988. **Source:** Commodity Systems, Inc. **Code:** STOCK45

AV   Common Stock Dividends: Minnesota Mining and Manufacturing; from July 1988. **Source:** Commodity Systems, Inc. **Code:** STOCK46

AW   Common Stock Prices: Novell; end of month closing price; adjusted for stock splits; from July 1988. **Source:** Commodity Systems, Inc. **Code:** STOCK47

AX   Common Stock Dividends: Novell; from July 1988. **Source:** Commodity Systems, Inc. **Code:** STOCK48

AY   Common Stock Prices: Pepsi–Cola; end of month closing price; adjusted for stock splits; from July 1988. **Source:** Commodity Systems, Inc. **Code:** STOCK49

AZ   Common Stock Dividends: Pepsi–Cola; from July 1988. **Source:** Commodity Systems, Inc. **Code:** STOCK50

BA   Common Stock Prices: Ryder System; end of month closing price; adjusted for stock splits; from July 1988. **Source:** Commodity Systems, Inc. **Code:** STOCK51

BB   Common Stock Dividends: Ryder System; from July 1988. **Source:** Commodity Systems, Inc. **Code:** STOCK52

BC   Common Stock Prices: Texaco; end of month closing price; adjusted for stock splits; from July 1988. **Source:** Commodity Systems, Inc. **Code:** STOCK53

BD   Common Stock Dividends: Texaco; from July 1988. **Source:** Commodity Systems, Inc. **Code:** STOCK54

BE   Common Stock Prices: United Air Lines; end of month closing price; adjusted for stock splits; from July 1988. **Source:** Commodity Systems, Inc. **Code:** STOCK55

BF   Common Stock Dividends: United Air Lines; from July 1988. **Source:** Commodity Systems, Inc. **Code:** STOCK56

BG   Common Stock Prices: Wal–Mart; end of month closing price; adjusted for stock splits; from July 1988. **Source:** Commodity Systems, Inc. **Code:** STOCK57

BH   Common Stock Dividends: Wal–Mart; from July 1988. **Source:** Commodity Systems, Inc. **Code:** STOCK58

BI   Common Stock Prices: Westinghouse; end of month closing price; adjusted for stock splits; from July 1988. **Source:** Commodity Systems, Inc. **Code:** STOCK59

BJ   Common Stock Dividends: Westinghouse; from July 1988. **Source:** Commodity Systems, Inc. **Code:** STOCK60

Money Market Yields
Spreadsheet: MONEYYLD.WK1   Monthly Data

A   Year of the observation **Code:** MMYYR

B   Month of the observation (1 = January; 2 = February; etc.) **Code:** MMYMO

C   Federal Funds (weighted average of rates on trades, average of daily figures, percent per annum); from January 1970. **Source:** *Federal Reserve Bulletin*, Table 1.35, various issues. **Code:** MMY001

D   Discount window borrowing (average of daily figures, rate for the Federal Reserve Bank of New York); from January 1970. **Source:** *Federal Reserve Bulletin*, Table 1.35, various issues. **Code:** MMY002

E   Commercial paper: 1–month (annualized, quoted on a discount basis, an average of rates for firms whose bond rating is AA or the equivalent);

from April 1971. **Source:** *Federal Reserve Bulletin*, Table 1.35, various issues. **Code:** MMY003

F   Commercial paper: 3–month (annualized, quoted on a discount basis, an average of rates for firms whose bond rating is AA or the equivalent); from April 1971. **Source:** *Federal Reserve Bulletin*, Table 1.35, various issues. **Code:** MMY004

G   Commercial paper: 6–month (annualized, quoted on a discount basis, an average of rates for firms whose bond rating is AA or the equivalent); from January 1970. **Source:** *Federal Reserve Bulletin*, Table 1.35, various issues. **Code:** MMY005

H   Commercial Paper Outstanding, Total, Financial and Non–Financial Companies; thousands of dollars; seasonally adjusted; from January 1983. **Source:** Federal Reserve Bank of New York, Domestic Reports Division, News Release—Commercial Paper in the United States, various issues. **Code:** MMY006

I   Commercial Paper Outstanding, Financial Companies; thousands of dollars; seasonally adjusted; from January 1983. **Source:** Federal Reserve Bank of New York, Domestic Reports Division, News Release—Commercial Paper in the United States, various issues. **Code:** MMY007

J   Commercial Paper Outstanding, Nonfinancial Companies; millions of dollars; seasonally adjusted; from January 1970. **Source:** Federal Reserve Bank of New York, Domestic Reports Division, News Release—Commercial Paper in the United States, various issues. **Code:** MMY008

K   Bankers' Acceptances: 3–month (annualized, quoted on a discount basis, representative closing yields for acceptances of the highest rated money center banks); from January 1970. **Source:** *Federal Reserve Bulletin*, Table 1.35, various issues. **Code:** MMY009

L   Bankers' Acceptances: 6–month (annualized, quoted on a discount basis, representative closing yields for acceptances of the highest rated money center banks); from January 1981. **Source:** *Federal Reserve Bulletin*, Table 1.35, various issues. **Code:** MMY010

M   Certificates of Deposit, secondary market: 1–month (annualized, an average of dealer offering rates on nationally traded certificates of deposit); from January 1970. **Source:** *Federal Reserve Bulletin*, Table 1.35, various issues. **Code:** MMY011

N   Certificates of Deposit, secondary market: 3–month (annualized, an average of dealer offering rates on nationally traded certificates of deposit); from January 1970. **Source:** *Federal Reserve Bulletin*, Table 1.35, various issues. **Code:** MMY012

O   Certificates of Deposit, secondary market: 6–month (annualized, an average of dealer offering rates on nationally traded certificates of deposit); from January 1970. **Source:** *Federal Reserve Bulletin*, Table 1.35, various issues. **Code:** MMY013

P   Eurodollar Deposit Rate (London); 7–Day; average of weekly averages week ending Wednesday; percent per annum; from January 1971. **Source:** Board of Governors of the Federal Reserve System, Division of International Finance, Selected Interest and Exchange Rates—Weekly Series of Charts—Chart 6, various issues. **Code:** MMY014

Q   Eurodollar Deposit Rate (London); 1–Month; average of weekly averages week ending Wednesday; percent per annum; from January 1970. **Source:** Board of Governors of the Federal Reserve System, Division of International Finance, Selected Interest and Exchange Rates—Weekly Series of Charts—Chart 6, various issues. **Code:** MMY015

R   Eurodollar Deposit Rate (London); 3–Month; average of weekly averages week ending Wednesday; percent per annum; from January 1970. **Source:** Board of Governors of the Federal Reserve System, Division of International Finance, Selected Interest and Exchange Rates—Weekly Series of Charts—Chart 6, various issues. **Code:** MMY016

S   Eurodollar Deposit Rate (London); 6–Month; average of weekly averages week ending Wednesday; percent per annum; from January 1970. **Source:** Board of Governors of the Federal Reserve System, Division of International Finance, Selected Interest and Exchange Rates—Weekly Series of Charts—Chart 6, various issues. **Code:** MMY017

T   Eurodollar Deposit Rate (London); 1 Year; average of weekly averages week ending Wednesday; percent per annum; from January 1971. **Source:** Board of Governors of the Federal Reserve System, Division of International Finance, Selected Interest and Exchange Rates—Weekly Series of Charts—Chart 6, various issues. **Code:** MMY018

U   U.S. Treasury bills; secondary market; 3–month; percent per annum; monthly average of daily figures; from January 1970. **Source:** *Federal Reserve Bulletin*, Table 1.35, various issues. **Code:** MMY019

V   U.S. Treasury bills; secondary market; 6–month; percent per annum; monthly average of daily figures; from January 1970. **Source:** *Federal Reserve Bulletin*, Table 1.35, various issues. **Code:** MMY020

W   U.S. Treasury bills; secondary market; 1 Year; percent per annum; monthly average of daily figures; from January 1970. **Source:** *Federal Reserve Bulletin*, Table 1.35, various issues. **Code:** MMY021

X   U.S. Treasury bills; Auction Average; percent per annum; Discount (Issue Date); 3–Month Bill; average of daily figures; from January 1970. **Source:** *Federal Reserve Bulletin*, Table 1.35, various issues. **Code:** MMY022

Y   U.S. Treasury bills; Auction Average; Discount (Issue Date); 6–Month Bill; average of daily figures; from January 1970. **Source:** *Federal Reserve Bulletin*, Table 1.35, various issues. **Code:** MMY023

Z   U.S. Treasury bills; Auction Average; Discount (Issue Date); 1–Year Bill; average of daily figures; from January 1970. **Source:** *Federal Reserve Bulletin*, Table 1.35, various issues. **Code:** MMY024

Bond Market Prices, Yields, and Activity
Spreadsheet: BONDYLD.WK1   Monthly Data
A   Year of the observation **Code:** BYLDYR

B   Month of the observation (1 = January; 2 = February; etc.) **Code:** BYLDMO

C   U.S. Treasury Notes and Bonds; constant maturities; 2–year (yields on actively traded issues adjusted to constant maturities); monthly average of daily figures; from June 1976. **Source:** *Federal Reserve Bulletin*, Table 1.35, various issues. **Code:** BYLD001

D   U.S. Treasury Notes and Bonds; constant maturities; 3–year (yields on actively traded issues adjusted to constant maturities); from January 1970. **Source:** *Federal Reserve Bulletin*, Table 1.35, various issues. **Code:** BYLD002

E   U.S. Treasury Notes and Bonds; constant maturities; 5–year (yields on actively traded issues adjusted to constant maturities); from January 1970. **Source:** *Federal Reserve Bulletin*, Table 1.35, various issues. **Code:** BYLD003

F   U.S. Treasury Notes and Bonds; constant maturities; 7–year (yields on actively traded issues adjusted to constant maturities); from January 1970. **Source:** *Federal Reserve Bulletin*, Table 1.35, various issues. **Code:** BYLD004

G   U.S. Treasury Notes and Bonds; constant maturities; 10–year (yields on actively traded issues adjusted to constant maturities); from January 1970. **Source:** *Federal Reserve Bulletin*, Table 1.35, various issues. **Code:** BYLD005

H   U.S. Treasury Notes and Bonds; constant maturities; 30–year (yields on actively traded issues adjusted to constant maturities); from March 1977. **Source:** *Federal Reserve Bulletin*, Table 1.35, various issues. **Code:** BYLD006

I   U.S. Treasury Notes and Bonds; composite; over 10 years (long–term); (unweighted average of rates on all outstanding bonds neither due nor callable in less than 10 years, including flower bonds); from January 1970. **Source:** *Federal Reserve Bulletin*, Table 1.35, various issues. **Code:** BYLD007

J   U.S. Treasury Notes and Bonds; Market Yield on Long–Term Treasury Bonds (10+ years); percent per annum; from January 1970. **Source:** U.S. Department of the Treasury, *Treasury Bulletin*, Table 1.35, various issues. **Code:** BYLD008

K   Composite Municipal Bond Yield (20 Year); percent per annum; average of daily figures; from January 1986. **Source:** Moody's Investors Service, *Bond Survey*, various issues. **Code:** BYLD009

L   AAA Municipal Bond Yield (20 Year); percent per annum; average of daily figures; from January 1970. **Source:** Moody's Investors Service, *Bond Survey*, various issues. **Code:** BYLD010

M   AAA Municipal Bond Yield (10 Year); percent per annum; average of daily figures; from January 1986. **Source:** Moody's Investors Service, *Bond Survey*, various issues. **Code:** BYLD011

N   AA Municipal Bond Yield (20 Year); percent per annum; average of daily figures; from January 1986. **Source:** Moody's Investors Service, *Bond Survey*, various issues. **Code:** BYLD012

O   AA Municipal Bond Yield (10 Year); percent per annum; average of daily figures; from January 1986. **Source:** Moody's Investors Service, *Bond Survey*, various issues. **Code:** BYLD013

P   A Municipal Bond Yield (20 Year); percent per annum; average of daily figures; from January 1986. **Source:** Moody's Investors Service, *Bond Survey*, various issues. **Code:** BYLD014

Q   BAA Municipal Bond Yield (20 Year); percent per annum; average of daily figures; from January 1986. **Source:** Moody's Investors Service, *Bond Survey*, various issues. **Code:** BYLD015

R   AAA Corporate Bonds, Average Yield; average of daily figures; percent per annum; from January 1970. **Source:** Moody's Investors Service, *Bond Survey*, various issues. **Code:** BYLD016

S   AA Corporate Bonds, Average Yield; average of daily figures; percent per annum; from January 1970. **Source:** Moody's Investors Service, *Bond Survey*, various issues. **Code:** BYLD017

T   A Corporate Bonds, Average Yield; average of daily figures; percent per annum; from January 1970. **Source:** Moody's Investors Service, *Bond Survey*, various issues. **Code:** BYLD018

U   BAA Corporate Bonds, Average Yield; average of daily figures; percent per annum; from January 1970. **Source:** Moody's Investors Service, *Bond Survey*, various issues. **Code:** BYLD019

V   Average Yield on Corporate Bonds; average of daily figures; percent per annum; from January 1970. **Source:** Moody's Investors Service, *Bond Survey*, various issues. **Code:** BYLD020

W   AAA Industrial Bonds, Average Yield; average of daily figures; percent per annum; from January 1970. **Source:** Moody's Investors Service, *Bond Survey*, various issues. **Code:** BYLD021

X   AA Industrial Bonds, Average Yield; average of daily figures; percent per annum; from January 1970. **Source:** Moody's Investors Service, *Bond Survey*, various issues. **Code:** BYLD022

Y   A Industrial Bonds, Average Yield; average of daily figures; percent per annum; from January 1970. **Source:** Moody's Investors Service, *Bond Survey*, various issues. **Code:** BYLD023

Z   BAA Industrial Bonds, Average Yield; average of daily figures; percent per annum; from January 1970. **Source:** Moody's Investors Service, *Bond Survey*, various issues. **Code:** BYLD024

AA   Average Yield on Industrial Bonds; average of daily figures; percent per annum; from January 1970. **Source:** Moody's Investors Service, *Bond Survey*, various issues. **Code:** BYLD025

AB   AA Utility Bonds, Average Yield; average of daily figures; percent per annum; from January 1970. **Source:** Moody's Investors Service, *Bond Survey*, various issues. **Code:** BYLD026

AC   A Utility Bonds, Average Yield; average of daily figures; percent per annum; from January 1970. **Source:** Moody's Investors Service, *Bond Survey*, various issues. **Code:** BYLD027

AD   BAA Utility Bonds, Average Yield; average of daily figures; percent per annum; from January 1970. **Source:** Moody's Investors Service, *Bond Survey*, various issues. **Code:** BYLD028

AE   Average Yield on Public Utility Bonds; average of daily figures; percent per annum; from January 1970. **Source:** Moody's Investors Service, *Bond Survey*, various issues. **Code:** BYLD029

Mortgage Market Prices, Yields, and Activity
Spreadsheet: MORTMKT.WK1   Monthly Data

A   Year of the observation **Code:** MOMKTYR

B   Month of the observation (1 = January; 2 = February; etc.) **Code:** MOMKTMO

C   Secondary Market Yield on FHA Loans; assumed prepayment of mortgages in 12 years; percent; from January 1970. **Source:** U.S. Department of Housing and Urban Development, Federal Housing Administration, *HUD News*, various issues. **Code:** MOMKT001

D   Conventional Home Mortgage Rates; Fixed Rate Loans Closed; percent; from July 1982. **Source:** Federal Housing Finance Board, *Federal Housing Finance Board News*, various issues. **Code:** MOMKT002

E   Conventional Home Mortgage Rates; Adjustable Rate Loans Closed; percent; from July 1982. **Source:** Federal Housing Finance Board, *Federal Housing Finance Board News*, various issues. **Code:** MOMKT003

F   Conventional Home Mortgage Rates; Loans Closed; National Average for All Major Lenders, percent; from July 1973. **Source:** Federal Housing Finance Board, *Federal Housing Finance Board News*, various issues. **Code:** MOMKT004

G   Mortgages by Institution; Federal National Mortgage Association; end of month; seasonally adjusted; millions of dollars; from January 1970. **Source:** *Federal Reserve Bulletin*, various tables, various issues. **Code:** MOMKT005

Foreign Exchange
Spreadsheet: FOREX.WK1   Monthly Data

A   Year of the observation **Code:** FOEXYR

B   Month of the observation (1 = January; 2 = February; etc.) **Code:** FOEXMO

C   Australia (Cents per Australian $); average of daily rates; from January 1970. **Source:** Board of Governors of the Federal Reserve System, *Foreign Exchange Rates*, G.5, various issues. **Code:** FOEX001

D   Belgium (Belgian Franc per U.S. $); average of daily rates; from January 1970. **Source:** Board of Governors of the Federal Reserve System, *Foreign Exchange Rates*, G.5, various issues. **Code:** FOEX002

E   Canada (Canadian Dollar per U.S. $); average of daily rates; from January 1970. **Source:** Board of Governors of the Federal Reserve System, *Foreign Exchange Rates*, G.5, various issues. **Code:** FOEX003

F   Denmark (Danish Krone per U.S. $); average of daily rates; from January 1970. **Source:** Board of Governors of the Federal Reserve System, *Foreign Exchange Rates*, G.5, various issues. **Code:** FOEX004

G   France (Franc per U.S. $); average of daily rates; from January 1970. **Source:** Board of Governors of the Federal Reserve System, *Foreign Exchange Rates*, G.5, various issues. **Code:** FOEX005

H   Ireland (Cents per Pound); average of daily rates; from January 1970. **Source:** Board of Governors of the Federal Reserve System, *Foreign Exchange Rates*, G.5, various issues. **Code:** FOEX006

I   Italy (Lira per U.S. $); average of daily rates; from January 1970. **Source:** Board of Governors of the Federal Reserve System, *Foreign Exchange Rates*, G.5, various issues. **Code:** FOEX007

J   Japan (Yen per U.S. $); average of daily rates; from January 1970. **Source:** Board of Governors of the Federal Reserve System, *Foreign Exchange Rates*, G.5, various issues. **Code:** FOEX008

K   Netherlands (Guilder per U.S. $); average of daily rates; from January 1970. **Source:** Board of Governors of the Federal Reserve System, *Foreign Exchange Rates*, G.5, various issues. **Code:** FOEX009

L   Norway (Krone per U.S. $); average of daily rates; from January 1970. **Source:** Board of Governors of the Federal Reserve System, *Foreign Exchange Rates*, G.5, various issues. **Code:** FOEX010

M   South Africa (Cents per Rand); average of daily rates; from January 1970. **Source:** Board of Governors of the Federal Reserve System, *Foreign Exchange Rates*, G.5, various issues. **Code:** FOEX011

N   Sweden (Krona per U.S. $); average of daily rates; from January 1970. **Source:** Board of Governors of the Federal Reserve System, *Foreign Exchange Rates*, G.5, various issues. **Code:** FOEX012

O   Switzerland (Swiss Franc per U.S. $); average of daily rates; from January 1970. **Source:** Board of Governors of the Federal Reserve System, *Foreign Exchange Rates*, G.5, various issues. **Code:** FOEX013

P   United Kingdom (Cents per Pound); average of daily rates; from January 1970. **Source:** Board of Governors of the Federal Reserve System, *Foreign Exchange Rates*, G.5, various issues. **Code:** FOEX014

Q   West Germany (Deutsche Mark per U.S.$); average of daily rates; from January 1970. **Source:** Board of Governors of the Federal Reserve System, *Foreign Exchange Rates*, G.5, various issues. **Code:** FOEX015

R   United States—Index of Weighted Average Exchange Value of U.S. Dollar Against the Currencies of the Industrial Countries; March 1973 = 100; Weights are 1972–76 Average Total Trade Shares of Each of the Industrial Countries; from January 1970. **Source:** Board of Governors of the Federal Reserve System, *Foreign Exchange Rates*, G.5, various issues. **Code:** FOEX016

S   Argentina (Pesos per U.S.$); average of daily rates; from January 1976. **Source:** International Monetary Fund, *International Financial Statistics*, various issues. **Code:** FOEX017

T   Colombia (Pesos per U.S.$); average of daily rates; from January 1974. **Source:** International Monetary Fund, *International Financial Statistics*, various issues. **Code:** FOEX018

U   Korea (Won per U.S.$); average of daily rates; from January 1970. **Source:** International Monetary Fund, *International Financial Statistics*, various issues. **Code:** FOEX019

V   Mexico (Pesos per U.S.$); average of daily rates; from January 1974. **Source:** International Monetary Fund, *International Financial Statistics*, various issues. **Code:** FOEX020

W   Saudi Arabia (Riyals per U.S.$); average of daily rates; from January 1974. **Source:** International Monetary Fund, *International Financial Statistics*, various issues. **Code:** FOEX021

Quarterly Financial Series
Spreadsheet: FINQU.WK1   Quarterly Data

A   Year of the observation **Code:** FQUYR

B   Quarter of the observation (3 = first quarter; 6 = second quarter; etc.) **Code:** FQUQU

C   M1: Sum of currency, demand deposits, travelers checks and other checkable deposits; averages of daily figures; billions of dollars; seasonally adjusted; from First Quarter 1959. **Source:** Board of Governors of the Federal Reserve System, *Statistical Release: Money Stock Measures and Liquid Assets,* H.6, various issues. **Code:** FQU001

D   M2: M1 plus overnight RP's and Eurodollars, MMMF balances, MMDA's, and savings and small time deposits; averages of daily figures; billions of dollars; seasonally adjusted; from First Quarter 1959. **Source:** Board of Governors of the Federal Reserve System, *Statistical Release: Money Stock Measures and Liquid Assets,* H.6, various issues. **Code:** FQU002

E   M3: M2 plus large time deposits, term RP's, term Eurodollars, and institution–only MMMF balances; averages of daily figures; billions of dollars; seasonally adjusted; from First Quarter 1959. **Source:** Board of Governors of the Federal Reserve System, *Statistical Release: Money Stock Measures and Liquid Assets,* H.6, various issues. **Code:** FQU003

F   L: M3 plus other liquid assets; averages of daily figures; billions of dollars; seasonally adjusted; from First Quarter 1959. **Source:** Board of Governors of the Federal Reserve System, *Statistical Release: Money Stock Measures and Liquid Assets,* H.6, various issues. **Code:** FQU004

G   Consumer Price Index: All Items (1982–84=100); seasonally adjusted; from First Quarter 1947. **Source:** U.S. Department of Labor, Bureau of Labor Statistics, *The Consumer Price Index*, various issues. **Code:** FQU005

H   Implicit Price Deflator, Gross National Product, 1987=100; seasonally adjusted; from First Quarter 1947. (Note break in series between 1958 and 1959.) **Source:** *Survey of Current Business*, various issues. **Code:** FQU006

I   U.S. Treasury bills; secondary market; 3–month; percent per annum; monthly average of daily figures; from First Quarter 1947. **Source:** *Federal Reserve Bulletin*, Table 1.35, various issues. **Code:** FQU007

J   U.S. Treasury Notes and Bonds, constant maturities; 30–year (yields on actively traded issues adjusted to constant maturities); from First Quarter 1977. **Source:** *Federal Reserve Bulletin*, Table 1.35, various issues. **Code:** FQU008

K   AAA Corporate Bonds, Average Yield; average of daily figures; percent per annum; from First Quarter 1947. **Source:** Moody's Investors Service, *Bond Survey*, various issues. **Code:** FQU009

L   Common Stock Prices: Dow Jones 30 Industrial Stocks; Average of Daily Closing Prices; from First Quarter 1947. **Source:** Dow Jones & Company, *The Wall Street Journal*, various issues. **Code:** FQU010

M   Common Stock Prices: Standard and Poor's Corporation: Composite (S&P's 500) 1941–43=10; monthly average of daily prices, from First Quarter 1947. **Source:** Standard and Poor's Corporation, *The Outlook*, various issues. **Code:** FQU011

N   Common Stock Prices: New York Stock Exchange: Composite (1965=50); monthly averages of daily closing rates; from January 1947. **Source:** *Federal Reserve Bulletin*, Table 1.36; various issues. **Code:** FQU012

The Real Sector

Macroeconomic Measures

Business Cycle Indicators
Spreadsheet: BUSCYCLE.WK1   Monthly Data

A   Year of the observation **Code:** BCYR

B   Month of the observation (1 = January; 2 = February; etc.) **Code:** BCMO

C   Composite index: 11 leading indicators; 1982=100; seasonally adjusted; from January 1970. **Source:** *Survey of Current Business*, Business Cycle Indicators, various issues. **Code:** BC001

D   Components: 11 leading indicators; Avg. Workweek of Production Workers, Mfg.; hours; seasonally adjusted; from January 1970. **Source:** *Survey of Current Business*, Business Cycle Indicators, various issues. **Code:** BC002

E   Components: 11 leading indicators; Avg. Weekly Initial Claims for Unemployment Insurance State Programs; thousands; seasonally adjusted; from January 1970. **Source:** *Survey of Current Business*, Business Cycle Indicators, various issues. **Code:** BC003

F   Components: 11 leading indicators; Value of Mgs' New Orders for Consumer Goods & Materials; billions of 1987 dollars; seasonally adjusted; from January 1970. **Source:** *Survey of Current Business*, Business Cycle Indicators, various issues. **Code:** BC004

G   Components: 11 leading indicators; Index, Stock Prices; 500 Common Stocks, (Standard & Poor's), 1941–43=10; from January 1970. **Source:** *Survey of Current Business*, Business Cycle Indicators, various issues. **Code:** BC005

H   Components: 11 leading indicators; Contracts and Orders for Plant & Equipment; seasonally adjusted; billions of 1987 dollars; from January

1970. **Source:** *Survey of Current Business*, Business Cycle Indicators, various issues. **Code:** BC006

I   Components: 11 leading indicators; Index; New Private Housing Units Authorized by Local Building Permit, 1967=100; seasonally adjusted; billions of 1987 dollars; from January 1970. **Source:** *Survey of Current Business*, Business Cycle Indicators, various issues. **Code:** BC007

J   Components: 11 leading indicators; Vendor Performance; % Companies Reporting Slower Deliveries; from January 1970. **Source:** *Survey of Current Business*, Business Cycle Indicators, various issues. **Code:** BC008

K   Components: 11 leading indicators; University of Michigan's Index of Consumer Expectations; seasonally adjusted; from January 1970. **Source:** *Survey of Current Business*, Business Cycle Indicators, various issues. **Code:** BC009

L   Components: 11 leading indicators; Change in Mfg. Unfilled Orders, Durable Goods, Smoothed (weighted 4–term moving average); billions of 1987 dollars; seasonally adjusted; from January 1970. **Source:** *Survey of Current Business*, Business Cycle Indicators, various issues. **Code:** BC010

M   Components: 11 leading indicators; Change in Sensitive Materials Price (%); Smoothed (weighted 4–term moving average); billions of 1987 dollars; seasonally adjusted; from January 1970. **Source:** *Survey of Current Business*, Business Cycle Indicators, various issues. **Code:** BC011

N   Components: 11 leading indicators; M–2; Money Supply; billions of 1987 dollars; seasonally adjusted; from January 1970. **Source:** *Survey of Current Business*, Business Cycle Indicators, various issues. **Code:** BC012

O   Components: 11 leading indicators; Change in Credit – Business and Consumer Borrowing; %; seasonally adjusted; from January 1970. **Source:** *Survey of Current Business*, Business Cycle Indicators, various issues. **Code:** BC013

P   Components: Capital Investment Commitments; Index of Net Business Formation (1967=100); seasonally adjusted; from January 1970. **Source:** *Survey of Current Business*, Business Cycle Indicators, various issues. **Code:** BC014

Q   Components: Capital Investment Commitments, Contracts & Orders for Plant & Equipment; billions of 1987 dollars; seasonally adjusted; from January 1970. **Source:** *Survey of Current Business*, Business Cycle Indicators, various issues. **Code:** BC015

R   Composite Index: 4 Coincident Indicators (1982=100); seasonally adjusted; from January 1970. **Source:** *Survey of Current Business*, Business Cycle Indicators, various issues. **Code:** BC016

S   Components: 4 Coincident Indicators; Number of Employees on Nonagricultural Payrolls; Establishment Survey; thousands; seasonally adjusted; from January 1970. **Source:** *Survey of Current Business*, Business Cycle Indicators, various issues. **Code:** BC017

T   Components: 4 Coincident Indicators; Index of Industrial Production; Total (1987=100); seasonally adjusted; from January 1970. **Source:** *Survey of Current Business*, Business Cycle Indicators, various issues. **Code:** BC018

U   Components: 4 Coincident Indicators; Personal Income Less Transfer Payments; billions of 1987$; seasonally adjusted; from January 1970. **Source:** *Survey of Current Business*, Business Cycle Indicators, various issues. **Code:** BC019

V   Components: 4 Coincident Indicators, Manufacturing & Trade Sales; millions of 1987 dollars; seasonally adjusted; from January 1970. **Source:** *Survey of Current Business*, Business Cycle Indicators, various issues. **Code:** BC020

W   Composite Index; 7 Lagging Indicators (1982=100); seasonally adjusted; from January 1970. **Source:** *Survey of Current Business*, Business Cycle Indicators, various issues. **Code:** BC021

X   Components: 7 Lagging Indicators; Ratio, Constant–Dollar Inventories to Sales, Manufacturing, and Trade (%); seasonally adjusted; from January 1970. **Source:** *Survey of Current Business*, Business Cycle Indicators, various issues. **Code:** BC022

Y   Components: 7 Lagging Indicators; Avg. (Mean) Duration Unemployment (weeks); seasonally adjusted; from January 1970. **Source:** *Survey of Current Business*, Business Cycle Indicators, various issues. **Code:** BC023

Z   Components: 7 Lagging Indicators; Ratio; Consumer Installment Debt to Personal Income (%); seasonally adjusted; from January 1970. **Source:** *Survey of Current Business*, Business Cycle Indicators, various issues. **Code:** BC024

AA   Components: 7 Lagging Indicators; Average Prime Rate Charged by Banks; %; from January 1970. **Source:** *Survey of Current Business*, Business Cycle Indicators, various issues. **Code:** BC025

AB   Components: 7 Lagging Indicators; Commercial and Industrial Loans Outstanding; millions of 1987 dollars; seasonally adjusted; from January 1970. **Source:** *Survey of Current Business*, Business Cycle Indicators, various issues. **Code:** BC026

AC   Components: 7 Lagging Indicators; Change in Consumer Price Index for Services; Smoothed; seasonally adjusted; from January 1970. **Source:** *Survey of Current Business*, Business Cycle Indicators, various issues. **Code:** BC027

National Product and Income
Spreadsheet: NATLPROD.WK1   Quarterly Data

A   Year of the observation **Code:** NPYR

B   Quarter of the observation (1 = First quarter; 2 = Second quarter; etc.) **Code:** NPQU

C   National Product: Gross Domestic Product: Total; billions of dollars; seasonally adjusted; from First quarter 1959. **Source:** *Survey of Current Business*, various issues. **Code:** NP001

D   National Product: Gross Domestic Product: Personal Consumption Expenditures; total; billions of dollars; seasonally adjusted; from First quarter 1946. **Source:** *Survey of Current Business*, various issues. **Code:** NP002

E   National Product: Gross Domestic Product: Personal Consumption Expenditures; durable goods; billions of dollars; seasonally adjusted; from First quarter 1946. **Source:** *Survey of Current Business*, various issues. **Code:** NP003

F   National Product: Gross Domestic Product: Personal Consumption Expenditures; nondurable goods; billions of dollars; seasonally adjusted; from First quarter 1946. **Source:** *Survey of Current Business*, various issues. **Code:** NP004

G   National Product: Gross Domestic Product: Personal Consumption Expenditures; services; billions of dollars; seasonally adjusted; from First quarter 1946. **Source:** *Survey of Current Business*, various issues. **Code:** NP005

H   National Product: Gross Domestic Product: Gross Private Domestic Investment; total; billions of dollars; seasonally adjusted; from First quarter 1946. **Source:** *Survey of Current Business*, various issues. **Code:** NP006

I   National Product: Gross Domestic Product: Gross Private Domestic Investment; fixed investment; billions of dollars; seasonally adjusted; from First quarter 1946. **Source:** *Survey of Current Business*, various issues. **Code:** NP007

J   National Product: Gross Domestic Product: Gross Private Domestic Investment; fixed investment; nonresidential; billions of dollars; seasonally adjusted; from First Quarter 1946. **Source:** *Survey of Current Business*, various issues. **Code:** NP008

K   National Product: Gross Domestic Product: Gross Private Domestic Investment; fixed investment; residential; billions of dollars; seasonally adjusted; from First Quarter 1946. **Source:** *Survey of Current Business*, various issues. **Code:** NP009

L   National Product: Gross Domestic Product: Change in Business Inventories; total; billions of dollars; seasonally adjusted; from First quarter 1946. **Source:** *Survey of Current Business*, various issues. **Code:** NP010

M   National Product: Gross Domestic Product: Change in Business Inventories; total; billions of 1987 dollars; seasonally adjusted; from First quarter 1959. **Source:** *Survey of Current Business*, various issues. **Code:** NP011

N   National Product: Gross Domestic Product: Change in Business Inventories: Nonfarm; billions of dollars; seasonally adjusted; from First quarter 1946. **Source:** *Survey of Current Business*, various issues. **Code:** NP012

O   National Product: Gross Domestic Product: Change in Business Inventories: Farm; billions of dollars; seasonally adjusted; from First quarter 1946. **Source:** *Survey of Current Business*, various issues. **Code:** NP013

P   National Product: Gross Domestic Product: Net Exports of Goods and Services; total; billions of dollars; seasonally adjusted; from First quarter 1946. **Source:** *Survey of Current Business*, various issues. **Code:** NP014

Q   National Product: Gross Domestic Product: Net Exports of Goods and Services: Exports; billions of dollars; seasonally adjusted; from First quarter 1946. **Source:** *Survey of Current Business,* various issues. **Code:** NP015

R   National Product: Gross Domestic Product: Net Exports of Goods and Services: Imports; billions of dollars; seasonally adjusted; from First quarter 1946. **Source:** *Survey of Current Business,* various issues. **Code:** NP016

S   National Product: Gross Domestic Product: Government Purchases of Goods and Services; total; billions of dollars; seasonally adjusted; from First quarter 1946. **Source:** *Survey of Current Business,* various issues. **Code:** NP017

T   National Product: Gross Domestic Product: Government Purchases of Goods and Services: Federal; billions of dollars; seasonally adjusted; from First quarter 1946. **Source:** *Survey of Current Business,* various issues. **Code:** NP018

U   National Product: Gross Domestic Product: Government Purchases of Goods and Services: Federal, National Defense; billions of dollars; seasonally adjusted; from First quarter 1946. **Source:** *Survey of Current Business,* various issues. **Code:** NP019

V   National Product: Gross Domestic Product: Government Purchases of Goods and Services: Federal, Nondefense; billions of dollars; seasonally adjusted; from First quarter 1946. **Source:** *Survey of Current Business,* various issues. **Code:** NP020

W   National Product: Gross Domestic Product: Government Purchases of Goods and Services: State and Local; billions of dollars; seasonally adjusted; from First quarter 1946. **Source:** *Survey of Current Business,* various issues. **Code:** NP021

X   National Product: Gross Domestic Product: Business; Total; billions of dollars; seasonally adjusted; from First quarter 1946. **Source:** *Survey of Current Business,* various issues. **Code:** NP022

Y   National Product: Gross Domestic Product: Business, Nonfarm; billions of dollars; seasonally adjusted; from First quarter 1946. **Source:** *Survey of Current Business,* various issues. **Code:** NP023

Z   National Product: Gross Domestic Product: Business, Farm; billions of dollars; seasonally adjusted; from First quarter 1946. **Source:** *Survey of Current Business,* various issues. **Code:** NP024

AA   National Product: Gross Domestic Product: Households and Institutions; billions of dollars; seasonally adjusted; from First quarter 1946. **Source:** *Survey of Current Business,* various issues. **Code:** NP025

AB   National Product: Gross Domestic Product: Households and Institutions, Private Households; billions of dollars; seasonally adjusted; from First quarter 1946. **Source:** *Survey of Current Business,* various issues. **Code:** NP026

AC   National Product: Gross Domestic Product: Households and Institutions, Nonprofit Institutions; billions of dollars; seasonally adjusted; from First quarter 1946. **Source:** *Survey of Current Business,* various issues. **Code:** NP027

AD   National Product: Gross Domestic Product: General Government; total; billions of dollars; seasonally adjusted; from First quarter 1946. **Source:** *Survey of Current Business,* various issues. **Code:** NP028

AE   National Product: Gross Domestic Product: General Government, Federal; billions of dollars; seasonally adjusted; from First quarter 1946. **Source:** *Survey of Current Business,* various issues. **Code:** NP029

AF   National Product: Gross Domestic Product: General Government, State and Local; billions of dollars; seasonally adjusted; from First quarter 1946. **Source:** *Survey of Current Business,* various issues. **Code:** NP030

AG   National Product: Gross National Product; total; billions of dollars; seasonally adjusted; from First quarter 1946. **Source:** *Survey of Current Business,* various issues. **Code:** NP031

AH   National Product: Gross National Product, Consumption of Fixed Capital; billions of dollars; seasonally adjusted; from First quarter 1946. **Source:** *Survey of Current Business,* various issues. **Code:** NP032

AI   National Product: Net National Product; billions of dollars; seasonally adjusted; from First quarter 1946. **Source:** *Survey of Current Business,* various issues. **Code:** NP033

AJ   National Product: Net National Product, Indirect Business Tax and Non–tax Liability; billions of dollars; seasonally adjusted; from First quarter 1946. **Source:** *Survey of Current Business,* various issues. **Code:** NP034

AK   National Product: Net Domestic Product; total; billions of dollars; seasonally adjusted; from First quarter 1959. **Source:** *Survey of Current Business,* various issues. **Code:** NP035

AL   National Product: Command–Basis Gross National Product; total; billions of dollars; seasonally adjusted; from First quarter 1959. **Source:** *Survey of Current Business,* various issues. **Code:** NP036

AM   National Product: Gross Domestic Product of Corporate Business; billions of dollars; seasonally adjusted; from First quarter 1946. **Source:** *Survey of Current Business,* various issues. **Code:** NP037

AN   National Product: Gross Domestic Product of Financial Corporate Business; billions of dollars; seasonally adjusted; from First quarter 1946. **Source:** *Survey of Current Business,* various issues. **Code:** NP038

AO   National Product: Gross Domestic Product of Nonfinancial Corporate Business; billions of dollars; seasonally adjusted; from First quarter 1946. **Source:** *Survey of Current Business,* various issues. **Code:** NP039

AP   National Income: total; billions of dollars; seasonally adjusted; from First quarter 1946. **Source:** *Survey of Current Business,* various issues. **Code:** NP040

AQ   National Income: Compensation of Employees; billions of dollars; seasonally adjusted; from First quarter 1946. **Source:** *Survey of Current Business,* various issues. **Code:** NP041

AR   National Income: Compensation of Employees; Wages and Salaries; billions of dollars; seasonally adjusted; from First quarter 1946. **Source:** *Survey of Current Business,* various issues. **Code:** NP042

AS   National Income: Proprietors' Income with Inventory Valuation and Capital Consumption Adjustment; billions of dollars; seasonally adjusted; from First quarter 1946. **Source:** *Survey of Current Business,* various issues. **Code:** NP043

AT   National Income: Proprietors' Income with Inventory Valuation and Capital Consumption Adjustment, Farm; billions of dollars; seasonally adjusted; from First quarter 1946. **Source:** *Survey of Current Business,* various issues. **Code:** NP044

AU   National Income: Proprietors' Income with Inventory Valuation and Capital Consumption Adjustment, Nonfarm; billions of dollars; seasonally adjusted; from First quarter 1946. **Source:** *Survey of Current Business,* various issues. **Code:** NP045

AV   National Income: Rental Income of Persons with Capital Consumption Adjustment; billions of dollars; seasonally adjusted; from First quarter 1946. **Source:** *Survey of Current Business,* various issues. **Code:** NP046

AW   National Income: Corporate Profits with Inventory Valuation Adjustment and Capital Consumption Adjustment; billions of dollars; seasonally adjusted; from First quarter 1946. **Source:** *Survey of Current Business,* various issues. **Code:** NP047

AX   National Income: Corporate Profits After Tax with Inventory Valuation Adjustment and Capital Consumption Adjustment; billions of dollars; seasonally adjusted; from First quarter 1946. **Source:** *Survey of Current Business,* various issues. **Code:** NP048

Personal Income and Consumption
Spreadsheet: PERINCOM.WK1   Quarterly Data

A   Year of the observation **Code:** PICYR

B   Quarter of the observation (1 = First quarter; 2 = Second quarter; etc.) **Code:** PICQU

C   Personal Income: Total Personal Income; billions of dollars; from First quarter 1946. **Source:** *Survey of Current Business,* various issues. **Code:** PIC001

D   Personal Income: Wage and Salary Disbursements; billions of dollars; from First quarter 1946. **Source:** *Survey of Current Business,* various issues. **Code:** PIC002

E   Personal Income: Wage and Salary Disbursements: Commodity–Producing Industries; billions of dollars; from First quarter 1946. **Source:** *Survey of Current Business,* various issues. **Code:** PIC003

F   Personal Income: Wage and Salary Disbursements: Distributive Industries; billions of dollars; from First quarter 1946. **Source:** *Survey of Current Business,* various issues. **Code:** PIC004

G   Personal Income: Wage and Salary Disbursements: Service Industries; billions of dollars; from First quarter 1946. **Source:** *Survey of Current Business,* various issues. **Code:** PIC005

H   Personal Income: Wage and Salary Disbursements: Government and Government Enterprises; billions of dollars; from First quarter 1946. **Source:** *Survey of Current Business*, various issues. **Code:** PIC006

I   Personal Income: Rental Income of Persons with Capital Consumption Adjustment; billions of dollars; from First quarter 1946. **Source:** *Survey of Current Business*, various issues. **Code:** PIC007

J   Personal Income: Personal Dividend Income; billions of dollars; from First quarter 1946. **Source:** *Survey of Current Business*, various issues. **Code:** PIC008

K   Personal Income: Personal Interest Income; billions of dollars; from First quarter 1946. **Source:** *Survey of Current Business*, various issues. **Code:** PIC009

L   Personal Income: Transfer Payments; billions of dollars; from First quarter 1946. **Source:** *Survey of Current Business*, various issues. **Code:** PIC010

M   Personal Income: Personal Tax and Nontax Payments; billions of dollars; from First quarter 1946. **Source:** *Survey of Current Business*, various issues. **Code:** PIC011

N   Personal Income: Personal Disposable Income; billions of dollars; from First quarter 1946. **Source:** *Survey of Current Business*, various issues. **Code:** PIC012

O   Personal Income: Personal Saving; billions of dollars; from First quarter 1946. **Source:** *Survey of Current Business*, various issues. **Code:** PIC013

P   Personal Consumption Expenditures: Total; billions of dollars; from First quarter 1946. **Source:** *Survey of Current Business*, various issues. **Code:** PIC014

Q   Personal Consumption Expenditures: Durable Goods; billions of dollars; from First quarter 1946. **Source:** *Survey of Current Business*, various issues. **Code:** PIC015

R   Personal Consumption Expenditures: Nondurable Goods; billions of dollars; from First quarter 1946. **Source:** *Survey of Current Business*, various issues. **Code:** PIC016

S   Personal Consumption Expenditures: Services; billions of dollars; from First quarter 1946. **Source:** *Survey of Current Business*, various issues. **Code:** PIC017

T   Personal Consumption Expenditures: Motor Vehicles and Parts; billions of dollars; from First quarter 1946. **Source:** *Survey of Current Business*, various issues. **Code:** PIC018

U   Personal Consumption Expenditures: Furniture and Household Equipment; billions of dollars; from First quarter 1946. **Source:** *Survey of Current Business*, various issues. **Code:** PIC019

V   Personal Consumption Expenditures: Food; billions of dollars; from First quarter 1946. **Source:** *Survey of Current Business*, various issues. **Code:** PIC020

W   Personal Consumption Expenditures: Clothing and Shoes; billions of dollars; from First quarter 1946. **Source:** *Survey of Current Business*, various issues. **Code:** PIC021

X   Personal Consumption Expenditures: Gasoline and Oil; billions of dollars; from First quarter 1946. **Source:** *Survey of Current Business*, various issues. **Code:** PIC022

Y   Personal Consumption Expenditures: Fuel Oil and Coal; billions of dollars; from First quarter 1959. **Source:** *Survey of Current Business*, various issues. **Code:** PIC023

Z   Personal Consumption Expenditures: Housing; billions of dollars; from First quarter 1946. **Source:** *Survey of Current Business*, various issues. **Code:** PIC024

AA   Personal Consumption Expenditures: Household Operation; billions of dollars; from First quarter 1946. **Source:** *Survey of Current Business*, various issues. **Code:** PIC025

AB   Personal Consumption Expenditures: Electricity and Gas; billions of dollars; from First quarter 1959. **Source:** *Survey of Current Business*, various issues. **Code:** PIC026

AC   Personal Consumption Expenditures: Transportation; billions of dollars; from First quarter 1946. **Source:** *Survey of Current Business*, various issues. **Code:** PIC027

AD   Personal Consumption Expenditures: Medical Care; billions of dollars; from First quarter 1947. **Source:** *Survey of Current Business*, various issues. **Code:** PIC028

Labor and Employment
Spreadsheet: EMPLOY.WK1   Monthly Data

A   Year of the observation **Code:** LEYR

B   Month of the observation (1 = January; 2 = February; etc.) **Code:** LEMO

C   Labor Statistics: Total; 16 years and over; Noninstitutional Population; thousands of persons; seasonally adjusted; from January 1970. **Source:** U.S. Department of Labor, Bureau of Labor Statistics, *The Employment Situation – Household Survey*, various issues. **Code:** LE001

D   Labor Statistics: Labor Force; thousands of persons; seasonally adjusted; from January 1970. **Source:** U.S. Department of Labor, Bureau of Labor Statistics, *The Employment Situation – Household Survey*, various issues. **Code:** LE002

E   Labor Statistics: Total employed; thousands of persons; seasonally adjusted; from January 1970. **Source:** U.S. Department of Labor, Bureau of Labor Statistics, *The Employment Situation – Household Survey*, various issues. **Code:** LE003

F   Labor Statistics: Employment–Population Ratio; thousands of persons; seasonally adjusted; (Total employment as a percent of the noninstitutional population) thousands of persons; from January 1970. **Source:** U.S. Department of Labor, Bureau of Labor Statistics, *The Employment Situation – Household Survey*, various issues. **Code:** LE004

G   Labor Statistics: Unemployed; seasonally adjusted; thousands of persons; from January 1970. **Source:** U.S. Department of Labor, Bureau of Labor

Statistics, *The Employment Situation – Household Survey*, various issues. **Code:** LE005

H   Labor Statistics: Unemployment Rate (Unemployment as a percent of the labor force including the resident Armed Forces); seasonally adjusted; thousands of persons; from January 1970. **Source:** U.S. Department of Labor, Bureau of Labor Statistics, *The Employment Situation – Household Survey*, various issues. **Code:** LE006

I   Labor Statistics: Labor Force, Men; seasonally adjusted; thousands of persons; from January 1970. **Source:** U.S. Department of Labor, Bureau of Labor Statistics, *The Employment Situation – Household Survey*, various issues. **Code:** LE007

J   Labor Statistics: Labor Force, Women; seasonally adjusted; thousands of persons; from January 1970. **Source:** U.S. Department of Labor, Bureau of Labor Statistics, *The Employment Situation – Household Survey*, various issues. **Code:** LE008

K   Labor Statistics: Total Employed, Men; seasonally adjusted; thousands of persons; from January 1970. **Source:** U.S. Department of Labor, Bureau of Labor Statistics, *The Employment Situation – Household Survey*, various issues. **Code:** LE009

L   Labor Statistics: Total Employed, Women; seasonally adjusted; thousands of persons; from January 1970. **Source:** U.S. Department of Labor, Bureau of Labor Statistics, *The Employment Situation – Household Survey*, various issues. **Code:** LE010

M   Labor Statistics: Unemployment Rate, Men; seasonally adjusted; thousands of persons; from January 1970. **Source:** U.S. Department of Labor, Bureau of Labor Statistics, *The Employment Situation – Household Survey*, various issues. **Code:** LE011

N   Labor Statistics: Unemployment Rate, Women; seasonally adjusted; thousands of persons; from January 1970. **Source:** U.S. Department of Labor, Bureau of Labor Statistics, *The Employment Situation – Household Survey*, various issues. **Code:** LE012

O   Employment Indicators: Diffusion Index: 12 Lead Indicator Components (1–mo. span); seasonally adjusted; 1967=100; from January 1970. **Source:** Center For International Business Cycle Research. **Code:** LE013

P   Employment Indicators: Initial Claims for Unemployment Insurance; seasonally adjusted; thousands; from January 1970. **Source:** U.S. Department of Labor, Employment Training Program, *Employment Insurance Claims – Covered Unemployment*, various issues. **Code:** LE014

Q   Labor Demand: Index of Help–Wanted Advertising in Newspapers; seasonally adjusted; 1967=100; from January 1970. **Source:** The Conference Board, *Help Wanted Advertising*, various issues. **Code:** LE015

R   Labor Demand: Ratio, Help–Wanted Advertising in Newspapers to Number of Unemployed; seasonally adjusted; 1967=100; from January 1970. **Source:** The Conference Board, *Help Wanted Advertising*, various issues. **Code:** LE016

Wages and Cost of Employment
Spreadsheet: WAGES.WK1   Quarterly Data

A   Year of the observation **Code:** WCEYR

B   Quarter of the observation (1 = First quarter; 2 = Second quarter; etc.)
Code: WCEQU

C   Employment Cost Index; Wages and Salaries; All Private Non–farm
Workers; (1989=100); from First quarter 1976. **Source:** Bureau of Labor
Statistics, *Employment Cost Index for Wages and Salaries*, Tables 8 & 9,
various issues. **Code:** WCE001

D   Employment Cost Index; Wages and Salaries; White–Collar Workers;
(1989=100); from First quarter 1976. **Source:** Bureau of Labor Statistics,
Employment Cost Index for Wages and Salaries, Tables 8 & 9, various issues.
Code: WCE002

E   Employment Cost Index; Wages and Salaries; Blue–Collar Workers;
(1989=100); from First quarter 1976. **Source:** Bureau of Labor Statistics,
Employment Cost Index for Wages and Salaries, Tables 8 & 9, various issues.
Code: WCE003

F   Employment Cost Index; Wages and Salaries; Manufacturing; (1989=100);
from First quarter 1976. **Source:** Bureau of Labor Statistics, *Employment
Cost Index for Wages and Salaries*, Tables 8 & 9, various issues. **Code:**
WCE004

G   Employment Cost Index; Wages and Salaries; Nonmanufacturing;
(1989=100); from First quarter 1976. **Source:** Bureau of Labor Statistics,
Employment Cost Index for Wages and Salaries, Tables 8 & 9, various issues.
Code: WCE005

H   Employment Cost Index; Wages and Salaries; Union Workers; (1989=100);
from First quarter 1976. **Source:** Bureau of Labor Statistics, *Employment
Cost Index for Wages and Salaries*, Tables 8 & 9, various issues. **Code:**
WCE006

I   Employment Cost Index; Wages and Salaries; Non–Union Workers;
(1989=100); from First quarter 1976. **Source:** Bureau of Labor Statistics,
Employment Cost Index for Wages and Salaries, Tables 8 & 9, various issues.
Code: WCE007

J   Employment Cost Index; Compensation: Civilian Workers; (1989=100);
from First quarter 1982. **Source:** Bureau of Labor Statistics, *Employment
Cost Index for Wages, Salaries, and Compensation*, Table 4, various issues.
Code: WCE008

K   Employment Cost Index; Compensation: Civilian White–Collar Workers;
(1989=100); from First quarter 1982. **Source:** Bureau of Labor Statistics,
Employment Cost Index for Wages, Salaries, and Compensation, Table 4,
various issues. **Code:** WCE009

L   Employment Cost Index; Compensation: Civilian Blue–Collar Workers;
(1989=100); from First quarter 1982. **Source:** Bureau of Labor Statistics,
Employment Cost Index for Wages, Salaries, and Compensation, Table 4,
various issues. **Code:** WCE010

M   Employment Cost Index; Compensation: Private Industrial Workers; (1989=100); from First quarter 1980. **Source:** Bureau of Labor Statistics, *Employment Cost Index for Wages, Salaries, and Compensation*, Table 4, various issues. **Code:** WCE011

N   Employment Cost Index; Compensation: Union Workers; (1989=100); from First quarter 1980. **Source:** Bureau of Labor Statistics, *Employment Cost Index for Private Industry Workers by Bargaining Status*, Table 6, various issues. **Code:** WCE012

O   Employment Cost Index; Compensation: Non–union Workers; (1989=100); from First quarter 1980. **Source:** Bureau of Labor Statistics, *Employment Cost Index for Private Industry Workers by Bargaining Status*, Table 6, various issues. **Code:** WCE013

P   Employment Cost Index; Benefits: Private Industry Workers (Total); (1989=100); from First quarter 1980. **Source:** Bureau of Labor Statistics, *Employment Cost Index for Wages, Salaries, and Compensation*, Table 10, various issues. **Code:** WCE014

Q   Employment Cost Index; Benefits: White–Collar Occupations; (1989=100); from First quarter 1980. **Source:** Bureau of Labor Statistics, *Employment Cost Index for Wages, Salaries, and Compensation*, Table 10, various issues. **Code:** WCE015

R   Employment Cost Index; Benefits: Blue–Collar Occupations; (1989=100); from First quarter 1980. **Source:** Bureau of Labor Statistics, *Employment Cost Index for Wages, Salaries, and Compensation*, Table 10, various issues. **Code:** WCE016

Government Receipts and Expenditures
Spreadsheet: FEDFISCL.WK1   Quarterly Data

A   Year of the observation **Code:** FISYR

B   Quarter of the observation (1 = First quarter; 2 = Second quarter; etc.) **Code:** FISQU

C   Federal Government: Receipts; billions of dollars; seasonally adjusted; from First quarter 1946. **Source:** U.S. Department of Commerce, Bureau of Economic Analysis, *Survey of Current Business*, various issues. **Code:** FIS001

D   Federal Government: Receipts: Personal Tax and Non–tax Receipts; billions of dollars; seasonally adjusted; from First quarter 1946. **Source:** U.S. Department of Commerce, Bureau of Economic Analysis, *Survey of Current Business*, various issues. **Code:** FIS002

E   Federal Government: Receipts: Personal Tax and Non–tax Receipts, Income Taxes; billions of dollars; seasonally adjusted; from First quarter 1946. **Source:** U.S. Department of Commerce, Bureau of Economic Analysis, *Survey of Current Business*, various issues. **Code:** FIS003

F   Federal Government: Receipts: Corporate Profits Tax Accruels; billions of dollars; seasonally adjusted; from First quarter 1946. **Source:** U.S. Department of Commerce, Bureau of Economic Analysis, *Survey of Current Business*, various issues. **Code:** FIS004

G   Federal Government: Receipts: Corporate Profits Tax Accruels; Federal Reserve Banks; billions of dollars; seasonally adjusted; from First quarter 1947. **Source:** U.S. Department of Commerce, Bureau of Economic Analysis, *Survey of Current Business*, various issues. **Code:** FIS005

H   Federal Government: Receipts: Indirect Business Tax and Non–tax Accruels; billions of dollars; seasonally adjusted; from First quarter 1946. **Source:** U.S. Department of Commerce, Bureau of Economic Analysis, *Survey of Current Business*, various issues. **Code:** FIS006

I   Federal Government: Receipts: Indirect Business Tax and Non–tax Accruels; Excise Taxes; billions of dollars; seasonally adjusted; from First quarter 1959. **Source:** U.S. Department of Commerce, Bureau of Economic Analysis, *Survey of Current Business*, various issues. **Code:** FIS007

J   Federal Government: Expenditures; billions of dollars; seasonally adjusted; from First quarter 1946. **Source:** U.S. Department of Commerce, Bureau of Economic Analysis, *Survey of Current Business*, various issues. **Code:** FIS008

K   Federal Government: Expenditures; Purchases of Goods and Services; billions of dollars; seasonally adjusted; from First quarter 1946. **Source:** U.S. Department of Commerce, Bureau of Economic Analysis, *Survey of Current Business*, various issues. **Code:** FIS009

L   Federal Government: Expenditures; Purchases of Goods and Services; National Defense; billions of dollars; seasonally adjusted; from First quarter 1946. **Source:** U.S. Department of Commerce, Bureau of Economic Analysis, *Survey of Current Business*, various issues. **Code:** FIS010

M   Federal Government: Expenditures; Purchases of Goods and Services; Nondefense; billions of dollars; seasonally adjusted; from First quarter 1946. **Source:** U.S. Department of Commerce, Bureau of Economic Analysis, *Survey of Current Business*, various issues. **Code:** FIS011

N   Federal Government: Expenditures; Transfer Payments (Net); billions of dollars; seasonally adjusted; from First quarter 1946. **Source:** U.S. Department of Commerce, Bureau of Economic Analysis, *Survey of Current Business*, various issues. **Code:** FIS012

O   Federal Government: Expenditures; Grants–in–Aid to State and Local Governments; billions of dollars; seasonally adjusted; from First quarter 1946. **Source:** U.S. Department of Commerce, Bureau of Economic Analysis, *Survey of Current Business*, various issues. **Code:** FIS013

P   Federal Government: Expenditures; Net Interest Paid; billions of dollars; seasonally adjusted; from First quarter 1946. **Source:** U.S. Department of Commerce, Bureau of Economic Analysis, *Survey of Current Business*, various issues. **Code:** FIS014

Q   Federal Government: Expenditures; Interest Paid; billions of dollars; seasonally adjusted; from First quarter 1960. **Source:** U.S. Department of Commerce, Bureau of Economic Analysis, *Survey of Current Business*, various issues. **Code:** FIS015

R   Federal Government: Expenditures; Interest Paid to Persons and Business; billions of dollars; seasonally adjusted; from First quarter 1960. **Source:**

U.S. Department of Commerce, Bureau of Economic Analysis, *Survey of Current Business*, various issues. **Code:** FIS016

S Federal Government: Expenditures; Interest Paid to Foreigners; billions of dollars; seasonally adjusted; from First quarter 1960. **Source:** U.S. Department of Commerce, Bureau of Economic Analysis, *Survey of Current Business*, various issues. **Code:** FIS017

T Federal Government: Surplus or Deficit (–), National Income and Product Accounts; billions of dollars; seasonally adjusted; from First quarter 1946. **Source:** U.S. Department of Commerce, Bureau of Economic Analysis, *Survey of Current Business*, various issues. **Code:** FIS018

U State and Local Government: Receipts; billions of dollars; seasonally adjusted; from First quarter 1946. **Source:** U.S. Department of Commerce, Bureau of Economic Analysis, *Survey of Current Business*, various issues. **Code:** FIS019

V State and Local Government: Expenditures; billions of dollars; seasonally adjusted; from First quarter 1946. **Source:** U.S. Department of Commerce, Bureau of Economic Analysis, *Survey of Current Business*, various issues. **Code:** FIS020

W State and Local Government: Surplus or Deficit (–), National Income and Product Accounts; billions of dollars; seasonally adjusted; from First quarter 1946. **Source:** U.S. Department of Commerce, Bureau of Economic Analysis, *Survey of Current Business*, various issues. **Code:** FIS021

Production and Capacity Utilization
Spreadsheet: INDUPROD.WK1   Monthly Data

A Year of the observation **Code:** IPYR

B Month of the observation (1 = January; 2 = February; etc.) **Code:** IPMO

C Industrial Production Indexes: Total Index; (1987=100); seasonally adjusted; from January 1970. **Source:** Board of Governors of the Federal Reserve System, *Industrial Production, Statistical Release G17*. **Code:** IP001

D Industrial Production Indexes: Durable Manufactures; (1987=100); seasonally adjusted; from January 1970. **Source:** Board of Governors of the Federal Reserve System, *Industrial Production, Statistical Release G17*. **Code:** IP002

E Industrial Production Indexes: Nondurable Manufactures; (1987=100); seasonally adjusted; from January 1970. **Source:** Board of Governors of the Federal Reserve System, *Industrial Production, Statistical Release G17*. **Code:** IP003

F Industrial Production Indexes: Consumer Goods; (1987=100); seasonally adjusted; from January 1970. **Source:** Board of Governors of the Federal Reserve System, *Industrial Production, Statistical Release G17*. **Code:** IP004

G Capacity Utilization: Manufacturing; (percent of capacity); seasonally adjusted; from January 1970. **Source:** Board of Governors of the Federal Reserve System, *Industrial Production and Capacity Utilization and Industrial Materials, Statistical Release G.3*. **Code:** IP005

H   Capacity Utilization: Durable Manufacturing; (percent of capacity); seasonally adjusted; from January 1970. **Source:** Board of Governors of the Federal Reserve System, *Industrial Production and Capacity Utilization and Industrial Materials, Statistical Release G.3.* **Code:** IP006

I   Capacity Utilization: Nondurable Manufacturing; (percent of capacity); seasonally adjusted; from January 1970. **Source:** Board of Governors of the Federal Reserve System, *Industrial Production and Capacity Utilization and Industrial Materials, Statistical Release G.3.* **Code:** IP007

J   Capacity Utilization: Mining; (percent of capacity); seasonally adjusted; from January 1970. **Source:** Board of Governors of the Federal Reserve System, *Industrial Production and Capacity Utilization and Industrial Materials, Statistical Release G.3.* **Code:** IP008

K   Capacity Utilization: Utilities; (percent of capacity); seasonally adjusted; from January 1970. **Source:** Board of Governors of the Federal Reserve System, *Industrial Production and Capacity Utilization and Industrial Materials, Statistical Release G.3.* **Code:** IP009

Foreign Industrial Production
Spreadsheet: FORPROD.WK1   Monthly Data

A   Year of the observation **Code:** FPYR

B   Month of the observation (1 = First quarter; 2 = Second quarter; etc.) **Code:** FPMO

C   Index of Industrial Production; United States (1987=100); from January 1970. **Source:** U.S. Department of Commerce, The Bureau of Economic Analysis, *The Survey of Current Business,* various issues. **Code:** FP001

D   Index of Industrial Production; OECD (1987=100); from January 1970. **Source:** U.S. Department of Commerce, The Bureau of Economic Analysis, *The Survey of Current Business,* various issues. **Code:** FP002

E   Index of Industrial Production; Japan (1987=100); from January 1970. **Source:** U.S. Department of Commerce, The Bureau of Economic Analysis, *The Survey of Current Business,* various issues. **Code:** FP003

F   Index of Industrial Production; West Germany (1987=100); from January 1970. **Source:** U.S. Department of Commerce, The Bureau of Economic Analysis, *The Survey of Current Business,* various issues. **Code:** FP004

G   Index of Industrial Production; France (1987=100); from January 1970. **Source:** U.S. Department of Commerce, The Bureau of Economic Analysis, *The Survey of Current Business,* various issues. **Code:** FP005

H   Index of Industrial Production; United Kingdom (1987=100); from January 1970. **Source:** U.S. Department of Commerce, The Bureau of Economic Analysis, *The Survey of Current Business,* various issues. **Code:** FP006

I   Index of Industrial Production; Italy (1987=100); from January 1970. **Source:** U.S. Department of Commerce, The Bureau of Economic Analysis, *The Survey of Current Business,* various issues. **Code:** FP007

J   Index of Industrial Production; Canada (1987=100); from January 1970. **Source:** U.S. Department of Commerce, The Bureau of Economic Analysis, *The Survey of Current Business,* various issues. **Code:** FP008

Key Economic Sectors

Energy
Spreadsheet: ENERGY.WK1   Monthly Data
- A   Year of the observation **Code:** ENYR
- B   Month of the observation (1 = January; 2 = February; etc.) **Code:** ENMO
- C   Energy Consumption: Total Energy Consumption; quadrillion BTUS; seasonally adjusted; from January 1974. **Source:** U.S. Department of Energy, *Monthly Energy Review*, various issues. **Code:** EN001
- D   Energy Consumption: Coal; quadrillion BTUS; seasonally adjusted; from January 1974. **Source:** U.S. Department of Energy, *Monthly Energy Review*, various issues. **Code:** EN002
- E   Energy Consumption: Natural Gas (Dry); quadrillion BTUS; seasonally adjusted; from January 1974. **Source:** U.S. Department of Energy, *Monthly Energy Review*, various issues. **Code:** EN003
- F   Energy Consumption: Petroleum; quadrillion BTUS; seasonally adjusted; from January 1974. **Source:** U.S. Department of Energy, *Monthly Energy Review*, various issues. **Code:** EN004
- G   Petroleum Production: Total Petroleum Products Supplied; thousands of barrels per day; from January 1974. **Source:** U.S. Department of Energy, *Monthly Energy Review*, various issues. **Code:** EN005
- H   Crude Oil – Refiners' Costs: Composite, dollars per barrel; from January 1974. **Source:** U.S. Department of Energy, *Monthly Energy Review*, various issues. **Code:** EN006
- I   Gasoline Prices: U.S. City Average: Retail, all types of gasoline; cents per gallon; from January 1978. **Source:** U.S. Department of Labor, Bureau of Labor Statistics, *Consumer Prices*, various issues. **Code:** EN007

Housing and Construction
Spreadsheet: HOUSING.WK1   Monthly Data
- A   Year of the observation **Code:** HOUSYR
- B   Month of the observation (1 = January; 2 = February; etc.) **Code:** HOUSMO
- C   Housing Starts: New Privately Owned Housing Units Started; total; (Nonfarm + Farm); thousands of units; seasonally adjusted; from January 1970. **Source:** U.S. Department of Commerce, Bureau of the Census, *Housing Starts and Building Permits*, (Monthly News Release), various issues. **Code:** HOUS001
- D   Housing Starts: Total Private Housing Units Started; thousands of units; seasonally adjusted; from January 1970. **Source:** U.S. Department of Commerce, Bureau of the Census, *Housing Starts and Building Permits*, (Monthly News Release), various issues. **Code:** HOUS002
- E   Housing Starts: Index of New Private Housing Authorized by Local Building Permits; (1967=100); seasonally adjusted; from January 1970. **Source:** U.S. Department of Commerce, Bureau of Economic Analysis, *Survey of Current Business*, various issues. **Code:** HOUS003

F   Housing: New Privately Owned Housing Units Completed; total; thousands of units; seasonally adjusted; from January 1970. **Source:** U.S. Department of Commerce, Bureau of the Census, *Housing Completions*, various issues. **Code:** HOUS004

G   Housing: New Privately Owned Housing Units Under Construction; total; thousands of units; seasonally adjusted; from January 1970. **Source:** U.S. Department of Commerce, Bureau of the Census, *Housing Completions*, various issues. **Code:** HOUS005

H   Construction: Value of New Construction; Total Private and Public Construction; millions of dollars; seasonally adjusted; from January 1970. **Source:** U.S. Department of Commerce, Bureau of the Census, *Value of New Construction Put in Place, Construction Reports*, various issues. **Code:** HOUS006

I   Construction: Value of New Construction, Private Residential Buildings; millions of dollars; seasonally adjusted; from January 1970. **Source:** U.S. Department of Commerce, Bureau of the Census, *Value of New Construction Put in Place, Construction Reports*, various issues. **Code:** HOUS007

J   Construction: Value of New Construction, Commercial and Industrial Buildings; millions of dollars; seasonally adjusted; from January 1970. **Source:** U.S. Department of Commerce, Bureau of the Census, *Value of New Construction Put in Place, Construction Reports*, various issues. **Code:** HOUS008

K   Construction: Value of New Construction, Public Construction; millions of dollars; seasonally adjusted; from January 1970. **Source:** U.S. Department of Commerce, Bureau of the Census, *Value of New Construction Put in Place, Construction Reports*, various issues. **Code:** HOUS009

L   Construction Indexes: Bureau of the Census Composite Fixed–Weight Price Index; (1987=100); seasonally adjusted; from January 1970. **Source:** U.S. Department of Commerce, Bureau of the Census, *Value of New Construction Put in Place, Construction Reports*, various issues. **Code:** HOUS010

M   Construction Indexes: Bureau of the Census Implicit Price Deflator; (1987=100); seasonally adjusted; from January 1970. **Source:** U.S. Department of Commerce, Bureau of the Census, *Value of New Construction Put in Place, Construction Reports*, various issues. **Code:** HOUS011

Automotive
Spreadsheet: AUTOS.WK1   Monthly Data

A   Year of the observation **Code:** AUTOYR

B   Month of the observation (1 = January; 2 = February; etc.) **Code:** AUTOMO

C   Domestic Trade: Retail Sales: Automotive Dealers; seasonally adjusted; millions of dollars; from January 1970. **Source:** U.S. Department of Commerce, Bureau of the Census, Current Business Reports:, *Monthly Retail Sales and Inventories, Manufacturing and Trade: Inventories and Sales*, various issues. **Code:** AUTO001

D   Domestic Trade: Retail Inventories: Automotive Dealers; seasonally adjusted; millions of dollars; from January 1970. **Source:** U.S. Department of Commerce, Bureau of the Census, Current Business Reports:, *Monthly Retail Sales and Inventories, Manufacturing and Trade: Inventories and Sales,* various issues. **Code:** AUTO002

E   Retail Automobile and Truck Sales: Total New Passenger Cars, millions of units; seasonally adjusted; millions of dollars; from January 1970. **Source:** U.S. Department of Commerce, Bureau of Economic Analysis, *Survey of Current Business,* various issues. **Code:** AUTO003

F   Retail Automobile and Truck Sales: Domestic New Passenger Cars; millions of units; seasonally adjusted; millions of dollars; from January 1970. **Source:** U.S. Department of Commerce, Bureau of Economic Analysis, *Survey of Current Business,* various issues. **Code:** AUTO004

G   Retail Automobile and Truck Sales: Foreign New Passenger Cars; millions of units; seasonally adjusted; millions of dollars; from January 1970. **Source:** U.S. Department of Commerce, Bureau of Economic Analysis, *Survey of Current Business,* various issues. **Code:** AUTO005

H   Inventory/Sales Ratio: New Passenger Car Units, Domestic; seasonally adjusted; from January 1970. **Source:** U.S. Department of Commerce, Bureau of Economic Analysis, Unpublished Printout: *Automobile Sales and Inventories,* **Code:** AUTO006

I   Average Expenditure per Car, Overall; ($/car) seasonally adjusted; from January 1970. **Source:** U.S. Department of Commerce, Bureau of Economic Analysis, Unpublished Printout: *Automobile Sales and Inventories,* **Code:** AUTO007

J   Average Expenditure per Car, Overall, Domestic; ($/car) seasonally adjusted; from January 1970. **Source:** U.S. Department of Commerce, Bureau of Economic Analysis, Unpublished Printout: *Automobile Sales and Inventories,* **Code:** AUTO008

K   Average Expenditure per Car, Overall, Foreign; ($/car) seasonally adjusted; from January 1970. **Source:** U.S. Department of Commerce, Bureau of Economic Analysis, Unpublished Printout: *Automobile Sales and Inventories,* **Code:** AUTO009

Manufacturing
Spreadsheet: MANUFAC.WK1   Monthly Data
A   Year of the observation **Code:** MANYR
B   Quarter of the observation (1 = First quarter; 2 = Second quarter; etc.) **Code:** MANMO
C   Manufacturing and Trade: Business Cycle Indicators, Sales; billions of dollars, seasonally adjusted; from January 1970. **Source:** U.S. Department of Commerce, Bureau of Economic Analysis, *Survey of Current Business,* various issues. **Code:** MAN001
D   Manufacturing and Trade: Business Cycle Indicators, Inventories (Book Value); billions of dollars; seasonally adjusted; from January 1970. **Source:**

U.S. Department of Commerce, Bureau of Economic Analysis, *Survey of Current Business*, various issues. **Code:** MAN002

E   Manufacturing and Trade: Business Cycle Indicators, Change in Inventories (Book Value); billions of dollars; seasonally adjusted; from January 1970. **Source:** U.S. Department of Commerce, Bureau of Economic Analysis, *Survey of Current Business*, various issues. **Code:** MAN003

F   Manufacturing and Trade: Inventories and Sales in Real Dollars, Inventories (end of month); Manufacturing; billions of 1987 dollars; seasonally adjusted; from January 1970. **Source:** U.S. Department of Commerce, Bureau of Economic Analysis, Unpublished Printout. **Code:** MAN004

G   Manufacturing and Trade: Inventories and Sales in Real Dollars, Inventories (end of month); Merchant Wholesalers; billions of 1987 dollars; seasonally adjusted; from January 1970. **Source:** U.S. Department of Commerce, Bureau of Economic Analysis, Unpublished Printout. **Code:** MAN005

H   Manufacturing and Trade: Inventories and Sales in Real Dollars, Inventories (end of month); Retail Trade; billions of 1982 dollars; seasonally adjusted; from January 1970. **Source:** U.S. Department of Commerce, Bureau of Economic Analysis, Unpublished Printout. **Code:** MAN006

I   Manufacturing and Trade: Inventories and Sales in Real Dollars, Sales (end of month); Manufacturing; billions of 1987 dollars; seasonally adjusted; from January 1970. **Source:** U.S. Department of Commerce, Bureau of Economic Analysis, Unpublished Printout. **Code:** MAN007

J   Manufacturing and Trade: Inventories and Sales in Real Dollars, Sales (end of month); Merchant Wholesalers; billions of 1987 dollars; seasonally adjusted; from January 1970. **Source:** U.S. Department of Commerce, Bureau of Economic Analysis, Unpublished Printout. **Code:** MAN008

K   Manufacturing and Trade: Inventories and Sales in Real Dollars, Sales (end of month); Retail Trade; billions of 1987 dollars; seasonally adjusted; from January 1970. **Source:** U.S. Department of Commerce, Bureau of Economic Analysis, Unpublished Printout. **Code:** MAN009

L   Manufacturing: Manufacturers' Shipments: Total Manufacturing Industries; millions of dollars; seasonally adjusted; from January 1970. **Source:** U.S. Department of Commerce, Bureau of Economic Analysis, *Current Industrial Reports, Manufacturers' Shipments, Inventories, and Orders*, various issues. **Code:** MAN010

M   Manufacturing: Inventories (end of month): Total Manufacturing Inventories; millions of dollars; seasonally adjusted; from January 1970. **Source:** U.S. Department of Commerce, Bureau of Economic Analysis, *Current Industrial Reports, Manufacturers' Shipments, Inventories, and Orders*, various issues. **Code:** MAN011

N   Manufacturing: New Orders: Total Manufacturing Inventories; millions of dollars; seasonally adjusted; from January 1970. **Source:** U.S. Department of Commerce, Bureau of Economic Analysis, *Current Industrial*

Reports, Manufacturers' Shipments, Inventories, and Orders, various issues. **Code:** MAN012

O   Manufacturing: Unfilled Orders (end of month): Total Manufacturing Inventories; millions of dollars; seasonally adjusted; from January 1970. **Source:** U.S. Department of Commerce, Bureau of Economic Analysis, *Current Industrial Reports, Manufacturers' Shipments, Inventories, and Orders,* various issues. **Code:** MAN013

Corporations

Corporate Profits
Spreadsheet: CORPPROF.WK1   Quarterly Data

A   Year of the observation **Code:** CPROFYR

B   Quarter of the observation (1 = First quarter; 2 = Second quarter; etc.) **Code:** CPROFQU

C   Corporate Profits with Inventory Valuation & Capital Consumption Adjustments; total; billions of dollars; seasonally adjusted; from First quarter 1946. **Source:** U.S. Department of Commerce, Bureau of Economic Analysis; *The National Income and Product Accounts of the United States, & The Survey of Current Business,* various issues. **Code:** CPROF001

D   Corporate Profits with Inventory Valuation & Capital Consumption Adjustments; Domestic Industries; billions of dollars; seasonally adjusted; from First quarter 1946. **Source:** U.S. Department of Commerce, Bureau of Economic Analysis; *The National Income and Product Accounts of the United States, & The Survey of Current Business,* various issues. **Code:** CPROF002

E   Corporate Profits with Inventory Valuation & Capital Consumption Adjustments; Domestic Industries, Financial; billions of dollars; seasonally adjusted; from First quarter 1946. **Source:** U.S. Department of Commerce, Bureau of Economic Analysis; *The National Income and Product Accounts of the United States, & The Survey of Current Business,* various issues. **Code:** CPROF003

F   Corporate Profits with Inventory Valuation & Capital Consumption Adjustments; Domestic Industries, Nonfinancial; billions of dollars; seasonally adjusted; from First quarter 1946. **Source:** U.S. Department of Commerce, Bureau of Economic Analysis; *The National Income and Product Accounts of the United States, & The Survey of Current Business,* various issues. **Code:** CPROF004

G   Corporate Profits with Inventory Valuation; Financial Institutions (excluding Federal Reserve Banks); billions of dollars; seasonally adjusted; from First quarter 1946. **Source:** U.S. Department of Commerce, Bureau of Economic Analysis; *The National Income and Product Accounts of the United States, & The Survey of Current Business,* various issues. **Code:** CPROF005

H   Corporate Profits with Inventory Valuation; Manufacturing; billions of dollars; seasonally adjusted; from First quarter 1946. **Source:** U.S. Department of Commerce, Bureau of Economic Analysis; *The National Income and*

Product Accounts of the United States, & The Survey of Current Business, various issues. **Code:** CPROF006

I   Corporate Profits with Inventory Valuation; Manufacturing, Durable Goods; billions of dollars; seasonally adjusted; from First quarter 1946. **Source:** U.S. Department of Commerce, Bureau of Economic Analysis; *The National Income and Product Accounts of the United States, & The Survey of Current Business,* various issues. **Code:** CPROF007

J   Corporate Profits with Inventory Valuation; Manufacturing, Nondurable Goods; billions of dollars; seasonally adjusted; from First quarter 1946. **Source:** U.S. Department of Commerce, Bureau of Economic Analysis; *The National Income and Product Accounts of the United States, & The Survey of Current Business,* various issues. **Code:** CPROF008

K   Corporate Profits with Inventory Valuation; Transportation and Public Utilities; billions of dollars; seasonally adjusted; from First quarter 1946. **Source:** U.S. Department of Commerce, Bureau of Economic Analysis; *The National Income and Product Accounts of the United States, & The Survey of Current Business,* various issues. **Code:** CPROF009

L   Corporate Profits with Inventory Valuation; Wholesale and Retail Trade; billions of dollars; seasonally adjusted; from First quarter 1946. **Source:** U.S. Department of Commerce, Bureau of Economic Analysis; *The National Income and Product Accounts of the United States, & The Survey of Current Business,* various issues. **Code:** CPROF010

Fixed Capital Investment
Spreadsheet: FXINVEST.WK1   Quarterly Data

A   Year of the observation **Code:** FCIYR

B   Quarter of the observation (1 = First quarter; 2 = Second quarter; etc.) **Code:** FCIQU

C   Fixed Capital Investment; Nonresidential; billions of dollars; seasonally adjusted; from First quarter 1946. **Source:** U.S. Department of Commerce, Bureau of Economic Analysis, *The Survey of Current Business,* various issues. **Code:** FCI001

D   Fixed Capital Investment; Nonresidential, Structures; billions of dollars; seasonally adjusted; from First quarter 1946. **Source:** U.S. Department of Commerce, Bureau of Economic Analysis, *The Survey of Current Business,* various issues. **Code:** FCI002

E   Fixed Capital Investment; Producers Durable Equipment; billions of dollars; seasonally adjusted; from First quarter 1946. **Source:** U.S. Department of Commerce, Bureau of Economic Analysis, *The Survey of Current Business,* various issues. **Code:** FCI003

F   Fixed Capital Investment; Producers Durable Equipment, Information Processing and Related Equipment; billions of dollars; seasonally adjusted; from First quarter 1947. **Source:** U.S. Department of Commerce, Bureau of Economic Analysis, *The Survey of Current Business,* various issues. **Code:** FCI004

G   Fixed Capital Investment; Industrial Equipment; billions of dollars; seasonally adjusted; from First quarter 1947. **Source:** U.S. Department of Commerce, Bureau of Economic Analysis, *The Survey of Current Business,* various issues. **Code:** FCI005

H   Fixed Capital Investment; Nonresidential Buildings, Excluding Farm; millions of dollars; from First quarter 1958. **Source:** U.S. Department of Commerce, Bureau of Economic Analysis, Unpublished Data. **Code:** FCI006

I   Fixed Capital Investment; Nonresidential Buildings, Excluding Farm, Industrial; millions of dollars; from First quarter 1959. **Source:** U.S. Department of Commerce, Bureau of Economic Analysis, Unpublished Data. **Code:** FCI007

J   Fixed Capital Investment; Nonresidential Buildings, Excluding Farm, Commercial, millions of dollars; from First quarter 1959. **Source:** U.S. Department of Commerce, Bureau of Economic Analysis, Unpublished Data. **Code:** FCI008

K   Fixed Capital Investment; Utilities, millions of dollars; from First quarter 1959. **Source:** U.S. Department of Commerce, Bureau of Economic Analysis, Unpublished Data. **Code:** FCI009

L   Fixed Capital Investment; Utilities, Telecommunications; millions of dollars; from First quarter 1959. **Source:** U.S. Department of Commerce, Bureau of Economic Analysis, Unpublished Data. **Code:** FCI010

M   Business Investment Expenditures; Wholesale and Retail Trade; billions of dollars; seasonally adjusted; from First quarter 1947. **Source:** U.S. Department of Commerce, Bureau of Economic Analysis, *Survey of Current Business.* **Code:** FCI011

N   Business Investment Expenditures; Finance and Insurance; billions of dollars; seasonally adjusted; from First quarter 1947. **Source:** U.S. Department of Commerce, Bureau of Economic Analysis, *Survey of Current Business.* **Code:** FCI012

O   Business Investment Expenditures; Personal and Business Services; billions of dollars; seasonally adjusted; from First quarter 1947. **Source:** U.S. Department of Commerce, Bureau of Economic Analysis, *Survey of Current Business.* **Code:** FCI013

P   Business Investment Expenditures; Communication; billions of dollars; seasonally adjusted; from First quarter 1947. **Source:** U.S. Department of Commerce, Bureau of Economic Analysis, *Survey of Current Business.* **Code:** FCI014

Business Inventories
Spreadsheet: INVENTOR.WK1   Quarterly Data

A   Year of the observation **Code:** INVYR

B   Quarter of the observation (1 = First quarter; 2 = Second quarter; etc.) **Code:** INVQU

C   Change in Business Inventories: Total; billions of dollars; from First quarter 1946. **Source:** U.S. Department of Commerce, Bureau of Economic Analysis, *Survey of Current Business*, various issues. **Code:** INV001

D   Change in Business Inventories: Total; Nonfarm, billions of dollars; from First quarter 1946. **Source:** U.S. Department of Commerce, Bureau of Economic Analysis, *Survey of Current Business*, various issues. **Code:** INV002

E   Change in Business Inventories: Manufacturing; billions of dollars; from First quarter 1946. **Source:** U.S. Department of Commerce, Bureau of Economic Analysis, *Survey of Current Business*, various issues. **Code:** INV003

F   Change in Business Inventories: Wholesale Trade; billions of dollars; from First quarter 1946. **Source:** U.S. Department of Commerce, Bureau of Economic Analysis, *Survey of Current Business*, various issues. **Code:** INV004

G   Change in Business Inventories: Retail Trade; billions of dollars; from First quarter 1946. **Source:** U.S. Department of Commerce, Bureau of Economic Analysis, *Survey of Current Business*, various issues. **Code:** INV005

H   Inventories (End of Quarter): Total; billions of dollars; from 4th quarter 1947. **Source:** U.S. Department of Commerce, Bureau of Economic Analysis, *Survey of Current Business*, various issues. **Code:** INV006

I   Inventories (End of Quarter): Total, Nonfarm; billions of dollars; from 4th quarter 1947. **Source:** U.S. Department of Commerce, Bureau of Economic Analysis, *Survey of Current Business*, various issues. **Code:** INV007

J   Inventories (End of Quarter): Manufacturing; billions of dollars; from 4th quarter 1947. **Source:** U.S. Department of Commerce, Bureau of Economic Analysis, *Survey of Current Business*, various issues. **Code:** INV008

K   Inventories (End of Quarter): Wholesale Trade; billions of dollars; from 4th quarter 1947. **Source:** U.S. Department of Commerce, Bureau of Economic Analysis, *Survey of Current Business*, various issues. **Code:** INV009

L   Inventories (End of Quarter): Retail Trade; billions of dollars; from 4th quarter 1947. **Source:** U.S. Department of Commerce, Bureau of Economic Analysis, *Survey of Current Business*, various issues. **Code:** INV010

Commodity Prices

Commodity Price Indexes
Spreadsheet: COMPRICE.WK1   Monthly Data

A   Year of the observation **Code:** COMYR

B   Month of the observation (1 = January; 2 = February; etc.) **Code:** COMMO

C   Commodity Research Bureau Spot Market Index: All Commodities; (1967=100); from January 1970. **Source:** Commodity Research Bureau, Inc., *CRB Commodity Index Report*, various issues. **Code:** COM001

D   Commodity Research Bureau Spot Market Index: Foodstuffs; (1967=100); from January 1970. **Source:** Commodity Research Bureau, Inc., *CRB Commodity Index Report,* various issues. **Code:** COM002

E   Commodity Research Bureau Spot Market Index: Raw Industrials; (1967=100); from January 1970. **Source:** Commodity Research Bureau, Inc., *CRB Commodity Index Report,* various issues. **Code:** COM003

F   Index of Prices Received by Farmers for All Farm Products; (1977=100); from January 1970. **Source:** U.S. Department of Agriculture, Crop Reporting Board, Statistical Reporting Service, *Agricultural Prices,* various issues. **Code:** COM004

G   Industrial Materials Price Index; (1985=100); from January 1970. **Source:** *Journal of Commerce,* various issues. **Code:** COM005

International Trade

Balance of Trade Statistics
Spreadsheet: TRADEBAL.WK1   Monthly Data

A   Year of the observation **Code:** INTYR

B   Month of the observation (1 = January; 2 = February; etc.) **Code:** INTMO

C   Exports, Domestic and Foreign Merchandise (Free Alongside Ship); millions of dollars; seasonally adjusted; from January 1984. **Source:** U.S. Department of Commerce, Bureau of the Census, *Summary of U.S. Export–Import Merchandise Trade,* various issues. **Code:** INT001

D   General Imports of Merchandise (Custom's Value); millions of dollars; seasonally adjusted; from January 1986. **Source:** U.S. Department of Commerce, Bureau of the Census, *Summary of U.S. Export–Import Merchandise Trade,* various issues. **Code:** INT002

E   Trade Balance: F.A.S. Exports; Customs Imports; millions of dollars; seasonally adjusted; from January 1986. **Source:** U.S. Department of Commerce, Bureau of the Census, *Summary of U.S. Export–Import Merchandise Trade,* various issues. **Code:** INT003

F   Total Exports: Food, Beverages, and Tobacco (F.A.S.); millions of dollars; from January 1970. **Source:** U.S. Department of Commerce, Bureau of the Census, *Summary of U.S. Export–Import Merchandise Trade,* various issues. **Code:** INT004

G   Total Exports: Crude Materials and Fuels (Including Fats and Oils), (F.A.S.); millions of dollars; from January 1970. **Source:** U.S. Department of Commerce, Bureau of the Census, *Summary of U.S. Export–Import Merchandise Trade,* various issues. **Code:** INT005

H   Total Exports: Manufactured Goods, (F.A.S.); millions of dollars; from January 1970. **Source:** U.S. Department of Commerce, Bureau of the Census, *Summary of U.S. Export–Import Merchandise Trade,* various issues. **Code:** INT006

I   Total Imports: Food, Beverage, and Tobacco, [F.A.S. (77–81), Customs Value, (81–Present)]; millions of dollars; from January 1970. **Source:** U.S.

Department of Commerce, Bureau of the Census, *Summary of U.S. Export–Import Merchandise Trade,* various issues. **Code:** INT007

J   Total Imports: Crude Materials and Fuels (Including Fats and Oils), [F.A.S. (77–81), Customs Value, (81–Present)]; millions of dollars; from January 1970. **Source:** U.S. Department of Commerce, Bureau of the Census, *Summary of U.S. Export–Import Merchandise Trade,* various issues. **Code:** INT008

K   Total Imports: Manufactured Goods, [F.A.S. (77–81), Customs Value, (81–Present)]; millions of dollars; from January 1970. **Source:** U.S. Department of Commerce, Bureau of the Census, *Summary of U.S. Export–Import Merchandise Trade,* various issues. **Code:** INT009

L   U.S. Trade Balance (Exports less Imports): Canada; millions of dollars; from January 1974. **Source:** U.S. Department of Commerce, Bureau of the Census, *Summary of U.S. Export–Import Merchandise Trade,* various issues. **Code:** INT010

M   U.S. Trade Balance (Exports less Imports): United Kingdom; millions of dollars; from January 1974. **Source:** U.S. Department of Commerce, Bureau of the Census, *Summary of U.S. Export–Import Merchandise Trade,* various issues. **Code:** INT011

N   U.S. Trade Balance (Exports less Imports): Federal Republic of Germany; millions of dollars; from January 1974. **Source:** U.S. Department of Commerce, Bureau of the Census, *Summary of U.S. Export–Import Merchandise Trade,* various issues. **Code:** INT012

O   U.S. Trade Balance (Exports less Imports): France; millions of dollars; from January 1974. **Source:** U.S. Department of Commerce, Bureau of the Census, *Summary of U.S. Export–Import Merchandise Trade,* various issues. **Code:** INT013

P   U.S. Trade Balance (Exports less Imports): Italy; millions of dollars; from January 1974. **Source:** U.S. Department of Commerce, Bureau of the Census, *Summary of U.S. Export–Import Merchandise Trade,* various issues. **Code:** INT014

Q   U.S. Trade Balance (Exports less Imports): Japan; millions of dollars; from January 1974. **Source:** U.S. Department of Commerce, Bureau of the Census, *Summary of U.S. Export–Import Merchandise Trade,* various issues. **Code:** INT015

REALDATA Exercises

Measures of the Money Supply

Contributed by Brian S. Wilson
Spreadsheet: MONEYSUP.WK1

Compute the percentage change of each component for the periods shown in the table below. According to M1, during which of the first four periods did the money supply expand the most? Which measure of the money supply has experienced the highest growth from January 1970 to December 1993? What are the components that make up this measure? Prepare a line graph that illustrates each of the money supply measures (M1, M2, M3, and L) from January 1970 through December 1993. (Let the X–axis run from 1970 to 1993, and set the Y–axis to run from 0 to 6000.)

Growth in the Money Supply From 1970–1993

Period	Percentage Growth in M1	Percentage Growth in M2	Percentage Growth in M3	Percentage Growth in L
Jan 1970–Dec 1974				
Jan 1975–Dec 1979				
Jan 1980–Dec 1984				
Jan 1985–Mar 1989				
Jan 1970–Dec 1993				

Exercise 2

Money in the U.S. Economy

Contributed by Ricardo J. Rodriguez
Spreadsheet: MONEYSUP.WK1

Using data from January 1970 through December 1993, find the correlation coefficient between each pair of money measures and complete the correlation matrix shown below. Based on the completed table, to what extent is one money measure a substitute for the other? Given the degree of correlation you have found, is there really any need for more than one of these indexes? Explain.

Correlation Matrix for the Various Definitions of Money

	M1	M2	M3	L
M1	1.00			
M2		1.00		
M3			1.00	
L				1.00

Exercise 3

Components of M2

Contributed by Brian S. Wilson
Spreadsheet: MONEYSUP.WK1

Complete the following table and prepare a pie graph showing the components of M2 for December 1993. (Do not divide M1 into components.) Which component makes up the largest proportion of M2? How can the Federal Reserve exert control over this component?

Components of M2

Component	Billions of Dollars	% of M2
M1		
Overnight Repurchase Agreements		
Overnight Eurodollars		
Money Market Mutual Fund Balances		
Savings Deposits		
Small Denomination Time Deposits		

Exercise 4

Currency and Demand Deposits

Contributed by Ricardo J. Rodriguez
Spreadsheet: MONEYSUP.WK1

The classical theory of money creation assumes that the ratio of currency in circulation to demand deposits is a constant, c. Compute the average and the standard deviation of the c–ratio over the entire period, as well as for each available complete decade, and complete the table below. Prepare a graph that shows the evolution of this ratio for 1970–1993. (Let the X–axis run from 1970:1 to 1993:12, and set the Y–axis to run from 0.0 to 1.) During which periods has the ratio of currency to demand deposits been approximately constant?

Ratio of Currency in Circulation to Demand Deposits

Period	Average	Standard Deviation
1970s		
1980s		
1970–1993		

Exercise 5

Overnight Repurchase Agreements and Overnight Eurodollars

Contributed by Ricardo J. Rodriguez
Spreadsheet: MONEYSUP.WK1

Consider the period from 1977–1993 for overnight repurchase agreements (repos) and Eurodollar deposits. Using linear regression over the entire period for each instrument, predict the use of these two financing sources in the year 2000. To perform the regression, create a time index by letting January 1977 be t = 1, February 1977 be t = 2, and so on. Then regress the column containing the repo data against the newly created index column. Do the same for the column containing the Eurodollar data. Based on the past growth patterns, how reliable do you think these projections are? What can you conclude about the relative importance of each of these instruments in the near future? Prepare a graph showing the evolution of these two financing techniques from 1977 through 1993. (Let the X–axis run from 1977:1 to 1993:12, and set the Y–axis to run from $0 to $80 billion.)

Exercise 6

The Evolution of Commercial Paper

Contributed by Ricardo J. Rodriguez
Spreadsheet: MONEYSUP.WK1

Prepare a graph showing the evolution of the level of commercial paper for 1970–1993. (Let the X–axis run from 1970:1 to 1993:12, and set the Y–axis to run from $0 to $400 billion.) Using linear regression over the entire period, predict the use of this source of financing in the year 2000. To perform the regression, create a time index by letting January 1970 be t = 1, February 1970 be t = 2, and so on. Then regress the column containing the commercial paper data against the newly created index column. Based on the past growth pattern of commercial paper, how reliable do you think this projection is?

Exercise 7

The Velocity of Money (M3)

Contributed by Brian S. Wilson
Spreadsheets: FINQU.WK1, NATLPROD.WK1

The average number of times a unit of money is used in one period is called the velocity of money. This is computed by dividing the GNP by a measure of the money supply. Prepare a line graph depicting the velocity of money from 1960:1 through 1993:4, using M3 as the money supply measure. Based on your visual analysis of the graph, how has the velocity of money changed throughout this period? What economic variables would influence the velocity of money?

Exercise 8

Money Velocity

Contributed by Ricardo J. Rodriguez
Spreadsheets: FINQU.WK1, NATLPROD.WK1

The velocity of money is defined as the ratio of the gross national product (GNP) to the money stock. Since there are four major definitions of money, there are also four measures of velocity. Compute the average velocity for each complete decade and for each of the four definitions of money, and complete the table shown below. What major characteristics of each of these velocity measures stand out? Which has been the most stable measure of velocity? Prepare a graph showing the evolution of the M1 and M2 velocity of money for 1959–1993. (Let the X–axis run from 1959:1 to 1993:4, and set the Y–axis to run from 1 to 8.)

Average Velocity of Money

Period	M1 Velocity	M2 Velocity	M3 Velocity	L Velocity
1960s				
1970s				
1980s				
1970–1993				

Exercise 9

The Money Multiplier

Contributed by Ricardo J. Rodriguez
Spreadsheets: MONEYSUP.WK1, RESERVES.WK1

The money multiplier is defined as the ratio of the money stock to the monetary base. Compute the average money multiplier for each complete decade and complete the table shown below. Prepare a graph showing the evolution of the money multiplier for 1970–1993. Use only M1 and M2 as the measure of money. (Let the X–axis run from 1970:1 to 1993:12, and set the Y–axis to run from 2 to 14.) Which of these two measures has been more stable?

The Money Multiplier for M1 and M2

Period	M1 Multiplier	M2 Multiplier
1970s		
1980s		
1970–1993		

Exercise 10

Vault Cash as a Percentage of Demand Deposits

Contributed by Ricardo J. Rodriguez
Spreadsheets: RESERVES.WK1, MONEYSUP.WK1

Consider the ratio of vault cash to demand deposits for 1970 through December 1993. Find the average and standard deviation for this ratio to complete the table shown below. Prepare a graph showing the evolution of the ratio of vault cash to demand deposits for 1970–1993. (Let the X–axis run from 1970:1 to 1993:12, and set the Y–axis to run from 2 to 13 percent.) Describe the main characteristics of this graph. Does the graph suggest any peculiar behavior in this ratio?

Ratio of Vault Cash to Demand Deposits

Period	Average	Standard Deviation
1970s		
1980s		
1970–1993		

Exercise 11

The Excess Reserves Ratio

Contributed by Ricardo J. Rodriguez
Spreadsheets: MONEYSUP.WK1, RESERVES.WK1

It is usually argued that banks hold very few of their assets in the form of excess reserves. The excess reserves ratio, e, is defined as the ratio of excess reserves to demand deposits. Consider the period from January 1970 through July 1993. Find the average excess reserves ratio for each complete decade and for the entire period. In similar fashion find the standard deviation for the same periods, as well as the coefficient of variation (standard deviation/average), and complete the table shown below. Do the data in the table support the idea that the excess reserves ratio is low and stable? Prepare a graph showing the evolution of the excess reserves ratio for 1970–1993. (Let the X–axis run from 1970:1 to 1993:12, and set the Y–axis to run from 0 to .009.)

The Excess Reserves Ratio

Period	Average	Standard Deviation	Coefficient of Variation
1970s			
1980s			
1970–1993			

Exercise 12

Excess Reserves and the Fed Funds Rate

Contributed by Brian S. Wilson
Spreadsheets: MONEYSUP.WK1, RESERVES.WK1, MONEYYLD.WK1

Complete the table below that compares the amount of excess reserves held by banks and the federal funds rate from January 1970 to December 1993. (HINT: Present the amount of excess reserves as a ratio to demand deposits.) Based on the table, do you see any correlation between the Federal Funds Rate and Excess Reserves? What other factors would influence the amount of Excess Reserves held by banks?

Excess Reserves and the Fed Funds Rate

Period	Average Fed Funds Rate	Average Ratio of Excess Reserves to Demand Deposits
Jan 1970–Dec 1974		
Jan 1975–Dec 1979		
Jan 1980–Dec 1984		
Jan 1985–Dec 1989		
Jan 1990–Dec 1993		

Exercise 13

The Required Reserves Ratio

Contributed by Ricardo J. Rodriguez
Spreadsheets: MONEYSUP.WK1, RESERVES.WK1

In many textbook models, the average required reserves ratio is defined as the ratio of required reserves to demand deposits. Prepare a graph showing the evolution of this required reserves ratio for 1970–1993. (Let the X–axis run from 1970:1 to 1993:12, and set the Y–axis to run from .07 to .17.) Find the mean of the average required reserves ratio for each complete decade and for the entire period. In similar fashion find the standard deviation and the coefficient of variation (standard deviation/average) for the same periods and complete the table shown below. Does the data suggest any substantial change in the required reserve ratio through time?

The Required Reserves Ratio

Period	Average	Standard Deviation	Coefficient of Variation
1970s			
1980s			
1970–1993			

Exercise 14

M1 and Inflation

Contributed by Brian S. Wilson
Spreadsheets: MONEYSUP.WK1, INFLATE.WK1

For 1980 to 1993, compute the annual percentage change of M1 and the annual percentage change in the CPI. Complete the following table and prepare a line graph depicting the CPI and M1 from January 1970 through December 1993. To make the series comparable, set the M1 value for June of 1983 equal to a base of 100. Does growth in inflation appear to be correlated with growth in M1?

Changes in M1 and Inflation

Period	Percent Change in M1	Percent Change in CPI
Jan–Dec 1980		
Jan–Dec 1981		
Jan–Dec 1982		
Jan–Dec 1983		
Jan–Dec 1984		
Jan–Dec 1985		
Jan–Dec 1986		
Jan–Dec 1987		
Jan–Dec 1988		
Jan–Dec 1989		
Jan–Dec 1990		
Jan–Dec 1991		
Jan–Dec 1992		
Jan–Dec 1993		

Exercise 15

The Distribution of Inflation

Contributed by Ricardo J. Rodriguez
Spreadsheet: INFLATE.WK1

For the period 1970–1993 prepare a histogram showing the distribution of monthly inflation by counting the number of months for which inflation fell within a certain range, and complete the table shown below. Describe the major characteristics of this distribution. What is the average inflation? What is the standard deviation of the distribution of inflation? Is the distribution skewed?

The Distribution of Monthly Inflation

Range (Percent)	Number of Months in the Range	Percentage of Months in the Range
–.6 to –.4		
–.4 to –.2		
–.2 to 0		
0 to .2		
.2 to .4		
.4 to .6		
.6 to .8		
.8 to 1		
1 to 1.2		
1.2 to 1.4		
1.4 to 1.6		
1.6 to 1.8		
1.8 to 2.0		

Exercise 16

Measures of Inflation

Contributed by Brian S. Wilson
Spreadsheets: FINQU.WK1, INFLATE.WK1

Complete the following table showing the CPI, PPI, and GNP deflator. For the CPI and PPI, use values from December for the year indicated. For the GNP deflator use values from the fourth quarter for the year indicated. By which measure has inflation increased the most from 1970 to 1990? Which measure contains the widest group of goods?

Measures of Inflation

Year	CPI Index: All Items (1982–1984 = 100)	PPI Index: All Commodities (1982–1984 = 100)	GNP Deflator (1987 = 100)
1970			
1975			
1980			
1985			
1990			
Average Annual Inflation Rate			

Exercise 17

The Correlation Among Various Consumer Price Indexes

Contributed by Ricardo J. Rodriguez
Spreadsheet: INFLATE.WK1

Find the correlation coefficient among the consumer price indexes for food and beverages, housing, and services, for January 1970 to December 1993, and complete the correlation matrix shown below. Based on the completed table, to what extent is one index a substitute for the other? Given the degree of correlation you have found, is there really any need for more than one of these indexes? Explain.

Correlation Matrix for the Consumer Price Indexes

	CPI Food & Beverages	CPI Housing	CPI Services
CPI Food & Beverages	1.00		
CPI Housing		1.00	
CPI Services			1.00

Exercise 18

Inflation in the United States and Japan

Contributed by Robert W. Kolb
Spreadsheet: FORINFLA.WK1

Complete the following table for inflation in the selected countries. What was the annualized rate of inflation in the United States and Japan for the decade of the 1980s (more specifically, the 120 month period from January 1980 to December 1989)? Prepare a graph showing the inflation indexes in the United States and Japan from January 1970 through December 1993. (Let the X–axis run from 1970 to 1993, and set the Y–axis to run from 0 to 160.)

Percentage Change in Consumer Price Index

Country	January 1970 to December 1979	January 1980 to December 1989
United States		
Japan		
Germany		
United Kingdom		
Italy		
Canada		

Exercise 19

Worldwide Correlations in Inflation

Contributed by Robert W. Kolb
Spreadsheet: FORINFLA.WK1

For the United States, Japan, Germany, and the United Kingdom, compute the monthly percentage change in the consumer price index for the period from February 1970 through the end of 1993. Using these percentage changes, compute the correlations in inflation among these four countries. Complete the table below by entering the correlations.

Correlation Matrix for Inflation Rates

	U.S.	Japan	Germany	U.K.
U.S.	1.0			
Japan		1.0		
Germany			1.0	
U.K.				1.0

Based on the completed table, to what extent is inflation a common phenomenon around the world? Is there really any tendency for the major economic powers to experience inflation simultaneously? Using the percentage changes that you computed, find the month of the highest and lowest inflation for each country. Complete the table below by indicating the percentage change that was the highest and lowest for each country in this period. Did any country experience deflation at any time? Explain.

Highest and Lowest Monthly Inflation for Four Countries, 1970–1993

	U.S.	Japan	Germany	U.K.
Highest Value				
Lowest Value				

Exercise 20

Banks and Consumer Credit

Contributed by Robert W. Kolb
Spreadsheet: CONSUMCR.WK1

For the period from January 1975 through the end of 1993, prepare a graph showing the percentage of total consumer installment credit outstanding that was financed at commercial banks. (Let the X–axis run from 1975 to 1993, and set the Y–axis to run from .4 to .55.) How has this changed over time? Can you explain why it might have changed as indicated? For December 1980 and December 1993, complete the following table that shows the amounts of revolving credit held by banks, retailers, and gasoline companies. How can you explain the differences that have arisen in the relative holdings of these three kinds of providers of credit?

**Holding of Revolving Consumer Credit, 1980 and 1989
(Millions of Dollars)**

	Banks	Retailers	Gasoline Companies	Total
December 1980				
December 1989				

Exercise 21

Mutual Fund Indexes

Contributed by Robert W. Kolb
Spreadsheet: LIPPER.WK1

For the period January 1987 through December 1993, compute the mean monthly growth in the mutual fund indexes and the standard deviation for the indexes shown in the table below. Do these values correspond to the risk levels implied by the type of fund? Explain.

Mutual Fund Index Performance

Fund Index	Mean Monthly Growth	Standard Deviation
Balanced		
Growth and Income		
Growth		
Small Company Growth		

Exercise 22

The Correlations Among Various Mutual Fund Indexes

Contributed by Ricardo J. Rodriguez
Spreadsheet: LIPPER.WK1

Find the correlation coefficient between the returns on Lipper mutual fund indexes for capital appreciation, growth, and gold, for 1987:1 to 1993:12, and complete the correlation matrix shown below. Based on the completed table, to what extent is one index a substitute for the other? Given the degree of correlation you have found, is there really any need for more than one of these indexes? Explain.

Correlation Matrix for the Lipper Mutual Fund Indexes

	Capital Appreciation	Growth	Gold
Capital Appreciation	1.00		
Growth		1.00	
Gold			1.00

Exercise 23

Net Asset Values of Fidelity Funds

Contributed by Ricardo J. Rodriguez
Spreadsheet: MUTUFUND.WK1

Prepare a graph that shows the net asset values (NAV) for Fidelity's capital appreciation fund, growth and income fund, high yield fund, and the Magellan fund for 1987–1993. To compare the relative performances of each index, create separate indexes for each of the funds as follows. Set the first observation (January 1987) of the capital appreciation fund so that it is equal to 1, by dividing it by itself. All other observations of this fund should also be divided by the first observation. Set the first observation of the growth and income fund to 2. For the high yield fund, set the first observation to 3, and for the Magellan fund, set it to 4. (Let the X–axis run from 1987:1 to 1993:12, and set the Y–axis to run from 0 to 6.) Find the correlation coefficient between each pair of asset values and complete the correlation matrix shown below. Based on the completed table, to what extent is one mutual fund a substitute for the other? Given the degree of correlation you have found, is there really any need to invest in more than one of these mutual funds?

Correlation for Net Asset Values of Selected Fidelity Mutual Funds

	Capital Appreciation	Growth and Income	High Yield	Magellan
Capital Appreciation	1.00			
Growth and Income		1.00		
High Yield			1.00	
Magellan				1.00

Exercise 24

Stock and Bond Issues

Contributed by Robert W. Kolb
Spreadsheet: PRIMMKT.WK1

Do U.S. corporations raise more funds by issuing stock or by selling bonds? For the period from January 1970 through December 1993, prepare a graph showing the ratio of funds raised by offering of bonds as a percentage of any new security issues. (Let the X–axis run from 1970 to 1993, and set the Y–axis to run from 0.2 to 1.0.) What do these results say about the relative importance of debt and equity in the financing of U.S. corporations? Comment on any extended trends that you observe in this proportion.

Exercise 25

Correlations Among Stock Indexes

Contributed by Robert W. Kolb
Spreadsheet: STKINDEX.WK1

For the Dow Jones Industrial Averages (DJIA), the New York Stock Exchange Composite Index (NYSE), and the S&P 500 index, compute the monthly percentage change in the consumer price index for the period from February 1970 through the end of 1993. Using these percentage changes, compute the correlations among these three indexes. Complete the table below by entering the correlations. Based on the completed table, to what extent is one index a substitute for another? Given the degree of correlation that you have found, is there really any need for more than one of these indexes? Explain.

Correlation Matrix for Major Stock Indexes

	DJIA	NYSE	S&P 500
DJIA	1.0		
NYSE		1.0	
S&P 500			1.0

Complete the table below by indicating the percentage change that was the highest and lowest for each index in this period.

Highest and Lowest Monthly Returns for Three Indexes, 1970–1993

	DJIA	NYSE	S&P 500
Highest Value			
Lowest Value			

Exercise 26

The Betas of Various Indexes Relative to the S&P 500 Index

Contributed by Ricardo J. Rodriguez
Spreadsheet: STKINDEX.WK1

Using the Standard and Poor's composite index of 500 stocks (the S&P 500) as a proxy for the market, calculate the beta of the Dow Jones industrial average of 30 stocks, of the New York stock exchange composite index, and of the S&P 500 index itself. Present the results of your calculation in the table below. You will need to prepare new columns for each of these variables that represent the monthly return for each of the indexes. In the process, the initial observation will be lost. Compute a single beta for each index using data from 1970 to 1993.

The Beta of Various Indexes

Index	Beta
DJIA 30	
NYSE Composite	
S&P 500	

The beta of any asset j can be calculated by performing the following regression:

$$R_{j,t} = \alpha_j + \beta_j R_{m,t} + \varepsilon_t$$

where:

$R_{j,t}$ = return on asset j in period t

$R_{m,t}$ = return on market portfolio in period t

Do these betas conform to your expectations?

Exercise 27

The Betas of Various Indexes
Relative to the New York Stock Exchange Composite Index

Contributed by Ricardo J. Rodriguez
Spreadsheet: STKINDEX.WK1

Using the New York stock exchange composite index as a proxy for the market, calculate the beta of the Dow Jones industrial average of 30 stocks, of the New York stock exchange composite index itself, and of the S&P 500 index. Present the results of your calculation in the table below. You will need to prepare new columns for each of these variables that represent the monthly return for each of the indexes. In the process, the initial observation will be lost. Compute a single beta for each index using data from 1970 to 1993.

The Beta of Various Indexes

Index	Beta
DJIA 30	
NYSE Composite	
S&P 500	

The beta of any asset j can be calculated by performing the following regression:

$$R_{j,t} = \alpha_j + \beta_j R_{m,t} + \varepsilon_t$$

where:
    $R_{j,t}$ = return on asset j in period t
    $R_{m,t}$ = return on market portfolio in period t

Do these betas conform to your expectations?

Exercise 28

Serial Correlation in Equity Returns

Contributed by Robert W. Kolb
Spreadsheet: STKINDEX.WK1

For the period from February 1970 to December 1993, compute the percentage change in the NYSE Composite Index (DELTANY). Regress the percentage change on the percentage change from the previous period, running the following regression:

$$DELTANY_t = \alpha + \beta DELTANY_{t-1} + \varepsilon_t$$

(Setting up this regression results in the loss of two observations. January 1970 is lost to form the return from January to February, and another observation is lost because of lagging by one period.) Based on the regression results, complete the following table. What do these regression results show about the tendency of stock market increases in one month to be followed by increases in the next month? To what extent is this result consistent with any version of the efficient markets hypothesis? Explain.

Using the same observations from the regression, prepare a graph that records $DELTANY^t$ on the vertical axis and $DELTANY^{t-1}$ on the X–axis. (Let the X–axis run from –0.16 to 0.16, and set the Y–axis to run from –0.16 to 0.16. Use the XY graph type, and show only symbols, not lines.) What does the graph reveal about the relationship of stock returns in one period relative to the next period?

**Results from Regressing the Percentage Change
of the NYSE Composite on its Lagged Values, 1970 to 1993**

	α	β	R^2
$\text{DELTANY}_t = \alpha + \beta \text{DELTANY}_{t-1} + \varepsilon_t$			

Exercise 29

Serial Correlation in Stock Market Levels

Contributed by Robert W. Kolb
Spreadsheet: STKINDEX.WK1

For the period from March 1970 to December 1993, regress the level of the NYSE composite index (NY) on the level of the index in the preceding period, running the following regression:

$$NY_t = \alpha + \beta NY_{t-1} + \varepsilon_t$$

Based on the regression results, complete the following table. What do these regression results show about the tendency of stock market levels in one month to be followed by a higher level in the next month? To what extent is this result consistent with any version of the efficient markets hypothesis? Does it shed any light on the efficient markets hypothesis? Explain. How can you interpret the large R^2 from this regression?

**Results from Regressing the Level of the NYSE Composite
on its Lagged Values, 1970 to 1993**

	α	β	R^2
$NY_t = \alpha + \beta NY_{t-1} + \varepsilon_t$			

Using the same observations from the regression, prepare a graph that records NY^t on the vertical axis and NY^{t-1} on the horizontal axis. (Let the X–axis run from 0 to 280, and set the Y–axis to run from 0 to 300. Use the XY graph type, and show only symbols, not lines.) What does the graph reveal about the relationship of stock prices in one period relative to the next period?

Exercise 30

The Distribution of S&P 500 Monthly Returns

Contributed by Ricardo J. Rodriguez
Spreadsheet: STKINDEX.WK1

Make a histogram of the distribution of monthly returns for the S&P 500 composite index by counting the number of months for which returns fell within a certain range and completing the table shown below. Do this for the period 1970–1993. Describe the major characteristics of this distribution. What is the average monthly return? What is the standard deviation of the distribution of returns? Is the distribution skewed?

The Distribution of Monthly Returns for the S&P 500 Index

Range (Percent)	Number of Months in the Range	Percentage of Months in the Range
−16 to −14		
−14 to −12		
−12 to −10		
−10 to −8		
−8 to −6		
−6 to −4		
−4 to −2		
−2 to 0		
0 to 2		
2 to 4		
4 to 6		
6 to 8		
8 to 10		
10 to 12		
12 to 14		
14 to 16		

Exercise 31

Corporate Profits and Stock Prices

Contributed by Brian S. Wilson
Spreadsheets: FINQU.WK1, NATLPROD.WK1

Prepare a line graph running from 1947:1 through 1993:4 depicting the ratio of the New York Stock Exchange Composite stock index to corporate profits before taxes. Then complete the table below. How has this relationship changed over time? In which period do stocks seem most depressed in comparison to corporate profits? In which period do stocks seem most inflated?

Corporate Profits and Stock Prices

Period	Average Ratio of the New York Stock Exchange Composite Index to Corporate Profits Before Taxes
1947:1–1949:4	
1950:1–1959:4	
1960:1–1969:4	
1970:1–1979:4	
1980:1–1989:4	
1990:1–1993:4	

Exercise 32

Dividend Yield

Contributed by Robert W. Kolb
Spreadsheet: STKINDEX.WK1

For January 1970 through the end of 1993, prepare a graph showing the dividend yield on the stocks in the S&P 500 common stock index. (Let the X–axis run from 1970 to 1993, and set the Y–axis to run from 0.2 to 0.7.) Find the average of all of these months, along with the month that had the highest and the lowest values. Use these figures to complete the following table.

S&P 500 Dividend Yield, 1970 to 1993

Average of all months

Highest month and yield for that month

Lowest month and yield for that month

Find the months of the biggest increase and the greatest drop in the dividend yield over the period from February 1970 through the end of 1993. Use these values to complete the following table. Were there any special market events that could explain these large changes? Explain.

S&P 500 Dividend Yield, 1970 to 1993

Month of largest increase and amount of the increase

Month of largest decrease and amount of the decrease

Exercise 33

The Stock Market Crash of October 1987

Contributed by Brian S. Wilson
Spreadsheets: STKINDEX.WK1

Complete the following table depicting the effects of the stock market crash of October 1987 on the stock indexes shown below. Which stock index value was most affected? Which stock index was least affected?

The Stock Market Crash of October 1987

Equity Market Component	Price or Index Value September 1987	Price or Index Value October 1987	Percent Change
DJIA			
NYSE Composite			
NYSE Industrial			
S&P 500			
NASDAQ Composite			

Exercise 34

The January Effect

Contributed by Ricardo J. Rodriguez
Spreadsheets: STKINDEX.WK1

It is said that returns in January are the highest of any month. This is the so–called January effect. Prepare a bar graph that shows the average return for each month of the year over the period from February 1970 through December 1993. Use the S&P 500 index to create a column of monthly returns for the market, and use those returns to test for the January effect. Be careful to note that the number of observations may not be identical for all months. Do your data support the January effect hypothesis?

Average Monthly Returns for the S&P 500

Month	Average Return
January	
February	
March	
April	
May	
June	
July	
August	
September	
October	
November	
December	

Exercise 35

The Nominal and Deflated S&P 500 Index

Contributed by Ricardo J. Rodriguez
Spreadsheets: STKINDEX.WK1, INFLATE.WK1

Prepare a graph showing the evolution of the nominal and real value of the Standard and Poor's 500 composite index for 1970–1993. Use the consumer price index for all items to deflate the nominal S&P 500 index. (Let the X–axis run from 1970:1 to 1993:12, and set the Y–axis to run from 0 to 500.) What noteworthy characteristics are apparent in the graph?

Exercise 36

Stock Exchange Activity

Contributed by Robert W. Kolb
Spreadsheet: STKACTIV.WK1

For the period from January 1977 to November 1993, prepare a graph showing the total market value of stocks sold on all registered exchanges. (Let the X–axis run from 1977 to 1993, and set the Y–axis to run from 0 to 300.) Based on a visual inspection of the graph you created, when was the approximate period of greatest increase in activity, as measured by market value? Explain. Prepare a second graph for the same period showing the market value activity of the New York Stock Exchange as a percentage of the total. (Let the X–axis run from 1977 to 1993, and set the Y–axis to run from .8 to .92.) How has this changed? What accounts for the relative stability or instability of this ratio?

Exercise 37

Growth in NYSE and NASDAQ Markets

Contributed by Robert W. Kolb
Spreadsheet: STKACTIV.WK1

For each month in the period from January 1983 to November 1993, find the combined market value of sales on the New York Stock Exchange and the

NASDAQ. Prepare a graph showing how the percentage of this total traded on the NASDAQ has changed over this period. (Let the X–axis run from 1983 to 1993, and set the Y–axis to run from 0 to .4.) Does the graph show a substantial trend? If so, what does it suggest about the future of organized exchanges like the NYSE relative to markets with a structure like the NASDAQ?

Exercise 38

Stock Market Volume Characteristics

Contributed by Robert W. Kolb
Spreadsheet: STKACTIV.WK1

For the New York Stock Exchange during the period from January 1974 through December 1993, prepare a graph showing the percentage of NYSE volume that was traded in lots of 5,000 shares or larger. (Let the X–axis run from 1974 to 1993, and set the Y–axis to run from 0 to 80 percent.) How has this changed over time? What do the results of your graph imply for the role of the individual shareholders a major force in the stock market?

Exercise 39

Foreign Stock Returns

Contributed by Robert W. Kolb
Spreadsheet: FORSTOCK.WK1

For the period from January 1970 to December 1993, create a stock index that has a value of 1.0 for January 1970 for the stock indexes of the United States, Japan, Germany, and the United Kingdom. (For each country, divide all of the observations by the value of the index for January 1970.) Based on the adjusted index that you have created, complete the following table. Do the values in this table reflect the total growth in the investment of $1 in each country's index? Explain. What does the table say about the relative performance of each country's stock market? Explain.

Adjusted Stock Index Values, December 1993

	U.S.	Japan	Germany	U.K.
December 1993				

Exercise 40

Correlations Among National Stock Market Returns

Contributed by Robert W. Kolb
Spreadsheet: FORSTOCK.WK1

For the period from February 1970 to December 1993, compute the percentage change in the stock indexes of the United States, Japan, Germany, and the United Kingdom. Compute the correlations in returns among these indexes, and use these values to complete the following correlation matrix. What do these correlations reveal about the prospects for reducing the risk of equity portfolios by investing outside one's home country? Which one country appears to offer the best diversification potential for an investor from Germany? Explain. Which pair of countries has the highest correlation? Can you explain why this might be the case?

Correlation Matrix for National Stock Market Returns, 1970 to 1993

	U.S.	Japan	Germany	U.K.
U.S.	1.0			
Japan		1.0		
Germany			1.0	
U.K.				1.0

Exercise 41

Riskiness of National Stock Market Returns

Contributed by Robert W. Kolb
Spreadsheet: FORSTOCK.WK1

For the period from February 1970 to December 1993, compute the percentage change in the stock indexes of the United States, Japan, Germany, and the United Kingdom. Compute the mean monthly returns and standard deviation of monthly returns for each index, and use those values to complete the following table.

Statistics for National Stock Market Returns, 1970 to 1993

	U.S.	Japan	Germany	U.K.
Mean Monthly Returns				
Standard Deviation				

Exercise 42

Riskiness of Two–Country Stock Portfolios

Contributed by Robert W. Kolb
Spreadsheet: FORSTOCK.WK1

For the period from February 1970 to December 1993, compute the percentage change in the stock indexes of the United States, Japan, Germany, and the United Kingdom. Compute the mean monthly returns and standard deviation of monthly returns for each index. Using the return series just computed, create returns series for two–country internationally diversified portfolios assuming equal division of investment between two countries for the country pairs shown in the table below and compute the statistics to complete the table. Create a graph showing each portfolio in risk/return space. (Let the X–axis run from 0.0 to 0.02, and set the Y–axis to run from 0.0 to 0.01. Use the XY graph type, and show only symbols, not lines.)

Statistics for Two–Country Portfolios, 1970 to 1993

	Mean Monthly Return	Standard Deviation
U.S./Japan		
U.S./Germany		
U.S./U.K.		
Japan/Germany		
Japan/U.K.		
Germany/U.K.		

Exercise 43

Riskiness of Internationally Diversified Stock Portfolios

Contributed by Robert W. Kolb
Spreadsheet: FORSTOCK.WK1

For the period from February 1970 to December 1993, compute the percentage change in the stock indexes of the United States, Japan, Germany, and the United Kingdom. Compute the mean monthly returns and standard deviation of monthly returns for each index. Using the return series just computed, create returns series for three–country internationally diversified portfolios assuming equal division of investment among the three countries shown in the table below and compute the statistics to complete the table. Also, make the same computations for the four–country portfolio.

Statistics for International Portfolios, 1970 to 1993

	Mean Monthly Return	Standard Deviation
U.S./Japan/Germany		
U.S./Germany/U.K.		
U.S./U.K./Japan		
Japan/Germany/U.K.		
All Countries		

Exercise 44

The Stock Market Crash of October 1987: Effect on Foreign Stocks

Contributed by Brian S. Wilson
Spreadsheet: FORSTOCK.WK1

Complete the following table depicting the effects of the stock market crash of October 1987 on the stock indexes of foreign countries. Do these index values provide evidence that the crash was felt worldwide?

Stock Price Index	Price or Index Value September 1987	Price or Index Value October 1987	Percent Change
United States			
Japan			
Germany			
France			
United Kingdom			
Italy			
Canada			

Exercise 45

Common Stock Returns

Contributed by Robert W. Kolb
Spreadsheet: STOCKS.WK1

For August 1989 through June 1994, compute monthly returns for the stocks shown in the table and complete the table. Be sure to include dividends, if any.

Common Stock Risk and Return

Stock	Average Monthly Return	Standard Deviation
Apple Computer		
FPL Group		
Homestake Mining		
Westinghouse Electric		

Exercise 46

Correlations Among Common Stock Returns

Contributed by Robert W. Kolb
Spreadsheet: STOCKS.WK1

For August 1989 through June 1994, compute the correlation among the monthly returns for the stocks shown in the table and complete the table. Be sure to include dividends, if any.

Correlation Matrix of Returns

Stock	American Express	Anheuser Busch	J.P. Morgan	Wal–Mart
American Express	1.00			
Anheuser Busch		1.00		
J.P. Morgan			1.00	
Wal–Mart				1.00

Exercise 47

Computing Betas

Contributed by Robert W. Kolb
Spreadsheets: STOCKS.WK1, STKINDEX.WK1

Based on returns for August 1989 through December 1993, compute the beta of each stock using the market model regression formula and complete the table shown below. Use the S&P 500 index as a proxy for the market portfolio.

The market model regression equation is:

$$R_{j,t} = \alpha_j + \beta_j R_{m,t} + \varepsilon_t$$

where:
$R_{j,t}$ = return on stock j in period t
$R_{m,t}$ = return on market portfolio in period t

Comment on the results in the table. Are the R^2s higher or lower than expected? Based on these results, which firm behaves most like the market? Which is the most aggressive?

Common Stock Betas

Stock	α	β	R^2
Apple Computer			
FPL Group			
Homestake Mining			
Westinghouse Electric			

Exercise 48

The Beta of the Risk–Free Asset

Contributed by Ricardo J. Rodriguez
Spreadsheets: STKINDEX.WK1, MONEYYLD.WK1

One of the basic assumptions of the Capital Asset Pricing Model is that the returns on the market are uncorrelated with the risk–free rate. This implies that the risk–free rate should have a beta of zero. Nevertheless, both the return on the market and the risk–free rate vary through time. Therefore, it is possible to find some correlation between the two rates, in which case the beta of the risk–free rate could be statistically different from zero. Using the 3–month Treasury bill rate as a proxy for the risk–free rate, and the return on the S&P 500 index (you need to calculate it from the price series), calculate the risk–free beta and present the results in the table below. To determine whether the beta coefficient is statistically significant, calculate its t–statistic (the ratio of the X coefficient to the standard error of the coefficient. Both of these values are part of the standard regression output). Normally, if the t–statistic has an absolute value greater than 1.96, we say that the coefficient is statistically different from zero at the 5 percent level.

The Beta of 3–Month T–Bills

Period	Beta	t–statistic
1970s		
1980s		
1970–1993		

The beta of any asset j can be calculated by performing the following regression:

$$R_{j,t} = \alpha_j + \beta_j R_{m,t} + \varepsilon_t$$

where:
$R_{j,t}$ = return on asset j in period t
$R_{m,t}$ = return on market portfolio in period t

Do these results conform to the CAPM?

Exercise 49

The Beta of Energy Companies

Contributed by Ricardo J. Rodriguez
Spreadsheets: STOCKS.WK1, STKINDEX.WK1

Using the Standard and Poor's composite index of 500 stocks (the S&P 500) as a proxy for the market, calculate the beta for Chevron, Exxon, Texaco, and for a portfolio of the three equally weighted stocks. Present the results of your calculation in the table below. You will need to prepare new columns for each of these variables that represent the monthly return for each of the stocks. This requires including both the price and the dividend series for each stock. In the process, the initial observation will be lost. Compute a single beta for each stock or portfolio using data from 1989:8 to 1993:12. Do these betas conform to your expectations?

The Beta of Various Energy Stocks and Portfolios

Stock	Beta
Chevron	
Exxon	
Texaco	
Equally–weighted Portfolio	

Exercise 50

The Beta of Food and Beverage Stocks

Contributed by Ricardo J. Rodriguez
Spreadsheets: STKINDEX.WK1, STOCKS.WK1

Using the Standard and Poor's composite index of 500 stocks (the S&P 500) as a proxy for the market, calculate the beta for Anheuser Busch, Coca–Cola, McDonald's, and Pepsi–Cola. Present the results of your calculation in the table below. You will need to prepare new columns for each of these variables that represent the monthly return for each of the stocks. This requires including both the price and the dividend series for each stock. In the process, the initial observation will be lost. Compute a single beta for each stock or portfolio using data from 1989:8 to 1993:12. Do these betas conform to your expectations?

The Beta of Various Food Stocks and Portfolios

Stock	Beta
Anheuser Busch	
Coca–Cola	
McDonald's	
Pepsi–Cola	

Exercise 51

The Beta of Computer Stocks

Contributed by Ricardo J. Rodriguez
Spreadsheets: STKINDEX.WK1, STOCKS.WK1

Using the Standard and Poor's composite index of 500 stocks (the S&P 500) as a proxy for the market, calculate the beta for Apple, Hewlett–Packard, Microsoft, IBM, and Novell. Present the results of your calculation in the table below. You will need to prepare new columns for each of these variables that represent the monthly return for each of the stocks. This requires including both the price and the dividend series for each stock. In the process, the initial observation will be lost. Compute a single beta for each stock or portfolio using data from 1989:8 to 1993:12. Do these betas conform to your expectations?

The Beta of Various Computer Stocks and Portfolios

Stock	Beta
Apple	
Hewlett–Packard	
Microsoft	
IBM	
Novell	

Exercise 52

Varying Volatilities Among Stocks in Different Industries

Contributed by Brian S. Wilson
Spreadsheets: STOCKS.WK1, STKINDEX.WK1

Complete the table below depicting the volatilities of stocks in various industries: Measure volatility by the standard deviation of monthly returns. Which company has the most volatile stock price in a single year? Which company has the least volatile in a single year? Do you think stock price volatility is somewhat related to the type of industry of the company?

Volatilities Among Stocks in Different Industries

Period	DJIA	FPL Group Inc.	Genentech	American Telephone and Telegraph	Microsoft Corp.
1990					
1991					
1992					
1993					
1990–1993					

Exercise 53

Two–Stock Portfolios

Contributed by Robert W. Kolb
Spreadsheet: STOCKS.WK1

Based on returns for August 1989 through December 1993, compute the correlation of monthly returns for the stocks shown in the table and complete the table. Be sure to include dividends, if any.

Correlation Matrix of Returns

	Apple Computer	Homestake Mining	FPL Group
Apple Computer	1.0000		
Homestake Mining		1.0000	
FPL Group			1.0000

For the two–stock portfolios shown in the table below, find the return and standard deviation of a portfolio composed of equal investment in each stock.

Portfolio Returns and Standard Deviations

Portfolio	Average Monthly Return	Standard Deviation
Apple/Homestake		
Apple/FPL		
Homestake/FPL		

Exercise 54

Fixed and Adjustable Mortgage Rates

Contributed by Ricardo J. Rodriguez
Spreadsheet: MORTMKT.WK1

Prepare a graph showing the evolution of fixed and adjustable mortgage rates closed for 1982–1993. (Let the X–axis run from 1982:7 to 1993:12, and set the Y–axis to run from 6 to 17 percent.) What is the general relationship between the two rates? Why?

Exercise 55

Commercial Paper Interest Rates

Contributed by Robert W. Kolb
Spreadsheet: MONEYYLD.WK1

For January 1980 to December 1993, compute the average yield on 1–month, 3–month, and 6–month maturities of commercial paper and use these values to complete the following table. Based on the information in the table, what can you say about the typical shape of the commercial paper yield curve? Is it possible to make any concrete inference? Based on the table, what inferences are possible regarding the relative volatility of long–term versus short–term interest rates?

Commercial Paper Interest Rates, 1980 to 1993

Maturity	Mean Rate	Standard Deviation
1–month		
3–month		
6–month		

Exercise 56

Issuers of Commercial Paper

Contributed by Robert W. Kolb
Spreadsheet: MONEYYLD.WK1

For the period from January 1983 to December 1993, create a graph showing the total amount of commercial paper outstanding and the total amount of commercial paper outstanding that is issued by financial companies. (Let the X–axis run from 1983 to 1993, and set the Y–axis to run from 0 to 600,000.) How has this changed? Can you offer a plausible explanation for any trend you may observe?

Exercise 57

Eurodollar Yield Curves

Contributed by Robert W. Kolb
Spreadsheet: MONEYYLD.WK1

For March 1980 and March 1993, find the Eurodollar deposit rates to complete this table. Based on the table, what can you say about the shape of the Eurodollar yield curve on these two dates?

Eurodollar Deposit Rates

Maturity	March 1980	March 1993
1–week		
1–month		
3–month		
6–month		
1–year		

Exercise 58

T–Bill Auction Rates

Contributed by Robert W. Kolb
Spreadsheet: MONEYYLD.WK1

For the period January 1980 through December 1993, prepare a graph showing the average auction rates on 3–month, 6–month, and 1–year T–bill rates. (Let the X–axis run from 1980 to 1993, and set the Y–axis to run from 0 to 18.) Compute the average rates for each maturity and the corresponding standard deviation. Use these values to complete the table below. What inferences can you make from the graph and your computations about the typical relationship between rates on different maturities of T–bills?

T–Bill Auction Interest Rates, 1980 to 1993

Maturity	Mean Rate	Standard Deviation
3–month		
6–month		
1–year		

Exercise 59

Treasury Yield Curves

Contributed by Robert W. Kolb
Spreadsheets: MONEYYLD.WK1, BONDYLD.WK1

For March 1977 to December 1993, compute the difference between the yields on 30–year U.S. T–bonds and 3–month secondary market T–bills. Prepare a graph showing both yields and the difference in the yields for the period specified. (Let the X–axis run from 1977 to 1993, and set the Y–axis to run from –4 to 17.) From the graph, does the yield differential appear to be greater when yield levels are higher or lower?

Regress the yield differential (YD) on the level of T–bill yields (TB) for this period as follows:

$$YD_t = \alpha + \beta TB_t + \varepsilon_t$$

For April 1977 to December 1993, compute the change in the T–bill yield (DELTATB) and the change in the yield differential (DELTAYD). With these values perform the similar regression:

$$DELTAYD_t = \alpha + \beta DELTATB_t + \varepsilon_t$$

Specify the values for α, β, and the R^2 from the two equations below. What can you conclude from these regressions? How can you explain the differences in the results?

Regressions of Yield Differential Levels and Changes on T–Bill Rates, 1977 to 1993

	α	β	R^2
$YD_t = \alpha + \beta TB_t + \varepsilon_t$			
$DELTAYD_t = \alpha + \beta DELTATB_t + \varepsilon_t$			

Exercise 60

Money Market Yields and the Inflation Rate

Contributed by Brian S. Wilson
Spreadsheets: INFLATE.WK1, MONEYYLD.WK1

Complete the following table depicting the correlation between the inflation rate and the yields on the various money market instruments indicated. For the inflation rate, use the monthly percentage change in the CPI. Then prepare a line graph from January 1970 through December 1993 depicting yields of each of the instruments shown in the table. For Bankers' Acceptances, use values from 1981. Which money market instrument is most highly correlated with the inflation rate? Which money market instrument is least highly correlated with the inflation rate?

Money Market Yields and the Inflation Rate

Money Market Instrument	Average Yield (1970–1993)	Correlation with Inflation Rate
6–month Commercial Paper		
6–month Bankers' Acceptances		
6–month Certificates of Deposit		
6–month Eurodollar Deposit Rate		
6–month U.S. Treasury Bills		

Exercise 61

Money Market Risk Differentials

Contributed by Robert W. Kolb
Spreadsheet: MONEYYLD.WK1

To explore the risk structure of interest rates in the money market, complete the following table. Use data for six–month maturities to avoid any term structure effects. Explain why the Eurodollar rate might be higher than the rate on certificates of deposit.

Money Market Risk Differentials

Pair of Instruments	January 1980–December 1989	January 1990–December 1993
Eurodollar rate – T–bill rate		
Commercial Paper rate – T–bill rate		
Certificate of Deposit – T–bill rate		
Eurodollar rate – Certificate of Deposit rate		

Exercise 62

Corporate Bond Risk Differentials

Contributed by Robert W. Kolb
Spreadsheet: BONDYLD.WK1

For January 1970 to December 1993, compute the difference between the yields on AAA and BAA corporate bonds. Prepare a graph showing both yields and the difference in the yields for the period specified. (Let the X–axis run from 1970 to 1993, and set the Y–axis to run from 0 to 18.) From the graph, does the yield differential appear to be greater when yield levels are higher or lower? Regress the yield differential (YD) on the level of AAA bond yields (AAA) for this period as follows:

$$YD_t = \alpha + \beta AAA_t + \varepsilon_t$$

For February 1970 to December 1993, compute the change in the AAA bond yield (DELTAAAA) and the change in the yield differential (DELTAYD). With these values perform the similar regression:

$$DELTAYD_t = \alpha + \beta DELTAAAA_t + \varepsilon_t$$

Specify the values for α, β, and the R^2 from the two equations below. What can you conclude from these regressions? How can you explain the differences in the results?

Regressions of Yield Differential Levels and Changes on AAA Bond Rates, 1970 to 1993

	α	β	R^2
$YD_t = \alpha + \beta AAA_t + \varepsilon_t$			
$DELTAYD_t = \alpha + \beta DELTAAAA_t + \varepsilon_t$			

Exercise 63

Bond Market Yields and the Inflation Rate

Contributed by Brian S. Wilson
Spreadsheets: INFLATE.WK1, BONDYLD.WK1

Complete the following table depicting the correlation between the inflation rate and the yields on the various bond market instruments indicated. For the inflation rate, use the monthly percentage change in the CPI. Then prepare a line graph from January 1970 through December 1993 depicting yields of each of the instruments shown in the table. For ten–year Municipals, use values from January 1986. Which bond market instrument is most highly correlated with the inflation rate? Which bond market instrument is least highly correlated with the inflation rate? How does the correlation with inflation vary with the level of average yield of bond market instruments? How does the correlation with inflation vary with the time remaining to maturity of the various instruments?

Bond Market Yields and the Inflation Rate

Bond Market Instrument	Average Yield (1970–1993)	Correlation with Inflation Rate
U.S. Treasury Notes and Bonds, 3–Year Maturity		
U.S. Treasury Notes and Bonds, 10–Year Maturity		
AAA Municipal Bond Yield (20–Year)		
AAA Municipal Bond Yield (10–Year)		
AAA Corporate Bonds, Average Yield		
BAA Corporate Bonds, Average Yield		

Exercise 64

Default Risk Premium

Contributed by Brian S. Wilson
Spreadsheet: BONDYLD.WK1

Prepare a line graph depicting the yields on AAA, AA, A, and BAA corporate bonds from January 1985 through December 1993. Do the yields on the various classifications of corporate bonds imply the presence of a default risk premium? Between which two neighboring categories is this premium greatest?

Exercise 65

Default Risk Premium by Type of Bond

Contributed by Brian S. Wilson
Spreadsheet: BONDYLD.WK1

For January 1980 through December 1993, prepare a line graph displaying the average yields on AA Corporate Bonds, Long–Term Treasury Bonds, AA Industrial Bonds, and AA Utility Bonds. According to the graph, which type of bond do investors perceive as most risky? Does the relationship or spread between these average yields stay relatively constant over this period?

Exercise 66

International Paper, Return and Risk

Contributed by Robert W. Kolb
Spreadsheet: STOCKS.WK1

For International Paper, find the monthly returns, including dividends, for each month in the years 1991–1993. Use these returns to complete the following table.

International Paper, Return and Risk, 1991–1993

Period	Arithmetic Mean Monthly Return	Geometric Mean Monthly Return	Standard Deviation of Returns
1991			
1992			
1993			
1991–1993			

Exercise 67

Genentech, Return and Risk

Contributed by Robert W. Kolb
Spreadsheet: STOCKS.WK1

For Genentech, find the monthly returns, including dividends, for each month in the years 1991–1993. Use these returns to complete the following table.

Genentech, Return and Risk, 1991–1993

Period	Arithmetic Mean Monthly Return	Geometric Mean Monthly Return	Standard Deviation of Returns
1991			
1992			
1993			
1991–1993			

Exercise 68

Disney, Inc., Return and Risk

Contributed by Robert W. Kolb
Spreadsheet: STOCKS.WK1

For Disney Inc., find the monthly returns, including dividends, for each month in the years 1991–1993. Use these returns to complete the following table.

Disney, Inc., Return and Risk, 1991–1993

Period	Arithmetic Mean Monthly Return	Geometric Mean Monthly Return	Standard Deviation of Returns
1991			
1992			
1993			
1991–1993			

Exercise 69

Currency Winners and Losers

Contributed by Robert W. Kolb
Spreadsheet: FOREX.WK1

For the period from January 1985 through December 1993, complete the following table, realizing that the values in the last row must be computed from the first two rows. Which currencies have appreciated relative to each other?

Swiss Francs, U.S. Dollars, and Italian Lira, 1985 to 1993

	January 1985	December 1993	Percentage Change in the Exchange Rate
Lira per dollar			
Swiss francs per dollar			
Lira per Swiss franc			

Exercise 70

Volatility of Exchange Rates

Contributed by Brian S. Wilson
Spreadsheet: FOREX.WK1

Complete the following table showing the volatility of exchange rates for Japan, West Germany, Mexico, and Brazil. Use standard deviation as a percent of the mean (coefficient of variation). In which country would an American multi–national corporation face the most currency risk? During which five–year period and in which country were exchange rates most volatile?

Volatility of Exchange Rates

Period	Standard Deviation of Yen per U.S. Dollar (percent of mean)	Standard Deviation of Deutsche Marks per U.S. Dollar (percent of mean)	Standard Deviation of Pesos per U.S. Dollar (percent of mean)
Jan 1975 to Dec 1979			
Jan 1980 to Dec 1984			
Jan 1985 to Dec 1989			
Jan 1975 to Dec 1993			

Exercise 71

Real and Nominal Exchange Rates

Contributed by Brian S. Wilson
Spreadsheets: FOREX.WK1, FORINFLA.WK1

Complete the following table deriving the nominal and real bilateral exchange rates between the United States and Japan with a base year of 1982. Prepare a graph that depicts the nominal and real exchange rate for each month from January 1972 to December 1993, with December 1982 values set equal to 100. Use data for January of the indicated year. The real exchange rate equals the nominal exchange rate (cents per yen) multiplied by the ratio of inflation abroad to inflation at home (CPI U.S./CPI Japan). According to the graph, do the nominal and real exchange rates correlate highly? What does a rise in the real exchange rate imply?

Real and Nominal Exchange Rates: U.S. and Japan

Period	Nominal Exchange Rate					Real Exchange Rate		
	Yen per U.S.$	Cents per Yen	Cents per Yen (1982 = 100)	CPI Japan	CPI U.S.	Ratio: CPI U.S. to CPI Japan	Ratio (1982 = 100)	
1972								
1974								
1976								
1978								
1980								
1982								
1984								
1986								
1988								
1990								
1992								
1993								

Exercise 72

Volatile Exchange Rates

Contributed by Brian S. Wilson
Spreadsheet: FOREX.WK1

Complete the following table depicting the coefficients of variation of the foreign exchange value of the South African Rand. Prepare a graph running from March of 1974 through December of 1993 of the exchange rate of South Africa.

Highly Volatile Exchange Rates

Period	Cents per Rand Standard Deviation (% of mean)
1–74 to 12–79	
1–80 to 12–84	
1–85 to 12–89	
1–74 to 12–93	

Exercise 73

Correlations Among Stock Indexes and Business Cycle Indexes

Contributed by Brian S. Wilson
Spreadsheets: STKINDEX.WK1, BUSCYCLE.WK1

Convert the Dow Jones Industrial Average to a base in which June of 1982 = 100. Use these converted values to complete the correlation matrix below containing the Composite Index of 4 Coincident Indicators, the Composite Index of 7 Lagging Indicators, and the Composite Index of 11 Leading Indicators. Use the period from January 1970 through December 1993 throughout. Based on the completed table, with which index does the Dow Jones Industrial Average have the highest correlation? As what kind of indicator, then, would you say the Dow Jones Industrial Average functions?

Correlation Matrix for Stock and Business Cycle Indexes

Business Cycle Index:	Correlation With DJIA (June 1982 = 100):
Leading Index	
Lagging Index	
Coincident Index	

Exercise 74

IBM versus Microsoft

Contributed by Robert W. Kolb
Spreadsheets: STOCKS.WK1

According to most news reports on the computer industry, Microsoft has prospered largely at the expense of IBM. For the period from August 1989 through December 1993, complete the following table.

IBM versus Microsoft, August 1989 through December 1993

	IBM	Microsoft
Mean Monthly Return		
Standard Deviation of Monthly Returns		
Mean Monthly Return of a Portfolio Long One Share of Each Stock		
Standard Deviation of Portfolio		
Mean Monthly Return of a Portfolio Long One Share of Microsoft and Short One Share of IBM		
Standard Deviation of Portfolio		

Exercise 75

Volatility of the Components of GNP

Contributed by Brian S. Wilson
Spreadsheet: NATLPROD.WK1

Complete the following table showing the respective means and coefficients of variation of the various components of GNP. Give the standard deviation as a percent of the mean. Based on your calculations, and a visual analysis of the table, which component of GNP is most erratic? During which period was GNP most volatile?

Volatility of the Components of GNP

	Consumption		Investment		Government Purchases		Net Exports	
Period	Mean	Std. Dev. % of Mean	Mean	Std. Dev. % of Mean	Mean	Std. Dev. % of Mean	Mean	Std. Dev. % of Mean
1970 to 1974								
1975 to 1979								
1980 to 1984								
1985 to 1990								

Exercise 76

Leveraging Microsoft

Contributed by Robert W. Kolb
Spreadsheets: STOCKS.WK1, MONEYYLD.WK1

Assume that on July 31, 1989 you had capital of $1,000,000, and that you were able to borrow $1,000,000 at the 1–month commercial paper rate. (That is, assume you borrow for August at the prevailing July rate, and so on.) Assume that you must refinance your borrowing each month at the new rate, and that you must pay the previous month's interest from the value of the portfolio. For the period from August 1989 through December 1993, complete the following table. For the leveraged portfolio, all values should reflect the repayment of borrowed funds.

Leveraging Microsoft

	All–Equity Portfolio $1 Million of Stock	Leveraged Portfolio $2 Million of Stock
Maximum Portfolio Value		
Minimum Portfolio Value		
Value of Portfolio on December 31, 1993		

Exercise 77

Components of GNP: The Expenditure Approach

Contributed by Brian S. Wilson
Spreadsheet: NATLPROD.WK1

Complete the following table and create a stacked–bar graph composed of the following GNP components according to the expenditure approach. How has the relationship between these components changed over time?

Components of GNP: The Expenditure Approach

Year	Consumption (% of Total)	Investment (% of Total)	Government Purchases (% of Total)	Net Exports (% of Total)
1950				
1960				
1970				
1980				
1990				

Exercise 78

Components of Investment Spending

Contributed by Brian S. Wilson
Spreadsheet: NATLPROD.WK1

Prepare a graph, from 1950:1 through 1993:4, depicting the following investment components as a percentage of GNP: Total Gross Private Domestic Investment, Non–residential Fixed Investment, Residential Fixed Investment, and Total Change in Business Inventories. During which decade has investment fallen the most as a percentage of GNP? During which decade was Total Gross Private Domestic Investment the highest as a percentage of GNP?

Exercise 79

Government Purchases and Gross Domestic Product

Contributed by Robert W. Kolb
Spreadsheet: NATLPROD.WK1

Prepare a graph that shows total seasonally adjusted government purchases of goods and services as a percentage of total seasonally adjusted gross domestic product for 1959–1989. (Let the X–axis run from 1959 to 1989, and set the Y–axis to run from .16 to .22.) Compute the mean of this percentage for the 1960s, 1970s, and 1980s, 1990s, and complete the following table. How has this relationship changed over time? The 1980s have the reputation of being a period of large tax cuts. Were these tax cuts accompanied by a relative decrease in government spending?

Decade	Mean Ratio of Total Government Purchases of Goods and Services to Total Gross Domestic Product
1960s	
1970s	
1980s	
1990s	

Exercise 80

Gross Domestic Product and Consumption

Contributed by Robert W. Kolb
Spreadsheet: NATLPROD.WK1

Prepare a graph that shows total personal consumption expenditures as a percentage of total seasonally adjusted gross domestic product for 1959–1993. (Let the X–axis run from 1959 to 1993, and set the Y–axis to run from .6 to .7.) Compute the mean of this percentage for the 1960s, 1970s, and 1980s and complete the table shown below. How has this relationship changed over time? The 1980s have the reputation of being a time of extreme consumption and self–indulgence. Do these statistics support the view that the 1980s were different from previous periods?

Decade	Mean Ratio of Total Personal Consumption to Total Gross Domestic Product
1960s	
1970s	
1980s	
1990s	

Exercise 81

National Income and Its Distribution

Contributed by Brian S. Wilson
Spreadsheet: NATLPROD.WK1

Complete the table below using data from the second quarter of each year listed. (Dollar amounts are in billions). How has the distribution of national income changed over time? How has the distribution of national income among proprietors and corporations changed since 1950?

National Income and Its Distribution

Year	Compensation of Employees $	%	Proprietor Income $	%	Rental Income $	%	Corporate Profits $	%
1950								
1960								
1970								
1980								
1990								

Exercise 82

The Personal Saving Rate

Contributed by Brian S. Wilson
Spreadsheet: PERINCOM.WK1

For the period from the 1960:1 through the 1993:4, prepare a line graph showing personal saving as a percent of personal disposable income. Did the tax cuts throughout the 1980s increase personal saving relative to personal disposable income?

Exercise 83

Real Personal Income

Contributed by Brian S. Wilson
Spreadsheets: FINQU.WK1, PERINCOM.WK1

Complete the table below by calculating the values for the descriptions given in the appropriate spreadsheets. For Average Personal Income for 1950, compute the average of the values for quarters one through four. The purchasing power of your real income is defined as current income adjusted for inflation according to the formula: Y(real) = Y(current)/(CPI/100). To complete the third column, compute real personal income in 1983 dollars for each year.

Real Personal Income

Year	Average Personal Income (Billions of Dollars)	Average CPI: All Items (1982–1984 = 100)	Real Personal Income (1983 Dollars)
1950			
1960			
1970			
1980			
1990			

Exercise 84

Personal Consumption Expenditures

Contributed by Brian S. Wilson
Spreadsheet: PERINCOM.WK1

Complete the following table using fourth quarter data. Based on an examination of the table, do you think that the U.S. economy is becoming increasingly service–oriented?

Personal Consumption Expenditures

Year	Personal Consumption Expenditures: Total	Personal Consumption Expenditures: Durable Goods (% of Total)	Personal Consumption Expenditures: Nondurable Goods (% of Total)	Personal Consumption Expenditures: Services (% of Total)
1946				
1950				
1955				
1960				
1965				
1970				
1975				
1980				
1985				
1990				
1993				

Exercise 85

Personal Consumption Expenditures: By Component

Contributed by Brian S. Wilson
Spreadsheet: PERINCOM.WK1

Complete the following table depicting the Components of Personal Consumption Expenditures as a percent of total during the period indicated. For electricity, use 1959, and for Medical Care, use 1947, instead of 1946. How have personal consumption expenditures changed since 1946? Is there a noticeable difference in consumption behavior during a recession or recovery?

Personal Consumption Expenditures: By Component

Component	Q2 1946	Average Q1 1981 to Q4 1983 (recession)	Average Q1 1984 to Q4 1986 (recovery)	Q2 1993
Durable Goods				
Nondurable Goods				
Services				
Food				
Clothing and Shoes				
Gas and Oil				
Housing				
Electricity & Gas				
Transportation				
Medical Care				

Exercise 86

Growth in Real GNP and the Employment Rate

Contributed by Brian S. Wilson
Spreadsheets: EMPLOY.WK1, NATLPROD.WK1, FINQU.WK1

Prepare a scatter diagram comparing the average quarterly percentage change in real GNP and the average quarterly percentage change in the employment rate for each year from 1971 through 1993. For the first quarter of each year, compute the percentage change from the fourth quarter of the prior year. Use the CPI from the FINQU.WK1 spreadsheet to compute real GNP. Set the Y–axis as the average quarterly growth rate of real GNP and set the X–axis as increase in employment rates (percentage points). Use the employment rate for March, June, September, and December to correspond to quarterly GNP. How do high and low rates of growth affect the employment rate?

Exercise 87

The Changing Labor Force

Contributed by Brian S. Wilson
Spreadsheet: EMPLOY.WK1

Prepare a bar graph showing the number of men employed as a percent of total, and the number of women employed as a percent of total for December of each year running from 1970 through 1993. (Set the X axis to run from 1970 to 1993. Set the Y–axis to run from 0% to 70%.) Does the graph you created give merit to the theory that more and more women are entering the work force?

Exercise 88

Corporate Tax Revenue and Employment

Contributed by Brian S. Wilson
Spreadsheets: FEDFISCL.WK1, EMPLOY.WK1, FINQU.WK1

Prepare two line graphs that illustrate Inflation Adjusted Corporate Tax Revenue and the Employment Rate from 1970:1 to 1993:4. For the Employment Rate use values from March, June, September, and December. (Let the X–axis for both graphs run from 1970:1 1993:4, and set the Y–axes to run from 40 to 120 for Corporate Tax Revenue and 89 to 97 for the Employment Rate. Do these series seem highly correlated? What could be the explanation for the correlation between these two factors? Hint: let the Employment Rate equal (100 – Unemployment Rate).

Exercise 89

The Discomfort Index

Contributed by Brian S. Wilson
Spreadsheets: EMPLOY.WK1, INFLATE.WK1

The Discomfort Index equals the inflation rate plus the overall unemployment rate. Complete the following table showing the discomfort index for the periods listed below. For the inflation rate, use the average annual percentage change in the CPI over the period, and for unemployment, use the average monthly unemployment rate for the period.

The Discomfort Index

Period	Average Inflation Rate	Average Unemployment Rate	Discomfort Index
Jan 1970–Dec 1974			
Jan 1975–Dec 1979			
Jan 1980–Dec 1984			
Jan 1985–Dec 1989			
Jan 1990–Dec 1993			

Exercise 90

Construction, Production, and the Employment Rate

Contributed by Brian S. Wilson
Spreadsheets: INDUPROD.WK1, HOUSING.WK1, EMPLOY.WK1

Complete the following correlation matrix using values from January 1970 to December 1993. For the employment rate, use one minus the unemployment rate setting the June of 1987 value equal to 100. Then prepare a line graph comparing the three indexes. Set the Y–axis equal to the respective index values, and the X–axis to run from January 1970 to December 1993. Is there any correlation between industrial production and construction? Is production or construction more correlated with the employment rate?

Correlation Matrix for Construction, Production, and Employment

	Construction Index: Composite Fixed– Weight Price Index (1987 = 100)	Industrial Production Index: Total Index (1987 = 100)	Employment Rate Index (1987 = 100)
Construction Index: Composite Fixed– Weight Price Index (1987 = 100)	1.0		
Industrial Production Index: Total Index (1987 = 100)		1.0	
Employment Rate Index (1987 = 100)			1.0

Exercise 91

Real Cost of Employment and Real Total Gross Domestic Product

Contributed by Brian S. Wilson
Spreadsheets: WAGES.WK1, NATLPROD.WK1, FINQU.WK1

Complete the following table depicting the average quarterly cost of employment indexes and real Gross Domestic Product from 1976 through 1993. As a measure of the cost of employment, use the employment cost index of the wages and salaries of all private non–farm workers. Use the CPI from the FINQU.WK1 spreadsheet to adjust each for inflation. Then prepare a graph depicting the levels of the Real Cost of Employment and the Real Total Gross Domestic Product. For the graph, set the Q2 1989 value of Total Real GDP equal to 100, and let the graph extend to Q4 1993. Let the X–axis run from 1976 to 1993, and let the Y–axis run from 72 to 106.) How have the cost of employment changes compared with changes in inflation? Have employees become more efficient based on changes in Gross Domestic Product?

Real Cost of Employment and Real Gross Domestic Product

Period	Avg. Percent Change in CPI Index	Avg. Percent Change in Nominal Cost of Employment Index	Avg. Percent Change in Nominal Gross Domestic Product	Avg. Percent Change in Real Cost of Employment Index	Avg. Percent Change in Real Gross Domestic Product
1976 to 1979					
1980 to 1984					
1985 to 1989					

Exercise 92

Changes in Real Wages

Contributed by Brian S. Wilson
Spreadsheets: WAGES.WK1, FINQU.WK1

Complete the following table comparing the percentage change in the nominal wages and salaries of White–Collar Workers, Blue–Collar Workers, and Union Workers with the percentage change in the Consumer Price Index. Also, prepare a line graph, running from 1976:1 through 1993:4, of the Indexes of the Wages and Salaries of White–Collar Workers, Blue–Collar Workers, and Union Workers adjusted for inflation. To convert the indexes to real values, divide the respective index by the CPI/100. Set the Y–axis equal to the various indexes, and set the X–axis to run from 1976:1 through 1993:4. Do increases in wages and salaries seem to correspond to increases in inflation? Which type of worker has seen the largest wage increases from 1976 to 1993? Compare the behavior of real wages in general by type of worker from 1976 to 1993.

Changes in Real Wages

Period	Avg. Percent Increase in Wages of White–Collar Workers	Avg. Percent Increase in Wages of Blue–Collar Workers	Avg. Percent Increase in Wages of Union Workers	Avg. Percent Increase in Consumer Price Index
1976 to 1979				
1980 to 1984				
1985 to 1993				
1976 to 1993				

Exercise 93

Federal Government: Receipts and Expenditures

Contributed by Brian S. Wilson
Spreadsheet: FEDFISCL.WK1

Create a line graph of the ratio of Federal government expenditures to Federal government receipts. let the X–axis run from 1950 to 1993. Let the Y–axis values be the average quarterly ratio of expenditures to receipts for the respective year. Then complete the following table. How has this ratio changed over time? Do you think this ratio can be maintained throughout the 21st century?

Federal Government: Receipts and Expenditures

Period	Average Receipts	Average Expenditures	Ratio of Average Expenditures to Average Receipts	% Change from 1950
1950				
1960				
1970				
1980				
1990				
1993				

Exercise 94

The Composition of Federal Outlays

Contributed by Brian S. Wilson
Spreadsheet: FEDFISCL.WK1

Prepare a line graph from 1950:1 to 1993:4 depicting Purchases of Goods and Services–Nondefense, National Defense, Net Transfer Payments, Grants–In–Aid to State and Local Governments, and Total Interest Paid, as a percentage of total expenditures. Complete the table below using first quarter data of the indicated year, showing components of expenditures as a percent of total expenditures. Which components of Federal expenditures increased relative to the others from 1950 to 1993? According to the graph, which component of Federal Government expenditures has shown the most variance as a percent of total?

The Composition of Federal Outlays

Year	National Defense	Nondefense	Transfer Payments	Grants–In–Aid	Net Interest Paid
1950					
1960					
1970					
1980					
1990					
1993					

Exercise 95

Federal Government: Net Interest Paid

Contributed by Brian S. Wilson
Spreadsheet: FEDFISCL.WK1

Using first quarter data, prepare a stacked–bar graph of the relationship between Federal Government Expenditures and Net Interest Paid by the Federal Government based on values that you compute to complete the following table. Let the graph cover the 1960 to 1990 period. Has this relationship changed over time? How does Net Interest Paid in the first quarter of 1990 compare with Total Expenditures in 1960?

Federal Government: Net Interest Paid

Year	Federal Government: Expenditures, Total	Federal Government: Expenditures, Net Interest Paid	Net Interest Paid as Percent of Total Expenditures
1960			
1970			
1980			
1990			

Exercise 96

The Budget Deficit and Real Interest Rates

Contributed by Brian S. Wilson
Spreadsheets: FINQU.WK1, FEDFISCL.WK1, NATLPROD.WK1

For the period from 1972 to 1993, create a graph depicting the real interest rate and the budget deficit as a percentage of GNP. The real interest rate is defined as the nominal interest rate minus the percentage rate of inflation. To complete your line graph, use the values you derive in the following table. What relationship do you observe between the deficit and real interest rates?

The Budget Deficit and Real Interest Rates

Year	Deficit	GNP	Deficit as % of GNP	Nominal Interest Rate	% Change in Inflation	Real Interest Rate
1972						
1974						
1976						
1978						
1980						
1982						
1984						
1986						
1988						
1990						
1992						
1993						

Exercise 97

The Budget Deficit and the Trade Deficit

Contributed by Brian S. Wilson
Spreadsheets: FEDFISCL.WK1, TRADEBAL.WK1

Prepare a line graph comparing the deficit to the trade balance from 1960:1 through 1993:4. Do you see a high correlation between these two series? What could this correlation be attributed to?

Exercise 98

The Correlation Between Sales and Output

Contributed by Brian S. Wilson
Spreadsheets: MANUFAC.WK1, NATLPROD.WK1, FINQU.WK1

Prepare a graph depicting inflation adjusted (real) Manufacturing and Trade Sales, Retail Trade, and GNP for 1970:1 through 1993:4. Adjust both series so that the first quarter of 1982 = 100. For sales data use the months March, June, September, and December. Use the CPI in the spreadsheet FINQU.WK1 to adjust GNP for inflation. According to the graph, do sales and output seem correlated? Using the values contained in the graph for the two series (1982 = 100), compute the correlation coefficient between the two variables.

Exercise 99

U.S. and Foreign Automobiles: Expenditures and Sales

Contributed by Brian S. Wilson
Spreadsheet: AUTOS.WK1

Prepare a line graph comparing retail automobile and truck sales of domestic and foreign new passenger cars from January 1970 to December 1993. Prepare another line graph comparing the average expenditure per car over the same period, and complete the following table using average monthly statistics. How has the relationship between foreign and domestic automobiles sold changed over time?

Have U.S. expenditures per automobile been historically higher than foreign expenditures per automobile?

U.S. and Foreign Automobiles: Expenditures and Sales

Year	Domestic Automobiles			Foreign Automobiles		
	Average Expenditure	Sales	Corr.	Average Expenditure	Sales	Corr.
1970						
1975						
1980						
1985						
1990						

Exercise 100

Inventory–to–Sales Ratio of the Automotive Industry

Contributed by Brian S. Wilson
Spreadsheets: AUTOS.WK1, MANUFAC.WK1

Complete the following table comparing the inventory–to–sales ratio of the automotive industry in comparison with the aggregate inventory–to–sales ratio of all retail trade. Prepare a line graph comparing the two ratios. Set the X–axis from January 1970 through December 1993, and let the Y–axis equal the inventory–to–sales ratio. On average, do automotive dealers hold more inventory than retailers as a whole? Is the inventory–to–sales ratio of automotive dealers more volatile? Has the amount of inventory held by automotive dealers or aggregate retailers changed over time?

Inventory–to–Sales Ratio of the Automotive Industry

Period	Average Inventory–to–Sales Ratio: Retail Trade	Mean Inventory–to–Sales Ratio: Automotive Dealers
Jan 70 to Dec 74		
Jan 75 to Dec 79		
Jan 80 to Dec 84		
Jan 85 to Dec 89		
Jan 90 to Dec 93		
Jan 70 to Dec 93		

Exercise 101

Corporate Profits by Industrial Sector

Contributed by Brian S. Wilson
Spreadsheets: CORPPROF.WK1, FINQU.WK1

Complete the following table depicting the mean and coefficient of variation of nominal and real quarterly corporate profits of the various industrial sectors shown from 1947:1 through 1993:4. The coefficient of variation is standard deviation as a percent of the mean. Which sector has shown the highest profit volatility?

Corporate Profits by Industrial Sector

Industrial Sector	Mean Nominal Quarterly Corporate Profits	Coefficient of Variation of Nominal Quarterly Corporate Profits	Mean Quarterly Real Corporate Profits	Coefficient of Variation of Real Quarterly Corporate Profits
Financial Institutions				
Manufacturing				
Transportation and Public Utilities				
Wholesale and Retail Trade				
Fiance				
Nonfinance				

Exercise 102

The Aggregate Inventory–to–Sales Ratio

Contributed by Brian S. Wilson
Spreadsheet: MANUFAC.WK1

Prepare a line graph running from January 1970 through December 1993 depicting the ratio of inventories (book value) to sales. Then complete the table below. How has this relationship changed over time? What does a high inventory–to–sales ratio imply?

The Aggregate Inventory–to–Sales Ratio

Period	Average Ratio of Inventories (Book Value) to Sales
January 1970–December 1974	
January 1975–December 1979	
January 1980–December 1984	
January 1985–December 1989	
January 1990–December 1993	

Exercise 103

Inventory as an Economic Indicator

Contributed by Brian S. Wilson
Spreadsheets: MANUFAC.WK1, BUSCYCLE.WK1

Prepare a line graph from January 1970 through December 1993 depicting the inventory–to–sales ratios of manufacturers, merchant wholesalers, and retailers. Then complete the following table. Based on the correlations you computed, do inventories appear to be leading, lagging, or coincident indicators. Does your conclusion vary by the type of inventory?

Inventory as an Economic Indicator

Definition of Inventory	Correlation with Composite Index of Leading Indicators	Correlation with Composite Index of Lagging Indicators	Correlation With Composite Index of Coincident Indicators
Manufacturing Inventories			
Inventories of Merchant Wholesalers			
Retail Trade Inventories			

Exercise 104

An Industrial Energy Efficiency Index

Contributed by Ricardo J. Rodriguez
Spreadsheets: ENERGY.WK1, INDUPROD.WK1

Prepare a graph showing the evolution of the ratio of total energy consumption to the total index of industrial production for 1974–1993. (Let the X–axis run from 1974:1 to 1993:4, and set the Y–axis to run from 0.05 to 0.11.) Notice that the index is only useful as a relative measure of energy usage. Thus, a downward trend would indicate that U.S. industry is more efficient in using energy. Notice also, that energy is used by other sectors of the economy, e.g., households, so this index captures more than industrial utilization. Based on the graph, what noteworthy patterns are apparent? Is the U.S. using its energy more efficiently now than in the recent past?

Exercise 105

Per Capita Energy Consumption

Contributed by Ricardo J. Rodriguez
Spreadsheets: ENERGY.WK1, EMPLOY.WK1

Prepare a graph showing the evolution of the ratio of total energy consumption to the total population of people 16 years and over for 1974–1993. (Let the X–axis run from 1974:1 to 1993:4, and set the Y–axis to run from 25 to 55 million BTUs per capita per year.) Based on the graph, what noteworthy patterns are apparent? Is the U.S. population using its energy more efficiently now than in the recent past? Compute the average per capita energy usage and complete the table shown below.

Per Capita Energy Consumption in the United States
(million BTUs per year)

Period	Average	Standard Deviation
1974–1979		
1980–1989		
1974–1993		

Exercise 106

The Nominal and Real Price of Gasoline

Contributed by Ricardo J. Rodriguez
Spreadsheets: ENERGY.WK1, INFLATE.WK1

Prepare a graph showing the evolution of the nominal and real prices of gasoline in U.S. cities at the retail level for 1978–1993. Use the consumer price index for all items to deflate nominal gas prices. (Let the X–axis run from 1978:1 to 1993:12, and set the Y–axis to run from 40 to 160 cents.) The graph should be in January 1978 dollars. What noteworthy characteristics are apparent in the graph?

Exercise 107

The Value of the Dollar and the Trade Balance with Germany and Japan

Contributed by Brian S. Wilson
Spreadsheet: FOREX.WK1, TRADEBAL.WK1

Complete the following table depicting the U.S. trade balance with Germany and Japan and the bilateral exchange rate of the U.S. dollar and the respective foreign currency. Prepare two line graphs, the first depicting the trade balance with Japan and the number of yen per dollar. Set the June of 1982 value for each series equal to 100. For the second graph, do the same for Germany. Set the X–axes to run from January 1975 through December 1993. In general, are the respective exchange rates and the respective trade balances correlated? Describe the general trend of the trade balances between the United States and Germany and Japan since 1975.

The Value of the Dollar and the Trade Balance with Germany and Japan

Period	Avg. U.S.– Japan Trade Balance	Avg. Yen per U.S. Dollar	Correlation Coefficient	Avg. U.S.– Germany Trade Balance	Avg. DM per U.S. Dollar	Correlation Coefficient
Jan 1975– Dec 1979						
Jan 1980– Dec 1984						
Jan 1985– Dec 1989						
Jan 1990– Dec 1993						